THE WORLD ALMANAC® ALMANAC® FOR KIDS 2005

WORLD ALMANAC BOOKS
A Division of World Almanac Education Group, Inc.
A WRC Media Company

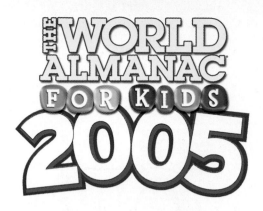

THE WORLD ALMANAC FOR KIDS 2005

EDITOR: Kevin Seabrooke

CURRICULUM CONSULTANT:
Eric S. Elkins, M.A., Youth Content Editor, Denver Newspaper Agency

CONTRIBUTORS: Elizabeth Barden, Laura C. Girardi, Joseph Gustaitis,
Sarah Janssen, Rachael Mason, Carol Moran, Donna Mulder, Kerria Seabrooke
Consultant: Lee T. Shapiro, Ph.D. (Astronomy)

KID CONTRIBUTORS: Joey Acosta, Emily Addison, Jon Bodi,
Ashley Bruggeman, Amanda Hatton, Emma Larson, Elana Metsch-Ampel, Kelly Moran,
Christin Mulder, Maya Master Park, Kristyn Romaine

Thanks to all the kids who wrote to us with their great ideas!

DESIGN: Bill SMITH STUDIO
Creative Director: Brian Kobberger **Project Director:** Sandra E. Will
Design: Eric Hoffsten, Ron Leighton, Scott Palmer
Photo Research: Christie Silver **Production:** James Liebman

WORLD ALMANAC BOOKS

Vice President–
Sales and Marketing
James R. Keenley

Editorial
Director
William McGeveran Jr.

Managing
Editor
Lori P. Wiesenfeld

Desktop Production Manager: Elizabeth J. Lazzara
Editorial Staff: Erik C. Gopel, Christopher Larson, Associate Editors

WORLD ALMANAC EDUCATION GROUP

Chief Executive Officer, WRC Media Inc.: Martin E. Kenney Jr.
Publisher: Ken Park
Director–Purchasing and Production/Photo Research: Edward A. Thomas
Director of Indexing Services: Marjorie B. Bank; **Index Editor:** Walter Kronenberg
Marketing Coordinator: Sarah De Vos

The World Almanac For Kids 2005
Copyright © 2004 by World Almanac Education Group, Inc.
The World Almanac and The World Almanac For Kids are registered trademarks of World Almanac Education Group, Inc.
ISBN (softcover): 0-88687-929-9
ISBN (hardcover): 0-88687-930-2
ISBN (Smyth-sewn edition): 0-88687-944-2
Printed in the United States of America
The softcover and hardcover editions are distributed to the trade in the United States by St. Martin's Press.
The Smyth-sewn edition is distributed by World Almanac Education, (800) 321-1147.
WORLD ALMANAC® BOOKS
An Imprint of World Almanac Education Group, Inc.
512 Seventh Avenue
New York, NY 10018
E-Mail: Waforkids@waegroup.com

Web site: **www.worldalmanacforkids.com**

The addresses and content of Web sites referred to in this book are subject to change.
Although The World Almanac For Kids carefully reviews these sites, we cannot take responsibility for their content.

CONTENTS

Holidays 96-98

Homework 99-103
Help

Inventions 104-106

Language 107-113

Military 114-117

Money 118-121

Movies 122-125
& TV

Museums 126-128

Science   197-205

Space   206-216

Sports   217-231

Transportation 232-237

Travel   238-242

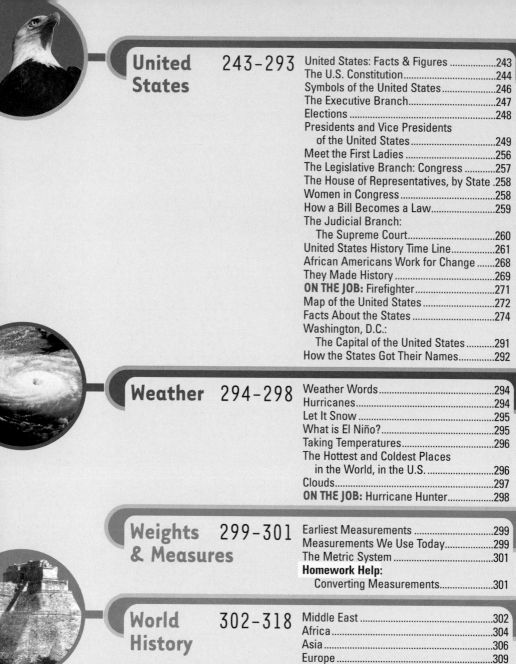

LISTEN UP!

NOT SO YESTERDAY

Hilary Duff's first CD, *Metamorphosis,* won her the 2004 Kids' Choice Award for Favorite Female Singer. She has also been busy making movies, including *A Cinderella Story* due out in summer 2004.

BOW WOW UNLEASHED

Rapper Bow Wow, a.k.a. Shad Gregory Moss, is now 17—and "Lil" no more. In between concerts and acting—*Johnson Family Vacation* opened in April 2004—Bow Wow finds time for his schoolwork and plans to go to college.

CLAY-NATION

Singer Clay Aiken may have been runner-up on season two of the TV show *American Idol,* but his *Measure of a Man* CD hit number one on the charts.

GRAMMY-LICIOUS

Beyoncé, shown here performing at the 2004 NBA All-Star Game, took home five Grammy Awards in February, including Best Contemporary R&B Album for *Dangerously in Love,* her first solo CD.

BIG SCREEN

SHREK IS BACK!

In *Shrek 2,* starring Mike Myers as everyone's favorite ogre, Fiona (Cameron Diaz) takes Shrek and Donkey (Eddie Murphy) home to meet her parents. Here Shrek gives the famous ogre-slayer Puss-in-Boots (Antonio Banderas) a big hug.

LORD OF THE OSCARS

The Return of the King, the blockbuster hit that concluded the Lord of the Rings trilogy, won a record-tying 11 Oscars in 2004, including Best Picture and Best Director. Shown here is Ian McKellen, as the wizard Gandalf.

MUSIC LESSONS

Jack Black (at the back) poses with kids from the hit comedy *School of Rock* —left to right—Kevin Clark, Miranda Cosgrove, Joey Gaydos and Rebecca Brown.

SMALL SCREEN

SHE'S ALL THAT AND MORE

Amanda Bynes, star of TV's *What I Like About You,* got a unique present for her 18th birthday. On April 3, the former *Amanda Show* star was named the Favorite Female Movie Actor at the 2004 Kids' Choice Awards (for 2003's *What a Girl Wants*).

AND THE WINNER IS....

On her popular Disney TV show, *That's So Raven,* Raven gets psychic glimpses of the future. Did the real-life 18-year-old know she was going to win a 2004 Kids' Choice Award for Favorite TV Actor? Maybe.

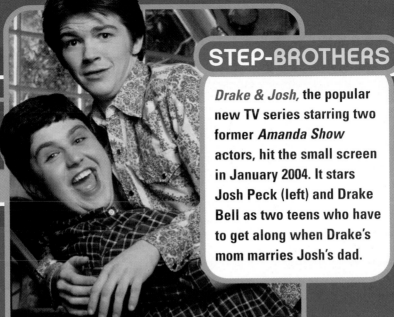

STEP-BROTHERS

Drake & Josh, the popular new TV series starring two former *Amanda Show* actors, hit the small screen in January 2004. It stars Josh Peck (left) and Drake Bell as two teens who have to get along when Drake's mom marries Josh's dad.

IT'S HIS HOUSE

Bernie Mac won an NAACP Image Award for Actor in a Comedy series in March 2004. The comedian and two-time Emmy Award nominee plays an uncle taking care of his sister's three kids in *The Bernie Mac Show.* Look for Bernie as a Hall of Fame baseball player in the movie *Mr. 3000.*

15

GOT GAME

TEEN ON TOP

In his first year out of high school, 19-year-old LeBron James, also known as "King James," was named NBA Rookie of the Year. This number one draft pick averaged 20.9 points per game.

ADU YOU BELIEVE THIS KID?

He's only 14, but Freddy Adu made his Major League Soccer debut for the D.C. United on April 3, 2004. He scored his first goal two weeks later against the NY/NJ MetroStars.

GOING FOR GOLD

Michael Phelps set five world records at the 2003 World Swimming Championships in Spain and won the Sullivan Award as the top amateur athlete in the U.S. In 2004, the 18-year-old from Baltimore hoped to win gold at the Olympics in Athens, Greece.

WIE, WOW

High school freshman **Michelle Wie** is six-feet tall and can drive a golf ball nearly 300 yards. In 2004, the 14-year-old became the youngest person and only the fourth woman to play in a men's PGA tournament.

UCONN CAN!

In 2004, the University of Connecticut became the first school ever to win the men's and women's NCAA basketball championships the same year. Diana Taurasi led the UConn women to their third straight national title and was named Most Outstanding Player of the Final Four. Emeka Okafor was the men's MOP.

THE LITTLE FISH THAT COULD

The Florida Marlins rush the field after winning Game Six—and the 2003 World Series. The Marlins ended their five-year string of losing seasons to beat the New York Yankees, 4 games to 2, and win their second championship since 1997.

NOT SO INSTANT REPLAY

New England kicker Adam Vinatieri celebrates his game-winning field goal in Super Bowl XXXVIII in Houston, Texas. As in 2002, Adam's kick on the last play of the game gave the Patriots an NFL title—this time over the Carolina Panthers, 32-29.

IN THE NEWS

THE BUSHES

President George W. Bush (R) was running for reelection in November 2004. He is shown here with first lady Laura Bush and their daughters, Barbara (left) and Jenna.

THE KERRYS

Senator John Kerry was hoping to capture the White House for the Democrats. He is shown here with—left to right—daughters Alexandra and Vanessa, wife Teresa Heinz Kerry, and stepson Chris Heinz.

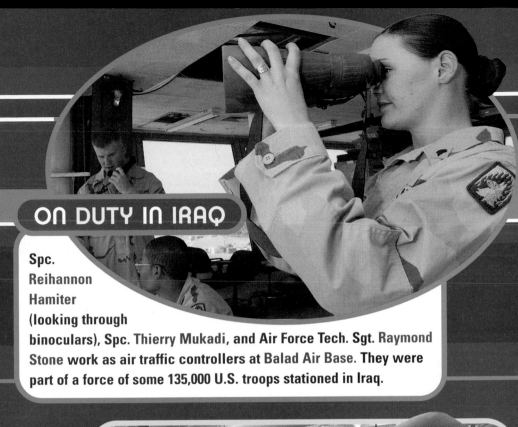

ON DUTY IN IRAQ

Spc. Reihannon Hamiter (looking through binoculars), Spc. Thierry Mukadi, and Air Force Tech. Sgt. Raymond Stone work as air traffic controllers at Balad Air Base. They were part of a force of some 135,000 U.S. troops stationed in Iraq.

KID POWER

Children exercise at the YMCA in Olathe, Kansas. They were part of a new fitness program in the Kansas City area aimed at fighting the growing problem of childhood obesity.

WAY OUT

DEEP, DEEP SPACE

Recent images from the Hubble Space Telescope offer the farthest look humankind has ever had into the universe. This view shows a spiral galaxy that existed about 1 billion years ago.

VIEW OF MARS

The panoramic camera of the Mars Exploration Rover *Spirit* offers a view of the "Columbia Hills," which were named in honor of the astronauts who died in the Space Shuttle *Columbia*.

HYPER-FAST

Shown here is an artist's conception of the X-43A scramjet, NASA's new hypersonic experimental vehicle. In March 2004, a 15-foot pilotless test version of the X-43A flew on its own at Mach 7—seven times the speed of sound—or about 5,000 mph, breaking the old airspeed record of Mach 3.3.

IT DRIVES, IT FLIES

The M400 Skycar, the world's only personal vertical takeoff and landing vehicle, hovers in the air at a demonstration. Its inventor, Dr. Paul Moller, hopes that someday cars developed from this model will become a reality.

Animals

What animal swims 68 mph? page 26

Animal Facts

▷ **CROCODILES** can go as long as a year without eating. Because they are cold-blooded animals, they can function at low body temperatures and use energy in food more efficiently than almost any other animal.

▷ **POLAR BEARS** swim faster than all other four-footed animals. They have been tracked at speeds up to 6 miles per hour, using their front paws to propel them through the water dog-paddle style. They have been known to swim over 60 miles without stopping. Their thick layer of fat keeps them warm while swimming in cold water. ▶

▷ The largest lizard is the **KOMODO DRAGON** of Indonesia. It can weigh up to 300 pounds and reach a length of 10 feet. This meat-eating lizard can eat up to 80% of its body weight during one meal.

▷ In 2003, scientists found a **PURPLE FROG** in India. Its scientific name translates as "frog with a nose." This newly discovered species, with tiny eyes and a pointy snout, is referred to as a "living fossil" because it belongs to a family of frogs that scientists thought was extinct. These primitive frogs were around as long as 130 million years ago, when dinosaurs still roamed Earth.

▷ The largest **FROG** today is the Goliath frog of Cameroon. It reaches a length of one foot. The gold frog of Brazil, which grows to only 3/8 of an inch, is the smallest.

▷ ▼The humps on a **CAMEL'S** back may look funny, but when food is hard to find, the camel draws energy from the fatty tissue in the hump. When this happens, the hump gets flabby and shrinks until the camel can eat and get some rest.

▷ The Japanese giant **SALAMANDER** which can reach a length of 6 feet long and weigh 140 pounds, is the largest amphibian.

▷ When a **HIPPOPOTAMUS** yawns, it doesn't mean it's ready for a nap. That wide mouth is actually a warning to stay away! And it's a good idea to do so. Hippos are very protective of their turf and their young. They kill more peole in Africa than any other wild animal. ▶

What Are Groups of Animals Called?

Here are some, often odd names for animal groups.

BEARS: *sleuth* of bears
CATTLE: *drove* of cattle
CROCODILES: *bask* of crocodiles
CROWS: *murder* of crows
ELKS: *gang* of elks
FISH: *school* of fish
FOXES: *skulk* of foxes
GEESE: *flock* or *gaggle* of geese
GNATS: *cloud* of gnats
HAWKS: *cast* of hawks

KITTENS: *kindle* or *kendle* of kittens
LEOPARDS: *leap* of leopards
LIONS: *pride* of lions
MULES: *span* of mules
NIGHTINGALES: *watch* of nightingales
OWLS: *parliament* of owls
PEACOCKS: *muster* of peacocks
SHARKS: *shiver* of sharks
RAVENS: *unkindness* of ravens
WHALES: *pod* of whales

Kool Koala Facts

▶ Koalas are not bears—although many people call them "koala bears." They are marsupials, a group of mammals that carry their young in a pouch.

▶ In the wild, koalas are found only in eucalyptus forests of eastern Australia.

▶ Eucalyptus leaves are poisonous for most animals, but koalas are able to eat them. In fact, these are almost their only food.

▶ Koalas do not need to drink. They get the moisture they need from eucalyptus leaves.

▶ Koalas live in trees and are nocturnal. They sleep during the day and move around and eat at night.

WHO AM I?

I was born near London on November 27, 1960. I've always loved animals, and had lots of pets as a boy, including a boa constrictor, a caiman (a kind of crocodile), and a magpie. I've worked in wildlife TV since I graduated from college. Now I travel all over the world to film animals, and I have my own show on The Discovery Channel, called "___'s Wild Wild World."

Answer: Nigel Marven

BIGGEST, SMALLEST, FASTEST

IN THE WORLD

WORLD'S BIGGEST ANIMALS

MARINE MAMMAL: blue whale (110 feet long, 209 tons)

LAND MAMMAL: African bush elephant (13 feet high, 8 tons)

TALLEST MAMMAL: giraffe (19 feet tall, 2 tons)

REPTILE: saltwater crocodile (16 feet long, 1,150 pounds)

SNAKE: Heaviest: anaconda (27 feet, 9 inches long, 500 pounds)
        Longest: reticulated python (26–32 feet long)

FISH: whale shark (41¼ feet long, 15 tons)

BIRD: ostrich (9 feet tall, 345 pounds)

INSECT: stick insect (15 inches long)

WORLD'S SMALLEST ANIMALS

MAMMAL: bumblebee bat
        (1.1 to 1.3 inches)

FISH: dwarf goby (length 0.3 inches)

BIRD: male bee hummingbird
        (2.2 inches)

SNAKES: thread snake and brahminy
        blind snake (4.25 inches)

LIZARD: Jaragua lizard (0.63 inches)

INSECT: fairy fly (0.01 inches)

FROG: Brazilian frog (0.33 inches)

WORLD'S FASTEST ANIMALS

MARINE MAMMAL: blue whale
        (30 miles per hour)

LAND MAMMAL: cheetah (70 miles per hour)

FISH: sailfish (68 miles per hour)

BIRD: peregrine falcon
        (100–200 miles per hour)

INSECT: dragonfly (36 miles per
        hour)

How Fast Do Animals Run?

Some animals can run as fast as a car. But a snail needs more than 30 hours just to go one mile. If you look at this table, you will see how fast some land animals can go. Humans at their fastest are still slower than many animals. The record for fastest speed for a human for a recognized race distance is held by Michael Johnson, who won the 1996 Olympic 200 meter dash in 19.32 seconds for an average speed of 23.16 mph.

	MILES PER HOUR
Cheetah	70
Antelope	60
Lion	50
Elk	45
Zebra	40
Rabbit	35
Reindeer	32
Cat	30
Elephant	25
Wild turkey	15
Squirrel	12
Snail	0.03

HOW LONG DO
ANIMALS LIVE?

Most animals do not live as long as human beings do. A monkey that is 14 years old is thought to be old. A person who is 14 is still considered young. The average life spans of some animals are shown here. The average life span of a human today is 65 to 70 years.

Galapagos tortoise	200+ years
Box turtle	100 years
Gray whale	70 years
Alligator	50 years
Humpback whale	50 years
Asian elephant	40 years
African elephant	35 years
Bottlenose dolphin	30 years
Chimpanzee	20 years
Horse	20 years
Polar bear	20 years
Black bear	18 years
Tiger	16 years
Lion	15 years
Cow	15 years
Tarantula	15 years
Leopard	12 years
Cat (domestic)	12 years
Dog (domestic)	12 years
Giraffe	10 years
Pig	10 years
Squirrel	10 years
Deer (white-tailed)	8 years
Kangaroo	7 years
Chipmunk	6 years
Rabbit (domestic)	5 years
Mouse	3 years
Opossum	1 year
Worker bee	4-5 weeks
Adult housefly	3-4 weeks

Animal Words

ANIMAL	MALE	FEMALE	YOUNG
bear	boar	sow	cub
cattle, giraffe, whale, hippo	bull	cow	calf
deer	buck, stag	doe	fawn
duck	drake	duck	duckling
ferret	hob	jill	kit
fox	reynard	vixen	kit, cub, pup
goat	buck	doe	kid
goose	gander	goose	gosling
gorilla	male	female	infant
hawk	tiercel	hen	eyas
horse	stallion	mare	foal, filly (female), colt (male)
pig	boar	sow	piglet
rabbit	buck	doe	kit, bunny
tiger	tiger	tigress	cub

Life on Earth

This time line shows how life developed on Earth and when land plants developed. The earliest animals are at the top of the chart. The most recent are at the bottom of the chart.

	YEARS AGO		ANIMAL LIFE ON EARTH
PRECAMBRIAN	4.5 BILLION		Formation of the Earth. No signs of life.
	2.5 BILLION		First evidence of life in the form of bacteria and algae. All life is in water.
PALEOZOIC	570–500 MILLION		Animals with shells (called trilobites) and some mollusks. Some fossils begin to form.
	500–430 MILLION		Jawless fish appear, oldest known animals with backbones (vertebrates).
	430–395 MILLION		Many coral reefs, jawed fishes, and scorpion-like animals. First land plants.
	395–345 MILLION		Many fishes. Earliest known insect. Amphibians (animals living in water and on land) appear.
	345–280 MILLION		Large insects appear. Amphibians increase in numbers. First trees appear.
	280–225 MILLION		Reptiles and modern insects appear. Trilobites, many corals, and fishes become extinct.
MESOZOIC	225–195 MILLION		Dinosaurs and turtles appear. Many reptiles and insects develop further. Mammals appear.
	195–135 MILLION		Many giant dinosaurs. Reptiles increase in number. First birds and crab-like animals appear.
	135–65 MILLION		Dinosaurs develop further and then become extinct. Flowering plants begin to appear.
CENOZOIC	65–2.5 MILLION		Modern-day land and sea animals begin to develop, including such mammals as rhinoceroses, whales, cats, dogs, apes, seals.
	2.5 MILLION–10,000		Earliest humans appear. Mastodon, mammoths, and other huge animals become extinct.
	10,000–PRESENT		Modern human beings and animals.

Animal Kingdom

The world has so many animals that scientists looked for a way to organize them into groups. A Swedish scientist named Carolus Linnaeus (1707–1778) worked out a system for classifying both animals and plants. We still use it today.

The animal kingdom is separated into two large groups—animals with backbones, called vertebrates, and animals without backbones, called invertebrates.

These large groups are divided into smaller groups called phyla. And phyla are divided into even smaller groups called classes. The animals in each group are classified together when their bodies are similar in certain ways.

Vertebrates
Animals With Backbones

FISH	Swordfish, tuna, salmon, trout, halibut
AMPHIBIANS	Frogs, toads, mud puppies
REPTILES	Turtles, alligators, crocodiles, lizards
BIRDS	Sparrows, owls, turkeys, hawks
MAMMALS	Kangaroos, opossums, dogs, cats, bears, seals, rats, squirrels, rabbits, chipmunks, porcupines, horses, pigs, cows, deer, bats, whales, dolphins, monkeys, apes, humans

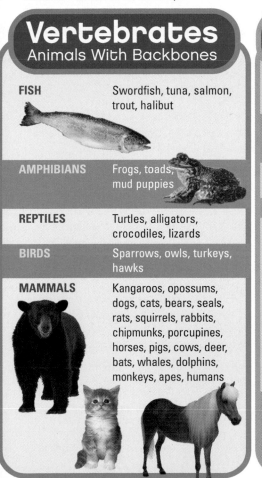

Invertebrates
Animals Without Backbones

PROTOZOA	The simplest form of animals
COELENTERATES	Jellyfish, hydra, sea anemones, coral
MOLLUSKS	Clams, snails, squid, oysters
ANNELIDS	Earthworms
ARTHROPODS	
Crustaceans:	Lobsters, crayfish
Centipedes and Millipedes	
Arachnids:	Spiders, scorpions
Insects:	Butterflies, grasshoppers, bees, termites, cockroaches
ECHINODERMS	Starfish, sea urchins, sea cucumbers

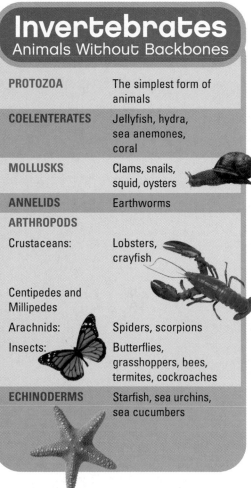

Homework Help

How can you remember the animal classifications from most general to most specific? Try this sentence:

King Philip Came Over From Great Spain.
K = Kingdom; **P** = Phylum; **C** = Class; **O** = Order; **F** = Family; **G** = Genus; **S** = Species.

It's A BUG'S World

Humans may be the smartest creatures on the planet, but they're greatly outnumbered! About half of all known living species are members of the class Insecta. If you could put all life on Earth on a scale all at once, insects would make up about 80% of the weight.

Insects are Arthropods (see page 29). Other Arthropods include crabs, spiders, lobsters, and scorpions.

You wouldn't mistake a crab for an insect, but many people think spiders are. To some people they're all just "bugs." One way to tell the difference is that spiders have 2 body segments and 8 legs, while insects have 3 body segments and 6 legs. Spiders are in their own class—Arachnida. (If you're afraid of a spider, it's *arachnophobia*.)

The BUZZ on Bees

The honeybee is about 1/2 inch long. It has a brownish, hairy thorax (mid-section) and orange-yellow and black bands on its abdomen, with "baskets" for carrying pollen on its hind legs. Honeybees are social insects. They live in fields, woods, and gardens in large colonies that are ruled by a **queen** bee. The queen is much bigger than the other bees, and her job is to lay eggs to populate the colony. She may lay 600 to 1,500 eggs a day in her three-to-four-year lifetime.

In honeybee society, stout male bees called **drones** have only one job: mating with the queen. The female **worker** bees have lots of jobs. These bees, as many as 50,000-60,000, build and repair the hive, feed the queen and larva (young), guard the entrance to the hive, help keep the hive cool by fanning their wings, and collect nectar to make honey. Bees use "dance language" to tell other bees where and how far away food is. There are two basic dances using tail wagging and

flying in circles. Bee experts have actually devised a robot bee that can speak to other bees by dancing!

Honeybees fly 15 miles per hour, visiting 50 to 100 flowers to collect nectar during one trip from the hive. They really are busy! In a single day, a honeybee may fly 12 miles and pollinate as many as 10,000 flowers! Bees store their collected nectar in a special honey stomach. When it's full, the bee returns to the hive to place its nectar in an empty honeycomb to be made into honey. Rather than hibernating, honeybees feed on stored honey and share body heat, clustering together in dense packs to survive the long winter months.

Bees are important to us not just because they're the only source of honey, but because in gathering nectar they move pollen from one plant to another. Without their help, many fruit and vegetable crops would not be able to reproduce.

BEE-LIEVE IT:

- ▶ There are more than 20,000 species of bees in the world.
- ▶ Bee wings beat 11,400 times per minute.
- ▶ Honeybees are the only insects that produce food eaten by humans.
- ▶ U.S. honey production averages over 200 million pounds per year.
- ▶ Bees have been making honey for at least 150 million years.
- ▶ Bees need to visit about 2 million flowers to make just 1 pound of honey.

REPTILES & AMPHIBIANS

Reptiles and amphibians are **vertebrates**, which means they have backbones. They are also **ectotherms**, which means they can't regulate their own body temperature. They need sunlight to warm them up and shade to cool them down if they get too hot. They get sluggish and don't move around too much in cold weather. In winter, some species hibernate.

Kinds of REPTILES

Reptiles have been around for millions of years and once were the most common vertebrate animals on Earth. Today, they are divided into **four main groups**: turtles and tortoises; lizards and snakes; crocodiles and alligators; and the tuatara. (A tuatara looks like a lizard, but it isn't. It's a species left over from a group of reptiles as old as dinosaurs. They live only in New Zealand and are in danger of becoming extinct.)

Some reptiles, like crocodiles and alligators, spend most of their time in water. Some turtles (like snapping turtles), snakes (like anacondas), and lizards (like marine iguanas) spend a lot of their time in water as well. But most species live on land. All have a scaly skin to protect them. Reptiles are found in all habitats except polar ice and tundra.

Reptiles usually lay their eggs in nests or holes dug in the ground. But some snakes, like rattlesnakes, let the eggs hatch inside the body and give birth to live babies.

Female alligators and crocodiles are very good mothers. They guard the nest and even help the hatchlings get a start in life. Some snakes do this too! But most reptiles lay their eggs and leave. The hatchlings, which are perfect miniature copies of their parents, are on their own. Baby rattlesnakes even have a supply of venom!

Kinds of AMPHIBIANS

Amphibians are cold-blooded animals that live part of their lives in water and part on land. They are divided into **three main groups**: salamanders, newts, and mudpuppies; caecilians; and frogs and toads. (Caecilians are sometimes called "rubber eels" and look like worms or small snakes without scales.) The skin of most amphibians is soft and moist. And though they are protected by mucus that comes out of the skin, amphibians usually must live near water or moist places to help keep them from drying out.

Unlike reptiles (or humans!), amphibians start life looking very different from their parents. A young amphibian is called a larva. It changes into an adult through a process called **metamorphosis**. The tadpole is a good example of a frog larva. It starts out with gills to breathe underwater (see page 202) and a tail for swimming. As it grows up, it develops lungs, legs, and a different mouth. Its eyes move up on its head. When it loses its tail, it is an adult frog, and will spend much of its time on land. Other amphibians go through similar changes.

All About... ANIMAL MIGRATION

Flock of swallows

The regular movement of animals during the year, usually following the seasons, is called **migration**. Animals travel at different times of the year to get the most from their surroundings. Their journeys range from tens of thousands of miles to only a few hundred yards!

Each year the **arctic tern** makes a 22,000-mile round-trip following the warmer weather from the northern Arctic polar region down to Antarctica. On the other hand, the **hummingbird** moves only a few hundred yards up or down a mountain. Arctic terns migrate over the sea— grabbing meals by diving into the water for fish. They stay in the Arctic only around 90 days before traveling south.

Other birds also log thousands of miles in search of warmth and food. The long-tailed **jaeger** flies 5,000 to 9,000 miles each way. Sandhill and whooping **cranes** fly as much as 2,500 miles each year, and barn **swallows**—which fly at speeds up to 46 mph—travel as far as 6,000 miles.

Swallows are among the first migrants each fall. Baby swallows and their parents learn each other's voices so they can stay together during migration. Most of the bird species that nest in the U.S. (520 out of 650 species) migrate south for the winter.

Monarch butterflies also travel long distances to stay warm, flying up to 3,000 miles to the same winter roosts— sometimes to the exact same trees! However, individual monarchs only make the round-trip once because their life span is only a few months. Their great-great-grandchildren return south the following fall. ▶

Some migrations take place over longer periods of time. **Salmon** begin their lives in freshwater streams and rivers, migrate to the ocean as adults, then return to the streams to breed. They use their sense of smell to find the exact stream in which they were born. Fish that are born in freshwater, live in saltwater, then return to freshwater to spawn are called **anadromous** (eh-NAD-ro-muss) fish. Eels do the opposite and are called **catadromous** (ca-TA-dra-muss). They are born in saltwater, and grow up and live in freshwater.

Whales travel to cold water for feeding and to warm water to give birth. Humpback whales prefer the warm subtropical water off Hawaii to give birth to their young, so they make trips there each fall. Then they head north to spend the summer near Alaska, where the food is plentiful. They average only about 1 mile an hour—taking plenty of time to rest and socialize along the way.

All About... DOGS

We know that dogs are humans' best friend—they love us and we love them. However, we're not so sure where they came from. Many scientists think they came from wolves 15,000 years ago. Although wolves are wild and dogs are tame, they're still a lot alike. Both wag their tails when happy and put their tails between their legs when scared. They also growl when angry, mark their territory, and want to be part of a "pack," or community. Other scientists think today's nearly 400 breeds of pet dogs came from wild dogs.

▲ Dog sledding through deep snow

No matter who their ancestors were, dogs have a "leg up" on their wilder cousins when it comes to reading humans' signals. In one experiment, conducted with chimpanzees, dogs, and wolves, food was hidden under one of two containers. The dogs did much better than the other animals because they watched the human experimenter, who pointed to, looked at, or tapped the container with food.

Dogs make great pets, but some are specially trained to do more than keep us company. "Working dogs" guide blind and wheelchair-bound people, help police sniff out bombs or drugs, herd sheep and cattle, lift the spirits of sick people, locate stranded travelers, and even act in movies or on TV!

▲ Wensleydale sheepdogs

The FBI uses working dogs because they're good at finding things using their keen senses. A dog's sense of hearing is 44 times more powerful than ours, and dogs can sometimes pick up a scent up to half a mile away, even if it's underground or underwater!

The FBI dogs are trained by Special FBI agents, or "handlers," to know what to search for. Handlers teach the dog how to find specific things in all different places like trees, woods, suitcases, or cars.

Pets At The Top

TOP TEN DOG BREEDS

Here are the ten most popular U.S. dog breeds with the numbers of dogs registered by the American Kennel Club in 2003:

1	Labrador retriever	144,934	6	Yorkshire terrier	38,256
2	Golden retriever	52,530	7	Boxer	34,136
3	Beagle	45,033	8	Poodle	32,176
4	German shepherd	43,950	9	Shih Tzu	26,935
5	Dachshund	39,473	10	Chihuahua	24,930

Zookeeper

Nicki Boyd is absolutely wild about her job! She's the Team Lead Zookeeper at the Children's Zoo in California's famous San Diego Zoo. Nicki trains and cares for creatures big and small. She also teaches people about the importance of protecting wildlife.

Q: How did you get where you are today?

I attended and graduated from Moorpark's Teaching Zoo in California and then went on to more schooling as a veterinary technician. I was hired at the San Diego Zoo two weeks after graduation. I have been at the zoo for 12 years. I was a keeper for nine years and have been a Team Lead Zookeeper for the last three years.

Q: What personality traits do you need to do this job well?

This job requires someone who is dedicated to animal care. I do a lot of public speaking, so being outgoing helps you get up in front of a large audience or a TV camera to teach people about the animals.

Q: Can you describe your typical day?

A typical day at the zoo is anything but typical. We always have the feeding and cleaning to do, but we do so much more. Some days, like yesterday, I have to take some monkeys to see the veterinarian for a checkup. Some days I take animals to the local news station to teach viewers about animals and conservation. We do daily training sessions so you can come to the Children's Zoo and meet the animals up close and in person. The variety is what makes this job so fun!

Q: What animals do you work with?

I work in the Children's Zoo, which has over 200 animals. I am responsible for all of them in some way. We have spider monkeys, red pandas, wombats, otters, birds of prey, parrots, naked mole rats, reptiles and so much more. I really like working with birds, mammals, and reptiles, and that's why I love working in the Children's Zoo!

Q: Which animal do you most like to work with? Why?

I have a few favorites. Our binturong (a relative of the meerkat and mongoose) and tree kangaroo both come out on leashes for animal presentations and walks. I also enjoy the red pandas and recently started training pygmy marmosets, which are the smallest monkeys in the world. That has been challenging and rewarding. Each animal and species has its own personality. It is interesting to train them because you get to see how they think.

Q: What's the best thing about your job?

The best part of my job is feeling that I make a difference in the world. The animals help me reach people about conservation. I hope that they recycle, don't buy animal products like fur, and continue to support conservation after making a connection with wildlife.

WEEKLY WR READER

From the *Weekly Reader*

THE MANY FACES OF BATS

There are almost a thousand species of bats worldwide. Bats come in different colors, shapes, and sizes. Some have huge ears and unusual faces. In fact, a bat's face can teach you about its habits. Take a closer look at some of these creatures.

Vampire Bat

Vampire bats can be found in Mexico, Central America, and South America. They drink blood, but it's usually from cattle and horses–not people. A heat sensor on its nose helps it find blood close to the surface of its victim's skin.

Egyptian Fruit Bat

Egyptian fruit bats live mainly in Asia and Africa. They eat fruit and nectar. Their long noses help them locate ripe fruit. Fruit bats use their sharp teeth to chew fruit.

American Long-Eared Bat

This bat's ears are almost as long as its head and body. It uses its ears to detect insects. This bat, which is found in parts of North America, feeds mainly on moths.

Echolocation

Some kinds of bats use echolocation (EHK-oh-loh-KAY-shun) to navigate in the dark and to find insects. The bats make sounds that can't be heard by humans. A bat knows where an insect is because the bat's sounds echo, or bounce off, an insect and return to the bat's ears. A bat can actually hear the footsteps of a tiny mosquito!

Bat Facts

▶ Bats are the only mammals that can fly.

▶ A little brown bat may eat as many as 1,000 mosquitoes in an hour.

▶ The tiniest bat is about the size of a penny. The largest bat has a 6-foot wingspan.

For more information about Weekly Reader, go to **WEB SITE** *www.weeklyreader.com*

Art

Can you name a "wrap" artist? page 38

Through Artists' Eyes

Artists look at the world in a new way. Their work can be funny or sad, beautiful or disturbing, real-looking or strange.

▶ Throughout history, artists have painted pictures of nature (called **landscapes**), pictures of people (called **portraits**), and pictures of flowers in vases, food, and other objects (known as **still lifes**). Today many artists create pictures that do not look like anything in the real world. These are examples of **abstract art**, or modern art.

▶ **Photography**, too, may be a form of art. Photos record both the commonplace and the exotic, and help us look at events in new ways.

▶ **Sculpture** is a three-dimensional form made from clay, stone, metal, or other material. Sculptures can be large, like the Statue of Liberty, or small. Some are real-looking. Others have no form you can recognize.

The Starry Night, *by Vincent van Gogh*

SOME FAMOUS WORKS of ART

Painting	Artist	When Painted	Where It Is
American Gothic	Grant Wood	1930	Art Institute of Chicago
Christina's World	Andrew Wyeth	1948	Museum of Modern Art, New York*
Guernica	Pablo Picasso	1937	Reina Sofía Museum, Madrid, Spain
Lavender Mist	Jackson Pollock	1950	National Gallery of Art, Washington, DC
Mona Lisa	Leonardo da Vinci	1503-1506	Louvre Museum, Paris, France
Nighthawks	Edward Hopper	1942	Art Institute of Chicago
The Scream	Edvard Munch	1893	National Gallery, Oslo, Norway
The Starry Night	Vincent van Gogh	1889	Museum of Modern Art, New York*

*The Museum of Modern Art (MoMA) in Manhattan is closed for renovation and rebuilding until late 2004. In the meantime, all the artwork is at MoMA QNS, The Museum of Modern Art in Queens.

Schools of Art

The style of a painting depends on many choices by the artist. What kind of paint and what colors to use. What brushes to use and how to make the strokes. How to use light and shadow. When a group of artists paint in a similar way, and sometimes paint the same kind of thing (a portrait or landscape), it is called a movement or "school" of painting. Here are some famous painters and the "schools" of art they belong to.

J.M.W. Turner (1775-1851), a **ROMANTIC** painter, often showed life in a dramatic and dreamy way. Unlike artists before him, Turner found new ways to paint light. He became an expert at painting the effects of different kinds of light, like moonlight and firelight. His work directly influenced the impressionists who came later.

Windsor Castle *by Turner* ▶

Winslow Homer (1836-1910), a **NATURALIST** painter, often painted landscapes but was most famous for his paintings of the sea. He, too, was interested in light, but wanted his scenes to look as much like real life as possible.

◀ Breezing Up *by Homer*

Claude Monet (1840-1926), like other **IMPRESSIONIST** painters, tried to capture what the eyes see in a single glance. Impressionists were fascinated by the play of light off things, especially water. Their paintings broke many "rules" of art. The bright colors, everyday subjects, and "messy" look shocked the public at first.

Regatta at Argenteuil *by Monet* ▶

Vincent van Gogh (1853-1890) was one of the most famous **POSTIMPRESSIONISTS**, so called because they came after the impressionists. They changed reality in their paintings to create an emotional effect. After them, **EXPRESSIONISTS**, like Edvard Munch (1863-1944), distorted reality much more, and paintings of **ABSTRACT EXPRESSIONISTS**, like Jackson Pollock (1912-1956), often do not show anything we can recognize at all. The colors and brushstrokes of these paintings are meant to create a mood or reaction in the person who views them.

◀ Cypress Road *by Van Gogh*

OUT-THERE ARTWORK!

Do you think wrapping a birthday gift is hard? Talk to Christo and Jeanne-Claude, the husband-and-wife art team who have dedicated their lives to wrapping whole buildings and large natural objects. Since 1961, they've wrapped all kinds of objects, including trees, building, bridges, and medieval towers. They created a running fence in Northern California, surrounded islands near Miami, Florida, with pink fabric, and they built a wall in Germany that was 26 feet high and made of 13,000 oil barrels of different colors. Their artwork is always outdoors, and usually very big.

In February 2005, Christo and Jeanne-Claude plan to install a new piece of art, *The Gates*, in New York City's Central Park. It will be made up of 7,500 saffron-colored fabric panels placed about 10 to 15 feet apart along the 23 miles of footpaths. The panels will be anywhere from 6 to 18 feet wide, and will hang about 7 feet above the ground. The Gates will stay there for 16 days, then will be taken down. Because it will be winter—and the trees will be bare—the streams of fabric will be visible around the park from different locations, creating what the artists hope will be a "golden river." They pay for all the expenses with their own money, and all the materials are recycled afterward.

The Gates, Project for Central Park, New York City

PAINTING ON WALLS

Painting a mural

If you drew on the walls when you were a little kid, you probably got into trouble. But did you know you were following a tradition thousands of years old? Humans have drawn and painted on walls for at least 17,000 years! Prehistoric people used earth pigments and animal fat to create animal scenes on walls of their caves. The most famous of these **cave paintings** today were discovered in 1940 in a cave near Lascaux in France.

Frescoes are another type of wall painting. They are made by painting on fresh, wet plaster. The most famous fresco in history was done by Michelangelo when Pope Julius II gave him the job of repainting the ceiling of the Sistine Chapel with scenes from the Bible. It took years for him to finish this masterpiece (1508-1512), which he painted lying on his back on a scaffold. You can still see his work today if you travel to Rome and visit the Vatican; in fact, it was recently restored to look just as it did when Michelangelo finished it.

Some murals today are aimed mainly at brightening a neighborhood. Others are done to remember special people or events. You don't need to be famous to paint on walls. You could join a community group that paints (with permission) on walls or the sides of buildings. Murals are a kind of art that is for the people and by the people.

Color Wheel

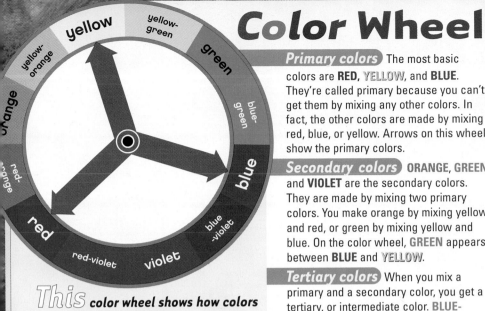

This color wheel shows how colors are related to each other.

Primary colors The most basic colors are **RED, YELLOW,** and **BLUE.** They're called primary because you can't get them by mixing any other colors. In fact, the other colors are made by mixing red, blue, or yellow. Arrows on this wheel show the primary colors.

Secondary colors ORANGE, GREEN, and **VIOLET** are the secondary colors. They are made by mixing two primary colors. You make orange by mixing yellow and red, or green by mixing yellow and blue. On the color wheel, **GREEN** appears between **BLUE** and **YELLOW.**

Tertiary colors When you mix a primary and a secondary color, you get a tertiary, or intermediate color. **BLUE-GREEN** and **YELLOW-GREEN** are intermediate colors.

More Color Terms

Values the lightness or darkness of a color is its value.

▶ **Tints** are light values made by mixing a color with white. **PINK** is a tint of **RED.**

▶ **Shades** are dark values made by mixing a color with black. **MAROON** is a shade of **RED.**

Complementary colors are contrasting colors that please the eye when used together. These colors appear opposite each other on the wheel and don't have any colors in common. **RED** is a complement to **GREEN,** which is made by mixing **YELLOW** and **BLUE.**

Analogous colors the colors next to each other on the wheel are from the same "family." **BLUE, BLUE-GREEN,** and **GREEN** all have **BLUE** in them and are analogous colors.

Cool Colors are mostly **GREEN, BLUE,** and **PURPLE.** They make you think of cool things like water and can even make you feel cooler.

Warm Colors are mostly **RED, ORANGE,** and **YELLOW.** They suggest heat and can actually make you feel warmer.

did you know?

The color wheel is used to show the mixing of pigments, as is done in paint or ink. If you mix all colors of paint, you will get black. It is different in the case of light. White light has all colors in it and black represents the absence of color.

Birthdays

Who shares your birthday?

JANUARY

January 27

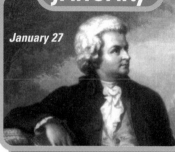

1 Paul Revere, *patriot*, 1735
2 Cuba Gooding Jr. , *actor*, 1968
3 J.R.R. Tolkien, *writer*, 1892
4 Dave Foley, *actor*, 1963
5 Warrick Dunn, *football player*, 1975
6 Joan of Arc, *warrior, saint*, 1412
7 Katie Couric, *newscaster*, 1957
8 Elvis Presley, *singer*, 1935
9 Steve Harwell, *singer*, 1967
10 George Foreman, *boxer*, 1949
11 John MacDonald, *Canada's 1st prime minister*, 1815
12 Jack London, *author*, 1876
13 Orlando Bloom, *actor*, 1977
14 Shannon Lucid, *astronaut*, 1943
15 Rev. Martin Luther King Jr., *civil rights leader*, 1929
16 Aaliyah, *singer*, 1979
17 Muhammad Ali, *boxer*, 1942
18 Kevin Costner, *actor*, 1955
19 Edgar Allan Poe, *writer*, 1809
20 Edwin "Buzz" Aldrin, *astronaut*, 1930
21 Jack Nicklaus, *golfer*, 1940
22 Diane Lane, *actress*, 1965
23 Edouard Manet, *painter*, 1832
24 Mary Lou Retton, *gymnast*, 1968
25 Alicia Keys, *singer*, 1981
26 Vince Carter, *basketball player*, 1977
27 Wolfgang Amadeus Mozart, *composer*, 1756
28 Elijah Wood, *actor*, 1981
29 Oprah Winfrey, *TV personality*, 1954
30 Jake Thomas, *actor*, 1990
31 Justin Timberlake, *singer*, 1981

FEBRUARY

1 Langston Hughes, *poet*, 1901
2 Garth Brooks, *singer*, 1962
3 Nathan Lane, *actor*, 1956
4 Rosa Parks, *civil rights activist*, 1913
5 Hank Aaron, *baseball player*, 1934
6 Babe Ruth, *baseball player*, 1895
7 Ashton Kutcher, *actor*, 1978
8 Seth Green, *actor*, 1974
9 David Gallagher, *actor*, 1985
10 Laura Dern, *actress*, 1967
11 Jennifer Aniston, *actress*, 1969
12 Arsenio Hall, *actor/host*, 1955
13 Chuck Yeager, *pilot*, 1923
14 Steve McNair, *football player*, 1973
15 Matt Groening, *cartoonist*, 1954
16 Jerome Bettis, *football player*, 1972
17 Michael Jordan, *basketball player*, 1963
18 John Travolta, *actor*, 1955
19 Jeff Daniels, *actor*, 1955
20 Brian Littrell, *singer*, 1975
21 Jennifer Love Hewitt, *actress*, 1979
22 Steve Irwin, *wildlife expert*, 1960
23 Dakota Fanning, *actress*, 1994
24 Jeff Garcia, *football player*, 1970
25 Sean Astin, *actor*, 1971
26 Johnny Cash, *musician*, 1932
27 Ralph Nader, *consumer activist*, 1934
28 Gilbert Gottfried, *actor*, 1955
29 Alex Rocco, *actor*, 1936

February 7 ▼

MARCH

March 18 ►

1 Ron Howard, *director*, 1954
2 Dr. Seuss, *author*, 1904
3 Jackie Joyner-Kersee, *Olympic champion*, 1962
4 Knute Rockne, *football player, coach*, 1888
5 Niki Taylor, *model*, 1975
6 Shaquille O'Neal, *basketball player*, 1972
7 Laura Prepon, *actress*, 1974
8 Freddie Prinze Jr., *actor*, 1976
9 Bow Wow, *rapper*, 1987
10 Shannon Miller, *Olympic gymnast*, 1987
11 Sam Donaldson, *TV journalist*, 1934
12 Amelia Earhart, *pilot*, 1905
13 William H. Macy, *actor*, 1950
14 Billy Crystal, *actor/comedian*, 1947
15 Sean Biggerstaff, *actor*, 1983
16 Jerry Lewis, *actor/comedian*, 1926
17 Mia Hamm, *soccer player*, 1972
18 Queen Latifah, *rapper/actress*, 1970
19 Wyatt Earp, *lawman*, 1848
20 Mr. (Fred) Rogers, *TV host*, 1928
21 Matthew Broderick, *actor*, 1962
22 Reese Witherspoon, *actress*, 1976
23 Jason Kidd, *basketball player*, 1973
24 Peyton Manning, *football player*, 1976
25 Sheryl Swoopes, *basketball player*, 1971
26 Keira Knightley, *actress*, 1985
27 Mariah Carey, *singer*, 1970
28 Reba McEntire, *singer, actress*, 1955
29 Jennifer Capriati, *tennis player*, 1976
30 Norah Jones, *musician*, 1979
31 Ewan McGregor, *actor*, 1971

APRIL

1 Ali MacGraw, *actress,* 1938
2 Emmylou Harris, *singer,* 1947
3 Amanda Bynes, *actress,* 1986
4 Maya Angelou, *poet,* 1928
5 Booker T. Washington, *educator,* 1856
6 John Ratzenberger, *actor,* 1947
7 Jackie Chan, *actor,* 1954
8 Kirsten Storms, *actress,* 1984
9 Dennis Quaid, *actor,* 1954
10 Mandy Moore, *singer,* 1984
11 Meshach Taylor, *actor,* 1947
12 Claire Danes, *actress,* 1979
13 Jane Leeves, *actress,* 1963
14 Sarah Michelle Gellar, *actress,* 1977
15 Emma Watson, *actress,* 1990
16 Wilbur Wright, *aviation pioneer,* 1867
17 Sean Bean, *actor,* 1959
18 Melissa Joan Hart, *actress,* 1976
19 Kate Hudson, *actress,* 1979
20 Joey Lawrence, *actor,* 1976
21 John Muir, *naturalist,* 1838
22 Jack Nicholson, *actor,* 1936
23 William Shakespeare, *playwright,* 1564
24 Kelly Clarkson, *singer,* 1982
25 Renee Zellweger, *actress,* 1969
26 Natrone Means, *football player,* 1972
27 Coretta Scott King, *activist,* 1927
28 Jay Leno, *TV host,* 1950
29 Andre Agassi, *tennis player,* 1970
30 Kirsten Dunst, *actress,* 1982

MAY

May 22

1 Tim McGraw, *musician,* 1967
2 The Rock, *wrestler,* 1972
3 James Brown, *singer,* 1933
4 Lance Bass, *singer,* 1979
5 Tammy Wynette, *singer,* 1942
6 Willie Mays, *baseball Hall of Famer,* 1931
7 Tim Russert, *TV journalist,* 1950
8 Enrique Iglesias, *singer,* 1975
9 Billy Joel, *songwriter,* 1949
10 Kenan Thompson, *actor,* 1978
11 Salvador Dali, *painter,* 1904
12 Tony Hawk, *skateboarder,* 1968
13 Stevie Wonder, *singer,* 1950
14 Cate Blanchett, *actress,* 1969
15 Emmitt Smith, *football player,* 1969
16 Pierce Brosnan, *actor,* 1953
17 Jordan Knight, *singer,* 1971
18 Spencer Breslin, *actor,* 1992
19 Malcolm X, *black nationalist, civil rights activist,* 1925
20 Cher, *singer/actress,* 1946
21 Fairuza Balk, *actress,* 1974
22 Sir Arthur Conan Doyle, *author,* 1859
23 Drew Carey, *actor/comedian,* 1958
24 Billy Gilman, *singer,* 1988
25 Mike Myers, *actor,* 1963
26 Sally Ride, *astronaut,* 1951
27 Wild Bill Hickok, *frontiersman,* 1837
28 Jim Thorpe, *Olympic champion,* 1888
29 Carmelo Anthony, *basketball player,* 1984
30 Wynonna Judd, *singer,* 1964
31 Clint Eastwood, *actor,* 1930

JUNE

1 Marilyn Monroe, *actress,* 1926
2 Dana Carvey, *comedian,* 1955
3 Lalaine (Varaga-Paras), *actress,* 1987
4 Angelina Jolie, *actress,* 1975
5 Mark Wahlberg, *actor,* 1971
6 Anson Carter, *hockey player,* 1974
7 Allen Iverson, *basketball player,* 1975
8 Frank Lloyd Wright, *architect,* 1867
9 Johnny Depp, *actor,* 1963
10 Maurice Sendak, *author/illustrator,* 1928
11 Shia LaBeouf, *actor,* 1986
12 Anne Frank, *diary writer,* 1929
13 Ashley and Mary-Kate Olsen, *actresses,* 1986
14 Donald Trump, *real estate executive,* 1946
15 Courteney Cox Arquette, *actress,* 1964
16 Kerry Wood, *baseball player,* 1977
17 Venus Williams, *tennis player,* 1980
18 Paul McCartney, *musician,* 1942
19 Paula Abdul, *singer,* 1963
20 John Goodman, *actor,* 1952
21 Prince William of Great Britain, 1982
22 Carson Daly, *TV personality,* 1973
23 Kurt Warner, *football player,* 1971
24 George Pataki, *N.Y. governor,* 1945
25 Dikembe Mutumbo, *basketball player,* 1966
26 Derek Jeter, *baseball player,* 1974
27 Tobey Maguire, *actor,* 1975
28 John Cusack, *actor,* 1966
29 Theo Fleury, *hockey player,* 1968
30 Mitch Richmond, *basketball player,* 1965

◄ *April 4*

June 11 ►

41

JULY

July 10 ▼

1 Jarome Iginla, *hockey player*, 1977
2 Lindsay Lohan, *actress*, 1986
3 Tom Cruise, *actor*, 1962
4 George Steinbrenner, *Yankees owner*, 1930
5 P. T. Barnum, *circus founder*, 1810
6 George W. Bush, *43rd president*, 1946
7 Michelle Kwan, *figure skater*, 1980
8 Kevin Bacon, *actor*, 1958
9 Tom Hanks, *actor*, 1956
10 Jessica Simpson, *singer*, 1980
11 Jeff Corwin, *wildlife expert*, 1967
12 Bill Cosby, *comedian*, 1937
13 Harrison Ford, *actor*, 1942
14 William Hanna, *cartoonist*, 1910
15 Rembrandt, *artist*, 1606
16 Will Ferrell, *actor*, 1967
17 David Hasselhoff, *actor*, 1952
18 Vin Diesel, *actor*, 1967
19 Edgar Degas, *artist*, 1834
20 Sir Edmund Hillary, *Everest climber*, 1919
21 Robin Williams, *actor/comedian*, 1952
22 David Spade, *actor*, 1965
23 Daniel Radcliffe, *actor*, 1989
24 Jennifer Lopez, *actress/singer*, 1970
25 Matt LeBlanc, *actor*, 1967
26 Sandra Bullock, *actress*, 1964
27 Alex Rodriguez, *baseball player*, 1975
28 Beatrix Potter, *author*, 1866
29 Martina McBride, *singer*, 1966
30 Lisa Kudrow, *actress*, 1963
31 J. K. Rowling, *author*, 1966

AUGUST

1 Ashley Angel, *singer*, 1981
2 Edward Furlong, *actor*, 1977
3 Tom Brady, *football player*, 1977
4 Jeff Gordon, *auto racer*, 1971
5 Neil Armstrong, *astronaut*, 1930
6 Lucille Ball, *comedian/actress*, 1911
7 Charlize Theron, *actress*, 1975
8 Joshua "JC" Chasez, *singer*, 1976
9 Chamiqua Holdsclaw, *basketball player*, 1977
10 Antonio Banderas, *actor*, 1960
11 Hulk Hogan, *wrestler*, 1953
12 Pete Sampras, *tennis player*, 1971
13 Annie Oakley, *markswoman*, 1860
14 Steve Martin, *actor/comedian*, 1945
15 Napoleon Bonaparte, *French emperor*, 1769
16 Vanessa Carlton, *singer*, 1980
17 Davy Crockett, *frontiersman*, 1786
18 Meriwether Lewis, *explorer*, 1774
19 Lil' Romeo, *rapper*, 1989
20 Todd Helton, *baseball player*, 1973
21 Kenny Rogers, *singer/actor*, 1938
22 Howie Dorough, *singer*, 1973
23 Shelley Long, *actress*, 1949
24 Rupert Grint, *actor*, 1988
25 Kel Mitchell, *actor/comedian*, 1978
26 Macaulay Culkin, *actor*, 1980
27 Alexa Vega, *actress*, 1988
28 Jack Black, *actor*, 1969
29 Michael Jackson, *singer*, 1958
30 Andy Roddick, *tennis player*, 1982
31 Hideo Nomo, *baseball player*, 1968

▼ August 13

SEPTEMBER

1 Tim Duncan, *basketball player*, 1966
2 Keanu Reeves, *actor*, 1964
3 Charlie Sheen, *actor*, 1965
4 Beyoncé Knowles, *musician*, 1981
5 Rose McGowan, *actress*, 1973
6 Tim Henman, *tennis player*, 1974
7 Briana Scurry, *soccer player*, 1971
8 Pink, *singer*, 1979
9 Adam Sandler, *actor*, 1966
10 Randy Johnson, *baseball player*, 1963
11 Harry Connick Jr., *musician/actor*, 1967
12 Yao Ming, *basketball player*, 1980
13 Roald Dahl, *author*, 1916
14 Adam Lamberg, *actor*, 1984
15 Prince Harry of Great Britain, 1984
16 Alexis Bledel, *actress*, 1982
17 John Ritter, *actor*, 1948
18 Lance Armstrong, *cyclist*, 1971
19 Trisha Yearwood, *singer*, 1964
20 Guy Lafleur, *hockey player*, 1951
21 Faith Hill, *singer*, 1967
22 Tom Felton, *actor*, 1987
23 Bruce Springsteen, *musician*, 1949
24 Eddie George, *football player*, 1973
25 Will Smith, *actor*, 1968
26 Serena Williams, *tennis player*, 1981
27 Avril Lavigne, *singer*, 1984
28 Hilary Duff, *actress*, 1987
29 Bryant Gumbel, *TV personality*, 1948
30 Lacy Chabert, *actress*, 1982

OCTOBER

1 Richard Harris, *actor*, 1932
2 Sting, *musician*, 1951
3 Gwen Stefani, *singer*, 1969
4 Alicia Silverstone, *actress*, 1976
5 Parminder K. Nagra, *actress*, 1975
6 Jack De Sena, *actor*, 1987
7 Priest Holmes, *football player*, 1973
8 Matt Damon, *actor*, 1970
9 Annika Sorenstam, *golfer*, 1970
10 Brett Favre, *football player*, 1969
11 Eleanor Roosevelt, *first lady*, 1884
12 Marion Jones, *Olympic champion*, 1975
13 Ashanti (Douglas), *singer*, 1980
14 Natalie Maines, *singer*, 1974
15 Emeril Lagasse, *TV chef*, 1959
16 Kordell Stewart, *football player*, 1972
17 Nick Cannon, *actor/comedian*, 1980
18 Peter Boyle, *actor*, 1935
19 Omar Gooding, *actor/host*, 1976
20 Viggo Mortensen, *actor*, 1958
21 Jeremy Miller, *actor*, 1976
22 Jonathan Lipnicki, *actor*, 1990
23 Stevie Brock, *singer*, 1990
24 Monica, *singer*, 1980
25 Pablo Picasso, *painter*, 1881
26 Hillary Rodham Clinton, *U.S. senator*, 1947
27 Kelly Osbourne, *TV personality*, 1984
28 Bill Gates, *Microsoft founder*, 1955
29 Richard Dreyfuss, *actor*, 1947
30 Diego Maradonna, *soccer player*, 1960
31 Peter Jackson, *director*, 1961

NOVEMBER

November 30

1 Stephen Crane, *author*, 1871
2 Daniel Boone, *frontiersman*, 1734
3 Roseanne, *actress*, 1952
4 Laura Bush, *first lady*, 1946
5 Javy Lopez, *baseball player*, 1970
6 James A. Naismith, *basketball inventor*, 1861
7 Marie Curie, *scientist*, 1867
8 Courtney Thorne-Smith, *actress*, 1968
9 Nick Lachey, *singer*, 1973
10 Sinbad, *actor/comedian*, 1956
11 Leonardo DiCaprio, *actor*, 1974
12 Sammy Sosa, *baseball player*, 1968
13 Whoopi Goldberg, *actress*, 1949
14 Prince Charles of Great Britain, 1948
15 Zena Grey, *actress*, 1988
16 Trevor Penick, *singer*, 1979
17 Danny DeVito, *actor*, 1944
18 Christina Vidal, *actress*, 1981
19 Gail Devers, *Olympic champion*, 1966
20 Ming-Na Wen, *actress*, 1967
21 Ken Griffey Jr., *baseball player*, 1969
22 Guion Bluford, *astronaut*, 1942
23 Billy the Kid, *outlaw*, 1859
24 Scott Joplin, *composer*, 1868
25 Jenna and Barbara Bush, *President Bush's daughters*, 1981
26 Charles Schulz, *cartoonist*, 1922
27 Anders Celsius, *scientist*, 1701
28 Randy Newman, *musician/composer*, 1943
29 Mariano Rivera, *baseball player*, 1969
30 Mark Twain, *author*, 1835

DECEMBER

1 Woody Allen, *actor/director*, 1935
2 Britney Spears, *singer*, 1981
3 Brendan Fraser, *actor*, 1967
4 Orlando Brown, *actor*, 1987
5 Frankie Muniz, *actor*, 1985
6 Tom Hulce, *actor*, 1953
7 Aaron Carter, *singer*, 1987
8 Teresa Weatherspoon, *basketball player*, 1965
9 Clarence Birdseye, *frozen food pioneer*, 1886
10 Raven Symone, *actress*, 1985
11 John Kerry, *U.S. senator*, 1943
12 Frank Sinatra, *singer/actor*, 1915
13 Jamie Foxx, *comedian*, 1967
14 Craig Biggio, *baseball player*, 1965
15 Mo Vaughn, *baseball player*, 1967
16 Ludwig van Beethoven, *composer*, 1770
17 Bill Pullman, *actor*, 1954
18 Steven Spielberg, *film producer*, 1947
19 William Parry, *Arctic explorer*, 1790
20 Rich Gannon, *football player*, 1965
21 Jane Kaczmarek, *actress*, 1955
22 Lady Bird Johnson, *first lady*, 1912
23 Scott Gomez, *hockey player*, 1979
24 Ricky Martin, *singer*, 1971
25 Clara Barton, *American Red Cross founder*, 1821
26 Susan Butcher, *sled dog racer*, 1954
27 Louis Pasteur, *scientist*, 1822
28 Denzel Washington, *actor*, 1954
29 Mary Tyler Moore, *actress*, 1936
30 LeBron James, *basketball player*, 1984
31 Henri Matisse, *painter*, 1869

December 11 ▶

◀ *October 20*

Books

What president lost a lot of teeth? page 46

DON'T READ THESE BOOKS!

Really, they are much too depressing, and there are ten of them. And another one, *The Grim Grotto,* is going to be published in September 2004.

There is also a movie starring Jim Carrey and Meryl Streep scheduled to open in December 2004. It's called *Lemony Snicket's A Series of Unfortunate Events.* It might be even more depressing!

▼ *Daniel Handler, a.k.a. Lemony Snicket*

Lemony Snicket

Did you never hear of the mysterious **Lemony Snicket** and his series of "unfortunate events" involving the **Baudelaire children**? His real name is Daniel Handler, and he's a rock musician with an odd sense of humor. In *Book the First: The Bad Beginning,* readers are warned, "If you are interested in stories with happy endings, you would be better off reading some other book. In this book there is no happy ending, there is no happy beginning, and very few happy things in the middle."

Violet, Klaus, and baby Sunny become orphans in the first book. They soon fall into the clutches of Count Olaf, a treacherous and evil man who, in many ridiculous disguises, chases the children through *The Reptile Room, The Wide Window, The Miserable Mill, The Austere Academy, The Ersatz Elevator, The Vile Village, The Hostile Hospital,* and *The Carnivorous Carnival.*

Along with the gloom and doom come some pretty good laughs. In all, 13 books are planned for the series—a most unfortunate number!

WHO AM I?

I was born in Boston on January 19, 1809. My parents died when I was little, and I was raised by my foster father, John Allan. I attended West Point briefly but was dismissed. Later, I worked as an editor in New York City and Philadelphia. I wrote many well-known poems, such as "The Raven" and "The Bells." I am most famous for my dark, scary tales, and I wrote the world's first detective story.

Answer: Edgar Allan Poe

Book Awards, 2003-2004

CALDECOTT MEDAL
For the artist of the best children's picture book
2004 winner: Mordicai Gerstein for ***The Man Who Walked Between the Towers***

NEWBERY MEDAL
For the author of the best children's book
2003 winner: ***The Tale of Despereaux***, by Kate DiCamillo

CORETTA SCOTT KING AWARD
For artists and authors whose works encourage expression of the African-American experience
2004 winners:
AUTHOR AWARD: ***The First Part Last***, by Angela Johnson
ILLUSTRATOR AWARD: ***Beautiful Blackbird***, illustrated by Ashley Bryan

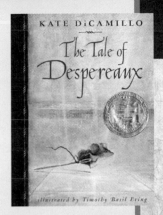

KATE DiCAMILLO
The Tale of Despereaux
illustrated by Timothy Basil Ering

BEST NEW BOOKS OF THE YEAR
Among those chosen in 2004 by the American Library Association

An American Plague: The True and Terrifying Story of the Yellow Fever Epidemic of 1793, by Jim Murphy (ages 11 and up). Art and newspaper headlines from the times help bring to life the story of the deadly yellow fever epidemic that hit Philadelphia, then the nation's capital, in 1793.

Granny Torrelli Makes Soup, by Sharon Creech (ages 9 and up). Granny's stories, and her cooking, always seem to make things better. They might be just the recipe to fix the broken friendship between 12-year-old Rosie and her best friend Bailey.

The Man Who Walked Between the Towers, by Mordicai Gerstein (ages 5 and up). This book tells about Philippe Petit, the French high-wire artist who walked between the twin towers of the World Trade Center from roof to roof across a tight rope in 1974. It also pays tribute to the buildings destroyed on September 11, 2001.

Silent Movie, by Avi (ages 9 and up). The black-and-white illustrations make this book look a bit like an old silent film. Set in the early 1900s, it's the story of Gustave and his mother, who are lost in New York City with no money, and cannot speak English. When Gustave gets a role in a silent movie, their fortunes starts to get better.

Snowed in with Grandmother Silk, by Carol Fenner (ages 9 and up). Ruddy finds out he has to spend ten days with Grandmother Silk while his parents are away, and he is not looking forward to it. She won't play games or watch TV with him, and she hates loud noise. When the two are snowed-in together one night and have no heat, light, or water, they finally get to know one another.

The Tale of Despereaux: Being the Story of a Mouse, a Princess, Some Soup, and a Spool of Thread, by Kate DiCamillo, illustrated by Timothy Basil Ering (ages 9 and up). Despereaux is a small mouse who is sent away by his family because his ears are too big. Forced to live in a dungeon, he meets and falls in love with Princess Pea. She makes friends with him even though her father doesn't like rodents.

45

Books to Enjoy

FICTION
Fiction is another word for invented stories. Some stories are set in a world of fantasy. Others seem more like real life.

Harry Potter and the Order of the Phoenix, by J.K. Rowling (ages 9 and up). In this, the fifth book in the famous Harry Potter series, Harry, now 15, continues his adventures at the Hogwarts School of Witchcraft and Wizardry.

Horse Hooves and Chicken Feet: Mexican Folktales, collected by Neil Philip and illustrated by Jacqueline Mair (ages 8 and up). Colorful paintings based on Mexican folk art bring to life these 15 folktales from Mexico and the American Southwest.

Inkheart, by Cornelia Funke (ages 10 and up). Twelve-year-old Meggie is in for a big surprise when she finds out her father has the magical ability to "read" characters out of books and into the real world.

The Merlin Conspiracy, by Diana Wynne Jones (ages 11 and up). This story is told in alternating chapters by Arianrhod "Roddy" Hyde and Nick Mallory. Though Roddy lives in an England that might have been, and Nick lives in our world, they are destined to meet.

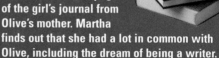

Olive's Ocean, by Kevin Henkes (ages 9 and up). After 12-year-old Olive dies when she is hit by a car, her classmate Martha receives a page of the girl's journal from Olive's mother. Martha finds out that she had a lot in common with Olive, including the dream of being a writer.

Stop the Train!, by Geraldine McCaughrean (ages 10 and up). Based partly on true events, this story is set in 1893, during the Oklahoma Land Rush. Townspeople try to persuade a train company to stop at their new town.

POETRY
Poems use language in new and imaginative ways, sometimes in rhyme.

Blues Journey, by Walter Dean Myers and illustrated by Christopher Myers (ages 10 and up). These poems tell us about a unique form of American music. The book has an introduction outlining the history, elements, and importance of the blues.

George Washington's Teeth, Deborah Chandra and Madeleine Comora (ages 7 and up). This illustrated book of poetry traces the dental problems of our first president, who lost on average a tooth a year from age 24.

Locomotion, by Jacqueline Woodson (ages 10 and up). A novel in verse, these 60 poems tell the life story of a New York City fifth grader who lives in a foster home and discovers he has a gift for poetry.

NONFICTION These books prove that facts can be fascinating.

Ben Franklin's Almanac: Being a True Account of the Good Gentleman's Life, by Candace Fleming (ages 9 and up). Put together like a scrapbook, this book is filled with portraits, sketches, cartoons, quotations, and facts both from and about this early American, who was a printer, statesman, diplomat, scientist, and writer.

Don't Hold Me Back: My Life and Art, by Winfred Rembert (ages 8 and up). The painter's words and images tell the story of his life as an African-American growing up in the South in the 1950s.

Hana's Suitcase: A True Story, by Karen Levine (ages 9 and up). Inspired by Japanese kids who wanted to know more about a suitcase in a museum, this book follows the real-life story of Hana Brady, a Czechoslovakian girl who died in the Holocaust.

Benjamin Franklin

Harvesting Hope: The Story of Cesar Chavez, by Kathleen Krull and illustrated by Yuyi Morales (ages 7 and up). Focusing on his 340-mile march of protest, this book tells the life story of the civil rights leader who fought to improve working conditions for migrant farm workers in California.

In Defense of Liberty: The Story of America's Bill of Rights, by Russell Freedman (ages 9 and up). This book offers a clear history how the Bill of Rights came about and what they mean in American life.

Jack: The Early Years of John F. Kennedy, by Ilene Cooper (ages 12 and up). The childhood biography—from birth through boarding school—of the boy from Massachusetts who grew up to be the 35th president of the United States.

John F. Kennedy

REFERENCE Many reference materials are stored on CD-ROMs and are also available on the Internet.

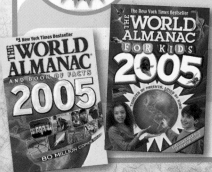

Almanac: A one-volume book of facts and statistics.

Atlas: A collection of maps.

Dictionary: A book of words in alphabetical order. Ilt gives meanings and spellings and shows how words are pronounced.

Encyclopedia: A place to go for information on almost any subject.

ALL ABOUT... BOOKS

If a Roman emperor wanted to read a book, he had to unroll it. Books were written on long **scrolls** (kind of like a roll of paper towels) that you unrolled as you went along. This was clumsy, especially if you were looking for a certain passage. Around **A.D.** 100 the **codex** was invented. It was made up of a stack of pages stitched together at the side and protected by a cover. The codex was easier to carry around, to store, and to search through. Books we read today look something like a codex.

In the Middle Ages books were made by monks who copied them by hand onto prepared animal skins called **parchment**. The monks often decorated the pages with beautiful color illustrations called "illuminations." Books were scarce, and few people who were not priests or monks could read. Even those who could read had to be rich to buy these hand-written books.

A big change came with the use of paper and printing, which were first invented in China. **Paper** came into Europe through the Muslim world and was common by the 14th century. Johann Gutenberg of Germany perfected **printing** in the 1450s. Once books no longer had to be copied by hand and could be printed on paper, they became less expensive and reading became more common.

At first books were still not easy to make and not cheap. Each letter was on a separate piece of type, and a typesetter had to put each piece into place individually. Once all the letters for the page were in place, they were covered with ink and printed, one at a time, by hand on a press. By the 19th century, however, steam-powered presses could print out hundreds of pages at a time. Another invention was the **linotype** machine, which stamped out individual letters and set them up much faster than a typesetter could. Now books had become truly affordable, and the skill of reading was something that everyone was expected to learn.

did you know?

The word "paper" comes from the ancient word "papyrus." Papyrus was a reed used in the ancient world to make writing material. It was made by slicing the stalks and gluing them together in a criss-cross pattern. The sheets were then glued together to make a scroll. Some ancient papyrus scrolls were over 30 feet long.

Buildings

Where can you find the world's largest greenhouse?

page 51

TALLEST *BUILDINGS* IN THE WORLD

Here are the world's tallest buildings, with the year each was completed. Heights listed here don't include antennas or other outside structures.

TAIPEI FINACIAL CENTER, Taipei, Taiwan (completed 2003) **Height**: 101 stories, 1,667 feet ▶

PETRONAS TOWERS 1 & 2, Kuala Lumpur, Malaysia (1998) **Height:** each building is 88 stories, 1,483 feet

SEARS TOWER, Chicago, Illinois (1974) **Height:** 110 stories, 1,450 feet

JIN MAO BUILDING, Shanghai, China (1998) **Height:** 88 stories, 1,381 feet

TWO INTERNATIONAL FINANCE CENTRE, Hong Kong, China (2003) **Height**: 88 stories, 1,352 feet

CITIC PLAZA, Guangzhou, China (1997) **Height**: 80 stories, 1,283 feet

WORLD'S TALLEST WHEN BUILT

The New York World Building, NY. Built 1890. Height: 309 feet. Torn down 1955.
- Home of the ***New York World*** newspaper, which started ***The World Almanac*** in 1868.

Metropolitan Life Insurance Tower, NY. Built 1909. Height: 700 feet.

Woolworth Building, NY. Built 1913. Height: 792 feet.

Chrysler Building, NY. Built 1930. Height: 1,046 feet.

Empire State Building, NY. Built 1931. Height: 1,250 feet.

World Trade Center Towers 1 & 2, NY. Built 1973. Height: 1,368 feet and 1,362 feet. Destroyed in September 2001.

THE TALLEST TOWERS

The world's **tallest free-standing structure** is the 1,815-foot **CN Tower** in Toronto, Canada. It is not exactly a *building* since it does not have stories. "Free-standing" means it supports its own weight and is not attached to anything. Brave visitors can walk across the glass floor at the 1,122-foot level!

The **tallest structure** is the **KVLY-TV tower** in Fargo, North Dakota. It's 2,063 feet tall (including the 113-foot antenna) and made of steel. The tower is anchored and supported by more than 7.5 miles of steel wires.

◀ CN Tower

A Short History of Tall Buildings

For over 4,000 years, the world's tallest structure was the 480-foot-tall Great Pyramid at Giza. Next to top the list was the cathedral spire in Cologne, Germany (513 ft., built in 1880), then the Washington Monument in Washington, D.C. (555 ft., 1884). These buildings all had thick stone walls, with not much space inside.

The biggest challenge to building tall was gravity. Whether made of mud, stone, brick, timber, or concrete, most buildings had load-bearing walls. This meant that the walls had to support their own weight, the roof, the floors, and everything in the building. The higher the walls, the thicker they needed to be, and too many windows would weaken the building.

By the 1880s, three **key factors in the evolution of tall buildings** were in place:

1. **A NEED FOR SPACE** Crowded cities had less space for building, and land got expensive. To create more space, buildings had to go up instead of out.

2. **BETTER STEEL PRODUCTION** Mass-producing steel made more of it available for construction. Long beams could be connected to make **columns**. These were braced with horizontal beams called **girders**. The columns and girders formed a strong three-dimensional grid called a **superstructure**. This type of building was lighter than a similar one made of stone or brick and its weight was directed down the columns, which were supported by a solid **foundation**.

3. **THE ELEVATOR** Too many stairs! The first elevator, powered by steam, was installed in a New York store in 1857. Electric elevators came along in 1880.

The first American "skyscraper" was built in Chicago in 1885. Though it was only 10 stories and 138 feet tall, the ◀ **Home Insurance Building** was the first tall building to have a metal superstructure and many windows.

As buildings got taller, a new problem sprang up—**wind**. Too much movement could damage buildings or make the people inside uncomfortable. Some tall buildings, like New York's Citicorp Center, actually have a counter-weight near the top. A computer controls a 400-ton weight, moving it back and forth to lessen the building's sway.

In California and Japan, **earthquakes** are a big problem and special techniques are needed to make tall buildings safer from quakes.

One of the most beautiful buildings in the world is the famous Taj Mahal, built on a riverbank outside Agra, India. It's actually a huge tomb. Made of white marble inlaid with gemstones, it was started in 1632 by the Mughal emperor Shah Jahan for his beloved wife who died in childbirth. Some 20,000 workers took 22 years to finish work on the tomb and surrounding buildings and grounds.

It's Not All About... TALL!

When it comes to buildings, the tall ones grab people's attention. But many other buildings are interesting and fun to look at. Here are a few really cool buildings.

KINGDOM CENTRE, Riyadh, Saudi Arabia

The first thing you notice about this unique skyscraper is its "missing" piece, which is visible from nearly all of Riyadh. It's covered in reflective glass, except for the opening, which is lined with aluminum and lit up at night with changing colored lights. A 200-foot observation bridge spans the top of the triangular hole. Because the city has a law against buildings with more than 30 floors, the designers made the top third of the Kingdom Centre just a decorative steel skeleton. This way they could build it as high as they wanted.

LA GRAND ARCHE DE LA DÉFENSE, Paris, France

The missing middle makes this 360-foot-tall cube hard to forget. Finished in 1989, this government office building was designed as a modern version of the city's famous military memorial, L'Arc de Triomphe. You could fit another famous Paris landmark, the Cathedral of Notre Dame (198.5 ft.), underneath the arch!

WALT DISNEY CONCERT HALL, Los Angeles, California

This latest addition to the Music Center of Los Angeles County, designed by the architect Frank O. Gehry, opened in October 2003 as the new home of the Los Angeles Philharmonic. On the outside it looks like a ship with its sail at full mast, and the auditorium with its curved wood ceiling looks like the hull of the ship. Not only does the curvy design *look* great; it also improves the acoustics, or the quality of the sound.

SYDNEY OPERA HOUSE, Sydney, Australia

Though it looks like a giant sea creature rising out of Sydney Harbor, architect Joern Utzon had the sections of an orange in mind when he designed this building. Finished in 1973, the shells were made of over 2,000 concrete sections held together by 217 *miles* of steel cable. The roof cover—bolted on in 4,240 sections—is covered with 1.5 million ceramic tiles.

EDEN PROJECT, Cornwall, England

The Eden Project is built on top of a huge clay pit in Western England. Its domes, or "biomes," look like they are bubbling out of the ground. The Humid Tropics Biome is the world's biggest greenhouse (11 of London's double-decker buses stacked on top of each other could fit inside!). It contains plants from the rain forest. The Warm Temperate Biome has plants from the world's Mediterranean regions. Millions of visitors have come here since the opening in March 2001 to learn about the importance of plants in different environments.

Camps

What is Bug Juice? page 53

Let's Go To Camp!

Do you want to learn how to do something completely new? Or maybe you want to improve at something you already know how to do, in sports, art, music, dance, or drama. Or, maybe you just want to have a whole lot of fun and make new friends!

Whatever the reason, camp is always in season. Each year more than 10 million kids and adults in the U.S. go to camp. Check out the camp choices in your area or anywhere in the U.S. at the American Camping Association's "Find a Camp" page at **WEB SITE** http://find.ACAcamps.org

Camp is for Everyone

No matter where or who you are, there is probably a camp near you. Here are some kinds of camps:

Resident Camp: Usually for kids age 7 or older. Campers stay overnight, usually in cabins, tents, or tepees. Stays can last a few days, a week, or more.

Day Camp: For kids as young as 4. Many of the same activities as a resident camp, but everyone goes home at the end of the day.

Specialty Camp: These are designed for learning a special skill, like horseback riding, water skiing, or dancing. There is a camp for just about every interest.

Special Needs Camp: No sort of disability should keep you from going to camp if you want to. Each year, more than a million kids with special needs go to summer camp.

You can find the ultimate summer adventure at camp. You can snowboard, skateboard, wakeboard, and mountain bike. American Camping Association-accredited High Cascade Snowboard Camp in Oregon is an example of summer fun in the snow! Find out more at **WEB SITE** *www.highcascade.com*

- Kids and families from all over the world go to camp. There are camps in Russia, Malaysia, Canada, Brazil, New Zealand, England, and many other countries.
- At camp, red Kool-Aid® is typically known as Bug Juice!

Camp Quiz

1 In what year did the first organized camp in the U.S. start?
- **A.** 1900
- **B.** 1999
- **C.** 1861
- **D.** 1300
- **E.** 1950

2 Which of these activities can you do at camp?
- **A.** scuba diving
- **B.** hiking
- **C.** learn about computers
- **D.** swimming
- **E.** all of the above

3 What should you bring to camp?
- **A.** camera and film
- **B.** water bottle
- **C.** journal
- **D.** swimming suit
- **E.** all of the above

ANSWERS ON PAGES 319-322. FOR MORE PUZZLES GO TO WWW.WORLDALMANACFORKIDS.COM

Let's Make S'mores!
A Fun and Popular Camp Treat

What you need:
- Graham Crackers
- Marshmallows
- Chocolate bars

CAUTION: Be sure to check with an adult before you try this.

Directions: Toast marshmallows on a stick (or in the microwave for 10 seconds); be careful not to flame the marshmallow. When golden brown (or soft), put the marshmallow and a piece of chocolate between two graham crackers. You'll probally want s'more.

THE AMERICAN CAMPING ASSOCIATION®
The American Camping Association is a resource for parents and kids to help them find the right camp to fit any need and budget. For more information, visit **WEB SITE** www.ACAcamps.org

Computers

What does :-@ sound like? **page 57**

Computers perform tasks by using programs called **software**. **Programs** tell the computer what to do when the user enters certain information or commands. This is called **input**.

The computer then processes the information and gives the user the results **(output)**. The computer can also save, or store, the information.

The machines that make up a computer system are kinds of **hardware**. The largest and most powerful computers are called **mainframes**. Most people are more familiar with personal computers (PCs). These can be used at a desk **(desktops)**, carried around **(laptops)**, worn on your belt **(wearable computers)**, or even held in your hand **(palm computers)**.

SOFTWARE

KINDS OF SOFTWARE When you write on a computer you use a type of software called a word processing program. This program can be selected by using the **keyboard** or a **mouse**.

Other common types of software include programs for doing math, keeping records, playing games, and creating pictures.

ENTERING DATA In a word processing program, you can input your words by typing on the **keyboard**. The backspace and delete keys are like erasers. You can also press special **function keys** or click on certain symbols **(icons)** to center or underline words, move words around, check spelling, print out a page, and do other tasks.

HARDWARE

INSIDE THE COMPUTER The instructions from the program you use are carried out inside the computer by the **central processing unit**, or **CPU**. The CPU is the computer's brain.

SEEING THE RESULTS The **monitor** and **printer** are the most commonly used output devices in a computer system. When you type a story, the words show up on a **monitor,** which is like a TV screen. Your story can be printed on paper by using a **printer**.

If you print out a story, you can mail it to a friend. But if you both have **modems**, it can get from your computer to your friend's computer. A **modem** allows information from a computer to travel over telephone or cable lines.

54

COMPUTER *TALK*

BIT The smallest unit of data.

BLOG is short for "Web log." It's a personal journal or diary that people put on a website for others to read.

BOOKMARK A feature in web browsers that lets the user save a favorite website. It can be used instead of typing in the URL.

BOOT To start up a computer.

BROWSER A program to help get around the Internet.

BUG OR GLITCH An error in a program or in the computer.

BYTE An amount of data equal to 8 bits.

CHIP A small piece of silicon holding the circuits used to store and process information.

COOKIE Some websites store information, like your passwords and other preferences, on your computer's hard drive. When you go back to that site later, your browser sends the information (the "cookie") to the website.

DATABASE A large collection of information organized so that it can be retrieved and used in different ways.

DESKTOP PUBLISHING The use of computers to design and produce magazines, newspapers, and books.

DOWNLOAD To transfer information from a host computer to a personal computer, often through a modem.

ENCRYPTION The process of changing information into a code, especially passwords, or financial or personal information, to keep others from reading it.

GIG OR GIGABYTE (GB) An amount of information equal to 1,024 megabytes.

HACKER A computer expert who likes to look at the code of operating systems and other programs to see how they work. Some hackers tamper with other people's information and programs illegally.

HTML The abbreviation for HyperText Markup Language, a computer language used to make web pages.

INTERNET A worldwide system of linked computer networks.

K Stands for *kilo,* or "thousands," in Greek. Used to represent bytes of data or memory.

MEGABYTE (MB) An amount of information equal to 1,048,516 bytes.

NETWORK A group of computers linked together so that they can share information.

PDA OR PERSONAL DIGITAL ASSISTANT A handheld computer that can store addresses, phone numbers, and other information that's useful to have handy.

PIXEL OR PICTURE ELEMENT The smallest unit of an image on a computer monitor. It can be used to measure the size of an image.

PORTAL A website that serves as a gateway to the Internet.

RAM OR RANDOM ACCESS MEMORY Memory your computer uses to open programs and store your work until you save it to a hard drive or disk. Information in RAM disappears when the computer is turned off.

ROM OR READ ONLY MEMORY Memory that contains permanent instructions for the computer and cannot be changed. The information in ROM stays after the computer is turned off.

SPAM Electronic junk mail.

THREAD A series of messages and replies that relate to a specific topic.

URL OR UNIFORM RESOURCE LOCATOR The technical name for a website address.

VIRUS A program that damages other programs and data. It gets into a computer through telephone lines or shared disks.

WI-FI OR WIRELESS FIDELITY Technology that allows people to link to other computers and the Internet from their computers without wires.

new Gadgets

Today's electronic devices not only do many different things, they are often small enough to hold in your hand or carry in your pocket. Here are some of the coolest gadgets around.

World's Smallest Hard Drive In 2004, Toshiba released the world's smallest hard drive, measuring only 0.85 of an inch across. Although it is only about the size of a postage stamp and weighs less than half an ounce, it can hold 2 to 4 gigabytes of digital information. Its small size will let it power a whole new generation of MP3 players, cell phones, PDAs, and digital cameras.

The Lightglove This wireless device worn on the underside of your wrists can sense finger and hand movements so you can remotely operate your computer instead of typing or using your mouse. If the devices are programmed for it, the Lightglove can operate stereos, telephones, video games, kitchen appliances, and lights. It can even open car doors!

The Smart Watch Microsoft's Smart Watch can pick up information from the Internet without being connected by wires. Information from a group of websites is broadcast over FM radio waves to the watch, sending the latest weather reports and news right to your wrist. The watch can even get text messages sent by friends. It runs on a rechargeable battery, and automatically updates the correct time, even if you change time zones.

Computer Games

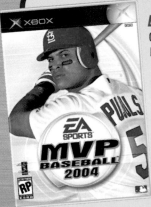

BACKYARD BASKETBALL 2004 Atari, for Windows and Mac. Choose from 30 backyard kids or 10 kid versions of real-life NBA stars like Kevin Garnett, Tracy McGrady, and Yao Ming. Pick from seven cool courts and shoot some hoop!

MVP BASEBALL 2004 Electronic Arts Sports, for Windows. Bring the stadium right into your room with this ultra-realistic game. Includes downloadable rosters of the most current line-ups for all Major League teams.

NANCY DREW: DANGER ON DECEPTION ISLAND Her Interactive, Inc., for Windows. Nancy Drew's ninth adventure takes you to an island in the North Pacific where you can explore by foot, bike, and kayak.

ZOO TYCOON: COMPLETE COLLECTION Microsoft Corp., for Windows. Includes Dinosaur Digs and Marine Mania, so you can build the ultimate zoo! Add prehistoric, marine, and even endangered species to your personal zoo.

SEARCHING *THE* INTERNET

Did you ever do a Web search and get too many results? Or be unable to find what you want? It could be that you aren't asking the search engine to look for the right terms. Here are some tips to help you find the website you want.

BE SPECIFIC Before you even start, think about what you want. Suppose you want information about birds. Do you want birds in general, or tropical birds in South America? If it's the latter, don't just type *birds*. Try *tropical birds South America* instead. Or if parrots are what you really want, try typing that first.

SOME WAYS TO SEARCH If you type in more than one word, most search engines will assume that you want only websites that show ALL the words. So *pet parrots* will work fine if you want only sites that have both those words somewhere.

Sometimes you may want websites with just ONE of the words. This can happen when there are different words for the same idea or when it is hard to figure out the best word to use. Some search engines will let you handle this by using OR in capital letters. For example, *parakeets* OR *budgerigars*.

If you want an exact phrase or title, just put quotation marks around your entry. To find websites that mention the fifth Harry Potter book, you can type *"Order of the Phoenix."*

You may want to remove certain information from your search. What if you need to read about parrots in the wild but not as pets? You can eliminate sites with the word *pet* by adding a hyphen (as a minus sign) right in front of the word *pet: parrots -pets.*

If a search gives you too many things, you can go back and use a minus sign to get rid of a word that crops up a lot in sites you do not want.

NEWS OR IMAGES ONLY

Most search engines will let you search within categories such as "Images" or "News." If you want to see pictures of parrots, you can enter *parrots* and click on "Images." Or, if you want to know if something about parrots is in the news right now, you can enter *parrots* and click on "News" for recent stories.

ADVANCED SEARCHES Some search engines give you a choice of making an Advanced Search. This may let you to do certain things easily, such as look for recent websites or for certain words that appear in the TITLE of the site. This can help narrow your search a lot. For example, lots of sites mention parrots, but only a smaller number will be about parrots and have that word in the title.

SHORTCUTS Each search engine has its own shortcuts and special keywords you can use to help find the right website. To find out more about these, go to the "Search tips" section.

Smileus

Smileys, or **emoticons**, are letters and symbols that look like faces when turned sideways. They tell things about yourself in messages you send. Here are a few with what they mean.

:-)	Smiling	:-o	Alarmed!	8-P	Yuck!
:+D	Laughing	:-]	Shocked	:-----}	Liar; Pinocchio
:-@	Screaming	:-S	Confused	:-[	Vampire
;-)	Winking	X-(	Mad	<*:-)	Magician
(:-<	Frowning	(((H)))	Big Hug	C=:-)	Chef
(:+(	Scared	I-0	Yawn		**57**

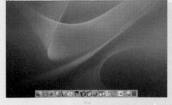

ALL ABOUT... APPLE

Almost 30 years ago in California's Silicon Valley, the "two Steves"—Steve Jobs and Steve Wozniak—made history when they built the Apple computer in Jobs's garage. At the time, personal computers (PCs) as we know them did not exist. There were large, expensive computers called *mainframes*, but they were used mostly by banks, scientists, and the military, for record-keeping, problem-solving, and statistics. To operate most computer systems, the user had to insert hundreds of paper punch cards containing instructions.

In 1975, the two Steves put all their money together, which was only about $1,300, and Wozniak began building the Apple I—the first PC to use a single circuit board. They began selling these in early 1976, for about $650 each. Over the next ten months, about 175 Apple I machines were sold at a local computer store. The Apple I couldn't produce graphics, only text. Since there were no disk drives or CD-ROMs back then, to save and load information, you used an audio cassette deck.

On January 3, 1977, Jobs and Wozniak created the company Apple Computer, Inc., and they released their next model, the Apple II, in April 1977. The Apple II was the first PC that had color graphics. Five years later, the company was worth about $500 million. In 1984, the two whizzes released the Macintosh, which included the first affordable *graphical user interface (GUI)*, using icons and symbols that are now used on all PCs.

COMPUTER MAZE

This is a "motherboard," the main circuit board inside your computer that holds the microchips and other electronic parts. Can you "complete the circuit" and find your way through?

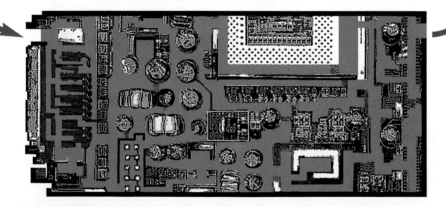

ANSWERS ON PAGES 319-322. FOR MORE PUZZLES GO TO WWW.WORLDALMANACFORKIDS.COM

Dinosaurs

Did a T-Rex ever eat a stegosaurus?) page 61

Dinosaurs last roamed the Earth some 65 million years ago. So how do we know so much about them?

Fossils: Clues to Ancient Life

Paleontologists are scientists who use fossils to study the past. **Fossils** are the remains of long-dead animals (like dinosaurs) or plants. Most fossils are formed from the hard parts of an animal's body, such as bones, shells, or teeth. Some fossils are **imprints**, like the outline of a leaf, or dinosaur footprints. Most fossils are found in **sedimentary rocks,** which form from the mud or sand (sediment) at the bottom of oceans, rivers, and lakes. Fossils have also been found in ice and tar. Insects that lived millions of years ago are sometimes found preserved in amber (hardened tree sap).

A fossil

EARLY DISCOVERIES

▶ In 1824 British geologist William Buckland recognized some fossils as part of a giant extinct reptile. He named this first dinosaur **Megalosaurus,** from the Greek words *megalos* ("big") and *sauros* ("lizard").

▶ In 1842 Sir Richard Owen used the Greek words *deinos* ("terrible") and *sauros* to coin the term "dinosaur."

▶ The partial skeleton of a **Hadrosaurus** was found in New Jersey in 1858. This was the first major dinosaur discovery in North America. The remains were made into a full dinosaur skeleton, the first ever displayed, at the Philadelphia Academy of Natural Sciences.

▶ Discovered in Germany in 1861, the **Archaeopteryx** is a link between dinosaurs and birds. It had bones, teeth, and a skull like a dinosaur's. But it also had feathers and could probably fly.

did you know?

Some of the best places to see dinosaurs and fossils in North America are the Academy of Natural Sciences (Philadelphia), the American Museum of Natural History (New York City), the Fernbank Museum of Natural History (Atlanta), the Field Museum of Natural History (Chicago), the National Museum of Natural History (Washington, D.C.), and the Royal Tyrrell Museum of Natural History (Drumheller, Alberta, Canada). Or you can visit the University of California at Berkeley's virtual Museum of Paleontology at

WEB SITE) *www.ucmp.berkeley.edu*

CELEBRITIES *of the*

Apatosaurus

Deceptive lizard
Plant-eating
Length: 70+ feet
Period: Jurassic
Found in: Western U.S.

Velociraptor

Speedy thief
Meat-eating
Length: 6 feet
Period: Cretaceous
Found in: Asia

Hadrosaurus

Big lizard
Plant-eating
Length: 30 feet
Period: Cretaceous
Found in: Asia, Europe, North and South America

WHEN DID **DINOSAURS LIVE?**

Dinosaurs roamed the Earth during the Mesozoic Era, which is divided into three periods:

TRIASSIC PERIOD
from 225 to 195 million years ago

►**Pangea**, Earth's one big continent, began to break up in this period.

►The earliest known mammals, such as the tiny, rat-like Morganucodon, began to appear.

►Evergreen plants were the most common vegetation.

►The earliest known dinosaur, **Eoraptor**, was a meat-eater only about 40 inches long. Herrersaurus, also a meat-eater, was about 10 feet long.

►Large reptiles, like long-necked **plesiosaurs** and dolphin-like **ichthyosaurs** (which were not dinosaurs), ruled the sea.

JURASSIC PERIOD
from 195 to 135 million years ago

►Flowering plants appeared.

►Plant-eating **sauropods**, like **Apatosaurus** and **Brachiosaurus**, were the biggest land creatures ever! These dinosaurs were eaten by meat-eaters like **Allosaurus** and **Megalosaurus**.

►**Archaeopteryx** was born— the earliest link between dinosaurs and birds.

►Flying reptiles called **pterosaurs**, close relatives of the dinosaur, dominated the sky.

CRETACEOUS PERIOD **from 135 to 65 million years ago**

►The climate was warm, with no polar ice caps.

►Meat-eating **theropods** like **Tyrannosaurus Rex** and **Giganotosaurus** walked on two legs.

►All dinosaurs and other reptiles such as **ichthyosaurs** and **pterosaurs** became extinct by the end of this period. It may have been because a huge asteroid or comet hit the Earth. This would have filled the atmosphere with dust and debris, blocking most of the sun's light and heat. As a result many plants and animals would have died out.

60

DINOSAUR WORLD

Tyrannosaurus Rex ("T-Rex")

King of the tyrant lizards
Meat-eating • Length: 40 feet
Period: Cretaceous
Found in: Western U.S., Canada, Asia

Triceratops

Three-horned face • **Plant-eating**
Length: 30 feet • **Period:** Cretaceous
Found in: North America

Stegosaurus

Plated lizard • **Plant-eating**
• **Length:** 30 feet • **Period:** Jurassic
• **Found in:** North America

DINOSAUR MYTHS

1. **Early humans hunted dinosaurs.** The last of the creatures we recognize as dinosaurs died out 65 million years ago. Our earliest human ancestors lived roughly 5 to 7 million years ago. You do the math!

2. **All big prehistoric animals were dinosaurs.** No, there were other big animals. One example is the 12-foot-long **Dimetrodon**. It was extinct before the first dinosaur ever lived! The body of this reptile looked a little like a crocodile's, with legs out to the side and a sail-like fin on its back. (Dinosaurs all had their legs directly under them.)

3. **Some dinosaurs swam or flew.** Large fish-like reptiles (*ichthyosaurs*) and flying reptiles (*pterodactyls*) lived at the same time as dinosaurs and were like them in some ways. But true dinosaurs did not fly or live in the water.

4. **All dinosaurs lived around the same time.** One example proves this wrong. Stegosaurs had been extinct for 80 million years before **Tyrannosaurus Rex** and **Apatosaurus** appeared!

5. **All dinosaurs died out 65 million years ago.** Many dinosaurs (like the **Stegosaurus**) were gone long before the mass extinction of 65 million years ago. The last dinosaurs did die out 65 million years ago, though birds have existed since then and are believed by some paleontologists to have evolved from dinosaurs.

Dino Word Search

```
A E R P E S R E J U R A S S I C E A R O
L P F F D F F D F F D F L D F F D P N D
M R A P T O R R A C S A M R A C R A C P
O A E T A O E A O P A O I A I E C L E R
B E I B O B I E O I S B L E B L E E I E
C D J C D S J T C U D C L D O J D O J H
E P A N G E A V R K V E I V E K I N K I
R E F I E R F U I F E I O E I F G T F S
J I C J E J A I R C I J N I J C I O C T
S J A C J S A J K U J K S J K A J L A O
F C I F O F Q K F Q S I F K F Q K O Q R
S R W G F C W F C W F C M F C W F G W I
T E E D I N O S A U R A A P A N C Y N C
A T O Q A Q O A Q O A T H E R O P O D S
S A T Y R A N N O S A U R U S I Q L T Q
E C A N W N A W N A S N E W N T N E A W
B E R O N O R N F D N O E N R R N T R N
U O J M E S O Z O I C M O I M O L O J S
C U K A M A K P S K M U A S A E M C K E
K S F R A R O A S F A S C O D R A Z I L
L R C A R R C R I C S E R N A O R R C I
A A Q E U E Q A L I A U J I E V A J Q T
N E W A E D E E C W S M G E D I E G W P
D D S V D A C D V C D V D D V N D D C E
F V E O R A P T O R V B F V B R V F E R
Q B I T B T I B T I B T Q B T A B Q I B
Z T H A D R O S A U R U S T L C T E R A
```

Can You Find These Words?

They go across, up, down, backward, and diagonally. Some letters are used for more than one word, and some are not used at all.

APATOSAURUS	FOSSIL	PREHISTORIC
BUCKLAND	HADROSAURUS	RAPTOR
CARNIVORE	IMPRINT	REPTILES
CRETACEOUS	JURASSIC	SAUROPODS
DEINOS	LIZARD	STEGOSAURUS
DIG	MESOZOIC	THEROPOD
DINOSAUR	MILLIONS	TRIASSIC
EARTH	MUSEUM	TRICERATOPS
EORAPTOR	PALEONTOLOGY	TYRANNOSAURUS
ERA	PANGEA	VOLCANO

Energy

Where do plants get their energy? | see answer below

The term **energy** comes from **energeia**, the Greek word for "work." Energy is defined as the capacity to do work.

Energy cannot be created or destroyed, but it can change form. Heat, light, and electricity are forms of energy. Other forms include **mechanical, chemical,** and **nuclear** energy. You can feel heat and see light, but most energy, like electricity, is invisible. We only see the result—like the lighting of a bulb.

All of the forms of energy we use come from the energy stored in natural resources. Sunlight, water, wind, petroleum, coal, and natural gas are natural resources. From these resources, we get heat, electricity, and mechanical power to run machines.

It STARTS with the SUN

All of our energy traces its source to the Sun. Inside the Sun, hydrogen atoms join together and become helium. This process releases energy that radiates into space in the form of waves. These waves give us heat and light. Energy from the sun is stored in plants and animals that we eat. Long before humans existed, trees and other plants absorbed the Sun's energy. Animals ate plants and smaller animals. After the plants and animals died, they got buried deeper and deeper underground. After millions of years, they turned into coal and petroleum—fossil fuels.

Plants absorb energy from the Sun (solar energy) and convert it to chemical energy for storage.

Animals eat plants and gain the stored chemical energy.

Food gives the body energy.

People eat plants and meat.

63

Sources of Energy

FOSSIL FUELS

Fuels are called "fossil" because they were formed from ancient plants and animals. The three basic fossil fuels are **coal, oil,** and **natural gas.** Most of the energy we use today comes from these sources. **Coal** is mined, either at the surface or deep underground. Pumpjacks pump **oil,** or petroleum, from wells drilled in the ground. **Natural gas,** which is made up mostly of a gas called methane, also comes from wells. Natural gas is a clean-burning fuel, and it has been used more and more. Oil and coal bring a greater risk of air pollution.

All fossil fuels have one problem: they are gradually getting used up. There are special problems about oil, because industrial countries must often import lots of it and can become greatly dependent on other countries for their supply.

▼ *A pumpjack*

Hoover Dam, on the Colorado River between Arizona and Nevada

A nuclear power plant

NUCLEAR ENERGY

Nuclear power is created by releasing energy stored in the nucleus of an atom. This process is nuclear **fission,** which is also called "splitting" an atom. Fission takes place in a **reactor,** which allows the nuclear reaction to be controlled. Nuclear power plants release almost no air pollution. Many countries today use nuclear energy.

Nuclear power does cause some safety concerns. In 1979 a nuclear accident at Three Mile Island in Pennsylvania led to the release of some radiation. A much worse accident at Chernobyl in Ukraine in 1986 led to the deaths of thousands of people.

WATER POWER

Water power is energy that comes from the force of falling or fast-flowing water. It was put to use early in human history. **Water wheels,** turned by rivers or streams, were common in the Middle Ages. They were used for tasks like grinding grain and sawing lumber.

Today water power comes from waterfalls or from specially built dams. As water flows from a higher to a lower level, it runs a turbine—a device that turns an electric generator. This is called **hydroelectric power** (hydro = water). Today, over half of the world's hydroelectric power is produced in five countries: Brazil, Russia, Canada, China, and the United States.

WIND ENERGY

People have used the wind's energy for a long time. **Windmills** were popular in Europe during the Middle Ages. Later, windmills became common on U.S. farms. Today, huge high-tech windmills with propeller-like blades are grouped together in **"wind farms."** Dozens of wind turbines are spaced well apart (so they don't block each other's wind). Even on big wind farms, the windmills usually take up less than 1% of the ground space. The rest of the land can still be used for farming or for grazing animals.

Wind power is a rapidly growing technology that doesn't pollute or get used up like fossil fuels. By 2003, there was nearly four times the generating capacity in the U.S. as there had been in 1996. Unfortunately, the generators only work if the wind blows.

GEOTHERMAL ENERGY

Geothermal energy comes from the heat deep inside the Earth. About 30 miles below the surface is a layer called the **mantle.** This is the source of the gas and lava that erupts from volcanoes. Hot springs and geysers, with temperatures as high as 700 degrees, are also heated by the mantle. Because it's so hot, the mantle holds great promise as an energy source, especially in areas where the hot water is close to the surface. Iceland, which has many active volcanoes and hot springs, uses lots of geothermal energy. About 85% of homes there are heated this way.

BIOMASS ENERGY

Burning wood and straw (materials known as **biomass**) is probably the oldest way of producing energy. It's an old idea, but it still has value. Researchers are growing crops to use as fuel. Biomass fuels can be burned, like coal, in a power plant. They can also be used to make **ethanol,** which is similar to gasoline. Most ethanol comes from corn, which can make it expensive. But researchers are experimenting with other crops, like "switchgrass" and alfalfa.

Recently, a biomass power plant was opened in Burlington, Vermont. It turns wood chips, solid waste, and switchgrass into a substance similar to natural gas.

SOLAR POWER

Energy directly from sunlight is a promising new technology. Vast amounts of this energy fall upon the Earth every day—and it is not running out. Energy from the sun is expected to run for some 5 billion years. Solar energy is also friendly to the environment. One drawback is space. To get enough light, the surfaces that gather solar energy need to be spread out a lot. Also, the energy can't be gathered when the sun isn't shining.

A solar cell is usually made of silicon, a **semiconductor.** That means it can change sunlight into electricity. The cost of solar cells has been dropping in recent years. Large plants using solar-cell systems have been built in several countries, including Japan, Saudi Arabia, the United States, and Germany.

◀ A solar power plant

Who **Produces** and **Uses** the **MOST ENERGY?**

The United States produces about 18% of the world's energy—more than any other country—and it also uses 24%. The table below on the left lists the world's top-ten energy-producers and the percent of the world's production that each nation was responsible for in 2001. The table on the right lists the world's top energy-users and the percent of the world's energy that each nation consumed.

Top Energy Producers	
United States	18%
Russia	11%
China	9%
Saudi Arabia	5%
Canada	5%
United Kingdom	3%
Iran	3%
Norway	3%
Australia	2%
Mexico	2%

Top Energy Users	
United States	24%
China	10%
Russia	7%
Japan	5%
Germany	4%
India	3%
Canada	3%
France	3%
United Kingdom	2%
Brazil	2%

WHERE **DOES** U.S. **ENERGY** COME FROM?

In 2002, most of the energy used in the U.S. came from fossil fuels (39% from petroleum, 24% from natural gas, and 23% from coal). The rest came mostly from hydropower (water power), nuclear energy, and renewable resources such as geothermal, solar, and wind energy, and from burning materials such as wood and animal waste.

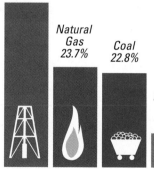

Petroleum
39.2%

Natural Gas
23.7%

Coal
22.8%

Nuclear power
8.4%

Hydro-power
2.7%

Other
3.2%

Homework Help

The different forms of energy fall into two main categories, and it helps to try and picture each one:

Kinetic Energy is the energy of objects in motion. Water in a river, electricity in a wire, and a sled going down a hill are good examples.

Potential energy is the energy of objects that are not moving—but could move. If you stretch a rubber band and hold it, it has potential energy. Let it go and its potential energy changes to kinetic energy with a snap! Natural gas, coal, and food are other examples of potential energy.

Environment

Who is "the person of the forest"? **page 70**

SHARING *the* EARTH

We share the planet with trees, flowers, insects, fish, whales, dogs, and many other plants and animals. Each species (type) of animal or plant has its place on Earth, and each one is dependent on many others. **Plants** give off oxygen that animals need to breathe. Animals pollinate plants and spread their seeds. **Animals** eat plants and are in turn eaten by larger animals. When plants and animals die, they become part of the soil in which new plants take root and grow.

People and the Environment

In **prehistoric times**, people killed animals for food and built fires to cook food and keep themselves warm. They cut down trees for fuel, and their fires released pollution into the air. But there were so few people that their activities had little impact on the environment.

In **modern times,** the world's population has been growing very fast. In 1850 there were around a billion people in the world. By 2004 there were about 6.3 billion. By 2050, according to United Nations estimates, there will be 8.9 billion people. Their activities have a big impact on the environment.

People are becoming more aware that human activities can seriously damage the planet and the animals and plants on it. Sometimes this damage can be reversed or slowed down. But it is often permanent. On the following pages you'll learn about the damage, and about some things that can be done to help clean up and protect our planet.

Every April 22, the world celebrates **Earth Day** to help make people aware of environment problems and ways they can help. There are many projects kids can get involved in. One example is the Earth Day Groceries Project, a cool Internet project your school or class can do. It's easy. Have your teacher borrow paper bags from a local grocery store. Each kid decorates a bag with pictures and messages about helping the environment. Then the bags go back to the store, where they will be used for shoppers' groceries on Earth Day.

WEB SITE For more information, go to http://www.earthdaybags.org

You can learn more about the environment at:
WEB SITE *http://www.epa.gov/students*

HOME SWEET BIOME

A "biome" is a large natural area that is the home to a certain type of plant. The animals, climate, soil, and even the amount of water in the region also help distinguish a biome. There are more than 30 kinds of biomes in the world. But the following types cover most of Earth's surface.

Forests

Forests cover about one-third of Earth's land surface. Pines, hemlocks, firs, and spruces grow in the cool **evergreen** forests farthest from the equator. These trees are called **conifers** because they produce cones.

Temperate forests have warm, rainy summers and cold, snowy winters. Here **deciduous trees** (which lose their leaves in the fall and grow new ones in the spring) join the evergreens. Temperate forests are home to maple, oak, beech, and poplar trees, and to wildflowers and shrubs. These forests are found in eastern United States, southeastern Canada, northern Europe and Asia, and southern Australia.

Still closer to the equator are the **tropical rain forests,** home to the greatest variety of plants on Earth. About 60 to 100 inches of rain fall each year. Tropical trees stay green all year. They grow close together, shading the ground. There are several layers of trees. The top, **emergent layer** has trees that can reach 200 feet in height. The **canopy,** which gets lots of sun, comes next, followed by the **understory.** The **forest floor,** covered with roots, gets little sun. Many plants cannot grow there.

Tropical rain forests are found mainly in Central America, South America, Asia, and Africa. They once covered more than 8 million square miles. Today, because of destruction by humans, fewer than 3.4 million square miles remain. More than half the plant and animal species in the world live there. Foods such as bananas and pineapples first grew there. Woods such as mahogany and teak also come from rain forests. Many kinds of plants there are used to make medicines.

When rain forests are burned, carbon dioxide is released into the air. This adds to the **greenhouse effect** (see page 75). As forests are destroyed, the precious soil is easily washed away by the heavy rains.

Emergent Layer

Canopy

Understory

Forest floor

A rain forest

Tundra & Alpine Region

In the northernmost regions of North America, Europe, and Asia surrounding the Arctic Ocean are plains called the **tundra.** The temperature rarely rises above 45 degrees Fahrenheit, and it is too cold for trees to grow there. Most tundra plants are mosses and lichens that hug the ground for warmth. A few wildflowers and small shrubs also grow where the soil thaws for about two months of the year. This kind of climate and plant life also exists in the **alpine** region, on top of the world's highest mountains (such as the Himalayas, Alps, Andes, and Rockies), where small flowers also grow.

WHAT IS THE TREE LINE? On mountains in the north (such as the Rockies) and in the far south (such as the Andes), there is an altitude above which trees will not grow. This is the **tree line** or **timberline.** Above the tree line, you can see low shrubs and small plants.

Deserts

The driest areas of the world are the **deserts.** They can be hot or cold, but they also contain an amazing number of plants. Cactuses and sagebrush are native to dry regions of North and South America. The deserts of Africa and Asia contain plants called euporbias. Dates have grown in the deserts of the Middle East and North Africa for thousands of years. In the southwestern United States and northern Mexico, there are many types of cactuses, including prickly pear, barrel, and saguaro.

▲ Arizona desert

Grasslands

▲ Grassland in Alberta, Canada

Areas that are too dry to have green forests, but not dry enough to be deserts, are called **grasslands.** The most common plants found there are grasses. Cooler grasslands are found in the Great Plains of the United States and Canada, in the steppes of Europe and Asia, and in the pampas of Argentina. The drier grasslands are used for grazing cattle and sheep. In the **prairies,** where there is a little more rain, wheat, rye, oats, and barley are grown. The warmer grasslands, called **savannas,** are found in central and southern Africa, Venezuela, southern Brazil, and Australia. Most savannas have moist summers and cool, dry winters.

Oceans

Coral reef ▶

Covering two-thirds of the earth, the **ocean** is by far the largest biome. Within the ocean are smaller biomes that include **coastal areas, tidal zones,** and **coral reefs.** Found in relatively shallow warm waters, the reefs are called the "rainforests of the ocean." Australia's Great Barrier Reef is the largest in the world. It is home to thousands of species of plant and animal life.

69

What Is BIODIVERSITY?

The Earth is shared by millions of species of living things. The wide variety of life on Earth, as shown by the many species, is called **"biodiversity"** (**bio** means "life" and **diversity** means "variety"). Human beings of all colors, races, and nationalities make up just one species, *Homo sapiens*.

Species, Species Everywhere

Here is just a sampling of how diverse life on Earth is. The numbers are only estimates, and more species are being discovered all the time!

ARTHROPODS (1.1 million species)
- insects: 750,000 species
  - moths & butterflies: 165,000 species
  - flies: about 122,000 species
  - cockroaches: about 4,000 species
- crustaceans: 44,000 species
- spiders: 35,000 species

FISH (24,500 species)
- bony fish: 23,000 species
- skates & rays: 450 species
- sharks: 350 species
- seahorses: 32 species

BIRDS (9,000 species)
- perching birds: 5,200-5,500 species
- raptors (eagles, hawks, etc.): 307 species
- penguins: 17 species
- ostrich: 1 species

MAMMALS (9,000 species)
- rodents: 1,700 species
- bats: 1,000 species
- monkeys: 242 species
- cats: 38 species
- apes: 21 species
- pigs: 14 species
- bears: 8 species

REPTILES (8,000 species)
- lizards: 4,500 species
- snakes: 2,900 species
- tortoises & turtles: about 294 species
- crocodiles & alligators: 23 species

AMPHIBIANS (5,000 species)
- frogs & toads: 4,500 species
- newts & salamanders: 470 species

PLANTS (260,000 species)
- flowering plants: 250,000 species
- evergreens: 550 species

Fascinating Bio Facts

▶ One out of every three **insects** on the planet is a beetle.

▶ The **Venus flytrap** turns the table on bugs by eating them. This "carnivorous plant" lives in poor soils in the southeastern U.S. It gets nourishing meals by luring bugs in with its sweet smell. When the bug steps on one part of the leaf, the leaf snaps shut.

▶ The tiniest known **seahorse**, only 0.6 inches long, was discovered on a coral reef in the Pacific in 2003. The biggest species grows up to 12 inches.

▶ The **orangutan** is a kid of ape. In the Malay language *orang* means "person" and *hutan* means "forest." So *orangutan* means "person of the forest."

ENDANGERED SPECIES

When a species becomes extinct, it reduces the variety of life on Earth. In the world today, 2,336 known species of animals (and even more plants) are endangered, according to the International Union for Conservation of Nature and Natural Resources. Humans have been able to save some endangered animals and are working to save more.

Some Endangered Animals

TIGER Only about 6,000 tigers still live in the wild. The biggest threat to the world's biggest cat is illegal hunting for body parts used in traditional Chinese medicines. In the 20th century, three of the eight subspecies of tigers became extinct.

ORANGUTAN The only member of the great ape family from Asia. Orangutans once lived throughout the rain forests of southeast Asia, but logging and the illegal pet trade reduced their numbers in the wild by 90% in the 20th century.

GIANT PANDA China's most loveable animal. As few as 1,000 of these creatures remain in the mountains of southwest China.

LEATHERBACK SEA TURTLE The largest living turtle in the world. These turtles are facing extinction. Habitat destruction, fishing nets, and the harvesting of its eggs are the biggest threats to their survival.

FACTORS THAT CAN MAKE A SPECIES ENDANGERED:

Deforestation in the Amazon rain forest.

HABITAT DESTRUCTION. As human populations grow, they need places to live and work. People build houses and factories in areas where plants and animals live. Filling in wetlands and clearing forests (**deforestation**) are examples of this threat.

OVER-HARVESTING. People may catch a kind of fish or hunt an animal until its numbers are too low to reproduce fast enough. Bison or buffalo once roamed over the entire Great Plains until they were almost hunted into extinction in the 19th century. They are now protected by law, and their numbers are increasing.

ALIEN SPECIES are plants and animals that have been moved by humans into areas where they are not naturally found. They may have no natural enemies there and can push out other native species. Red fire ants, zebra mussels, and kudzu are examples of alien species.

POLLUTION in the air, water, and land can affect plants and animals. It can poison them or make it hard for them to grow or reproduce. Factories are not the only source. Oil, salt, and other substances sprayed or spilled on roads can wash into streams, rivers, and lakes. Acid rain damages and kills trees, especially in the mountains where acidic clouds and fog often surround them.

WHERE **GARBAGE** GOES

Most of the things around you will be thrown away someday. Skates, clothes, the toaster, furniture—they can break or wear out, or you may get tired of them. Where will they go when they are thrown out? What kinds of waste will they create?

LOOK at WHAT Is NOW in U.S. LANDFILLS

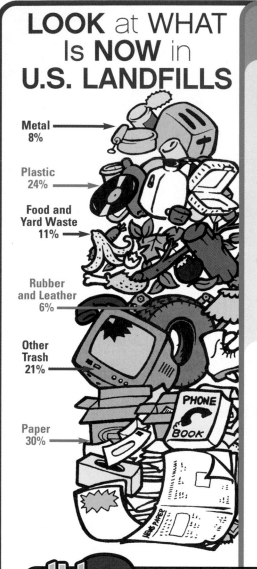

Metal
8%

Plastic
24%

Food and
Yard Waste
11%

Rubber
and Leather
6%

Other
Trash
21%

Paper
30%

WHAT **HAPPENS** TO THINGS WE **THROW AWAY?**

Landfills

Most of our trash goes to places called landfills. A **landfill** (or dump) is a low area of land that is filled with garbage. Most modern landfills are lined with a layer of plastic or clay to try to keep dangerous liquids from seeping into the soil and ground water supply.

The Problem with **Landfills**

More than half of the states in this country are running out of places to dump their garbage. Because of the unhealthful materials many contain, landfills do not make good neighbors, and people don't want to live near them. Many landfills are located in poor neighborhoods. But where can cities dispose of their waste? How can hazardous waste — material that can poison air, land, and water — be disposed of in a safe way?

Incinerators

One way to get rid of trash is to burn it. Trash is burned in a furnace-like device called an **incinerator.** Because incinerators can get rid of almost all of the bulk of the trash, some communities would rather use incinerators than landfills.

The Problem with **Incinerators**

Leftover ash and smoke from burning trash may contain harmful chemicals, called **pollutants**, and make it hard for some people to breathe. They can harm plants, animals, and people.

did you know?

Waste from pig farms is getting to be a big problem. One pig can create thousands of pounds of waste in a year. Hauling away the smelly sludge takes time and money. And this waste can't be used to fertilize crops meant for people. North Carolina has more than 6,000 waste ponds, or lagoons. Researchers there have an idea that may help: using poplar trees. One acre of these trees absorbs about 3,000 gallons of waste per day! Even with this method, however, researchers estimate that it would be 10 years before the land would be usable again.

Reduce, Reuse, Recycle

You can help reduce waste by reusing containers, batteries, and paper. You can also recycle a newspaper, glass, and plastics to provide materials for making other products. Below are some of the things you can do.

	TO REDUCE WASTE	TO RECYCLE
Paper	Use both sides of the paper. Use cloth towels instead of paper towels.	Recycle newspapers, magazines, comic books, and junk mail.
Plastic	Wash food containers and store leftovers in them. Reuse plastic bags.	Return soda bottles to the store. Recycle other plastics.
Glass	Keep bottles and jars to store other things.	Recycle glass bottles and jars.
Clothes	Give clothes to younger relatives or friends. Donate clothes to thrift shops.	Cut unwearable clothing into rags to use instead of paper towels.
Metal	Keep leftovers in storage containers instead of wrapping them in foil. Use glass or stainless steel pans instead of disposable pans.	Recycle aluminum cans and foil trays. Return wire hangers to the dry cleaner.
Food/ Yard Waste	Cut the amount of food you throw out. Try saving leftovers for snacks or meals later on.	Make a compost heap using food scraps, leaves, grass clippings, and the like.
Batteries	Use rechargeable batteries for toys and games, radios, tape players, and flashlights.	Find out about your town's rules for recycling or disposing of batteries.

What is made from RECYCLED MATERIALS?

- ▶ *From* RECYCLED PAPER we get newspapers, cereal boxes, wrapping paper, cardboard containers, and insulation.
- ▶ *From* RECYCLED PLASTIC we get soda bottles, tables, benches, bicycle racks, cameras, backpacks, carpeting, shoes, and clothes.
- ▶ *From* RECYCLED STEEL we get steel cans, cars, bicycles, nails, and refrigerators.
- ▶ *From* RECYCLED GLASS we get glass jars and tiles.
- ▶ *From* RECYCLED RUBBER we get bulletin boards, floor tiles, playground equipment, and speed bumps.

THE AIR WE

The air surrounding the Earth is made up of different gases: about 78% nitrogen, 21% oxygen, and 1% carbon dioxide, water vapor, and other gases. All human beings and animals need air to survive. Plants also need air. Plants use sunlight and the carbon dioxide in air to make food, and then give off oxygen.

Humans breathe more than 3,000 gallons of air a day. Because air is so basic to life, it is important to keep it clean. Air pollution causes health problems and may bring about acid rain, smog, global warming, and a breakdown of the ozone layer.

What is Acid Rain?

Acid rain is a kind of air pollution caused by chemicals in the air. Eventually these can make rain, snow, or fog more acidic than normal. The main sources of these chemicals are exhaust from cars, trucks, and buses, waste incinerators, factories, and some electric power plants, especially those that burn fossil fuels, such as coal. When these chemicals mix with moisture and other particles, they create sulfuric acid and nitric acid. The wind often carries these acids many miles before they fall to the ground in rain, snow, and fog, or even as dry particles.

Acid rain can harm people, animals, and plants. It is especially harmful to lakes. Thousands of lakes in Canada, Finland, Norway, and Sweden have been declared "dead." Not even algae can live in them. Birds and other species that depend on the lakes for food are also affected. Acid rain can also affect crops and trees. Buildings, statues, and cars can be damaged as it eats away metal, stone, and paint.

What is Smog?

The brownish haze seen mostly in the summer and especially around big cities is **smog**. The main ingredient in smog is ozone. When ozone is high up in the atmosphere, it helps protect us from the Sun's stronger rays. But near the ground, ozone forms smog when sunlight and heat interact with oxygen and particles produced by the burning of fossil fuels. Smog makes it hard for some people to breathe, especially those with asthma. "Ozone Alerts" are not just for Los Angeles (famous for its smog). Many cities in the U.S. issue them through newspapers, TV, and radio stations to let people know when the air can be unhealthy for outdoor activities. For more information visit http://www.epa.gov/airnow/aqikids

What is the Ozone Layer?

Our atmosphere is made up of different layers. One layer, between 6 and 30 miles above the Earth, is made up of ozone gas. This **ozone layer** protects us from the Sun's harshest rays, called **ultraviolet** or **UV rays**. These rays can cause sunburn and skin cancer.

When refrigerators, air conditioners, and similar items are thrown away, gases from them (called **chlorofluorocarbons,** or CFCs) rise into the air and destroy some of the ozone in this layer. Most countries no longer produce CFCs, but the gas can stay in the atmosphere for years—destroying ozone and adding to the greenhouse effect.

Each August, a **hole in the ozone layer** forms over Antarctica (it usually closes by December). Since it was discovered in the 1980s, it has doubled to about the size of North America. It sometimes extends over southern Chile and Argentina. On some days, people in Punta Arenas, Chile (the world's southernmost city), may limit their sun exposure to no more than 20 minutes between noon and 3 P.M. Other days, they don't go out at all!

BREATHE

What is Global Warming?

The average surface temperature on Earth was 58°F in 2003. That's about 1°F higher than it was 100 years ago. Since accurate record-keeping began in 1880, the hottest year in history was 1998. The nine hottest years have all been since 1990. This gradual rise is called **global warming**. On that much, scientists agree. Where they can't agree is on the cause. Some think it is part of a natural cycle of warming and cooling. But most scientists believe that increased gases in the air play a big role.

The **greenhouse effect** is a natural process, needed for life to exist on Earth. Certain gases in the atmosphere act like the glass walls of a greenhouse: they let the rays of the Sun pass through to the Earth's surface but hold in some of the heat that radiates from the Sun-warmed Earth. These naturally occurring greenhouse gases are water vapor, carbon dioxide, methane, nitrous oxide, and ozone. Without these gases, Earth's average temperature would be 60°F colder and we couldn't live here.

Heat from the Sun

Most heat is trapped in atmosphere

Carbon dioxide, other gases from cars and factories trap extra heat.

Some heat escapes

Human activity is putting more of these gases into the air. As cities have grown in size and population, people have needed more and more electricity, cars, and manufactured things of all kinds. As industries have grown, more greenhouse gases have been produced by the burning of fossil fuels such as oil, coal, and natural gas. The increases in these gases make greenhouse "glass" thicker, causing more heat to be trapped than in the past.

It doesn't seem like much, but a slight warming could cause changes in the climate of many regions. If the climate changed enough, the plants and animals that normally live there could no longer survive. Many scientists think average temperatures could rise as much as 6°F over the next 100 years. This warming could cause a lot of ice near the North and South Poles to melt, making more water go into the oceans. Many areas along the coasts would be flooded.

WATER, WATER EVERYWHERE

Earth is the water planet. More than two-thirds of its surface is covered with water, and every living thing on it needs water to live. Water is not only part of our life (drinking, cooking, cleaning, bathing); it makes up 75% of our brains and 60% of our whole bodies! Humans can survive for about a month without food, but only for about a week without water. People also use water to cool machines in factories, to produce power, and to irrigate farmland.

HOW MUCH IS THERE TO DRINK? **Seawater** makes up 97% of the world's water. Another 2% of the water is frozen in ice caps, icebergs, glaciers, and sea ice. Half of the 1% left is too far underground to be reached. That leaves only 0.5% of **freshwater** for all the people, plants, and animals on Earth. This supply is renewable only by rainfall.

WHERE DOES DRINKING WATER COME FROM? Most smaller cities and towns get their freshwater from **groundwater**—melted snow and rain that seeps deep into the ground and is drawn out from wells. Larger cities usually rely on lakes or **reservoirs** for their water. Some areas of the world with little fresh water are turning to a process called **desalinization** (removing salt from seawater) as a solution. But this process is slow and expensive.

THE HYDROLOGICAL CYCLE: WATER'S ENDLESS JOURNEY Water is special. It's the only thing on Earth that exists naturally in **all three physical states**: solid (ice), liquid, and gas (water vapor). It never boils naturally (except around volcanoes), but it evaporates (turns into a gas) easily into the air. These unique properties send water on a cycle of repeating events.

HOW DOES WATER GET INTO THE AIR? Sunlight causes surface water in oceans, lakes, swamps, and rivers to turn into water vapor. This is called **evaporation**. Plant photosynthesis releases water vapor into the air. Animals also release a little bit when they breathe. This is **transpiration**.

clouds

rain

evaporation

snow

ocean

HOW DOES WATER COME OUT OF THE AIR? Warm air holds more water vapor than cold air. As the air rises into the atmosphere, it cools and the water vapor **condenses**—changes back into a tiny water droplets. These form clouds. As the drops get bigger, gravity pulls them down as **precipitation** (rain, snow, sleet, fog, and dew are all types of precipitation).

WHERE DOES THE WATER GO? Depending on where the precipitation lands, it can: **1.** evaporate back into the atmosphere; **2.** run off into streams and rivers; **3.** be absorbed by plants; **4.** soak down into the soil as ground water; **5.** fall as snow on a glacier and be trapped as ice for thousands of years.

Why We Need Wetlands

Wetlands are—you guessed it—**wet lands**. They are wet (covered with water, or with water at or near the surface) at least part of every year. Bogs, swamps, and marshes are all kinds of wetlands.

Wetlands have at least three important functions:

▶ **storing water.** They absorb water like giant sponges and hold it in, releasing it slowly. During floods an acre of wetland can hold in 1.5 million gallons of water.

▶ **cleaning up water.** They slow water flow down and let harmful sediments drop to the bottom. Plant roots and tiny organisms remove human and animal waste.

▶ **providing habitats.** They are home to huge numbers of plants, fish, and wildlife. More than one-third of all threatened and endangered species in the U.S. live only in wetlands.

There are about 100 million acres of wetlands left in the lower 48 states, less than half of what there were in 1600. Wetlands are lost when people drain and fill them in for farmland, dam them up to form ponds and lakes, or pave and build up surrounding areas.

◀ *Wetlands, Everglades National Park*

WATER WOES

Pollution Polluted water can't be used for drinking, swimming, watering crops, or provide a habitat for plants and animals. Major sources of water pollutants are sewage, chemicals from factories, fertilizers and weed killers, and landfills that leak. In general, anything that anyone dumps on the ground finds its way into the water cycle. Each year, the United Nations promotes March 22 as **"World Water Day"** to remind people how important it is to protect precious freshwater.

Overuse Using water faster than nature can pass it through the hydrological cycle can create other problems. When more water is taken out of lakes and reservoirs (for drinking, bathing, and other uses) than is put back in, the water levels begin to drop. Combined with lower than normal rainfall, this can be devastating. In some cases, lakes become salty or dry up completely.

The Dreaded Dripping Faucet: Just one faucet, dripping very slowly (once a minute), can waste 38 gallons a year. Multiply that by several million houses and apartments, and you see a lot of water going down the drain!

Games & Toys

When was Barbie "born"? page 79

Want to **Play?**

It's a safe bet that games and toys have been around as long as people have. The first games were probably similar to tag and hide and seek, but archaeologists (scientists who study the past) have little evidence of when they first began. The earliest toys were probably natural things kids found lying around: bones, sticks, and stones. Most of our clues about the earliest games come from things ancient peoples left behind. Baked clay marbles dating back to 3,000 B.C. have been found in prehistoric caves.

Kids still play with simple things like blocks, clay, and sticks, but toys and games sure have come a long way in the age of machines and computers!

A TIME-LINE OF VIDEO GAMES

1961—*Spacewar!*, played on an early microcomputer, is the first fully interactive video game.

1974—Atari's *Pong*, one of the first home video games, has "paddles" to hit a white dot back and forth on-screen.

1980—*Pac-Man*, *Space Invaders*, and *Asteroids* (first to let high scorers enter initials) invade arcades.

1985—Russian programmer Alex Pajitnov develops *Tetris* for play on a PC.

1986—Nintendo Entertainment System comes to the U.S. *Super Mario Bros.* is a huge hit!

1987—*Legend of Zelda* game released.

1989—Nintendo's hand-held video game system, Game Boy, debuts. *Adventures of Link* game released.

1990—The Sega Genesis system comes out.

1991—Sega's *Sonic the Hedgehog* makes his debut.

1996—Nintendo 64 is released.

1998—Game Boy Color and *Pokémon* hit the U.S.

2000—Sony's Playstation 2 arrives.

2001—Microsoft's XBOX and Nintendo's GameCube hit the shelves. *Luigi's Mansion* and *Super Smash Bros. Melee* make a big splash.

For more information about computer games, see page 56.

did you know?

Introduced in 1980, Pac-Man was an instant hit and is still one of the most popular video games ever. The only known perfect score of 3,333,360 was set in 1999 by 33-year-old Florida resident Billy Mitchell. It took Billy six hours to go through all 256 screens, gobbling up every dot, energy blob, ghost, and fruit—without losing a single life!

TOP-SELLING VIDEO GAMES OF 2003

Source: The NPD Group/NPD Funworld®/TRSTS®
(Sales ranked by total units sold in the U.S.)

1. **Madden NFL 2004** by Electronic Arts (Playstation 2)
2. **Pokémon Ruby** by Nintendo (Game Boy Advance)
3. **Pokémon Sapphire** by Nintendo (Game Boy Advance)
4. **Need for Speed: Underground** by Electronic Arts (Playstation 2)
5. **Zelda: The Wind Waker** by Nintendo (Gamecube)

TIMELESS TOYS

You may be surprised to find out how long some popular toys have been around.

In 1902, Rose Michtom made stuffed bears to sell in a store she ran with her husband in Brooklyn. She named them after President Teddy (Theodore) Roosevelt, and started a big trend. Stieff (1903) and Gund (1906) are the oldest **TEDDY BEAR** makers in business today.

Edwin Binney and C. Harold Smith made their first box of **CRAYOLA CRAYONS** in 1903. There were 8 colors—compared to 120 today. The Crayola factory in Easton, Pennsylvania, now turns out more than 3 billion crayons each year (an average of 12 million per day!).

Some Classic Toys

Erector Set	1913
Tinker Toys	1914
Raggedy Ann doll	1915
Lincoln Logs	1916
Yo-Yos	1929
Tonka Trucks	1947
Silly Putty	1950
Matchbox cars	1952
Mr. Potato Head	1952
Wiffle Ball	1953
Easy-Bake Oven	1963
G.I. Joe	1963
Twister	1966
Battleship	1967
Rubik's Cube	1979
Cabbage Patch Kids	1983

Plastic **LEGO** bricks were invented in Denmark by Ole Kirk Christiansen in 1949. The company, whose name comes from the Danish words "LEg GOdt" (play well) has since made more than 206 billion of them! Imagine if you had to clean up that many in your room.

HOT WHEELS brand cars hit the scene in 1968. Emphasizing speed and racetrack building made this brand the hottest selling toy car ever.

One of the most popular toys in history, the **BARBIE DOLL** was "born" in 1959. Created by Mattel, Inc., founders Ruth and Elliot Handler, the doll was named after their daughter Barbie. Ken, named after their son, came out in 1961.

PLAY-DOH started out as a wallpaper cleaner! It was first sold as a toy in 1956 at a department store in Washington, D.C. It only came in off-white. Red, yellow, and blue were added in 1957. The original formula is still a secret!

Its inventor, Arthur Granjean, called it "L' Ecran Magique" (the magic screen), but it hit the toy stores in 1960 as **ETCH A SKETCH®**. When you turn the knobs, a stylus scrapes aluminum powder off the inside of the screen to draw a line.

Made of polyurethane foam, the first **NERF** ball hit the scene (and didn't break any lamps!) in 1969. This indoor/outdoor ball sold 4 million in its first year. In 1972, the king of all Nerf toys—the Nerf football—was introduced.

A **Dice** Game **You** "Probably" **Know**

YAHTZEE is a popular dice game for 2 or more players. Players roll any or all dice up to three times per turn. Points are scored by rolling different combinations of dice (some borrowed from poker, like "straight," "full house," and "three of a kind"). Rolling the same number on all five dice is a "yahtzee." Scores are added in 13 categories and the player with the highest point total wins.

According to Yahtzee's maker, Hasbro, the game was invented in 1956 by a wealthy Canadian couple who played a "yacht game" with friends on their yacht.

Homework Help

LUCKY 7:
UNDERSTANDING PROBABILITY

Probability can be a fun subject, and it may be a little more fun and easier to learn about if you think of it in terms of the dice you use to play games with.

A single die has six different faces, numbered **1** through **6**. Each has an equal chance of coming up. So the chance, or **probability,** of rolling any one of the numbers with one die is one in six. We write this as a ratio or fraction: 1/6.

There were six possible **outcomes,** and of these, one was "favorable"—that is, was the one you wanted or were talking about.

What if you roll two dice? There are 36 possible outcomes, because each die can come out one of six ways; 6 x 6 = 36. The lowest possible outcome would be 2 (a **1** on each die). The highest possible outcome would be 12 (a **6** on each die).

With two dice, some totals are more likely to come up than others because there are more possible outcomes that add up to those totals. Pretend that the dice are red and blue. The the only way to roll a total of 2 ("snake eyes") is for the red die to come up as a **1** and the blue die to come up as a **1**. So the probability of shaking 2 is 1 in 36 (1/36). But there are two ways to shake a 3. The red die could have a **1** and the blue die could have a **2**, or the red die could be a **2** and the blue die could be a **1**. So the probability shaking a 3 is 2 in 36 (2/36, which equals 1/18).

Look below for your chances of shaking each total with two dice.	
2	1 in 36
3	2 in 36
4	3 in 36
5	4 in 36
6	5 in 36
7	6 in 36
8	5 in 36
9	4 in 36
10	3 in 36
11	2 in 36
12	1 in 36

The total that has the most possible outcomes is 7. The red die can be any of the numbers from **1** to **6**, and the blue die can be the number that makes seven when added to the number on the red die (**1** and **6**, **2** and **5**, **3** and **4**, **4** and **3**, **5** and **2**, **6** and **1**). Since there are six possible combinations to total 7, the chances of rolling a 7 are 6 in 36 (6/36, which equals 1/6, or one out of six).

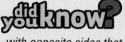

Dice have been around for thousands of years and were very popular in Roman times—even with the emperors! Modern dice, with opposite sides that add to seven, are basically the same design as the "tesserae" the ancient Romans carved out of bone, ivory, and wood.

What's the deal?

Where Our Playing Cards Come From

People have been playing cards for at least 700 years!

Cards first appeared in Europe around the late 1300s. They are thought to have come from Egypt, India, or China. Scholars believe that cards were originally used for magical purposes as well as for markers in games simulating battle maneuvers.

At first the suits (symbols used on a number of different cards) were not spades diamonds, clubs, or hearts but swords, batons, coins, and cups.

The first playing cards were hand painted, so only the very wealthy could afford them. However, once woodcuts were invented in the 14th century, cards were much cheaper to produce and more folks could play.

The first packs of cards in Europe contained 52 cards in four different suits, with three court cards in each suit (king, knight, and foot-servant).

spades

diamonds

clubs

hearts

How to play SPIT!
(a card game for 2 players)*

- ♦ Deal two piles of four cards each face down (these are the "spit" piles).

- ♠ Deal the rest of the cards face down to each player (you should end up with 22 each). These will be the players' "draw" piles.

- ♥ Each player picks up and holds four cards, called a "hand," from the top of her draw pile.

- ♣ Turn over the top card on both spit piles. Each player then tries to play any card next in order to the face-up card on either spit pile. (For example, if a spit card is a 10, players could play either a 9 or a jack. Suit does NOT matter.)

- ♦ After a card is played, the player may replace it with one from his draw pile. Remember: no more than four cards in your hand at one time!

- ♠ Play continues until neither player can put down a card. At that point, each turns over a new card from their spit pile. The first player to play all 22 cards wins.

How to play CRAZY EIGHTS!
(a card game for 2 or more players)*

- ♥ Each player is dealt 8 cards and picks them up into a hand.

- ♣ The rest of the cards go face down in a stack called the draw pile.

- ♦ The top card on the draw pile is turned over. The first player (to the right of dealer) has to play a card that matches the suit or value of the upturned card. (For example, if the card is the 6 of spades, a player could play a 6 of any suit or a spade of any value.)

- ♠ Eights are wild! Play an 8 at any time and you can name any suit to be played next.

- ♥ A player who can't put down a card must take a card, or cards, from the draw pile (and keep them) until one is found that can be played. The first player to run out of cards is the winner.

* These rules show one good way to play. Rules for the game may vary.

Geography

Which hemispheres do you live in? page 84

Sizing up THE EARTH

The word "geography" comes from the Greek word *geographia*, meaning "writing about the earth." It was first used by the Greek scholar Eratosthenes, who was head of the great library of Alexandria in Egypt. Around 230 B.C., when many people believed the world was flat, he did a remarkable thing. He calculated the circumference of the Earth. His figure of 25,000 miles was close to the modern measurement 24,870 miles!

Actually, the Earth is not perfectly round. It's flatter at the poles and bulges out a little at the middle. This bulge around the equator is due to centrifugal force from the Earth's rotation. ("Centrifugal" means "moving away from the center." Think of how a merry-go-round pushes you to the outside as it spins). The Earth's diameter is 7,926 miles across the equator, but only 7,900 miles from North Pole to South Pole. The total surface area of the Earth is 196,950,000 square miles.

Geography 1-2-3

LONGEST RIVERS	1. Nile (Egypt and Sudan)— 4,160 miles 2. Amazon (Brazil and Peru)— 4,000 miles 3. Chang (China)— 3,940 miles (formerly called the Yangtze)
TALLEST MOUNTAINS	1. Mount Everest (Tibet and Nepal)— 29,035 feet 2. K2 (Kashmir)— 28,250 feet 3. Kanchenjunga (India and Nepal)— 28,208 feet
BIGGEST ISLANDS	1. Greenland (Atlantic Ocean)— 840,000 square miles 2. New Guinea (Pacific Ocean)— 306,000 square miles 3. Borneo (Pacific Ocean)— 280,100 square miles
BIGGEST DESERT REGIONS	1. Sahara Desert (North Africa)— 3.5 million square miles 2. Australian Deserts—1.3 million square miles 3. Arabian Peninsula—1 million square miles
BIGGEST LAKES	1. Caspian Sea (Europe and Asia)— 143,244 square miles 2. Superior (U.S. and Canada)— 31,700 square miles 3. Victoria (Kenya, Tanzania, Uganda)— 26,828 square miles
HIGHEST WATERFALLS	1. Angel Falls (Venezuela)— 3,212 feet 2. Tugela Falls (South Africa)— 2,800 feet 3. Monge Falls (Norway)— 2,540 feet

THE **SEVEN CONTINENTS** AND **FOUR OCEANS**

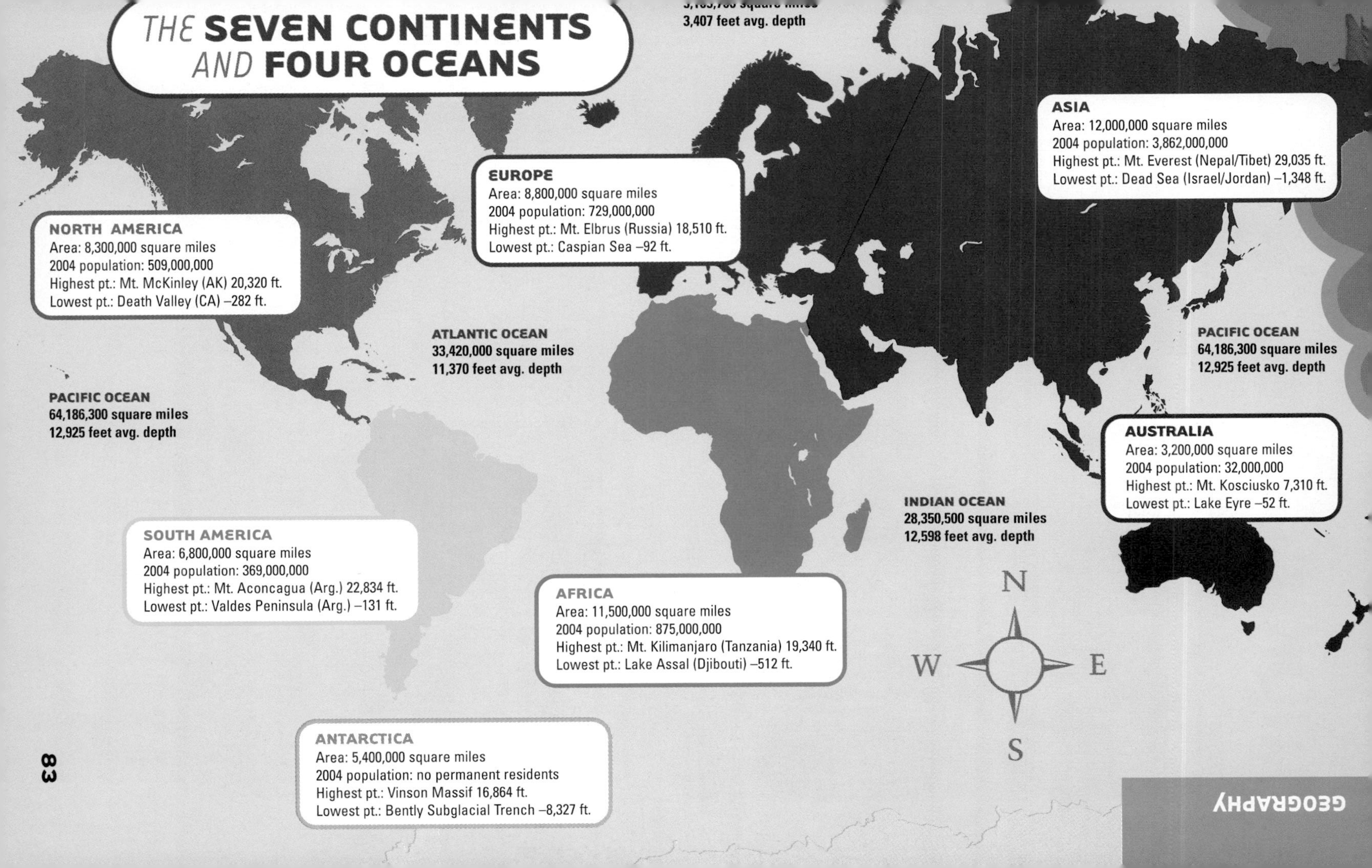

ASIA
Area: 12,000,000 square miles
2004 population: 3,862,000,000
Highest pt.: Mt. Everest (Nepal/Tibet) 29,035 ft.
Lowest pt.: Dead Sea (Israel/Jordan) −1,348 ft.

PACIFIC OCEAN
64,186,300 square miles
12,925 feet avg. depth

AUSTRALIA
Area: 3,200,000 square miles
2004 population: 32,000,000
Highest pt.: Mt. Kosciusko 7,310 ft.
Lowest pt.: Lake Eyre −52 ft.

INDIAN OCEAN
28,350,500 square miles
12,598 feet avg. depth

EUROPE
Area: 8,800,000 square miles
2004 population: 729,000,000
Highest pt.: Mt. Elbrus (Russia) 18,510 ft.
Lowest pt.: Caspian Sea −92 ft.

ATLANTIC OCEAN
33,420,000 square miles
11,370 feet avg. depth

AFRICA
Area: 11,500,000 square miles
2004 population: 875,000,000
Highest pt.: Mt. Kilimanjaro (Tanzania) 19,340 ft.
Lowest pt.: Lake Assal (Djibouti) −512 ft.

3,407 feet avg. depth

NORTH AMERICA
Area: 8,300,000 square miles
2004 population: 509,000,000
Highest pt.: Mt. McKinley (AK) 20,320 ft.
Lowest pt.: Death Valley (CA) −282 ft.

PACIFIC OCEAN
64,186,300 square miles
12,925 feet avg. depth

SOUTH AMERICA
Area: 6,800,000 square miles
2004 population: 369,000,000
Highest pt.: Mt. Aconcagua (Arg.) 22,834 ft.
Lowest pt.: Valdes Peninsula (Arg.) −131 ft.

ANTARCTICA
Area: 5,400,000 square miles
2004 population: no permanent residents
Highest pt.: Vinson Massif 16,864 ft.
Lowest pt.: Bently Subglacial Trench −8,327 ft.

N
E
S
W

83

LOOKING *at our* WORLD

THINKING GLOBAL

Shaped like a ball or sphere, a globe is a model of our planet. Like Earth, it's not perfectly round. It is an oblate spheroid (called a "geoid") that bulges a little in the middle.

In 1569, Gerardus Mercator found a way to project the Earth's curved surface onto a flat map. One problem with a Mercator map is that land closer to the poles appears bigger than it is. Australia looks smaller than Greenland on this type of map, but in reality it's not.

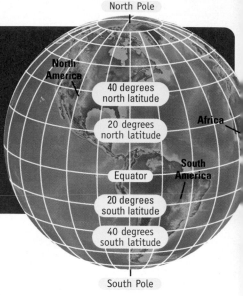

North Pole

North America

40 degrees north latitude

20 degrees north latitude

Africa

Equator

South America

20 degrees south latitude

40 degrees south latitude

South Pole

LATITUDE AND LONGITUDE

Imaginary lines that run east and west around Earth, parallel to the equator, are called **parallels**. They tell you the **latitude** of a place, or how far it is from the equator. The equator is at 0 degrees latitude. As you go farther north or south, the latitude increases. The North Pole is at 90 degrees **north latitude**. The South Pole is at 90 degrees **south latitude**.

Imaginary lines that run north and south around the globe, from one pole to the other, are called **meridians**. They tell you the degree of **longitude**, or how far east or west a place is from an imaginary line called the **Greenwich meridian** or **prime meridian** (0 degrees). That line runs through the city of Greenwich in England.

Which Hemispheres Do *You* Live In?

Draw an imaginary line around the middle of Earth. This is the **equator**. It splits Earth into two halves called **hemispheres**. The part north of the equator, including North America, is the **northern hemisphere**. The part south of the equator is the **southern hemisphere**.

You can also divide Earth into east and west. North and South America are in the **western hemisphere**. Africa, Asia, and most of Europe are in the **eastern hemisphere**.

THE **TROPICS** OF **CANCER** AND **CAPRICORN**

If you find the equator on a globe or map, you'll see two dotted lines running parallel to it, one above and one below (see pages 139 and 148-149). The top one marks the Tropic of Cancer, an imaginary line marking the latitude (23.5° North) where the sun is directly overhead on the summer solstice, June 21 or 22. Below the equator is the Tropic of Capricorn (23.5° South). This line marks the sun's path directly overhead at noon on the winter solstice, December 21 or 22. The area between these dotted lines is the tropics, where it is consistently hot because the sun's rays shine more directly than they do farther north or south.

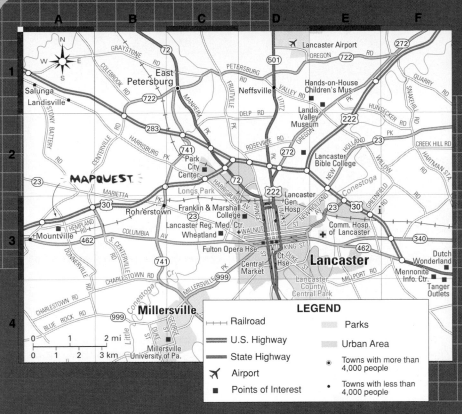

LEGEND

┝┼┼┼ Railroad		Parks
═══ U.S. Highway		Urban Area
─── State Highway	⊙	Towns with more than 4,000 people
✈ Airport		
■ Points of Interest	•	Towns with less than 4,000 people

READING A **MAP**

DIRECTION Maps usually have a **compass rose** that shows you which way is north. On most maps, like this one, it's straight up. The compass rose on this map is in the upper left corner.

DISTANCE Of course the distances on a map are much shorter than the distances in the real world. The **scale** shows you how to estimate the real distance. This map's scale is in the lower left corner.

PICTURES Maps usually have little pictures or symbols to represent real things like roads, towns, airports, or other points of interest. The map **legend** (or **key**) tells what they mean.

FINDING PLACES Rather than use latitude and longitude to locate features, many maps, like this one, use a **grid system** with numbers on one side and letters on another. An **index**, listing place names in alphabetical order, gives a letter and a number for each. The letter and number tell you which square to look for a place on the map's **grid**. For example, Landisville can be found at A-1 on this map.

USING THE MAP People use maps to help them travel from one place to another. What if you lived in East Petersburg and wanted to go to the Hands-on-House Children's Museum? First, locate the two places on the map. East Petersburg is in C-1, and Hands-on-House is in E-1. Next, look at the roads that connect them and decide on the best route. (There could be several different ways to go.) One possibility is to take Route 722 northeast to Petersburg Road. Take that east to Valley Road. And, finally, travel southeast on Valley Road until you get to the museum.

EARTHQUAKES

Earthquakes may be so weak that they are hardly felt, or strong enough to do great damage. There are thousands of earthquakes each year, but most are too small to be noticed. About 1 in 5 can be felt, and about 1 in 500 causes damage.

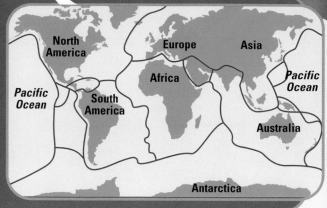

WHAT CAUSES EARTHQUAKES? The Earth's outer layer, its **crust**, is divided into huge pieces called **plates** (see map). These **plates**, made of rock, are constantly moving—away from each other, toward each other, or past each other. A crack in Earth's crust between two plates is called a **fault**. Many earthquakes occur along faults where two plates collide as they move toward each other or grind together as they move past each other. Earthquakes along the **San Andreas Fault** in California are caused by the grinding of two plates.

MEASURING EARTHQUAKES

The Richter scale goes from 0 to more than 8. These numbers indicate the strength of an earthquake. Each number means the quake releases about 30 times more energy than the number below it. An earthquake measuring 6 on the scale is about 30 times stronger than one measuring 5 and 900 times stronger than one measuring 4. Earthquakes that are 4 or above are considered major. (The damage and injuries caused by a quake also depend on other things, such as whether the area is heavily populated and built up.)

MAJOR EARTHQUAKES

The earthquakes listed here are among the largest and most destructive recorded in the past 100 years.

Year	Location	Magnitude	Deaths (approximate)
2003	Iran (southeastern)	6.5	41,000+
2002	Afghanistan (northern)	6.1	1,000+
2001	India (western)	7.9	30,000+
1999	Turkey (western)	7.4	17,200+
1998	Afghanistan (northeastern)	6.9	4,700+
	Afghanistan (northeastern)	6.1	2,323
1995	Japan (Kobe)	6.9	5,502
1994	United States (Los Angeles area)	6.8	61
1993	India (southern)	6.3	9,748
1990	Iran (western)	7.7	40,000+
1989	United States (San Francisco area)	7.1	62
1988	Soviet Armenia	7.0	55,000
1985	Mexico (Michoacan)	8.1	9,500
1976	China (Tangshan)	8.0	255,000
1970	Peru (northern)	7.8	66,000
1939	Chile (Chillan)	8.3	28,000
1927	China (Nan-Shan)	8.3	200,000
1923	Japan (Yokohama)	8.3	143,000
1920	China (Gansu)	8.6	200,000
1906	Chile (Valparaiso)	8.6	20,000
	United States (San Francisco)	8.3	3,000+

VOLCANOES

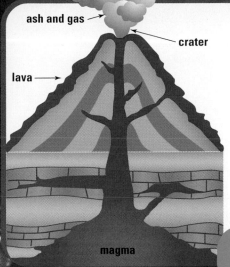

ash and gas

crater

lava

magma

A volcano is a mountain or hill (**cone**) with an opening on top known as a **crater**. Hot melted rock (**magma**), gases, and other material from inside the Earth mix together miles underground, rising up through cracks and weak spots. When enough pressure builds up, the magna may blast out, or erupt, through the crater. The magma is called **lava** when it reaches the air. This lava may be hotter than 2,000° Fahrenheit. The cone of this volcano is made of layers of lava and ash that have erupted, then cooled.

Some islands, like the Hawaiian, are really the tops of undersea volcanoes.

Where *is the* Ring of Fire?

The hundreds of active volcanoes found on the land near the edges of the Pacific Ocean make up what is called the **Ring of Fire**. They mark the boundary between the plates under the Pacific Ocean and the plates under the continents around the ocean. (The plates of the Earth are explained on page 86, with the help of a map.) The Ring of Fire runs all along the west coast of South and North America, from the southern tip of Chile to Alaska. The ring also runs down the east coast of Asia, starting in the far north in Kamchatka. It continues down past Australia.

SOME FAMOUS VOLCANIC ERUPTIONS

Year	Volcano (place)	Deaths (approximate)
79	Mount Vesuvius (Italy)	16,000
1586	Kelut (Indonesia)	10,000
1792	Mount Unzen (Japan)	14,500
1815	Tambora (Indonesia)	10,000
1883	Krakatau or Krakatoa (Indonesia)	36,000
1902	Mount Pelée (Martinique)	28,000
1980	Mount St. Helens (U.S.)	57
1982	El Chichón (Mexico)	1,880
1985	Nevado del Ruiz (Colombia)	23,000
1986	Lake Nyos (Cameroon)	1,700
1991	Mt. Pinatubo (Philippines)	800

There are three types of rock:

IGNEOUS rocks form from underground magma (melted rock) that cools and becomes solid. Granite is an igneous rock made from quartz, feldspar, and mica.

SEDIMENTARY rocks form on low-lying land or the bottom of seas. Layers of small particles harden into rock such as limestone or shale over millions of years.

METAMORPHIC rocks are igneous or sedimentary rocks that have been changed by chemistry, heat, or pressure (or all three). Marble is a metamorphic rock formed from limestone.

87

EARLY EXPLORATION

AROUND 1000	**Leif Ericson**, from Iceland, explored "Vinland," which may have been the coasts of northeast Canada and New England.
1271-95	**Marco Polo** (Italian) traveled through Central Asia, India, China, and Indonesia.
1488	**Bartolomeu Dias** (Portuguese) explored the Cape of Good Hope in southern Africa.
1492-1504	**Christopher Columbus** (Italian) sailed four times from Spain to America and started colonies there.
1497-98	**Vasco da Gama** (Portuguese) sailed farther than Dias, around the Cape of Good Hope to East Africa and India.
1513	**Juan Ponce de León** (Spanish) explored and named Florida.
1513	**Vasco Núñez de Balboa** (Spanish) explored Panama and reached the Pacific Ocean.
1519-21	**Ferdinand Magellan** (Portuguese) sailed from Spain around the tip of South America and across the Pacific Ocean to the Philippines, where he died. His expedition continued around the world.
1519-36	**Hernando Cortés** (Spanish) conquered Mexico, traveling as far west as Baja California.
1527-42	**Alvar Núñez Cabeza de Vaca** (Spanish) explored the southwestern United States, Brazil, and Paraguay.
1532-35	**Francisco Pizarro** (Spanish) explored the west coast of South America and conquered Peru.
1534-36	**Jacques Cartier** (French) sailed up the St. Lawrence River to the site of present-day Montreal.
1539-42	**Hernando de Soto** (Spanish) explored the southeastern United States and the lower Mississippi Valley.
1603-13	**Samuel de Champlain** (French) traced the course of the St. Lawrence River and explored the northeastern United States.
1609-10	**Henry Hudson** (English), sailing from Holland, explored the Hudson River, Hudson Bay, and Hudson Strait.
1682	**Robert Cavelier**, sieur de La Salle (French), traced the Mississippi River to its mouth in the Gulf of Mexico.
1768-78	**James Cook** (English) charted the world's major bodies of water and explored Hawaii and Antarctica.
1804-06	**Meriwether Lewis and William Clark** (American) traveled from St. Louis along the Missouri and Columbia rivers to the Pacific Ocean and back.
1849-59	**David Livingstone** (Scottish) explored Southern Africa, including the Zambezi River and Victoria Falls.

ALL ABOUT... LEWIS and CLARK

It's been 200 years since Meriwether Lewis and William Clark set out across the uncharted western lands of North America. They started near St. Louis in May 1804. President Thomas Jefferson called the brave group "The Corps of Discovery." They were to explore for the U.S. the vast unknown territory between the Mississippi and the Rocky Mountains which Jefferson had bought from France a year before (in the "Louisiana Purchase"). In addition to political and military objectives, they also had hoped to find a water route to the Pacific (but, of course, there isn't one).

Jefferson appointed Captain Lewis, his personal secretary and an Army veteran, to head the expedition. As co-commander Lewis chose his friend Clark, another soldier, who was a skilled boatman and mapmaker. Together they led a group of 34 adventurers more than 4,000 miles to the Pacific coast of the Oregon Territory, which they reached in November 1805—then another 4,000 miles back! Among hazards they faced on the long trip (2 years, 4 months, 9 days) were winter cold and storms, mountains, rapids, bears, diseases, and sometimes unfriendly Indian tribes. While risking their lives they also took time to learn about Indian customs and record descriptions of more than 300 species of previously unknown plants and animals.

Sacagawea, a Shoshone Indian woman, was a valuable guide and translator. Among other things, she helped the expedition trade for the horses they needed to cross the Rockies.

did you know?

A large collection of objects, journals, maps, and equipment that the explorers carried or brought back are on a cross-country tour from 2004 to 2006. The exhibit started in early 2004 in St. Louis and was slated to move to Philadelphia; Denver; Portland, Oregon; ending up Washington, D.C.

Quick Quiz

1. **Which part of a map tells what the symbols on it mean?**
   A legend B scale C compass rose D grid

2. **On a Mercator projection map, where do the land shapes look too big?**
   A near the poles B near the equator C at the meridians D nowhere

3. **If you were at 0° latitude, where would you be?**
   A the North Pole B the prime meridian C the equator D the South Pole

4. **A degree of latitude is equal to how much of the earth's circumference?**
   A 1/90 B 1/100 C 1/360 D 1/720

5. **If you were at 0° longitude, where would you be?**
   A the North Pole B the prime meridian C the equator D the South Pole

6. **What latitude is halfway between the equator and the North Pole?**
   A 45° N B 45° S C 45° E D 45° W

Answers on Pages 319–322. For more puzzles go to
WWW.WORLDALMANACFORKIDS.COM

Health

Which are less fatty, pretzels or potato chips?

page 91

The Right FOODS

To stay healthy, it is important to eat the right foods and to exercise. To help people choose the right foods for good health and fitness, the U.S. government developed the food pyramid shown below. The food pyramid shows the groups of foods that everyone should eat every day.

The foods at the bottom of the pyramid are the ones everyone needs to eat in the biggest amounts. At the top are the foods to be eaten in the smallest amounts. The number of servings needed depends on your age and body size. Younger, smaller people need fewer servings. Older, larger people need more.

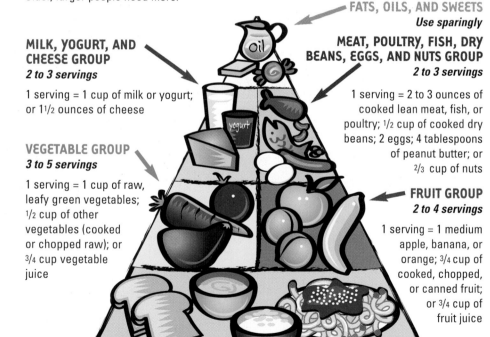

FATS, OILS, AND SWEETS
Use sparingly

MILK, YOGURT, AND CHEESE GROUP
2 to 3 servings

1 serving = 1 cup of milk or yogurt; or 1 1/2 ounces of cheese

MEAT, POULTRY, FISH, DRY BEANS, EGGS, AND NUTS GROUP
2 to 3 servings

1 serving = 2 to 3 ounces of cooked lean meat, fish, or poultry; 1/2 cup of cooked dry beans; 2 eggs; 4 tablespoons of peanut butter; or 2/3 cup of nuts

VEGETABLE GROUP
3 to 5 servings

1 serving = 1 cup of raw, leafy green vegetables; 1/2 cup of other vegetables (cooked or chopped raw); or 3/4 cup vegetable juice

FRUIT GROUP
2 to 4 servings

1 serving = 1 medium apple, banana, or orange; 3/4 cup of cooked, chopped, or canned fruit; or 3/4 cup of fruit juice

BREAD, CEREAL, RICE, AND PASTA GROUP
6 to 11 servings
1 serving = 1 slice of bread; 1 ounce of ready-to-eat cereal; or 1/2 cup of cooked cereal, rice, or pasta

We Are What We Eat

Have you ever noticed the labels on the packages of food you and your family buy? The labels provide information people need to make healthy choices about the foods they eat. Below are some terms you may see on labels.

NUTRIENTS ARE NEEDED

Nutrients are the parts of food the body can use for growth, for energy, and for repairing itself. Carbohydrates, fats, proteins, vitamins, minerals, and water are different kinds of nutrients found in food. **Carbohydrates** and **fats** provide energy. **Proteins** aid growth and help maintain and repair the body. **Vitamins** help the body use food, help eyesight and skin, and aid in fighting off infections. **Minerals** help build bones and teeth and aid in such functions as muscle contractions and blood clotting. **Water** helps with growth and repair of the body. It also helps the body digest food and get rid of wastes.

CALORIES COUNT

A **calorie** is a measure of how much energy we get from food. The government recommends the number of calories that should be taken in each day. Kids aged 7 to 12 and teenaged girls should eat about 2,200 calories daily. Teenaged boys need around 2,800. Active people—who play sports, for instance—may need more.

To maintain a **healthy weight,** it is important to balance the calories in the food you eat with the calories you use up. The more active you are, the more calories your body burns. If you eat more calories than your body uses, you will gain weight.

Junk food is a term for foods (such as candy, soda, and most desserts) that have lots of calories but not many nutrients.

Nutrition Facts

Serving Size 1/2 cup (1 oz.) = (30g)
Servings per container 14

Amount Per Serving	Cereal	Cereal w/ 1/2 cup Lowfat Milk
Calories	100	150
Calories from Fat	10	25
	% Daily Value**	
Total Fat 1g*	2%	4%
Saturated Fat 0g	0%	5%
Cholesterol 0mg	0%	3%
Sodium 50mg	2%	5%
Total Carbohydrates 20g	7%	9%
Dietary Fiber 2g	8%	8%
Sugars 5g		
Protein 4g		
Vitamin A	0%	6%
Vitamin C	0%	2%
Calcium	0%	15%
Iron	2%	4%

* Amount in Cereal. One half cup lowfat milk contributes an additional 50 calories, 1.5g total fat (1g saturated fat), 9 mg cholesterol, 60mg sodium, 6g total carbohydrates (6g sugars), and 3g protein.
** Percents (%) of a Daily Value are based on a 2,000 calorie diet. Your Daily Values may vary higher or lower depending on your calorie needs:

Nutrient	Calories	2,000	2,500
Total Fat	Less than	65g	80g
Sat Fat	Less than	20g	25g
Cholesterol	Less than	300mg	300mg
Sodium	Less than	2,400mg	2,400mg
Total Carbohydrates		300g	375g
Dietary Fiber		25g	30g

Calories per gram:
Fat 9 • Carbohydrate 4 • Protein

Some lower-fat foods

chicken or turkey hot dog

tuna fish canned in water

baked potato

pretzels

apple

plain popcorn (with no butter)

skim milk or 1% or 2% milk

Some fatty foods

beef or pork hot dog

fried hamburger

french fries

potato chips

tuna fish canned in oil

buttered popcorn

whole milk

A Little Fat Goes a Long Way

A little bit of fat keeps your body warm. It gives the muscles energy. It helps keep the skin soft and healthy. But the body needs only a small amount to do all these things. Less than one-third of your calories should come from fat, if you're over two years old.

Cholesterol. Eating too much fat can make some people's bodies produce too much **cholesterol** (ka-**less**-ter-all). This waxy substance can build up over the years on the inside of arteries. Too much cholesterol keeps blood from flowing freely through the arteries and can cause serious health problems such as heart attacks.

Body Basics:

Your body is made up of many different parts that work together every minute of every day and night. It's more amazing than any machine or computer. Even though everyone's body looks different outside, people have the same parts inside. Each system of the body has its own job. Some of the systems also work together to keep you healthy and strong.

CIRCULATORY SYSTEM In the circulatory system, the **heart** pumps **blood**, which then travels through tubes, called **arteries**, to all parts of the body. The blood carries the oxygen and food that the body needs to stay alive. **Veins** carry the blood back to the heart.

DIGESTIVE SYSTEM The digestive system moves food through parts of the body called the **esophagus**, **stomach**, and **intestines**. As the food passes through, some of it is broken down into tiny particles called **nutrients**, which the body needs. Nutrients enter the bloodstream, which carries them to all parts of the body. The digestive system then changes the remaining food into waste that is eliminated from the body.

ENDOCRINE SYSTEM
The endocrine system includes **glands** that are needed for some body functions. There are two kinds of glands. **Exocrine** glands produce liquids such as sweat and saliva. **Endocrine** glands produce chemicals called hormones. **Hormones** control body functions, such as growth.

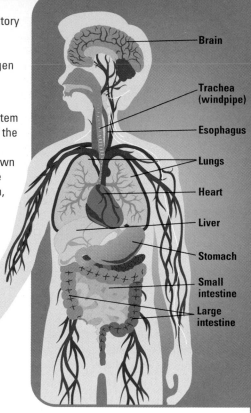

Brain

Trachea (windpipe)

Esophagus

Lungs

Heart

Liver

Stomach

Small intestine

Large intestine

NERVOUS SYSTEM The nervous system enables us to think, feel, move, hear, and see. It includes the **brain**, the **spinal cord**, and **nerves** in all parts of the body. Nerves in the spinal cord carry signals back and forth between the brain and the rest of the body. The brain tells us what to do and how to respond. It has three major parts. The **cerebrum** controls thinking, speech, and vision. The **cerebellum** is responsible for physical coordination. The **brain stem** controls the respiratory, circulatory, and digestive systems.

RESPIRATORY SYSTEM The respiratory system allows us to breathe. Air comes into the body through the nose and mouth. It goes through the **windpipe** (or **trachea**) to two tubes (called **bronchi**), which carry air to the **lungs**. Oxygen from the air is taken in by tiny blood vessels in the lungs. The blood then carries oxygen to the cells of the body.

What the Body's Systems Do

SKELETAL SYSTEM
The skeletal system is made up of the **bones** that hold your body upright. Some bones protect organs, such as the ribs that cover the lungs.

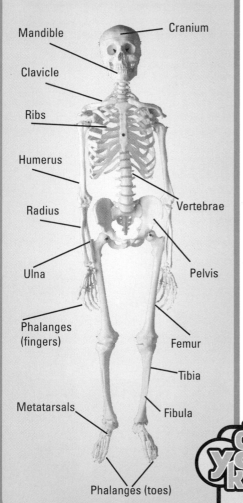

- Mandible
- Cranium
- Clavicle
- Ribs
- Humerus
- Radius
- Ulna
- Phalanges (fingers)
- Metatarsals
- Vertebrae
- Pelvis
- Femur
- Tibia
- Fibula
- Phalanges (toes)

MUSCULAR SYSTEM
Muscles are made up of elastic fibers There are three types of muscle: **skeletal, smooth,** and **cardiac.** The skeletal muscles help the body move—they are the large muscles we can see. Smooth muscles are found in our digestive system, blood vessels, and air passages. Cardiac muscle is found only in your heart. Smooth and cardiac muscles are **involuntary** muscles—they do their job without us having to think about them.

REPRODUCTIVE SYSTEM
Through the reproductive system, adult human beings are able to create new human beings. Reproduction begins when a **sperm** cell from a man fertilizes an **egg** cell from a woman.

URINARY SYSTEM
This system, which includes the **kidneys**, cleans waste from the blood and regulates the amount of water in the body.

IMMUNE SYSTEM
The immune system protects your body from diseases by fighting against certain substances that come from outside, or **antigens.** This happens in different ways. For example, white blood cells called **B lymphocytes** learn to fight certain viruses and bacteria by producing **antibodies,** which spread around the body to attack them. Sometimes, as in **allergies,** the immune system makes a mistake and creates antibodies to fight a substance that's really harmless.

did you know?
The "funny bone" is not funny at all—it's humerus (the Latin name for the bone). The ulnar nerve running along your arm rests against the humerus bone; that's why it hurts when you hit it.

Exercise It's What You do!

The CDC reports that the average kid spends 4.5 hours a day in front of some sort of screen (TV, video game, computer). That's 31.5 hours a week. In a year, that time adds up to 1,642.5 hours or 68.4 days! Can you find at least 30 minutes in your day to get some moderate exercise?

If you watch TV in the afternoons after school or on Saturday mornings, you've probably seen the "VERB. It's What You Do" ads. They're part of a seven-year campaign sponsored by the government to encourage kids age 9-13 to get more exercise.

Why does the U.S. Department of Health and Human Services' Centers for Disease Control and Prevention (CDC) think exercise is important for kids? In 2002, the National Center for Health Statistics reported that an estimated 8.8 million U.S. kids age 6–19 were overweight. Being overweight increases a risk of developing high blood pressure, diabetes, and heart disease.

But daily exercise has other benefits too: it makes you feel good. Exercise also helps you think better, sleep better, and feel more relaxed. Regular exercise will make you stronger and help you improve at physical activities. Breathing deeply during exercise gets more oxygen into your lungs with each breath. Your heart pumps more oxygen-filled blood all through your body with each beat. Muscles and joints get stronger and more flexible as you use them.

Organized sports are a good way to get a lot of exercise, but not the only way. You can shoot hoops, jog, ride a bike, or skate without being on a team. If you can't think of anything else, try walking in a safe place. Walk with friends or even try to get the adults in your life to put down the remote and join you. They could probably use the exercise!

Below are some activities, with a rough idea of how many calories a 100-pound person would burn per minute while doing them.

ACTIVITY	CALORIES PER MINUTE
Jogging (6 miles per hour)	8
Jumping rope (easy)	7
Playing basketball	7
Playing soccer	6
Bicycling (9.4 miles per hour)	5
Skiing (downhill)	5
Raking the lawn	4
Rollerblading (easy)	4
Walking (4 miles per hour)	4
Bicycling (5.5 miles per hour)	3
Swimming (25 yards per minute)	3
Walking (3 miles per hour)	3

If you're interested in running, try **WEB SITE** http://www.kidsrunning.com/
There you'll find advice, activities, stories, poems, and more—all about running.

1 *Your lacrimal (LAH-kruh-mul) glands help you to:*
A sweat   B taste   C cry   D spit

2 *Which of the following is not one of the four blood types:*
A type A   B type B   C type AB   D type Z

3 *We're born with more than 300 bones, but many of them grow together as we get older. How many bones does a full-grown adult have?*
A 150   B 206   C 175   D 250

4 *About how many muscles are in the human body?*
A 1,000   B 500   C 650   D 300

5 *Where would find the stirrup bone (only about a tenth of an inch long), your body's smallest?*
A foot   B jaw   C hand   D ear

6 *In what part of your body would you find the femur, the longest human bone?*
A leg   B arm   C chest   D back

7 *Cardiac muscle is found only in which part of your body?*
A brain   B lungs   C liver   D heart

8 *Your first set of "baby" teeth numbers 20. How many are in a normal set of adult teeth?*
A 32   B 42   C 20   D 30

9 *Which of the following is not one of the four taste zones on your tongue?*
A sweet   B sour   C bitter   D spicy

10 *As an adult, you'll have about five feet of large intestine in your body. About how many feet of the much narrower small intestine will you have?*
A 50   B 25   C 100   D 10

Optical Illusions

Optical illusions trick your eyes or fool your brain into seeing things as they're not.

Do you see a circle in this grid?

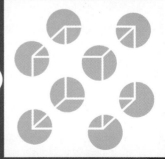

Do you see a cube?

Would you have any trouble eating with this impossible fork? How many tines does it have?

Answers on Pages 319–322. For more puzzles go to
WWW.WORLDALMANACFORKIDS.COM

Holidays

Where is Juneteenth celebrated? page 97

Holidays in the United States

There are no official holidays for the whole U.S. But most states celebrate the holidays listed below on the days shown. These are the federal holidays, when workers for the federal government get the day off. Many offices, and most banks and schools, in the 50 states are closed on these days.

NEW YEAR'S DAY The U.S. and most other countries celebrate the beginning of the new year on January 1.

MARTIN LUTHER KING JR. DAY Observed on the third Monday in January, this holiday marks the birth (January 15, 1929) of the African-American civil rights leader Rev. Martin Luther King Jr. In 2005, it will be celebrated on January 17.

PRESIDENTS' DAY On the third Monday in February (February 21, 2005), most states celebrate the births of both George Washington (born February 22, 1732) and Abraham Lincoln (born February 12, 1809).

MEMORIAL DAY OR DECORATION DAY Memorial Day, observed on the last Monday in May (May 30, 2005), is set aside to remember men and women who died serving in the military.

FOURTH OF JULY OR INDEPENDENCE DAY July 4 is the anniversary of the day in 1776 when the American colonies signed the Declaration of Independence. Kids and grownups celebrate with bands and parades, picnics, barbecues, and fireworks.

LABOR DAY Labor Day, the first Monday in September, honors the workers of America. It was first celebrated in 1882. It falls on September 6 in 2004 and September 5 in 2005.

COLUMBUS DAY Celebrated on the second Monday in October, Columbus Day is the anniversary of October 12, 1492, the day Christopher Columbus was traditionally thought to have arrived in the Americas (on the island of San Salvador). It falls on October 11 in 2004 and October 10 in 2005.

VETERANS DAY Veterans Day, November 11, honors veterans of wars. First called Armistice Day, it marked the armistice (agreement) that ended World War I. This was signed on the 11th hour of the 11th day of the 11th month of 1918.

THANKSGIVING Thanksgiving was first observed by the Pilgrims in 1621 as a harvest festival and a day for thanks and feasting. In 1863, Abraham Lincoln revived the tradition. It comes on the fourth Thursday in November— November 25 in 2004 and November 24 in 2005.

CHRISTMAS Christmas is both a religious holiday and a legal holiday. It is celebrated on December 25.

Election Day

Election Day, the first Tuesday after the first Monday in November (November 2 in 2004 and November 8 in 2005), is also a holiday in some states.

Other **Special** Holidays

VALENTINE'S DAY February 14 is a day for sending cards or gifts to people you love.

MOTHER'S DAY AND FATHER'S DAY Mothers are honored on the second Sunday in May. Fathers are honored on the third Sunday in June.

HALLOWEEN In ancient Britain, Druids wore grotesque costumes on October 31 to scare off evil spirits. Today, "trick or treating" children ask for candy, or money for UNICEF, the United Nations Children's Fund.

HANUKKAH (ALSO CHANUKAH) This eight-day Jewish festival begins on the evening of December 7 in 2004 and December 25 in 2005. It recalls when the Jews, in 165 B.C., recaptured the Temple of Jerusalem. Today, people light candles each night until the menorah, an eight-branched candle holder, is filled. And children get gifts!

KWANZAA This seven-day African-American festival begins on December 26. It celebrates seven virtues: unity, self-determination, collective work and responsibility, cooperative economics, purpose, creativity, and faith.

DON'T FORGET THESE DAYS!

You can chase away the "back-to-school blues" by observing **Hobbit Day** or **Elephant Appreciation Day** on September 22. Here are a few other odd "days" you've probably never heard of (dates are for 2005):

January 18, Pooh Day (A.A. Milne's birthday)	July 17, National Ice Cream Day
February 14, Ferris Wheel Day	August 6, National Fresh Breath Day
March 1, National Pig Day	September 19, Talk Like a Pirate Day
April 14, International Moment of Laughter Day	October 26, Mule Day
May 2, Sibling Appreciation Day	November 14, National American Teddy Bear Day
June 2, National Bubba Day	December 31, Make Up Your Mind Day

Special note: September 1-30 is Be Kind to Writers and Editors Month!

The holiday "Juneteenth" celebrates June 19, 1865. That's when Union General Gordon Granger read President Lincoln's Emancipation Proclamation in Galveston, Texas, letting the people there know that the Civil War was over and the slaves were free. So far, only Texas has made Juneteenth an official holiday, but it is celebrated by many African-Americans around the U.S.

HOLIDAYS Around the World

BASTILLE DAY On July 14, the French celebrate the fall of the Bastille, a prison in Paris, in 1789. This was the start of the French Revolution.

BOXING DAY December 26 is a holiday in Britain, Australia, Canada, and New Zealand. On this day, gifts were once given out in boxes to servants, tradespeople, and the poor.

CANADA DAY Canada's national holiday, July 1, commemorates the union of Canadian provinces in 1867.

CHINESE NEW YEAR China's biggest holiday starts the first month in the Chinese lunar calendar and falls on February 9 in 2005. Celebrations include parades, fireworks, and traditional meals.

CINCO DE MAYO Mexicans remember May 5, 1867, when Mexico defeated its French rulers and became independent.

Calendar Basics

Holidays and calendars go hand in hand. Using a calendar, you can see what day of the week it is, and watch out for the next special day. Calendars divide time into days, weeks, months, and years. A year is the time it takes for one revolution of Earth around the Sun. Early calendars were lunar—based on the movements of the Moon across the sky. The ancient Egyptians were probably the first to develop a solar calendar, based on the movements of Earth around the Sun.

THE JULIAN AND GREGORIAN CALENDARS

In 46 B.C., the emperor Julius Caesar decided to use a calendar based on movements of the Sun. This calendar, called the **Julian calendar**, fixed the normal year at 365 days and added one day every fourth year (leap year). It also established the months of the year and the days of the week.

Pope Gregory XIII revised the Julian calendar in A.D. 1582 because the year was 11 minutes, 14 seconds too long. This added up to about 3 extra days every 400 years. To fix it, he made years ending in 00 leap years only if they can be divided by 400. Thus, 2000 was a leap year, but 2100 will not be. The **Gregorian calendar** is the one used today in most of the world.

JEWISH, ISLAMIC, AND CHINESE CALENDARS

The **Jewish calendar**, which began almost 6,000 years ago, is the official calendar of Israel. The year 2004 is the same as 5764-5765 on the Jewish calendar, which starts at Rosh Hashanah, usually in September. The **Islamic calendar** started in A.D. 622. The year 2004 is equivalent to 1424-1425 on the Islamic calendar, which begins with the month of Muharram, usually in February or March. The **Chinese calendar** has years named after animals. There are 12 of them: Rat, Ox, Tiger, Rabbit, Dragon, Snake, Horse, Sheep, Monkey, Rooster, Dog, and Pig. On January 22, 2004, the Year of the Monkey began. On February 9, 2005, the Year of the Rooster starts.

BIRTHSTONES

MONTH	BIRTHSTONE
January	Garnet
February	Amethyst
March	Aquamarine
April	Diamond
May	Emerald
June	Pearl
July	Ruby
August	Peridot
September	Sapphire
October	Opal
November	Topaz
December	Turquoise

Here's a useful way to keep your months straight:

30 days hath September,
April, June, and November.
All the rest have 31,
Except the second month alone.
February has 28 days time,
Til leap year makes it 29.

THE NAMES OF THE MONTHS

January	named for the Roman god Janus, guardian of gates (often shown with two faces, looking backward and forward)
February	named for Februalia, a Roman time of sacrifice
March	named for Mars, the Roman god of war (the end of winter meant fighting could begin again)
April	"aperire," Latin for "to open," as in flower buds
May	named for Maia, the goddess of plant growth
June	"Junius," the Latin word for the goddess Juno
July	named after the Roman ruler Julius Caesar
August	named for Augustus, the first Roman emperor
September	"septem," the Latin word for seven
October	"octo," the Latin word for eight
November	"novem," the Latin word for nine
December	"decem," the Latin word for ten

Homework Help

What are some good search engines? page 102

If you need to study for an exam, write a research paper, or do a diorama, there are helpful hints in this chapter.

In other chapters, you can find lots of information on topics you may write about or study in school. **Facts About Nations,** pages 154-173, and **Facts About U.S. States,** pages 274-290, are good places to look. For math tips and formulas, look up the chapter on **Numbers**. For good books to read, and write about, see the **Books** chapter. Plus, there are many other study and learning tips throughout the book. Look for the **"Homework Help" icon**! ▶

Those Tricky Tests

Getting Ready

Being prepared for a test can relieve some of your jitters and can make test taking a lot easier! Here are some tips to help you get ready.

▶ Take good notes in class and keep up with assignments, so you don't have to learn material at the last minute! Just writing down the notes helps you remember the information.

▶ Make a study schedule and stick to it! Don't watch TV or listen to distracting music while studying.

▶ Start reviewing early if you can—don't wait until the night before the test.

▶ Go over the headings, summaries, and questions in each chapter to review key points. Read your notes and highlight the most important topics.

▶ Take study breaks so you can concentrate and stay alert.

▶ Get a good night's sleep and eat a good breakfast before the test.

The Big Event

Follow these suggestions for smooth sailing during test time:

▶ Take a deep breath and relax! That will help calm your nerves.

▶ Skim through the entire exam so you know what to expect and how long it may take.

▶ As you start each part, read directions carefully.

▶ Read each question carefully before answering. For a multiple choice question, check every possible answer before you decide on one. The best answer could be the last one!

▶ Don't spend too much time on any one question. Skip hard questions and go back to them at the end.

▶ Keep track of time so you can pace yourself. Use any time left at the end to go back and review your answers. Make sure you've written the answer you meant to select.

How to write a research paper

Picking a Topic

Sometimes you not only have to research a topic and write about it—you have to pick the topic in the first place. Here are a few tips to keep in mind.

► **Start out by brainstorming.** Let your brain flow freely with ideas of ALL kinds and write them down. Even if an idea seems doubtful, write it down anyway. You can be more picky later on.

► **Don't make the topic too big.** For example: "American Presidents" may be too big because it includes over 40 people; it would be better to narrow it down to just one.

► **Consider picking a subject you already like.** If you're already interested in something, like soccer or recycling or Sherlock Holmes, you'll enjoy writing about it and might well do a better job.

► **But don't rule out something unfamiliar or unusual.** Writing on a subject you don't know anything about is a great way to learn. And picking an unusual topic can add interest. For example, instead of writing about Abraham Lincoln, you could try James Buchanan, or Franklin Pierce!

Doing Research

Once you have a topic, the next step is to read all about it. Try to find information from as many sources as you can. If you can't come up with at least a few good sources, then the topic is too narrow. If you're overwhelmed with information about the topic, you need to go back and narrow the topic down.

► **Encyclopedias are a good place to start.** They can give you a good overview of the subject.

► **The electronic catalog** of your school or town library will probably be your main source for finding material about your subject. Keep in mind that books are not as current as magazines and newspapers, but they can still give you information you can use.

► **Check your library's indexes** for magazine or newspaper articles. *The Reader's Guide to Periodic Literature* can be a big help in finding articles; there's even an online version.

► You can also use **the Internet** as a research tool. For more details, see "Research on the Internet" (page 102).

► Don't be afraid to ask **the librarian** for help if you get stuck!

► As you read each source, **write down the facts and ideas** that you may need. You might try using 3x5 index cards.

► **Make sure** your cards show the title and author for each source and the page numbers for where you found the particular information.

Hint: Use quotation marks when you think you may want to use the same words as the author.

Writing It Down

The next step is to organize your facts. See which cards you still need and try to put them in the order you want to use. **Develop a rough outline** of your main ideas in the order in which they'll appear.

Now you're ready for the **first draft**. It can be a rough draft that gets your ideas down while they're fresh. You can worry about the exact wording, the spellings, and so forth later on.

Your paper should contain three main parts:

INTRODUCTION The introduction, or first paragraph, explains your topic and your point of view on it. It should draw readers into the paper and let them know what to expect.

BODY The body of the paper develops your ideas. Use specific facts, examples, and details to make your points clear and convincing. Use separate paragraphs for each new idea and use words and phrases that link one paragraph to the next so your ideas flow smoothly.

CONCLUSION Summarize your main points in the final paragraph, or conclusion.

Put your first draft aside for a few days, then go back and re-read it. You'll be able to make corrections more easily after seeing it with fresh eyes. After you're done making your **revisions,** read the paper (slowly!) to check for misspellings and mistakes in grammar or punctuation.

Showing Your Sources

▶ It is important in a paper to show what sources you used. This can be done with **footnotes** that go on the same page as the information itself and say where you got each key fact or quote.

▶ You may need to do a **bibliography** at the end. This is a list of all the sources you used to prepare the report—even some that you may not have actually ended up using in what you wrote.

▶ In the box below are samples of what you might put in your bibliography for a book, magazine article, or Internet source you used in your research. Your teacher will tell you exactly what format to use for showing your sources.

Hint: You usually will not have a reason to use the same wording as your source. If you do, refer to your source and use quotation marks.

FOR A BOOK: *Author(s). title (in italics). city published: publisher, year.*
Kwek, Karen. *Welcome to Chile.* Milwaukee, Wisc.: Gareth Stevens, 2004.

FOR A MAGAZINE OR NEWSPAPER ARTICLE: *Author. article title (in quotation marks). name of publication (in italics). date of issue: article page numbers.*
Michael Silver. "Super Bowl XXXVIII: Fight to the Finish." *Sports Illustrated.* February 9, 2004: 42-52.

FOR ON-LINE (INTERNET): *Author. title of page used (in quotation marks). website address (http://...). date.*
Environmental Protection Agency. "Learn About Chemicals Around Your House." *http://www.epa.gov/kidshometour.* April 10, 2003.

Homework Help
Research on the INTERNET

Using Library Resources
Your school or public library is a great place to start. It probably has a list (catalog) of its books and periodicals (newspapers and magazines) available from computers at the library, or even from home over the Internet through your library's web site. You can search using **keywords** (words that describe your subject) in three basic ways: by **author**, by **title**, or by **subject**.

For example, doing a subject search for "Benjamin Franklin" will give you a list of books and articles about him, along with their locations in the library.

Your library may also subscribe to on-line reference databases that companies like The World Almanac create especially for research. These are accessible over the Internet and could contain almanacs, encyclopedias, other reference books, or collections of articles. You can access these databases from the library, and maybe even from home from your library's web site.

When you write your report, don't copy directly from books, articles, or the Internet—that's **plagiarism**. Keep track of all your **sources**—the books, articles, and web sites you use—and list them in a **bibliography**. (See page 101 for some examples.)

Why shouldn't I just search the Internet?
The library's list may look just like other information on the Internet. But these sources usually have been checked by experts. This is not true of all the information on the Internet. It could come from almost anybody, and may not be trustworthy.

When can I use the Internet?
The Internet is still a great way to look things up. You can find addresses or recipes, listen to music, or find things to do. You can look up information on hobbies or musical instruments, or read a magazine or newspaper online.

If you search the internet on your own, make sure the web site you find is reliable. A U.S. government site or a site produced by a well-known organization or publication may be your best bet.

Using a Search Engine
The best way to find web sites is to use a search engine. Here are some helpful ones:

Yahooligans (www.yahooligans.com)
Kidsclick (www.kidsclick.org)
Lycos Zone (lycoszone.lycos.com)
Ask Jeeves Kids (www.ajkids.com)

Start by typing one or two search terms—words that describe your topic. The search engine scans the Internet and gives you a list of sites that contain them. The results appear in a certain order, or **rank**. Search engines use different ways of measuring which web sites are likely to be the most helpful. One way is by counting how many times your search terms appear on each site. The site that's listed first may not have what you want. Explore as many of the sites as possible.

You might have to narrow your search by using more keywords. Or try using **directories** to help find what you need.

THE WORLD ALMANAC FOR KIDS has its own website at:
WEB SITE *http://www.worldalmanacforkids.com*

HOW TO MAKE A DIORAMA

A diorama is a small model of a real-life scene that has lifelike details and a realistic background. It could be anything from the habitat of a white Bengal tiger (see below) to a Native American village to a spaceship landing on the Moon.

After you choose the scene that you want to re-create, make a base for the model using a thin piece of board or cardboard, a shoebox, or a larger box. Make sure your base is the right size—the pieces of your model will look too cluttered if the base is too small or too empty if the base is too big. Here are some other tips to keep in mind when you're doing the layout:

▶ Put the buildings or vehicles in the scene at an angle to the sides of the base.

▶ Put bigger items in the back, leaving the front of the scene clear and easy to see.

▶ To draw attention to one particular part of the scene, have all the figures look in the same direction as the section you want to highlight. That way, the viewer's eyes will also focus there.

▶ Keep the scene "balanced"—don't put all the larger items on one side and the smaller items on the other.

After you finish the layout, gather all the figures and materials together that you want to use. Some of the supplies you might need include a shoe box or a slightly larger box, crayons or markers, paste or a glue stick, a pencil, scissors, tape, thread, a darning needle, a hole punch, acrylic paint, and pipe cleaners.

▶ If you use cutouts made of thin paper for the figures, paste them onto poster board or thin cardboard (like an old cereal box) so they stand up better.

▶ Hang flying animals or fish from the top of a box using invisible thread, tape, or pipe cleaners.

▶ Green and brown pipe cleaners work well as plants, and cotton puffs make great clouds or snow!

Make sure you use the same care and attention with the little details in the small items and figures as you use with the larger items—like the buildings and vehicles—so the overall look is complete and well thought out.

Diorama showing the habitat of a white Bengal tiger

Inventions

When was TV invented? page 105

A lot of the world's inventions came before history was written. These include the wheel, pottery, many tools, and the ability to make fire. More recent inventions help us to travel faster, communicate better, and live longer.

Invention TIME LINE

YEAR	INVENTION	INVENTOR (COUNTRY)
105	paper	Ts'ai Lun (China)
1250	magnifying glass	Roger Bacon (England)
1447	moveable type	Johann Gutenberg (Germany)
1590	2-lens microscope	Zacharias Janssen (Netherlands)
1608	telescope	Hans Lippershey (Netherlands)
1709	piano	Bartolomeo Cristofori (Italy)
1714	mercury thermometer	Gabriel D. Fahrenheit (Germany)
1752	lightning rod	Benjamin Franklin (U.S.)
1780	bifocal lenses for glasses	Benjamin Franklin (U.S.)
1785	parachute	Jean Pierre Blanchard (France)
1795	modern pencil	Nicolas Jacques Conté (France)
1800	electric battery	Alessandro Volta (Italy)
1807	steamboat (practical)	Robert Fulton (U.S.)
1815	safety lamp for miners	Sir Humphry Davy (England)
1819	stethoscope	René T.M.H. Laënnec (France)
1829	steam locomotive	George Stephenson (England)
1834	refrigeration	Jacob Perkins (England)
1837	telegraph	Samuel F.B. Morse (U.S.)
1842	anesthesia (ether)	Crawford W. Long (U.S.)
1845	rotary printing press	Richard M. Hoe (U.S.)
1846	sewing machine	Elias Howe (U.S.)
1851	cylinder (door) lock	Linus Yale (U.S.)
1852	elevator brake	Elisha G. Otis (U.S.)
1863	fire extinguisher	Alanson Crane (U.S.) ▶
1867	typewriter	Christopher Sholes, Carlos Glidden, & Samuel W. Soulé (U.S.)
1870s	*telephone ▶	Antonio Meucci (Italy), Alexander G. Bell (U.S.)
1877	phonograph	Thomas A. Edison (U.S.)
1877	microphone	Emile Berliner (U.S.)
1879	practical lightbulb	Thomas A. Edison (U.S.)
1885	bicycle (modern)	James Starley (England)
1885	motorcycle	Gottlieb Daimler (Germany)
1886	automobile (gasoline)	Karl Benz (Germany)
1886	dishwasher	Josephine Cochran (U.S.)
1888	ballpoint pen	John Loud (U.S.)
1888	portable camera	George Eastman (U.S.)
1891	escalator	Jesse W. Reno (U.S.)
1891	submarine (modern)	John Holland (U.S.)
1893	moving picture viewer	Thomas A. Edison (U.S.)

YEAR	INVENTION	INVENTOR (COUNTRY)
1894	motion picture projector	Charles F. Jenkins (U.S.)
1895	diesel engine	Rudolf Diesel (Germany)
1895	X ray	Wilhelm Roentgen (Germany) ▶
1899	tape recorder	Valdemar Poulsen (Denmark)
1901	washing machine	Langmuir Fisher (U.S.)
1903	propeller airplane	Orville & Wilbur Wright (U.S.)
1903	windshield wipers	Mary Anderson (U.S.)
1907	vacuum cleaner	J. Murray Spangler (U.S.)
1911	air conditioning	Willis H. Carrier (U.S.)
1913	modern radio receiver	Reginald A. Fessenden (U.S.)
1917	practical zipper	Gideon Sundback (Canada)
1922	insulin	Sir Frederick G. Banting (Canada)
1923	television**	Vladimir K. Zworykin** (U.S.)
1924	frozen packaged food	Clarence Birdseye (U.S.)
1926	rocket engine	Robert H. Goddard (U.S.)
1929	penicillin	Alexander Fleming (Scotland)
1930	cyclotron (atom smasher)	Ernest O. Lawrence (U.S.)
1937	xerography copies	Chester Carlson (U.S.)
1939	helicopter	Igor Sikorsky (U.S.)
1939	jet airplane	Hans van Ohain (Germany)
1942	electronic computer	John V. Atanasoff & Clifford Berry (U.S.)
1943	Aqua Lung	Jacques-Yves Cousteau & Emile Gagnan (France)
1944	auto sequence computer	Howard H. Aiken (U.S.)
1947	transistor	William Shockley, Walter H. Brattain, & John Bardeen (U.S.)
1947	Tupperware	Earl Silas Tupper (U.S.)
1948	Velcro	Georges de Mestral (Switzerland)
1952	airbag	John Hetrick (U.S.)
1954	antibiotic for fungal diseases	R. F. Brown & E. L. Hazen (U.S.)
1955	fiber optics	Narinder S. Kapany (England)
1955	polio vaccine	Jonas E. Salk (U.S.)
1958	laser	A. L. Schawlow & C. H. Townes (U.S.)
1963	pop-top can	Ermal C. Fraze (U.S.)
1965	word processor	IBM (U.S.)
1968	computer mouse	Douglas Engelbart (U.S)
1969	cash machine (ATM)	Don Wetzel (U.S.)
1969	videotape cassette	Sony (Japan)
1969	battery operated smoke detector	Randolph Smith & Kenneth House (U.S.)
1971	food processor	Pierre Verdon (France)
1972	compact disc (CD)	RCA (U.S.)
1972	video game (Pong)	Noland Bushnell (U.S.)
1973	CAT scanner	Godfrey N. Hounsfield (England)
1973	Jet Ski®	Clayton Jacobsen II (U.S)
1977	space shuttle	NASA (U.S.)
1978	artificial heart	Robert K. Jarvik (U.S.)
1979	cellular telephone	Ericsson Company (Sweden)
1979	Walkman	Sony (Japan)
1980	rollerblades	Scott Olson (U.S.)
1980	Post-its	3M Company (U.S.)
1987	laptop computer	Sir Clive Sinclair (England) ▶
1987	meningitis vaccine	Connaught Lab (U.S.)
1994	digital camera	Apple Computer, Kodak (U.S.)
1995	DVD (digital video disk)	Matsushita (Japan)
2002	robot vacuum	iRobot Corp. (U.S.)

X ray of human hand

*Meucci developed a version of the telephone (early 1870s); Bell received a patent for another version.
**Others who helped invent television include Philo T. Farnsworth (1926) and John Baird (1928).

New 'bots on the Block

In 2003, Sony wowed the world with its humanoid robot QRIO. Pronounced like "curio," the name is short for "quest for curiosity." Besides dancing and jogging, the three-foot-tall QRIO can recognize human faces and hold a short conversation in Japanese. In January 2004, QRIO got his first acting job, doing a voice-over for the TV cartoon "Astro Boy." QRIO has also visited China, Russia, and the U.S.

Toyota introduced its own robot to the world in 2004. This four-foot robot (not given a name at first) may have show biz ambitions too: it can play the trumpet! The robot toots its horn with a machine inside its "head" that blows air with enough force to play the notes. At its debut in Japan in February, the robot played a sparkling rendition of the classic "When You Wish Upon a Star." Toyota hopes to put together an all-robot band that will play at the World Exposition to be held in Aichi, Japan, in 2005. (Do you think they will perform better than live musicians?)

Both companies hope to eventually use the robots to serve as assistants, and possibly to help out the elderly and disabled.

INVENTIONS CROSSWORD

ACROSS
1. This device, invented in 1837, uses Morse Code
4. People movers invented in 1891
8. To be safe, every home should have a device to detect this
9. _ _ _ -Top Can was invented by Ermal C. Fraze
10. Inventor of the telephone who received a patent in 1876
11. Fiber or nerve
13. Company that invented the CD in 1972
15. First name of Edison, inventor of the phonograph and practical lightbulb
16. Instrument played by the Toyota robot

DOWN
2. A cylinder version was invented by Linus Yale
3. A type of airplane
5. A safety _ _ _ _ was invented by Sir Davy to help miners see in the mines
6. Inventor of the first polio vaccine
7. A laptop is a type of this
12. Pong is one of these
14. What you get from an ATM

ANSWERS ON PAGES 319–322. FOR MORE PUZZLES GO TO WWW.WORLDALMANACFORKIDS.COM

Language

What is the Horse Corral Code?) page 112

Words about words

An **acronym** is an abbreviation formed from the first letters or syllables of a group of words.

"Radar" comes from "radio detection and ranging"

An **anagram** is a word or phrase made by rearranging the letters from another word or phrase, or perhaps from nonsense letters.

From "Clint Eastwood" you can get the anagram "Old West Action."

Antonyms are words that have opposite meanings.

big and small
early and late

A **cliché** is a saying or expression that has been used so often by so many people, it has lost its interest.

She works like a dog.
Dry as dust

An **eponym** is a word that comes from the name of a person or thing.

"Sandwich" comes from the Earl of Sandwich (1718-1792), who ate these when he was too busy gambling to stop for long.

A **euphemism** is a pleasant word or phrase used in place of a harsher word or phrase.

Instead of "old person": senior citizen
Instead of "used car": pre-owned vehicle

Homophones are words that sound alike but have different meanings and spellings.

hear/here
hair/hare
right/write

A **palindrome** is a word, phrase, or sentence that has exactly the same letters when spelled backward or forward.

no lemons, no melon
Ma has a ham.

A **pseudonym** is a name someone makes up and uses to hide his or her true identity.

Daniel Handler, the author of *A Series of Unfortunate Events*, uses the pseudonym Lemony Snicket.

A **pun** is the use of a word with two different meanings, in a way that's humorous.

The baker said, "I think I'll loaf around all day."
Avoidable: What a bullfighter tries to do.

Synonyms are words that have the same or almost the same meanings.

quick and fast
tired and sleepy

The English Language

Facts about English

▶ According to the Oxford English Dictionary, the English language contains between 250,000 and 750,000 words. The number depends on whether you count different meanings of the same word as separate words and on how many obscure technical terms you count.

▶ The most frequently used letters of the alphabet are E, T, A, and O, in that order.

▶ Here are the 30 most common English words: the, of, and, a, to, in, is, that, it, was, he, for, as, on, with, his, be, at, you, I, are, this, by, from, had, have, they, not, or, one

▶ English has borrowed many words from different languages. For example, here are a few food words from other languages:

from Arabic:	from Chinese:	from German:	from Spanish:
apricot, candy, coffee, sherbet, spinach, sugar, syrup, tuna	chopsticks, chow, chow mein, soy, tea, wok, wonton	delicatessen, frankfurter, hamburger, pretzel, sauerkraut, seltzer	avocado, burrito, chili, chocolate, cocoa, maize, tomato, tamale, tortilla

New Words

English is always changing as new words are born and old ones die out. Many new words come from the field of electronics and computers, from the media, or from slang.

funplex: an entertainment complex with sports facilities, games, and often restaurants. ("The new funplex at the mall was so crowded we couldn't get in.")

pumped: filled with excitement and enthusiasm. ("I'm so pumped that I made the run through the half-pipe without falling!")

s'more: a dessert usually made of toasted marshmallow and pieces of a chocolate bar sandwiched between two graham crackers. ("One of my favorite things about camping is sitting around the fire after dinner and making s'mores.") (See the "Camps" chapter, page 53.)

unplugged: music played on an instrument whose sound is not electrically modified. ("Guitarist Eric Clapton's album, *Unplugged*, is still one of the most popular unplugged CDs ever.")

In Other Words: IDIOMS

Idioms are phrases that mean more than their words put together. Here are some:

barking up the wrong tree—"looking in the wrong place" Some dogs are trained to show a hunter where an animal is by barking at the tree it's hiding in. If the animal jumps from one tree to another and escapes, the dogs are left barking up the wrong tree.

dog days of summer—"the hottest days of summer" Sirius, the "dog star," rises with the Sun from early July to mid-August every year. The Romans used this expression because they believed that the star added its heat to the Sun's, making the weather even hotter.

keeping up with the Joneses—"trying to have the same material things your neighbor has" A. R. "Pop" Momand's comic strip, *Keeping Up with the Joneses* first ran in *The New York World* newspaper in 1913 and was later in papers across the U.S. The title came from Momand's own efforts to compete with his neighbors.

GETTING TO THE ROOT

Many English words and parts of words can be traced back to Latin or Greek. If you know the meaning of a word's parts, you can probably guess what it means. A **root** (also called a stem) is the part of the word that gives its basic meaning, but can't be used by itself. Roots need other word parts to complete them: either a **prefix** at the beginning, or a **suffix** at the end, or sometimes both. The following tables give some examples of Greek and Latin roots, prefixes, and suffixes.

Latin

root	basic meaning	example
-aqua-	water	aquarium
-ject-	to throw	reject
-mem-	to keep in mind	memory
-port-	to carry	transport
-scrib-/ -script-	to write	prescription

prefix	basic meaning	example
co-	together	cooperate
de-	away, off	defrost
inter-	between, among	international
pre-	before	prevent
re-	again, back	rewrite
sub-	under	subway

suffix	basic meaning	example
-able/-ible	capable or worthy of	workable
-fy/-ify	make or cause to become	horrify
-ly	like, to the extent of	highly
-ous	full of	wondrous
-ty/-ity	state of, power to	purity

Greek

root	basic meaning	example
-chron-	time	chronology
-bio-	life	biology
-dem-	people	democracy
-phon-	sound	telephone
-psych-	mind, soul, spirit	psychology
-scope-	to see	telescope

prefix	basic meaning	example
a-/an-	without, not	anaerobic, amoral
auto-	self	autopilot
geo-	Earth	geography
micro-	small	microscope
tele-	far off	television

suffix	basic meaning	example
-ism	act, state, theory of	realism
-ist	one who believes in, practices	capitalist
-graph	write, draw, describe, record	photograph
-logy	talk, speech, study	biology
-meter	measure, measuring device	kilometer

Homework Help

I before *E* except after *C*,

or when sounded like *A*, as in **neighbor** or **weigh**.

This is a pretty good rule and helpful in remembering how to spell lots of words. *Believe, receive,* and *sleigh* are just a few examples. But you do have to learn a few exceptions—cases where the rule doesn't work. The exceptions include *weird, either, neither, height,* and *leisure.*

TOP TEN LANGUAGES

Would you have guessed that Mandarin, the principal language of China, is the most common spoken language in the world? You may find more surprises in the chart below, which lists languages spoken in 2000 by at least 100,000,000 native speakers (those for whom the language is their first language, or mother tongue) and some of the places where each one is spoken.

Privyet! (Russian)

LANGUAGE	WHERE SPOKEN	NATIVE SPEAKERS
Mandarin	China, Taiwan	874,000,000
Hindi	India	366,000,000
English	U.S., Canada, Britain	341,000,000
Spanish	Spain, Latin America	322,000,000
Arabic	Arabian Peninsula	207,000,000
Bengali	India, Bangladesh	207,000,000
Portuguese	Portugal, Brazil	176,000,000
Russian	Russia	167,000,000
Japanese	Japan	125,000,000
German	Germany, Austria	100,000,000

LANGUAGE USED AT HOME	SPEAKERS OVER 5 YEARS OLD
❶ Speak only English	215,423,557
❷ Spanish	28,101,052
❸ Chinese	2,022,143
❹ French	1,643,838
❺ German	1,383,442
❻ Tagalog (Philippines)	1,224,241
❼ Vietnamese	1,009,627
❽ Italian	1,008,370
❾ Korean	894,063
❿ Russian	706,242
⓫ Polish	667,414
⓬ Arabic	614,582
⓭ Portuguese	564,630
⓮ Japanese	477,997
⓯ French Creole	453,368
⓰ Greek	365,436
⓱ Hindi	317,057
⓲ Persian	312,085
⓳ Urdu	262,900
⓴ Gujarathi	235,988

(spoken in India & parts of Africa)

Which LANGUAGES Are SPOKEN in the UNITED STATES?

Since the beginning of American history, immigrants have come to the United States from all over the world. They have brought their native languages with them.

¡Hola! That's how more than 28 million Americans say "hi" at home. Still, 215 million Americans only speak English.

The table at left lists the other most frequently spoken languages in the United States, as of the 2000 census.

Hello! (English)

Bonjour! (French)

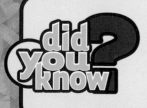

Did you know?

One of the oldest forms of writing is called cuneiform, which was invented in the Middle East around 3000 B.C. The term comes from the Latin words for "wedge shaped" because the writer used a special tool to make wedge-shaped strokes on a wet clay tablet. The tablets were then baked or dried. Scholars began figuring out how to read cuneiform tablets in the 19th century, and now they are a big help in learning more about ancient history.

Language Express

Surprise your friends and family with words from other languages.

English	Spanish	French	German	Chinese
January	enero	janvier	Januar	yi-yue
February	febrero	fevrier	Februar	er-yue
March	marzo	mars	Marz	san-yue
April	abril	avril	April	si-yue
May	mayo	mai	Mai	wu-yue
June	junio	juin	Juni	liu-yue
July	julio	juillet	Juli	qi-yue
August	agosto	aout	August	ba-yue
September	septiembre	septembre	September	jiu-yue
October	octubre	octobre	Oktober	shi-yue
November	noviembre	novembre	November	shi-yi-yue
December	diciembre	decembre	Dezember	shi er-yue
Monday	lunes	lundi	Montag	Xingqiyi
Tuesday	martes	mardi	Dienstag	Xingqier
Wednesday	miércoles	mercredi	Mittwoch	Xingqisan
Thursday	jueves	jeudi	Donnerstag	Xingqisi
Friday	viernes	vendredi	Freitag	Xingqiwu
Saturday	sábado	samedi	Samstag	Xingqiliu
Sunday	domingo	dimanche	Sonntag	Xingqitian
blue	azul	bleu	blau	lan
red	rojo	rouge	rot	hong
green	verde	vert	grun	lu
yellow	amarillo	jaune	gelb	huang
black	negro	noir	schwarz	hei
white	blanco	blanc	weiss	bai
happy birthday!	¡feliz cumpleaños!	bonne anniversaire!	Glückwunsch zum Geburtstag!	sheng-ri kuai le!
hello!	¡hola!	bonjour!	hallo!	ni hao!
good-bye!	¡adios!	au revoir!	auf Wiedersehen!	zai-jian!
dog	perro	chien	Hund	gou
cat	gato	chat	Katze	mao
bear	oso	ours	Bar	xiong
one	uno	un	eins	yi
two	dos	deux	zwei	er
three	tres	trois	drei	san
four	cuatro	quatre	vier	si
five	cinco	cinq	funf	wu
six	seis	six	sechs	liu
seven	siete	sept	sieben	qi
eight	ocho	huit	acht	ba
nine	nueve	neuf	neun	jiu
ten	diez	dix	zehn	shi

Sign language

Many people who are deaf or hearing-impaired use American Sign Language (ASL) to talk to each other. ASL is not just a form of English turned into gestures. It's a unique language with its own vocabulary, grammar, and punctuation. The position and movement of the hands and arms, facial expressions, and even moving your whole body is part of the language. To ask a question, for example, an ASL user might lean forward with raised eyebrows.

Below is the American Manual Alphabet, a system of "finger spelling" originally developed in France by Abbe Charles Michel De l'Epee in the late 1700s, the manual alphabet was later brought to the United States by Laurent Clerc (1785-1869), a Frenchman who taught people who were deaf.

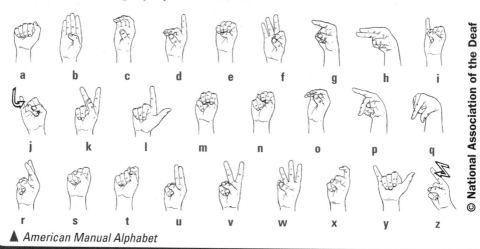

© National Association of the Deaf

▲ *American Manual Alphabet*

Codes have been used since ancient times to send secret messages, especially military plans. Most of the codes used today by the military and by banks (for ATM machines) are electronic, but there are many types of codes you can use. **The Horse Corral Code** is fun because it looks like you're writing in a strange ancient language. The name comes from the way that your answer key looks sort of like the letter pairs are horses in a corral (at least they did to the inventors of the code!).

First, make a grid like this one. Each letter is represented by the lines that surround it. If it's meant to be the second letter in the box, a dot is used.

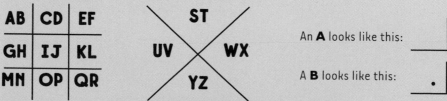

AB	CD	EF
GH	IJ	KL
MN	OP	QR

An **A** looks like this:

A **B** looks like this:

Can you decode the messages below?

Jokes & Riddles

Why did the T-rex cross the road?

Dan: "My report card was all wet."
Jan: "How did that happen?"
Dan: "It was below C level."

What's a boxer's favorite drink?

Which nail does a carpenter hate to hit?

Why did the tomato blush?

What do you call a 100-year-old ant?

Which day of the week starts with the letter "Y"?

What did the sick freight elevator say?

What's a tree's favorite drink?

What's black and white and eats like a horse?

What's broken when you say it?

What can travel around the world without leaving the corner?

What kind of street does a ghost live on?

Why did the cow cross the road?

Why did the turkey cross the road?

How do you stop a bull from charging?

Why was the computer cold at night?

Two legs I have, and this will confound: only at rest do they touch the ground! What am I?

How far can a deer run into the woods?

I run but cannot walk. I have hands but no arms, and a face but no head. What am I?

If you spell out the numbers, how far do you have to go before you need the letter "a"?

Can you name a word in the English language that has 8 consonants and one vowel?

Which side of a chicken has the most feathers?

ANSWERS ON PAGES 319–322.
FOR MORE PUZZLES GO TO
WWW.WORLDALMANACFORKIDS.COM

113

Military

What kind of ship costs $5 billion to build? page 117

Soldiers risk their lives to fight for their nation or cause, often to defend the lives and freedom of others. Since the beginning of the Revolutionary War, more than 2.6 million U.S. soldiers have been killed or wounded in wars (almost as many people as now live in Arkansas).

In the Iraq War that began March 19, 2003, U.S. special operations forces on the ground got information, or "intelligence," to help pinpoint bombing targets. This helped U.S.-led troops defeat the Iraqi forces quickly while suffering fewer casualties. New technology also made it possible to bomb targets more precisely, reducing civilian casualties.

However, flawed intelligence beforehand may have led the U.S. to overestimate how important it was to wage the war in the first place. And after the main fighting ended, despite the U.S. technology, some Iraqi groups continued to wage attacks on troops and sometimes civilians. As of March 19, 2004, 572 U.S. troops had died in Iraq, while civilian casualties continued.

Long before Iraq, intelligence and technology, as well as tactics and just plain stubbornness, have proven important in war.

INTELLIGENCE

During World War II, U.S. military intelligence broke a Japanese naval code used to send secret messages by radio. Americans thus learned of a planned attack on the U.S.-held island of Midway, northwest of Hawaii. Planes from U.S. aircraft carriers were able to ambush the Japanese fleet before it got in shooting range of the island.

TECHNOLOGY

English forces in France used the longbow to defeat the French in the Battle of Agincourt, in 1415. Longbows, which were as tall as the archers themselves, could hurl heavy arrows 200 yards or more, or the length of two modern football fields.

TACTICS

The tactics of General Robert E. Lee led to a Southern victory in the Civil War Battle of Chancellorsville, Virginia, in May 1863. Trapped between two much larger Union forces, Lee divided his army into three parts and launched a surprise flanking attack that made the Northerners retreat.

STUBBORNNESS

Soldiers and civilians in the Russian city of Stalingrad (Volgograd) held off an invading German army in 1942–43. The Russians refused to surrender the city despite terrible casualties and hardships. Eventually, Russian troops launched a counterattack, and the Germans retreated.

OUT *OF THE* ORDINARY

WHAT ARE SPECIAL OPERATIONS? "Special operations" is a term for missions not part of normal warfare. In war, two large forces usually face each other, with thousands of troops fighting at once. "Special Ops" forces work in small units, often deep inside enemy territory. They can fight anywhere, from baking deserts to steaming jungles to snow-covered mountains. Most are parachute-trained, and some are trained in underwater operations. They know foreign languages. They are some of the finest troops in any army.

U.S. SPECIAL OPERATIONS FORCES The U.S. has the most special-operation forces in the world. The Army, Navy, Air Force, and Marines have units. All are under the Defense Department's Special Operations Command at MacDill Air Force Base in Florida.

Army The Army's Special Forces and Rangers are part of its 75th Regiment. Rangers specialize in larger-unit operations—like the raid on Taliban headquarters on October 19, 2001. More than 100 Rangers and other Special Forces troops took part in the first U.S. ground operations in Afghanistan. Their history goes back to "Roger's Rangers," a group of American frontiersmen who fought bravely in the French and Indian War (1754–63).

Formed in 1952, the Army's Special Forces **"Green Berets"** get their name from the caps they wear with their uniforms. Today, the Army has four active-duty Special Forces Groups, with about 700 men each.

The basic unit of a Special Forces Group is the Alpha Detachment, or "A-Team." Each A-Team has a captain, a lieutenant, and 10 sergeants. Each member has one main specialty (operations, intelligence, medicine, weapons, demolitions, or radio operations) and is also trained in a second one. For example, a Green Beret might be a radio operator and also trained in medicine or in using explosives.

Air Force The Air Force has a variety of units that provide transportation and air cover for U.S. commandos. These units include the 1st Special Operations Wing and two Special Operations Squadrons.

Marines Every Marine Expeditionary Unit (of about 1,000 troops) has a Force Recon unit (about 150 troops) to act as its eyes and ears in the field.

Navy Organized during World War II, the Navy's SEALs were originally called underwater demolition teams, or UDTs. SEAL stands for "Sea-Air-Land," reminding us that these Navy warriors can fight anywhere they are needed.

SADDAM CAPTURED While resistance continued inside Iraq, the occupying forces did manage to catch many key figures in the former Iraqi regime, including its ruler, Saddam Hussein. On December 13, 2003, Saddam was found in a crude hideout, a 6-foot-deep hole just big enough for one person to lie down in. About 600 troops and a number of Special Op forces had joined in a search of the area, aided by a tip from a prisoner. Saddam gave up without a fight; two rifles and $750,000 in U.S. money were found nearby. The hideout was near a two-room mud hut about 9 miles from the city of Tikrit.

Here are some of the aircraft used by the U.S. in Afghanistan and in the war in Iraq.

B-2A SPIRIT This is the long-range "stealth bomber." Its shape, high-altitude flight, and stealth technology make it almost impossible for enemy radar to detect it. The B-2 can fly 6,000 miles without refueling. B-2s are part of the 509th Bomb Wing. Missions are usually flown from Whiteman Air Force Base in Missouri, but for operations in Iraq, they were based on Diego Garcia Island in the Indian Ocean. The B-2 can travel close to the speed of sound (about 700 mph) and fly as high as 50,000 feet. It carries a crew of two: a pilot and a bombardier. It is 69 feet long, 17 feet high, and weighs 336,500 lbs. fully loaded. Its wingspan is 172 feet.

B-1B LANCER These are long-range, multi-role bombers. Each B-1B can carry up to 84 500-pound bombs or 20 Cruise missiles. It is difficult for enemy radar to detect. The plane's four turbo-fan engines can push it as high as 30,000 feet, at speeds over 900 miles per hour. The B-1B carries a crew of four: a commander, a co-pilot, plus offensive and defensive systems officers. It is 146 feet long, 34 feet high, and weighs 190,000 lbs. (empty). Its wingspan is 137 feet.

RQ-1 PREDATOR This unmanned, propeller-driven aircraft is used mostly for observation. It has video cameras, an infrared camera (for night vision), and radar. It can see through dense clouds and smoke. It may carry Hellfire missiles to strike targets on the ground. The Predator is 27 feet long, weighs 950 pounds, and has a wingspan of 27 feet. It has a cruising range of 424 miles, at 84 miles per hour, and can fly as high as 25,000 feet. It has a crew of zero.

The RQ-4 Global Hawk is another plane without a pilot that was used in Iraq in 2003. Unlike the Predator, the Global Hawk is a jet-powered, high-altitude spy plane. It has a range of 4,000 miles and can fly as high as 60,000 feet. It has a wingspan of 116 feet and can stay in the air for 24 hours.

F-117A NIGHTHAWK This was the first plane to use "low-observable" technology. It's called the "stealth fighter," but it doesn't engage in battles with other planes. In Iraq, F-117s flew into heavily protected areas with two 2,000-pound laser-guided missiles, to take out difficult military targets like radar centers, ammunition factories, and Saddam Hussein's command bunker. F-117s are used at the beginning of a big attack to clear the way for other forces to follow. The F-117 is 63 feet long, 12 feet high, and has a wingspan of 43 feet. It weighs 52,500 pounds (empty) and flies just under the speed of sound.

At **Sea**

USS Harry S. Truman

AIRCRAFT CARRIER Six carriers were deployed in the Persian Gulf or eastern Mediterranean Sea during the war with Iraq. They were the *USS Abraham Lincoln, USS Theodore Roosevelt, USS Harry S. Truman, USS Constellation, USS Kitty Hawk,* and *USS Nimitz.* These ships are designed to carry up to 80 airplanes, which take off from and land on their huge decks. The *USS Abraham Lincoln*, stationed in the Persian Gulf, had 1,600 missions flown from its deck to Iraq. Carriers are the heart of the modern navy. They are so expensive to build (nearly $5 billion!), though, that very few countries have them. A modern carrier is about as long as the Empire State Building is tall (1,092 feet) and its flight deck is 4.5 acres. A carrier is sometimes called a "floating city" because it can hold 6,000 people and has many of the same services as a regular town—restaurants, stores, gyms, a barbershop, a drug store, a dentist, a TV station, a hospital, and even a brig (jail). Because most carriers are nuclear powered, they can be at sea for months without refueling. This lets military planners be prepared for air strikes almost anywhere in the world.

On the **Ground**

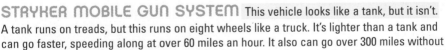

M1 ABRAMS MAIN BATTLE TANK The Abrams tank is called the backbone of the armored forces of the U.S. military. Along with the M-2 Bradley Infantry Fighting Vehicle (an armored troop carrier), it was the main ground force in Iraq in 2003. It is named after General Creighton W. Abrams, a famous tank commander of World War II and later Army chief of staff. The Abrams tank carries a crew of four (commander, gunner, loader, and driver) and weighs more than 60 tons. It uses a lot of fuel—about 3 gallons per mile—but it's a highly mobile vehicle that can fire shells while moving at fast speeds over rough ground. The tank also has special vision devices that allow its gunner to see a target at night. Over 8,000 of them have been built, not only for the United States, but also for some of its allies.

STRYKER MOBILE GUN SYSTEM This vehicle looks like a tank, but it isn't. A tank runs on treads, but this runs on eight wheels like a truck. It's lighter than a tank and can go faster, speeding along at over 60 miles an hour. It also can go over 300 miles without

refueling—much farther than a tank. It's also quieter, which means the enemy is less likely to hear it coming. The Stryker is small enough to be carried in a C-130 transport plane, something a tank can't do. The first Strykers were delivered in the summer of 2002, making it one of the newest vehicles added to the U.S. armored forces. These state-of-the-art machines went to Iraq in December 2003 to support the U.S. operations there.

Money

Whose picture is on a five-dollar bill? **page 120**

History of Money

Why Did People Start Using Money?

At first, people bartered, which means they traded goods they had for things they needed. A farmer who had cattle might want to have salt to preserve meat, or cloth to make clothing. For this farmer, a cow became a "medium of exchange"—a way of getting things the farmer did not make or grow. Cattle became a form of money. Whatever people agreed to use for trade became the earliest kinds of money.

What Objects Have Been Used as Money?

► knives, rice, and spades in China around 3000 B.C.

► cattle and clay tablets in Babylonia around 2500 B.C.

► wampum (beads) and beaver fur by Native Americans of the northeast around A.D. 1500

► tobacco by early American colonists around 1650

► whales' teeth by the Pacific peoples on the island of Fiji, until the early 1900s

▲ *Wampum used by Native Americans*

Why Did Governments Start Issuing Money?

Governments started issuing money because the money itself had value. If a government could gain control over the manufacture of money, it could increase its own wealth—often simply by making more money.

The first government to make coins that looked alike and use them as money is thought to be the Greek city-state of Lydia in the 7th century B.C. These Lydian coins were actually bean-shaped lumps made from a mixture of gold and silver.

By the Middle Ages (about A.D. 800-1100), gold had become a popular medium for trade in Europe. But gold was heavy and difficult to carry, and the cities and the roads of Europe at that time were dangerous places to carry large amounts of gold. So merchants and goldsmiths began issuing notes promising to pay gold to the person carrying the note. These "promissory notes" were the beginning of paper money in Europe.

In the early 1700s, France's government became the first in Europe to issue paper money that looked alike. Paper money was probably also invented in China, where the explorer Marco Polo saw it in the 1280s.

did you know?

The nickel is being redesigned for the first time in over 60 years. The front still shows Thomas Jefferson, but two new designs are being put on the back. The first design, which marks the 200th anniversary of the 1803 Louisiana Purchase, is based on the "Peace Medal" that Jefferson sent to Indian tribes. It shows clasped hands, a tomahawk, and a peace pipe. The second depicts the explorers Lewis and Clark on their journey to the West in 1804-1806. The new designs aren't permanent, though. Jefferson's home, Monticello, will return in 2006.

Money Around the World

When you go to a foreign country, one of the first things you may notice is what the money looks like. Many countries have colorful bills in different shapes and sizes. They often show queens or presidents or other famous people. But you also may find a rhinoceros, tiger, or elephant (India), a sea turtle (Brazil), cows and fruit (Nigeria), a map of the North Pole (Norway), or even schoolchildren (Taiwan).

All About... The Euro

Twelve countries in Europe—all members of the European Union—now all have the same currency; all their coins and paper money are **euros**. The euro is used in Austria, Belgium, Finland, France, Germany, Greece, Ireland, Italy, Luxembourg, the Netherlands, Portugal, and Spain. The one-euro coin is now a common sight. The front (obverse) side of the coin has the word "euro" and a map of the euro area. On the other side (reverse), each euro country has a national symbol, such as the Irish harp for Ireland, and a portrait of the king for Spain.

People in France and Italy miss their francs and lire. But now money flows easily from one country to another. This makes it easier to complete big financial deals between countries. And tourists can use the same kind of money to pay for a slice of pizza whether it's in Italy or in Belgium.

The euro has been increasing in value in comparison to the dollar. This makes it more expensive for Americans to go to Europe! The euro was worth about $1.22 in spring 2004.

What are Exchange Rates

When one country exports goods to another, the payment from the country buying the goods must be changed into the currency of the country selling them. People traveling to other countries usually need to convert their money into the local currency. In some countries, like Canada, stores will accept U.S. money for purchases, but will give change in Canadian money. How do they know how much change to give you? An exchange rate—that gives the price of one currency in terms of another—is used. For example, in March 2004 one U.S. dollar could buy 1.22 Canadian dollars.

Here are the exchange rates in 1990 and 2004 between the U.S. dollar and the currency of some of the country's biggest trading partners.

What A U.S. Dollar Bought

COUNTRY	IN 1990	IN 2004
Canada	1.2 Canadian dollars	1.34 Canadian dollars
Great Britain (UK)	0.56 pound	0.56 pound
European Union*	—	1.22 euros
Japan	144.8 yen	110.8 yen
Mexico	2.8 pesos	10.96 pesos

United States   Japan

*The euro is used in 12 countries of the European Union (see above). Only 3 EU countries do not use the euro: Great Britian, Denmark, and Sweden.

Making Money

What Is the U.S. Mint?

The U.S. Mint, founded in 1792, is part of the Treasury Department. The Mint makes all U.S. coins and safeguards the nation's $100 million in gold and silver **bullion** (uncoined bars of metal). Reserves of these precious metals are held at West Point, New York, and Fort Knox, Kentucky. The Mint turns out coins at four production facilities (Denver, Philadelphia, San Francisco, and West Point). For more information, visit the U.S. Mint's website at

WEB SITE *http://www.usmint.gov*

What Kinds of Coins Does the Mint Make?

Branches of the U.S. Mint in Denver and Philadelphia currently make coins for "circulation," or everyday use. In 2003, these two facilities made 12 billion coins, including 6.8 billion pennies! A tiny "D" or "P" near the year, called a mint mark, tells you which one made the coin. A Lincoln cent or "penny" with no mint mark was probably made at the Philadelphia Mint, which has by tradition never marked pennies. The U.S. Mint also makes commemorative coins in honor of events, like the Olympics, or people, like Christopher Columbus.

What is the Bureau of Engraving and Printing?

The Bureau of Engraving and Printing (BEP), established in 1862, is also part of the Treasury Department. The BEP designs and prints all U.S. paper money. It also prints U.S. postage stamps and other official certificates. The BEP's production facilities in Washington, D.C., and Ft. Worth, Texas, made more than 8 billion bills in 2003. About 95% of them are used to replace worn out money. Even though bills are made of a special paper that is 75% cotton and 25% linen, they wear out pretty fast if they are used a lot. The $1 bill only lasts an average of 18 months, while $50 and $100 bills last about 9 years. For more information visit the BEP's website at

WEB SITE *http://www.moneyfactory.com*

Whose portraits are on our money?

The table below shows which presidents and other famous Americans appear on the front of all U.S. money.

Denomination	Portrait	Denomination	Portrait
1¢	Abraham Lincoln, 16th President	$2	Thomas Jefferson, 3rd President
5¢	Thomas Jefferson, 3rd President	$5	Abraham Lincoln, 16th President
10¢	Franklin D. Roosevelt, 32nd President	$10	Alexander Hamilton, 1st Treasury Secretary
25¢	George Washington, 1st President		
50¢	John F. Kennedy, 35th President	$20	Andrew Jackson, 7th President
$1 (COIN)	Sacagawea, Native American woman	$50	Ulysses S. Grant, 18th President
$1 (BILL)	George Washington, 1st President	$100	Benjamin Franklin, inventor, U.S. patriot

U.S. State Quarters

From 1999 to 2008, five new quarter designs are being minted each year. George Washington will stay on the front, but a design honoring one of the 50 states will appear on the back. The quarters for each state are coming out in the order in which the states joined the Union. In 2004, Michigan, Florida, Texas, Iowa, and Wisconsin were coming out. California, Minnesota, Oregon, Kansas, and West Virginia are due in 2005.

How Much Money Is In Circulation?

As of June 2003, the total amount of money in circulation in the United States came to $693,371,342,186. More than 33 billion dollars was in coins, the rest in paper money.

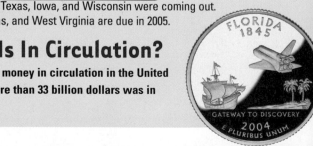

FLORIDA 1845 / GATEWAY TO DISCOVERY / 2004 / E PLURIBUS UNUM

The U.S. $1 Bill: An Owner's Manual

Everybody knows that George Washington is on the U.S. one-dollar bill, but did you ever wonder what all that other stuff is? Here's a guide:

Plate position
Shows where on the 32-note plate this bill was printed.

The Treasury Department seal: The balancing scales represent justice. The pointed stripe across the middle has 13 stars for the original 13 colonies. The key represents authority.

Plate serial number
Shows which printing plate was used for the face of the bill.

Serial number
Each bill has its own

Federal Reserve District Number
Shows which district issued the bill.

Secretary of the Treasury Signature

Treasurer of the U.S. Signature

Series indicator (year note's design was first used)

(Since 1949, every Treasurer of the U.S. has been a woman.)

Federal Reserve District Seal
The name of the Federal Reserve Bank that issued the bill is printed in the seal. The letter tells you quickly where the bill is from. Here are the letter codes for the 12 Federal Reserve Districts:

A: Boston
B: New York
C: Philadelphia
D: Cleveland
E: Richmond
F: Atlanta
G: Chicago
H: St. Louis
I: Minneapolis
J: Kansas City
K: Dallas
L: San Francisco

Front of the Great Seal of the United States: The bald eagle is the national bird. The shield has 13 stripes for the 13 original colonies. The eagle holds 13 arrows (symbol of war) and an olive branch (symbol of peace). Above the eagle is the motto "E Pluribus Unum," Latin for "out of many, one," and a constellation of 13 stars.

Plate serial number
Shows which plate was used for the back.

Reverse of the Great Seal of the United States:
The pyramid symbolizes something that lasts for ages. It is unfinished because the U.S. is always growing. The eye, known as the "Eye of Providence," probably comes from an ancient Egyptian symbol. The pyramid has 13 levels; at its base are the Roman numerals for 1776, the year of American independence. "Annuit Coeptis" is Latin for "God has favored our undertaking." "Novus Ordo Seclorum" is Latin for "a new order of the ages." Both phrases are from the works of the Roman poet Vergil.

Movies & TV

What film company uses a desk lamp as part of its logo?

page 124

Film Facts

Black Maria

- In 1893, Thomas Edison ▶ built the first movie studio, nicknamed "Black Maria," in West Orange, New Jersey.

- Nickelodeon is not just a TV channel. Around 1903-1915, nickelodeons were popular storefront theaters showing short films for a nickel.

- The first widely released, fully animated cartoon was *Gertie the Dinosaur*, made by Windsor McCay in 1914.

- The first full-length movie with sound was *The Jazz Singer*, released in 1927.

- The first popular full-length color film was 1935's *Becky Sharp*.

- The 1939 films *The Wizard of Oz* and *Gone With the Wind* were filmed in color, not colorized later by computer.

- *Toy Story*, release in 1995, was the first full-length film animated only by computer.

All-Time Top Movies*

1. *Titanic*, 1997
2. *Star Wars*, 1977
3. *E.T.: The Extra-Terrestrial*, 1982
4. *Star Wars: Episode I— The Phantom Menace*, 1999
5. *Spider-Man*, 2002
6. *Lord of the Rings: The Return of the King*, 2003
7. *Jurassic Park*, 1993
8. *Lord of the Rings: The Two Towers*, 2002
9. *Finding Nemo*, 2003
10. *Forrest Gump*, 1994

*As of April 1, 2004, based on U.S. ticket sales.

All-Time Top Animated Movies*

1. *Finding Nemo*, 2003
2. *The Lion King*, 1994
3. *Shrek*, 2001
4. *Monsters, Inc.*, 2001
5. *Toy Story 2*, 1999
6. *Aladdin*, 1992
7. *Toy Story*, 1995
8. *Ice Age*, 2002
9. *Tarzan*, 1999
10. *A Bug's Life*, 1998

*As of April 1, 2004, based on U.S. ticket sales.

Some Movie Hits of 2003

Agent Cody Banks (PG)

Bringing Down the House (PG-13)

Brother Bear (G)

Bruce Almighty (PG-13)

Cheaper by the Dozen (PG)

Daddy Day Care (PG)

Dr. Seuss' The Cat in the Hat (PG)

Elf (PG)

Finding Nemo (G)

Freaky Friday (PG-13)

The Haunted Mansion (PG)

Holes (PG)

The Hulk (PG-13)

The Jungle Book 2 (G)

Kangaroo Jack (PG)

The Lizzie McGuire Movie (PG)

Lord of the Rings: The Return of the King (PG-13)

Pirates of the Caribbean: The Curse of the Black Pearl (PG-13)

Rugrats Go Wild (G)

School of Rock (PG-13)

Seabiscuit (PG-13)

Spy Kids 3D: Game Over (PG)

X2: X-Men United (PG-13)

SOME MOVIES TO LOOK FOR

Here are a dozen films set for release by the end of 2004.*

Which movie will make the top of your list?

Agent Cody Banks 2: Destination London—Frankie Muniz is back as the coolest junior secret agent (March).

A New York Minute—The Olsen twins hit the Big Apple on the big screen (May).

Shrek 2—Everyone's favorite ogre is back, and trying not to fall on his donkey (May) ▶

Harry Potter and the Prisoner of Azkaban—More of Harry's adventures at Hogwarts (June).

Spider-Man 2—The sequel to 2002's biggest hit swings into theaters (June).

I, Robot—Will Smith stars in this film based on Isaac Asimov's popular stories (July).

Yu-Gi-Oh!—The popular anime TV cartoon hits the big screen for the first time (August).

Shark Tale—Animated underwater adventure, from Dreamworks Studios, makers of *Shrek* (October).

The Incredibles—A superhero family stars in this animated film from Pixar Studios, makers of *Finding Nemo* (November).

The Polar Express—The popular book hits the big screen, with Tom Hanks as star (November).

The SpongeBob SquarePants Movie—The title says it all (November).

Lemony Snicket's A Series of Unfortunate Events—Based on the popular books and starring Jim Carrey as Count Olaf (December).

*The month of planned release is shown in parentheses. It may change.

One of the Edison Company's most famous films was The Great Train Robbery *(1903). It was the first "western" and the first movie with a plot and suspense. Based on a real train robbery committed by Butch Cassidy's gang in 1900, the movie was just 10 minutes long, with 14 scenes. It was filmed in New Jersey, not the West!*

People to Watch

Christy Carlson Romano

Born: March 20, 1984, in Milford, Conn.

Known for: "Ren Stevens" on Disney TV show *Even Stevens*; voice of Kim in the cartoon *Kim Possible;* "Belle" in Broadway's *Beauty and the Beast*.

didyouknow?

Christy sings the song "Say the Word" on the *Kim Possible CD*

• She's not related to Ray Romano!

Angus T. Jones

Born: October 8, 1993, in Austin, Texas.

Known for: "Jake" in TV show *Two and a Half Men*; "George Jr." in *George of the Jungle 2*; "Georgey" in *Bringing Down the House;* "Hunter" in *The Rookie*.

didyouknow? Angus began acting in TV commercials at age 4 • He got his first big role at 6, in *See Spot Run*.

All About...
Pixar Animation Studios

Twenty years ago, a man named John Lasseter left Disney to work for director George Lucas's computer special-effects group. Two years after that, in 1986, Steve Jobs (the Apple computer head) bought the computer graphics group and named it "Pixar." There were about 44 people working at the company then. That same year, Pixar released its first short film, *Luxo Jr.*, about a baby lamp and his father. The film was nominated for an Academy Award for Best Short Film. (It didn't win, but two years later, Pixar's *Tin Toy* did.

For the next nine years, Pixar made award-winning short films and commercials. The company pioneered many new techniques in computer graphics for film, and designed their own software. But most people had probably never heard of Pixar. That all changed in 1995, with the release of *Toy Story*—the first full-length film animated entirely by computer.

Next came *A Bug's Life* (1998), *Toy Story 2* (1999), *Monsters, Inc.* (2001), and *Finding Nemo* (2003). All these films were award winners and on the top 10 list of biggest animated hits ever. Not only did *Finding Nemo* win an Oscar for Best Animated Film for 2003, it passed *The Lion King* (1994) as the biggest animated hit of all time.

Today, there are more than 600 people working at Pixar's studio in Emeryville, California. In 2001, the studio won an Oscar "for significant advancements to the field of motion picture rendering." There is even a Pixar University, where employees can learn new animation and film-making skills.

The animators at Pixar are hard at work on a new film, *Cars*, set for release in late 2005.

Most Popular TV Shows in 2003-2004

(source: Nielsen Media Research; as of April 4, 2004)

Cable TV Shows

AGES 6-11

1. *Drake & Josh*
2. *The Amanda Show*
3. *SpongeBob SquarePants*
4. *The Adventures of Jimmy Neutron: Boy Genius*
5. *The Fairly OddParents*

AGES 12-17

1. *Dragon Ball GT*
2. *Lizzie McGuire*
3. *Yu Yu Hakusho*
4. *Dragon Ball Z*
5. *Pimp My Ride*

Network TV Shows

AGES 6-11

1. *American Idol*
2. *Survivor: All-Stars*
3. *Survivor: Pearl Islands*
4. *The Simpsons*
5. *Fear Factor*

AGES 12-17

1. *American Idol*
2. *The Simpsons*
3. *My Big Fat Obnoxious Fiancé*
4. *The O.C.*
5. *Malcolm in the Middle*

Movie & TV Match-Ups

Can you match these animated duos with the film or TV show they belong in?

Monsters, Inc.

The Fairly OddParents

Jimmy Neutron: Boy Genius

Toy Story

Woody & Buzz

Pumbaa & Timon

Jackie Chan Adventures

SpongeBob SquarePants

Manfred & Sid

Carl & Sheen

Jade & Uncle

Cosmo & Wanda

Patrick & Squidward

Eustace & Muriel

Ice Age

Finding Nemo

Donkey & Fiona

Bart & Lisa

Mike & Sully

Marlin & Dory

Courage The Cowardly Dog

The Lion King

Shrek

The Simpsons

Answers on Pages 319–322. For more puzzles go to
WWW.WORLDALMANACFORKIDS.COM

Museums

Where can you find a Trash-o-saurus? page 128

The word museum comes from a Greek word that means "temple of the Muses." The Muses were the Greek goddesses of art and science.

The oldest museum in the U.S. is The Charleston Museum, founded in South Carolina in 1773. The U.S. now has about 16,000 museums. Some are described here. For others, look in the Index under "Museums." You can also check out the Association of Children's Museums on the Internet at

WEB SITE *http://www.childrensmuseums.org*

The Smithsonian Institution

In 1835, the people of the United States received a unique gift from an English scientist. In his will, James Smithson left $508,318 to the U.S. to set up an institution for the "increase and diffusion of knowledge." No one knew exactly what he had in mind or why he was interested in giving money to this new foreign country. At first, nobody knew what to do about the gift. President Andrew Jackson was not even sure if it was legal for him to accept it. He had Congress pass a measure allowing him to do so. In 1846 Congress finally passed another bill, signed by President James Polk, establishing the Smithsonian. The Smithsonian's original building, known as "the castle," wasn't finished until 1855.

Today, the Smithsonian is the biggest museum complex in the world, with museums devoted to aviation and space exploration, American history, the arts, natural history, postal history, cultural history, and other fields. In addition to its 16 museums and 7 research centers, the Smithsonian also includes the National Zoo. Admission is free for all Smithsonian museums in Washington, D.C.

New things to check out at the Smithsonian:

✔ On September 21, 2004, the National Museum of the American Indian (see page 178) is scheduled to open. It's right in front of the U.S. Capitol on the National Mall in Washington and will be home to one of the largest collections of Indian art and artifacts in the world.

✔ The Museum of American History opened its new exhibit "America on the Move," in November 2003. The exhibit explains the role of transportation throughout U.S. history (see page 236). Get a close-up look at a 92-foot Southern Railway locomotive!

✔ The Air & Space Museum's Udvar-Hazy Center at Washington Dulles International Airport opened in December 2003. It's home a lot of really big air and spacecraft like the first U.S. Space Shuttle, *Enterprise*.

Living History Exhibits

These places to visit have been restored or re-created to look the way they did many years ago. Museum staff wear costumes and show visitors what life was like in those days.

Plimoth Plantation, Plymouth, Massachusetts. Come and see what life was like in this 1627 village, a re-creation of the Pilgrim's first settlement in the New World.

St. Augustine Historic District, St. Augustine, Florida. Visit the oldest permanent European settlement in America—and the Castillo de San Marcos, a fort built between 1672 and 1695.

Colonial Williamsburg, Williamsburg, Virginia. Learn about life in the American colonies in this restored version of Williamsburg, which was the capital of Virginia (1699 to 1780). Nearby is a re-creation of **Jamestown**, founded 1607, the first permanent English settlement in America.

Calico Ghost Town

Calico Ghost Town, near Barstow, California. Experience the Old West in this real mining town (a third of the buildings are original) that sprang up in 1881 when silver was discovered.

Stuhr Museum of the Prairie Pioneer, Grand Island, Nebraska. This restored railroad town, Pawnee-Indian earth lodge, and pioneer settlement captures the flavor of life in Nebraska at the end of the 1800s.

Lower East Side Tenement Museum, New York, New York. Learn about the lives of 4 immigrant families who lived her and worked in the garment industry at different times between the 1870s and 1930s.

Ethnic Museums

These museums show the culture and history of different groups.

Ellis Island Immigration Museum, New York Harbor • This museum tells the story of the 12 million immigrants who passed through Ellis Island from 1892 to 1954.

The Jewish Museum, New York, New York • Has exhibits covering many centuries of Jewish history and culture.

Japanese American National Museum, Los Angeles, California • Hundreds of objects and photos show the 130-year history of Japanese Americans.

The Heard Museum, Phoenix, Arizona • Displays art by Native Americans, primarily from the southwestern U.S., such as the Apache, Hopi, and Navajo.

The Latin American Art Museum, Miami, Florida • Celebrates artwork, music, poetry, and dance performances by Hispanic and Latin American artists of today.

Charles H. Wright Museum of African American History, Detroit, Michigan • Features a large model of a slave ship, inventions by African Americans, music by black composers, and the space suit worn by the first U.S. black female astronaut.

did you know? *You might be able to stay overnight at a museum, zoo, or aquarium near you. More than 200 institutions across the U.S. have some kind of sleepover program. At the New Jersey State Aquarium, for example, you can even sleep with the fishes—sort of. Guests spend the night near a 760,000-gallon tank with more than 1,500 fish, including 12 sharks!*

Odd Museums

Houdini Historical Center, Appleton, Wisconsin. Located in the adopted hometown of the famous magician and escape artist, it holds most of the magic equipment and papers of the man whose real name was Ehrich Weiss.

WEB SITE *http://www.foxvalleyhistory.org/houdini/index.html*

Cockroach Hall of Fame, Plano, Texas. See live Madagascar Hissing Cockroaches 3 to 4 inches long, and many "art" displays featuring preserved roaches—ugh!

WEB SITE *http://www.pestshop.com/cockroaches.html*

National Farm Toy Museum, Dyersville, Iowa. More than 30,000 items and exhibits, including toy tractors, tools, trucks, miniature farm dioramas, and pedal tractors are on display around the museum.

WEB SITE *http://www.nationalfarmtoymuseum.com*

The National Yo-Yo Museum in Chico, California, claims to have the world's biggest working wooden yo-yo—Big-Yo weighs 256 pounds and has a diameter of 50 inches.

WEB SITE *http://www.nationalyoyo.org/museum/index.htm*

Museums of all kinds

The Museum of Television and Radio has two locations: New York, New York, and Los Angeles, California. You can watch TV or listen to the radio in this museum, which has more than 100,000 programs, including news, drama, documentaries, the performing arts, children's shows, sports, comedy, and even advertising. The programs are selected for their artistic, cultural, and historical significance. **WEB SITE** *http://www.mtr.org*

The National Cowboy and Western Heritage Museum, Oklahoma City, Oklahoma. The American Cowboy gallery traces the history and culture of this way of life from Spanish colonial times to the 20th century. There are also galleries for Western art and sculpture. Other galleries depict Native American life and customs and life on the frontier.

WEB SITE *http://www.nationalcowboymuseum.com*

The Garbage Museum, Stratford, Connecticut. A 30-foot-long Trash-o-saurus greets you at the door of this center, run by the Connecticut Resources Recovery Authority. Get a first-hand look at what happens to your garbage after it leaves your house.

WEB SITE *http://www.crra.org/education.html*

The Computer Museum of America, La Mesa, California. Collects and preserves historic computer equipment and houses the Computer Hall of Fame.

WEB SITE *http://www.computer-museum.org*

The Center for Puppetry Arts, Atlanta, Georgia. This museum has more than 1,000 puppets in its permanent collection. Learn about the history of puppetry and see puppets from around the world.

WEB SITE *http://www.puppet.org*

Music & Dance

When did the Beatles first come to America? page 131

Musical Instruments

There are many kinds of musical instruments. Instruments in an orchestra are divided into four groups, or sections: string, woodwind, brass, and percussion.

PERCUSSION INSTRUMENTS

Percussion instruments make sounds when they are struck. The most common percussion instrument is the drum. Others include cymbals, triangles, gongs, bells, and xylophone. Keyboard instruments, like the piano, are sometimes thought of as percussion instruments.

BRASSES

Brass instruments are hollow inside. They make sounds when air is blown into a mouthpiece shaped like a cup or a funnel. The trumpet, French horn, trombone, and tuba are brasses.

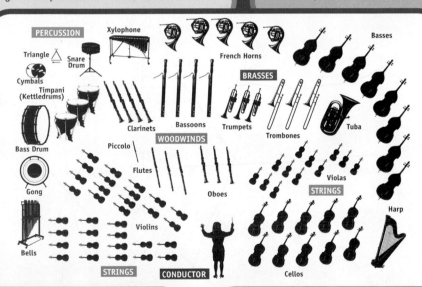

WOODWINDS

Woodwind instruments are long and round and hollow inside. They make sounds when air is blown into them through a mouth hole or a reed. The clarinet, flute, oboe, bassoon, and piccolo are woodwinds.

STRINGS

Stringed instruments make sounds when the strings are either stroked with a bow or plucked with the fingers. The violin, viola, cello, bass, and harp are used in an orchestra. The guitar, banjo, and mandolin are other stringed instruments.

POPULAR MUSIC

►**POP** Pop music (short for popular music) puts more emphasis on melody (tune) than does rock and has a softer beat. **Famous pop singers:** Frank Sinatra, Barbra Streisand, Madonna, Michael Jackson, Mariah Carey, Brandy, 'N Sync, Beyoncé Knowles, Jennifer Lopez, Britney Spears, Jessica Simpson.

►**RAP and HIP-HOP** In rap, words are spoken or chanted to a fast, hip-hop beat, with the emphasis on rhythm rather than melody. Rap was created in inner cities. The lyrics show strong feelings and may be about anger and violence. Hip-hop often includes "samples," which are pieces of music from other songs. **Famous rappers:** Eminem, Coolio, LL Cool J, TLC, The Fugees, Will Smith, Nelly, Jay-Z, Nas.

►**JAZZ** Jazz has its roots in the work songs, spirituals, and folk music of African-Americans. It began in the South in the early 1900s. **Famous jazz artists:** Louis Armstrong, Fats Waller, Jelly Roll Morton, Duke Ellington, Benny Goodman, Billie Holiday, Sarah Vaughan, Ella Fitzgerald, Dizzy Gillespie, Charlie Parker, Miles Davis, John Coltrane, Thelonious Monk, Wynton Marsalis.

►**ROCK** (also known as Rock 'n' Roll) Rock music, which started in the 1950s, is based on black rhythm and blues and country music. It often uses electronic instruments and equipment. Folk rock, punk, heavy metal, and alternative music are types of rock music. **Famous rock musicians:** Elvis Presley, Bob Dylan, Chuck Berry, The Beatles, Janis Joplin, The Rolling Stones, Joni Mitchell, Bruce Springsteen, Pearl Jam, Matchbox 20.

►**BLUES** The music called "the blues" developed from work songs and religious folk songs (spirituals) sung by African-Americans. It was introduced early in the 1900s by African-American musicians. Blues songs are usually sad. (A type of jazz is also called "the blues.") **Famous blues performers:** Ma Rainey, Bessie Smith, Billie Holiday, B. B. King, Muddy Waters, Robert Johnson, Howling Wolf, Etta James.

►**COUNTRY** American country music is based on Southern mountain music. Blues, jazz, and other musical styles have also influenced it. Country music became popular through the *Grand Ole Opry* radio show in Nashville, Tennessee, during the 1920s. **Famous country artists:** Hank Williams, Willie Nelson, Vince Gill, Reba McEntire, Tim McGraw, Faith Hill, Lee Ann Womack, Billy Gilman, Alan Jackson, Shania Twain, Dixie Chicks.

Rock and Roll Hall of Fame

The Rock and Roll Hall of Fame and Museum, in Cleveland, Ohio, honors rock-and-roll musicians with exhibits and multi-media presentations. Musicians cannot be included until 25 years after their first record. The class of 2004 includes George Harrison, Prince, ZZ Top, Jackson Browne, the Dells, Bob Seger, and Traffic. George Harrison is the third member of the Beatles to be inducted as a solo performer. John Lennon entered in 1992 and Paul McCartney in 1999. The whole group was inducted in 1988.

BRITISH INVASION OF 1964

On February 7, 1964, just over 40 years ago, four guys from England landed in New York City and were greeted by thousands of screaming fans. They were John, Paul, George, and Ringo—The Beatles! Already a big hit in Europe, they were in the U.S. for the first time. The first stop for John Lennon, Paul McCartney, George Harrison, and Ringo Starr was an appearance on *The Ed Sullivan Show* on Feb. 9. They sang five songs, including "I Want to Hold Your Hand" and "She Loves You." Nearly 40% of the U.S. watched—a record 73 million people. In 2004, that show was still 24th on the list of the most watched TV shows in history.

"Beatlemania"—the excitement created by the band— had hit the U.S. on December 26, 1963. That's when "I Want to Hold Your Hand" was first played on U.S. radio. Millions of kids and teenagers heard it and went crazy. The single went to the top of the charts, selling millions in a couple of weeks—on one day in New York City, as many as 10,000 an hour were sold! For a week in March of 1964, the "Fab Four" had all top five songs on the charts. No other music act has *ever* done that. The Beatles came back to the U.S. for more concerts in the summer and by the end of the year, they'd had six number one hits.

The Beatles launched the so-called "British Invasion" in music. Other British groups like The Rolling Stones, The Who, and The Dave Clark Five were soon big hits in America.

Some TOP ALBUMS of 2003

Beyoncé

1. *Come Away With Me*, Norah Jones
2. *Up!*, Shania Twain
3. *Home*, Dixie Chicks
4. *Let Go*, Avril Lavigne
5. *Meteora*, Linkin Park
6. *Fallen*, Evanescence
7. *Tim McGraw and the Dancehall Doctors*, Tim McGraw
8. *Justified*, Justin Timberlake
9. *A Rush of Blood to the Head*, Coldplay
10. *Dangerously in Love*, Beyoncé

131

Dance

Dancers perform patterns of movement, usually to music or rhythm. Dance may be a form of art, or part of a religious ceremony. Or it may be done just for fun.

►**BALLET** Ballet is a kind of dance based on formal steps. The movements are often graceful and flowing. Ballets are almost always danced to music, are performed for an audience, and often tell a story. In the 15th century, ballet was part of the elaborate entertainment performed for the rulers of Europe. In the 1700s dancers wore bulky costumes and shoes with high heels. Women danced in hoopskirts—and so did men! In the 1800s ballet steps and costumes began to look the way they do now. Many of the most popular ballets today date back to the middle or late 1800s.

►**BALLROOM DANCING** Social dancing has been around since at least the Middle Ages, when it was popular at fairs and festivals. In the 1400s social dance was part of fancy court pageants. It developed into ballroom dances like the minuet and the waltz during the 1700s. More recent dances include the Charleston, lindy, twist, and tango, as well as disco dancing, break dancing, line dancing, and dances such as the macarena and electric slide.

►**MODERN DANCE** Modern dance differs from classical ballet. It is often less concerned with graceful, flowing movement and with stories. Modern dance steps are often not performed in traditional ballet. Dancers may put their bodies into awkward, angular positions and turn their backs on the audience. Many modern dances are based on ancient art, such as Greek sculpture, or on dance styles found in Africa and Asia.

►**FOLK DANCE** Folk dance is the term for a dance that is passed on from generation to generation and is part of the culture or way of life of people from a particular country or ethnic group. Virginia reel (American), czardas (Hungarian), jig, and the Israeli hora are some folk dances.

►**HIP HOP DANCE** Like the music, the driving rhythms and athletic moves of hip hop dance grew out of urban culture in New York City in the 1970s—break dancing and robot-like "popping and locking," are part of this tradition.

Some **FAMOUS** Ballets

Giselle *Giselle* is a classic romantic ballet that is as popular now as when it was first performed over 160 years ago (1841). It combines drama and dancing with mystery, romance, and magic. Adolphe Adam composed the music.

The Sleeping Beauty This 1890 ballet carries the audience into a mystical world where spells are cast and a fairy comes to the aid of a handsome prince. Tchaikovsky composed the beautiful score.

The Nutcracker When this ballet was first performed in St. Petersburg in 1892, it was a flop. It has since become so popular that it is danced in many places every year at holiday time in December.

Swan Lake First danced in St. Petersburg, Russia, in 1895 to music by Tchaikovsky. Perhaps the most popular ballet ever, *Swan Lake* is the story of a prince and his love for a maiden who was turned into a swan by an evil magician.

On the Job

Violinist

Violinist Midori got her big break when she was just 11 years old: She performed with the legendary New York Philharmonic in New York City and received rave reviews. Since then, the violin has really taken her places!

For more than 20 years, the New Yorker has played with most of the world's leading orchestras and given recitals in the U.S., Europe, and her native Japan. Midori also records CDs, teaches violin, and through her nonprofit work, helps kids value music and themselves.

Q: What was it like to perform with the New York Philharmonic when you were a child?
It is always a thrill to play a public concert. Playing with an orchestra creates such a wonderful sensation in my body. Different instruments' sounds vibrate in and around me throughout.

Q: Whose work do you most like to play?
I like many different composers, and I listen to many different kinds of music. Not everything I like I get to play, but there is so much that I could play that I am never bored . . . . I enjoy, within the classical genre, works from Baroque, classical, Romantic, to contemporary. I'm also keen on working with living composers and playing their works, which include pieces written specifically at my request.

Q: How old is your violin, and is it the only one you use?
I always play (perform and practice) on a violin that was made by an Italian violin maker, Guarnerius del Gesù, in 1734. The violin is on loan to me from a private foundation in Japan called the Hayashibara Foundation. I've had it since 1999. When I first saw the violin, it was in London in 1999. I immediately knew that this was the right violin for me.

Q: When and why did to start your first non-profit group, Midori & Friends?
I started the first of my three organizations in 1992. I wanted to take an active role in challenging the decrease of the arts education in the public schools, particularly music education in New York City. In order to advocate effectively for music education to be made available to more children—if not all children—I needed the structural support of an organization. This way, I was able to design a comprehensive program in music education, and not simply coordinate a performance at a school. It also enabled me to encourage my colleagues to participate in our programs. (The description of my other two organizations, Music Sharing and Partners in Performance, can be found on my web site, www.GoToMidori.com.)

Q: To what do you owe your success?
My desire to keep searching for more has kept me disciplined, motivated, and encouraged. There is so much to know in this world. The more I try to know, the more I know how little I know.

Mythology

What dog had three heads? **page 135**

MYTHS *of the* GREEKS

As the ancient Greeks went about their daily lives, they believed that a large family of gods and goddesses were in their home on Mount Olympus, watching over them. Farmers planting crops, sailors crossing the sea, and poets writing verses thought that these immortal beings could make their tasks succeed or fail. The stories of these gods and goddesses are called **myths**. Some of the oldest myths came from the *Iliad* and *Odyssey*, long poems in Greek composed around 700 B.C.

After the Romans conquered Greece in 146 B.C., they adopted Greek myths but gave Roman names to the main gods and goddesses. Long after worship of these gods faded, their stories continued to fascinate people. If you visit any large art museum, you will see many works devoted to figures and stories from Greek and Roman mythology.

Head of Zeus

The MAJOR GODS of OLYMPUS

The family of Greek and Roman gods and goddesses was large. Their family tree would have more than 50 figures on it. Here are some major gods. Those with * are children of Zeus (Jupiter).

Greek Name	Roman Name	Description
*Aphrodite	Venus	Goddess of beauty and of love.
*Apollo	Phoebus	God of prophecy, music, and medicine.
*Ares	Mars	God of war; protector of the city.
*Artemis	Diana	Goddess of the Moon; a great huntress.
*Athena	Minerva	Goddess of wisdom and of war.
Demeter	Ceres	Goddess of crops and harvest, sister of Zeus (Jupiter).
*Dionysus	Bacchus	God of wine, dancing, and theater.
Hades	Pluto	Ruler of the underworld, brother of Zeus (Jupiter).
*Hephaestus	Vulcan	God of fire.
Hera	Juno	Queen of the gods, wife of Zeus (Jupiter), goddess of marriage.
*Hermes	Mercury	Messenger god, had winged helmet and sandals.
Poseidon	Neptune	God of the sea and of earthquakes, brother of Zeus (Jupiter).
Zeus	Jupiter	Sky god, ruler of gods and mortals.

MAKING SENSE of the WORLD

Unlike folklore or fables, myths were once thought to be true. The Greeks and Romans explained many of the things in nature by referring to the gods. (So did other ancient peoples, such as the Egyptians and the Norse). To the Greeks a rough sea meant that **POSEIDON** was angry. Lightning was the work of **ZEUS**, ruler of the universe. The sun went across the sky because **APOLLO** was driving the chariot of the sun.

One of the most famous nature stories is about **PERSEPHONE**, or Proserpina, who was the daughter of Zeus and **DEMETER**. **HADES**, who fell in love with her, kidnapped her and carried her off to the underworld (where people went after death). The gods asked Hades to bring her back, but while in the underworld Persephone had eaten part of a pomegranate (the food of the dead), which meant she could not return. Eventually the gods worked out a deal. She could spend half of every year on earth and half in the underworld. When Persephone is on earth, flowers bloom and crops grow, but when she is with Hades, plants wither and die. This is how the Greeks explained the seasons.

A famous place in ancient Greece was the **TEMPLE OF APOLLO AT DELPHI**. Inside it was a sacred stone that the Greeks believed to be the center of the world. The most important thing about Delphi, however, was its oracle. This was a priestess through whom, it was believed, Apollo spoke.

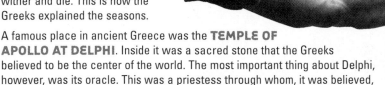

Statue of Poseidon

Ancient Heroes

Besides the gods, Greek and Roman mythology has many stories about "heroes" who had superhuman qualities. They were somewhere between ordinary humans and full-blown gods. Often, a hero became famous for destroying some kind of monster:

- **THESEUS** went into the great maze known as the Labyrinth and killed the **Minotaur**, a man-eating creature with the head of a bull and the body of a man.

- **PERSEUS** cut off the head of **Medusa**, a terrifying woman who had snakes for hair and whose stare turned people to stone.

- **BELLEROPHON**, with the help of the famous winged horse **Pegasus**, killed the fire-breathing Chimaera.

But the most popular hero was Herakles, or **Hercules**. The most famous of his deeds were his twelve labors. They included his killing of the **Hydra**, a many-headed monster, and his capture of the horrible three-headed dog **Cerberus**, who guarded the gates of the underworld. Hercules was so great a hero that the gods granted him immortality. When his body lay on his funeral pyre, Athena came and carried him off to Mount Olympus in her chariot.

Nations

Where is the "Shoestring Republic?" page 159

KIDS
AROUND THE WORLD
ENGLAND

England, along with Scotland and Wales, make up Great Britain, which along with Northern Ireland is the nation officially known as the United Kingdom of Great Britain and Northern Ireland. (It's often called Great Britain for short.) During its long history many people from northern and western Europe settled in England. More recently, immigrants from former British colonies in Asia and Africa have also come. The United Kingdom has a queen and royal family, but it is also one of the world's oldest democracies. Children in England lead similar lives to kids in the U.S., and love soccer and rugby (a sport similar to American football). They must take a big test when they are 16, to see whether they can go on to college or not. It's usually cool in England, especially at the beach. But in the summer of 2003, there was a record heat wave. The temperature in London reached 100° F for the first time!

INDIA

With over a billion people, India has the second biggest population in the world, just behind China. It is also the birthplace of two major world religions—Buddhism and Hinduism. About 800 languages are spoken in India—12 are official—including English because the country was ruled by Great Britain for many years in the 19th and 20th centuries. Elephants still roam freely in parts of India, but are often hit by cars or cause damage to villages. Working elephants, used in logging, began wearing "rear reflectors" for safety in 2003. Indians of all ages love to go to the movies. India's movie-making town is in the city of Mumbai (Bombay) and is called "Bollywood." In the spring many people celebrate the festival of Holi, known as the "carnival of colors." Children, friends, and neighbors run out onto the streets and throw colored water or powder all over each other.

JAMAICA

Jamaica is an island in the Caribbean Sea. Most Jamaicans are descendents of slaves brought from West Africa for Spanish and British colonists. Most of the people today speak a dialect, or local version, of English. It is a mixture of English with African languages, Spanish, and French. Storytelling is a big part of the traditional culture. Anansi the spider, who uses his cleverness to outsmart bigger opponents, is famous in Jamaican folklore. Jamaica enjoys warm weather all year round and is a popular vacation spot. Kids there like to play soccer, go snorkeling, and compete in track and field. Dominoes is a popular game.

JORDAN

Jordan is a kingdom located in the Middle East, and is bordered by Iraq, Israel, Saudi Arabia, and Syria. Its history goes back thousands of years, and it has had many different rulers. Most of the people are Arabs, who practice Islam. Roughly 90% of the people live in the cities, although some Bedouin nomads still live in tents in the desert. About half of the population is Palestinian. Since much of the country is too dry for farming, and lacks natural resources, Jordan depends a lot on foreign aid and tourism. Family life is very important in Jordan, and children live with their extended families. Almost half of the population is under the age of 20. Each year, thousands of tourists flock to the ruins of Petra, an ancient city over 2,000 years old, carved from red sandstone cliffs.

NEPAL

Nepal is a small kingdom in Central Asia, between India and China. Part of the country lies in the tallest mountain range in the world—the Himalayas. Most of the people are Hindus. Visitors come from all over the world to climb the world's tallest mountain, Mt. Everest. Despite its dramatic scenery, Nepal is one of the poorest nations in the world. Half of all the children have to leave school before the fifth grade to go to work. Nepal has an interesting holiday called Tihar, a festival of lights, during which brothers and sisters, or children who are the same age, put red powder on each other's foreheads as a blessing, and then exchange gifts.

137

Maps & Flags
of the Nations of the World

Maps showing the continents and nations of the world appear on pages 138-149. Flags of the nations appear on pages 150-153. A map of the United States appears on pages 272-273.

AUSTRALIA

- ⊛ National Capital
- ★ State Capital
- • Other City

PACIFIC ISLANDS

⍟ National Capital

★ Territorial Capital

● Other City

1:84,569,000

| 0 | 500 | 1,000 mi |
| 0 | 500 | 1,000 km |

Miller Projection

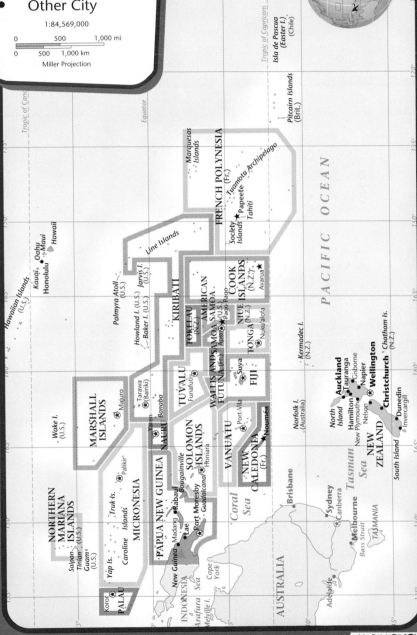

Tropic of Cancer

Equator

Tropic of Capricorn

Sala y Gomez (Chile)

Isla de Pascua (Easter I.) (Chile)

Pitcairn Islands (Brit.)

Marquesas Islands

FRENCH POLYNESIA (Fr.)

Tuamotu Archipelago

Society Islands
★ Papeete
Tahiti

PACIFIC OCEAN

Hawaii
Kauai Oahu Maui
Honolulu

Hawaiian Islands (U.S.)

Line Islands

Jarvis I. (U.S.)

Palmyra Atoll (U.S.)

Howland I. (U.S.)
Baker I. (U.S.)

KIRIBATI

Wake I. (U.S.)

Tarawa (Bairiki)
Banaba

MARSHALL ISLANDS

Majuro

TOKELAU (N.Z.)

AMERICAN SAMOA (U.S.)

COOK ISLANDS (N.Z.)
Avarua ★

NIUE (N.Z.)

WALLIS AND FUTUNA (Fr.)

SAMOA
Apia ★ Pago Pago

TUVALU
Funafuti

Suva

FIJI

TONGA
Nuku'alofa

Kermadec I. (N.Z.)

Chatham Is. (N.Z.)

Auckland Tauranga
Hamilton Gisborne
New Plymouth Napier
Nelson Wellington
Christchurch
Dunedin
Invercargill

North Island

South Island

NEW ZEALAND

Tasman Sea

Yap Is. Palikir ⍟

Truk Is.

Caroline Islands

MICRONESIA

NORTHERN MARIANA ISLANDS
Saipan
Tinian (U.S.)
Guam (U.S.)

PAPUA NEW GUINEA
Madang Lae
Rabaul
Port Moresby

Bougainville

SOLOMON ISLANDS
Honiara
Guadalcanal

NAURU
Yaren ⍟

VANUATU
Port-Vila

NEW CALEDONIA (Fr.)
★ Nouméa

Norfolk I. (Australia)

Coral Sea

New Guinea

Cape York

INDONESIA
Arafura Sea
Melville I.

PALAU
Koror

AUSTRALIA

Brisbane

Sydney
Canberra

Melbourne

Adelaide

TASMANIA

Bass Strait

© MAPQUEST.COM

139

SWEDEN

NORWAY

GREAT BRITAIN

ICELAND

Denmark Strait

Cape Farewell

Arctic Circle

Tasiilaq

Greenland Sea

Spitsbergen

Cape Morris Jessup

North Pole
+

Arctic Ocean

Nord

Knud Rasmussen Land

Qaanaaq (Thule)

GREENLAND (KALAALLIT NUNAAT) (Den.)

Nuuk

Grise Fiord

Ellesmere I.

Alert

Davis Strait

Baffin Bay

Pangnirtung

Iqaluit

Baffin Island

Pond Inlet

Arctic Bay

Labrador Sea

Hebron

NEWFOUNDLAND AND LABRADOR

St. Anthony

Happy Valley-Goose Bay

Conne Brook

St. Pierre & Miquelon (Fr.)

St. John's

Island of Newfoundland

Anticosti I.

Schefferville

Labrador City

Sept-Îles

QUÉBEC

Chibougamau

CANADIAN SHIELD

Powungnituk

Ungava Peninsula

Belcher Is.

James Bay

Mooseonee

Hudson Strait

Hudson Bay

Repulse Bay

Southampton

Churchill

York Factory

L. Winnipeg

MANITOBA

Thompson

Flin Flon

Lynn Lake

Queen Elizabeth Islands

Resolute

Cambridge Bay

Victoria I.

Holman

Banks I.

Kugluktuk

NUNAVUT

CANADA

Prince Albert

Saskatoon

SASK.

Uranium City

La Ronge

Saskatchewan

La Loche

Yellowknife

Ft. Smith

Hay River

Ft. Simpson

Délîne

Great Bear L.

Great Slave L.

NORTHWEST TERRITORIES

ALBERTA

Peace River

Ft. McMurray

Edmonton

Athabasca

L. Athabasca

GREA

ROC KY

Calgary

Jasper

Sachs Harbour

Beaufort Sea

Inuvik

Fort McPherson

Mackenzie

Point Barrow

Barrow

Kotzebue

BROOKS RANGE

Fort Yukon

Yukon

Fairbanks

Dawson

Mayo

Carmacks

YUKON

Whitehorse

Watson Lake

BRITISH COLUMBIA

Williams Lake

COAST MOUNTAINS

Point Hope

Nome

Bethel

ALASKA

Mt. McKinley 6,194 m. (20,320 ft.)

ALASKA RANGE

Anchorage

Valdez

Mt. Logan 5,959 m. (19,551 ft.)

Yakutat

Skagway

Juneau

Sitka

Ketchikan

Prince Rupert

Kitimat

Queen Charlotte Is.

Vancouver I.

Vancouver

Victoria

Kenai

Seward

Kodiak

Gulf of Alaska

RUSSIA

Bering Strait

Arctic Circle

Bering Sea

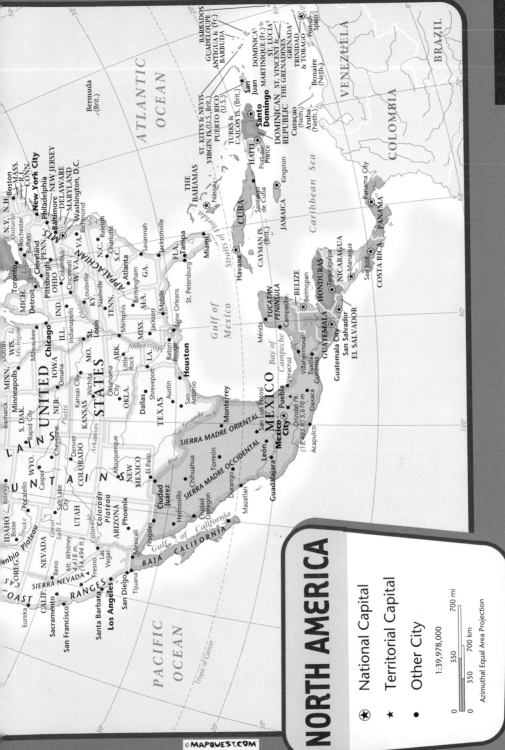

NORTH AMERICA

⊛ National Capital

★ Territorial Capital

• Other City

1:39,978,000

| 0 | 350 | 700 mi |
| 0 | 350 | 700 km |

Azimuthal Equal Area Projection

©MAPQUEST.COM

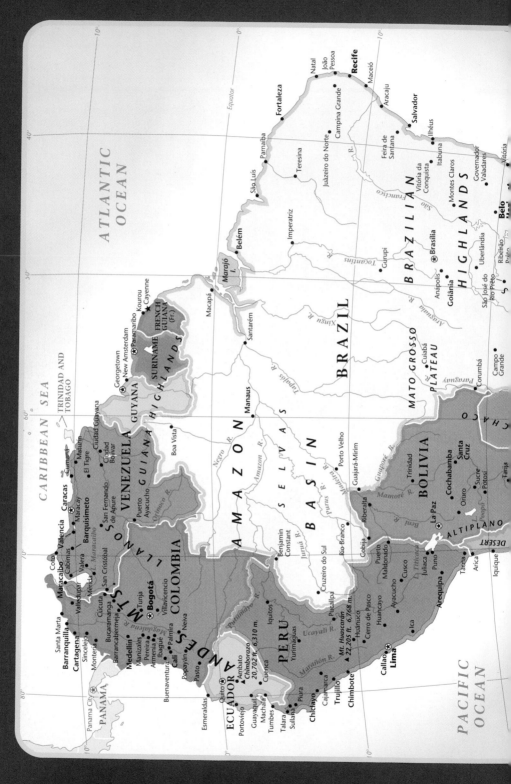

ATLANTIC OCEAN

CARIBBEAN SEA

TRINIDAD AND TOBAGO

PANAMA

Panama City

Santa Marta
Barranquilla
Cartagena
Sincelejo
Montería
Barrancabermeja
Medellín
Manizales
Pereira
Armenia
Ibagué
Cali
Palmira
Buenaventura
Popayán
Pasto

Maracaibo
Cabimas
Valledupar
Valera
Mérida
San Cristóbal
Cúcuta
Bucaramanga
Tunja
Bogotá
Villavicencio
Neiva

Coro
Valencia
Maracay
Caracas
Cumaná
Maturín
El Tigre
Ciudad Guayana
Ciudad Bolívar
San Fernando de Apure
Puerto Ayacucho

VENEZUELA

COLOMBIA

LLANOS

ANDES MTS.

Esmeraldas
Quito
ECUADOR
Portoviejo
Guayaquil
Machala
Tumbes
Talara
Sullana
Piura
Chiclayo
Chimbote
Trujillo
Cajamarca
Ambato
Chimborazo
20,702 ft. 6,310 m.
Cuenca
Yurimaguas
Iquitos
Pucallpa
PERU
Mt. Huascarán
22,205 ft. 6,768 m.
Huánuco
Cerro de Pasco
Huancayo
Ayacucho
Ica
Cusco
Arequipa
Tacna
Arica
Iquique

Callao
Lima

GUYANA

GUIANA HIGHLANDS

SURINAME
Paramaribo
New Amsterdam
Georgetown

FRENCH GUIANA (Fr.)
Cayenne
Kourou

Boa Vista

Macapá

Marajó I.

Belém

São Luís

Santarém

Manaus

Negro R.

Amazon R.

AMAZON BASIN

SELVAS

Putumayo R.

Caquetá R.

Benjamin Constant

Cruzeiro do Sul

Rio Branco

Purus R.

Madeira R.

Porto Velho

Guajará-Mirim

Riberalta

Cobija

Puerto Maldonado

Juliaca
Puno

Lake Titicaca

La Paz

BOLIVIA

ALTIPLANO

Trinidad

Cochabamba
Oruro
Sucre
Potosí
Tarija

Santa Cruz

Lake Poopó

DESERT

Equator

Natal
João Pessoa
Recife
Maceió
Aracaju
Salvador
Ilhéus
Itabuna

Campina Grande
Fortaleza

Parnaíba
Teresina
Juàzeiro do Norte

Feira de Santana

São Francisco R.

Vitória da Conquista
Montes Claros
Governador Valadares
Vitória

Belo

BRAZILIAN HIGHLANDS

Imperatriz

Gurupi

Tocantins R.

Anápolis
Brasília
Goiânia
São José do Rio Preto
Uberlândia
Ribeirão Prêto

BRAZIL

Xingu R.

Tapajós R.

Araguaia R.

MATO GROSSO PLATEAU

Cuiabá

Corumbá

Campo Grande

Paraguay R.

Guaporé R.

Mamoré R.

Beni R.

CHACO

PACIFIC OCEAN

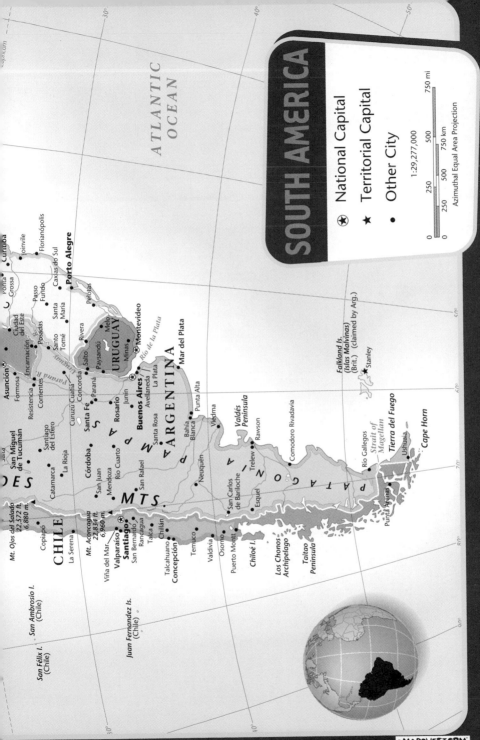

SOUTH AMERICA

⊛ National Capital
★ Territorial Capital
• Other City

1:29,277,000

| 0 | 250 | 500 | 750 mi |
| 0 | 250 | 500 | 750 km |

Azimuthal Equal Area Projection

ATLANTIC OCEAN

Curitiba
Joinvile
Florianópolis
Ponta Grossa
Passo Fundo
Caxias do Sul
Porto Alegre
Santa Maria
Pelotas
Ciudad del Este
Posadas
Santo Tomé
Rivera
Melo
⊛ Montevideo
Encarnación
Santa
Fe
Corrientes
Formosa
⊛ Asunción
Resistencia
Curuzú Cuatiá
Concordia
Paraná
Paysandú
Salto
URUGUAY
Minas
Río de la Plata
Mar del Plata
La Plata
Buenos Aires
Avellaneda
Junín
Rosario
Santa Rosa
Punta Alta
ARGENTINA
Bahía Blanca
Viedma
Neuquén

Valdés Peninsula

Rawson
Trelew

Comodoro Rivadavia

Falkland Is.
(Islas Malvinas)
(Brit.) (claimed by Arg.)
• Stanley

San Carlos de Bariloche
Esquel

PATAGONIA

Río Gallegos
Strait of Magellan
Punta Arenas
Ushuaia
Tierra del Fuego
Cape Horn

Santiago del Estero
Córdoba
La Rioja
Catamarca
San Miguel de Tucumán
Salta

San Ambrosio I.
(Chile)

San Félix I.
(Chile)

Juan Fernandez Is.
(Chile)

Mt. Ojos del Salado
22,572 ft.
6,880 m.
Copiapó
La Serena
CHILE
ES
San Juan
Mendoza
Río Cuarto
San Rafael
M
Mt. Aconcagua
22,834 ft.
6,960 m.
Viña del Mar
Valparaíso
⊛ Santiago
Rancagua
San Bernardo
Talca
Chillán
Talcahuano
Concepción
Temuco
Valdivia
Osorno
Puerto Montt
Chiloé I.

Los Chonos Archipelago
Taitao Peninsula

M T S .

A
N
D
E
S

© MAPQUEST.COM

143

EUROPE

★ National Capital

• Other City

1:22,107,000

```
0        250        500 mi
|----|----|----|----|
0    250    500 km
```

Azimuthal Equal Area Projection

ICELAND
Reykjavík · Akureyri

Arctic Circle

Norwegian *Sea*

Faroe Is.
(Den.)

Trondheim

Shetland Is.
(Brit.)

NORWAY
Bergen

Bodø

Sundsvall

SWEDE

Orkney Is.

Stavanger · Oslo ★

Uppsala

Stockholm
Linköping

Skagerrak

Göteborg

Gotla

Hebrides

Aberdeen

Glasgow
Edinburgh

Belfast · Newcastle
GREAT BRITAIN

Dublin · Leeds
IRELAND ★ Liverpool (UNITED KINGDOM)
Cork · Manchester · Sheffield

Irish Sea

North Sea

Jutland · Århus
Copenhagen ★ Helsingborg
DENMARK · Odense · Malmö

Ba

Gdar
Szczecin

Birmingham
Cardiff · Bristol
Land's End · Portsmouth · London ★

NETHERLANDS
Amsterdam ★
Antwerp · Rotterdam

Hamburg
Bremen
Hannover

★ Berlin

Pozna

ATLANTIC OCEAN

English Channel
Channel Is.
(Brit.) · Le Havre
Brest · Rouen
LUXEMBOURG
Paris ★
Nantes

Brussels ★
Lille
BELGIUM · Liège
Bonn
Luxembourg ★

Essen
Cologne
GERMANY
Leipzig
Frankfurt
Mannheim

Dresden

Prague ★
CZECH REP.
Brno ·

Katowi
Ostra

Wro

Loire

Strasbourg
Dijon · Bern ★
Zürich

Stuttgart
Munich
LIECHTENSTEIN
SWITZERLAND
AUSTRIA

Linz · Vienna ★ Bratisl
SLOV

FRANCE

Cape Finisterre

Vigo · Gijón

Bay of Biscay

Bordeaux

Geneva
Lyon ★

Graz
SLOVENIA
Ljubljana ★ · Zagreb ★

Buda
HUNG
Pécs

Porto · Bilbao
Valladolid

Toulouse

Mt. Blanc
4807 m
(15,771 ft)

ALPS
Milan
Turin · Verona · Venice
Po

DINARIC
CROATIA
BOSNIA
HERZEGO

PORTUGAL
Lisbon ★
Badajoz

IBERIAN
Zaragoza
Pico de Aneto
3404 m
(11,168 ft)
Madrid ★
PENINSULA

PYRENEES
ANDORRA
Barcelona

Marseille
Nice
Toulon
MONACO

Genoa
Bologna
Florence
Ligurian Sea

APENNINES
SAN MARINO

Split
Sarajevo ·

Adriatic

Dubrovnik ·
Podg

Córdoba
Sevilla
Cádiz

SPAIN
Valencia
Alicante
Granada

Balearic Sea
Majorca
Palma
Minorca
Balearic Is.
(Sp.)

Corsica
(Fr.)

Elba

VATICAN ★ ★ **Rome**
CITY

ITALY
Naples ·
Salerno

Bari

Sea

Cape
St. Vincent

Málaga
GIBRALTAR (Brit.)

Strait of Gibraltar

Sardinia
(It.)

Cagliari

Tyrrhenian Sea

Palermo

Ion

M e d i t e r r a n e a n

Rabat ★
Casablanca

Algiers ★

Tunis ★

Catania
Sicily

Mt. Etna
3323 m
(10,902 ft)

MOROCCO

ATLAS

MOUNTAINS
ALGERIA

TUNISIA

Valletta ★
MALTA

Sea

North Cape
mmerfest
LAND
Barents Sea
Nar'yan-Mar
Pechora
Murmansk
KOLA PENINSULA
Apatity
White Sea
Ukhta
R U S S I A
Arctic Circle
Oulu
Belomorsk
Arkhangel'sk
Syktyvkar
Serov
FINLAND
Kotlas
Bereznıki
Petropavl
Yekaterinburg
Tampere
Lake Onega
Petrozavodsk
Perm'
Chelyabinsk
Lahti
Lake Ladoga
Kirov
Izhevsk
Ufa
Qostanay
Helsinki
St. Petersburg
Vologda
Cherepovets
Naberezhnyye Chelny
Magnitogorsk
Tallinn
Velikiy Novgorod
Yaroslavl'
Kazan
ESTONIA
Ivanovo
Nizhniy Novgorod
Tartu
Tver'
Pskov
Ul'yanovsk
Tol'yatti
Orenburg
Orsk
LATVIA
Moscow
Saransk
Samara
Daugavpils
Ryazan'
Penza
Aktobe
HUANIA
Vitsyebsk
Smolensk
Tula
Tambov
Oral
KAZAKHSTAN
nas
Vilnius
Mahilyow
Lipetsk
Saratov
ad
Hrodna
Bryansk
Voronezh
Minsk
Kursk
BELARUS
Homyel'
Atyraū
Aral Sea
saw
Brest
Volgograd
Kiev
Kharkiv
UZBEKISTAN
ND
Luhans'k
Astrakhan
Aktaū
L'viv
UKRAINE
Dnieper
Donets'k
Dnipropetrovs'k
Zaporizhzhia
Caspian
THIAN
Chernivtsi
Kryvyy Rih
Mariupol'
Rostov na Donu
Makhachkala
ice
MOLDOVA
Mykolaiv
Sea of Azov
Stavropol'
TURKMENISTAN
ebrecen
Iaşi
Chişinău
Krasnodar
Groznyy
Türkmenbashy
ROMANIA
Odesa
CRIMEA
Sea
nişoara
Simferopol'
CAUCASUS
Baku
Ploieşti
Sevastopol'
GEORGIA
ade
Bucharest
Constanţa
Tbilisi
AZERBAIJAN
Black Sea
ARMENIA
RO
Danube
Varna
Trabzon
Yerevan
BULGARIA
Burgas
Tabriz
Tehran
Skopje
Sofia
Plovdiv
ONIA
İstanbul
Ankara
TURKEY
IRAN
AN
Thessaloniki
ULA
Larisa
İzmir
Adana
IRAQ
ECE
Athens
Baghdad
PONNESE
Cyclades
SYRIA
Euphrates
Rhodes
Nicosia
Sea of Crete
LEBANON
Crete
Iraklion
CYPRUS
Beirut
Damascus
Persian

ATLANTIC OCEAN

IRELAND
PORTUGAL
GREAT
BRITAIN
SPAIN
NORWAY
MOROCCO
BEL. NETH. DEN.
FRANCE
GERMANY
SWEDEN
Barents
Sea
ALGERIA
SWITZ.
CZECH
REP.
FINLAND
Murmansk
ITALY
AUS. POLAND LITH. LAT.
ESTONIA
Arkhangel'sk
St. Petersburg
TUNISIA
HUNG.
BELARUS
SERB. &
MONT.
ALB.
ROM.
MOL.
Moscow
R U S S
U R A L   M O U N T A I N S
LIBYA
GREECE
BUL.
UKRAINE
Istanbul
Izmir
Ankara
Black
Sea
Volgograd
Volga
Yekaterinburg
Chelyabinsk
Magnitogorsk
Irtysh
Omsk
Novosibi
TURKEY
GEORGIA
Tbilisi
Astrakhan'
Caspian
Sea
KAZAKHSTAN
Astana
Karaganda
Semey
(Semipalatinsk)
Pavlo
CYPRUS
LEBANON
Nicosia
ARMENIA
Yerevan
AZERBAIJAN
Aral
Sea
Lake
Balkhash
CHAD
Beirut
Tel Aviv
Jerusalem
ISRAEL
SYRIA
Damascus
Amman
Tabriz
Baku
TURKMENISTAN
Ashgabat
UZBEKISTAN
Bishkek
Almaty
EGYPT
Sinai
JORDAN
IRAQ
Baghdad
Tehran
Mashhad
Tashkent
Dushanbe
KYRGYZSTAN
Kashi
A F R I C A
Red
Sea
SAUDI
ARABIA
Al Basrah
Kuwait City
Esfahan
IRAN
Mashhad
AFGHANISTAN
Kabul
TAJIKISTAN
Takla M
Dese
KUWAIT
Manama
Shiraz
Kerman
Islamabad
Kandahar
Srinagar
XIZA
(TIB
Jeddah
Mecca
Riyadh
BAHRAIN
QATAR
Doha
Abu Dhabi
Lahore
Amritsar
Delhi
H I M A L A
SUDAN
UNITED ARAB
EMIRATES
Gulf of Oman
PAKISTAN
Sukkur
New Delhi
NEPAL
Kathmand
ERITREA
Sanaa
Muscat
OMAN
Karachi
Hyderabad
Jaipur
Kanpur
Luckn
Gan
ETHIOPIA DJI.
Aden
YEMEN
Gulf of Aden
Socotra
(Yemen)
Arabian
Sea
Ahmadabad
I N D I A
Nagpur
SOMALIA
Mumbai
Hyderabad
Bangalore
Madras
(Chennai)
Lakshadweep
(India)
Kochi
Madurai
SRI LANK
Colombo
Male
MALDIVES
INDIAN
OCEA

Equator

ASIA

⊛ National Capital

• Territorial Capital

• Other City

1:51,084,000

500   1,000 mi

500   1,000 km

Two-Point Equidistant Projection

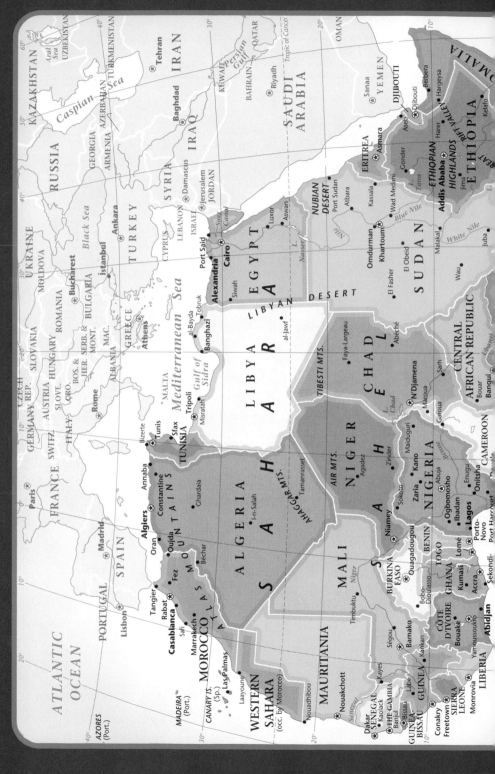

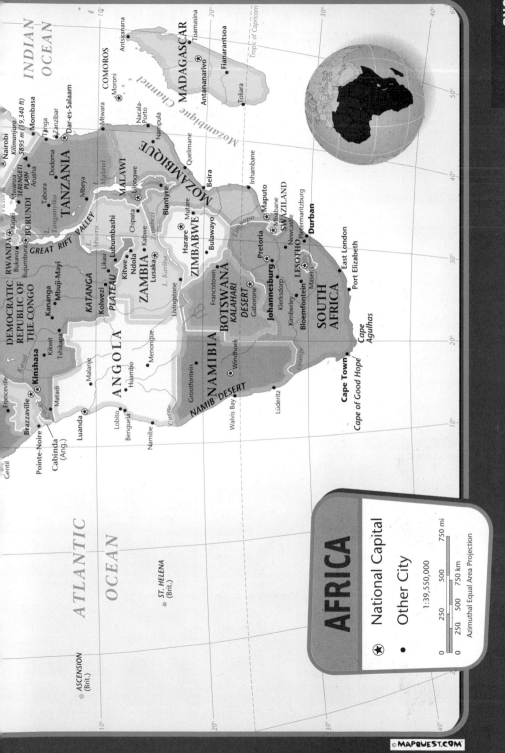

AFRICA

⊛ National Capital

• Other City

1:39,550,000

0 250 500 750 mi
0 250 500 750 km
Azimuthal Equal Area Projection

©MAPQUEST.COM

AFGHANISTAN

ALBANIA

ALGERIA

ANDORRA

ANGOLA

ANTIGUA AND BARBUDA

ARGENTINA

ARMENIA

AUSTRALIA

AUSTRIA

AZERBAIJAN

THE BAHAMAS

BAHRAIN

BANGLADESH

BARBADOS

BELARUS

BELGIUM

BELIZE

BENIN

BHUTAN

BOLIVIA

BOSNIA AND HERZEGOVINA

BOTSWANA

BRAZIL

BRUNEI

BULGARIA

BURKINA FASO

BURUNDI

CAMBODIA

CAMEROON

CANADA

CAPE VERDE

CENTRAL AFRICAN REPUBLIC

CHAD

CHILE

CHINA

COLOMBIA

COMOROS

CONGO, DEMOCRATIC REP. OF THE

CONGO, REP. OF THE

COSTA RICA

CÔTE D'IVOIRE

CROATIA

CUBA

CYPRUS

CZECH REPUBLIC

DENMARK

DJIBOUTI

DOMINICA

DOMINICAN REPUBLIC

FLAGS *of the* NATIONS *of the* WORLD
(EAST TIMOR–LIECHTENSTEIN)

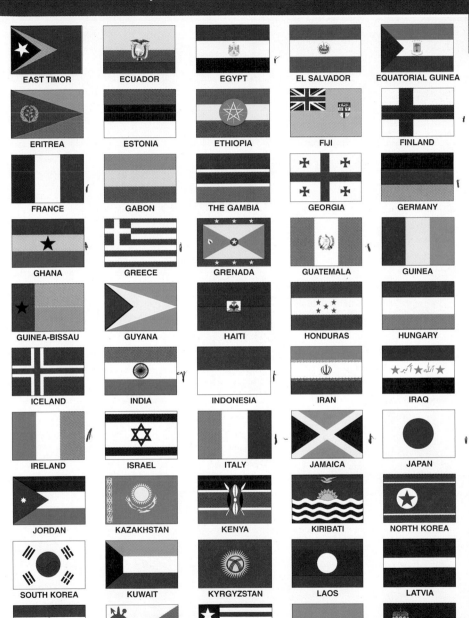

EAST TIMOR	ECUADOR	EGYPT	EL SALVADOR	EQUATORIAL GUINEA
ERITREA	ESTONIA	ETHIOPIA	FIJI	FINLAND
FRANCE	GABON	THE GAMBIA	GEORGIA	GERMANY
GHANA	GREECE	GRENADA	GUATEMALA	GUINEA
GUINEA-BISSAU	GUYANA	HAITI	HONDURAS	HUNGARY
ICELAND	INDIA	INDONESIA	IRAN	IRAQ
IRELAND	ISRAEL	ITALY	JAMAICA	JAPAN
JORDAN	KAZAKHSTAN	KENYA	KIRIBATI	NORTH KOREA
SOUTH KOREA	KUWAIT	KYRGYZSTAN	LAOS	LATVIA
LEBANON	LESOTHO	LIBERIA	LIBYA	LIECHTENSTEIN

FLAGS *of the* NATIONS *of the* WORLD
(LITHUANIA–SAUDI ARABIA)

LITHUANIA

LUXEMBOURG

MACEDONIA

MADAGASCAR

MALAWI

MALAYSIA

MALDIVES

MALI

MALTA

MARSHALL ISLANDS

MAURITANIA

MAURITIUS

MEXICO

MICRONESIA

MOLDOVA

MONACO

MONGOLIA

MOROCCO

MOZAMBIQUE

MYANMAR (BURMA)

NAMIBIA

NAURU

NEPAL

NETHERLANDS

NEW ZEALAND

NICARAGUA

NIGER

NIGERIA

NORWAY

OMAN

PAKISTAN

PALAU

PANAMA

PAPUA NEW GUINEA

PARAGUAY

PERU

PHILIPPINES

POLAND

PORTUGAL

QATAR

ROMANIA

RUSSIA

RWANDA

ST. KITTS AND NEVIS

ST. LUCIA

ST. VINCENT AND
THE GRENADINES

SAMOA

SAN MARINO

SÃO TOMÉ AND PRÍNCIPE

SAUDI ARABIA

152

FLAGS *of the* NATIONS *of the* WORLD
(SENEGAL–ZIMBABWE)

 SENEGAL

 SERBIA & MONTENEGRO

 SEYCHELLES

 SIERRA LEONE

 SINGAPORE

 SLOVAKIA

 SLOVENIA

 SOLOMON ISLANDS

 SOMALIA

 SOUTH AFRICA

 SPAIN

 SRI LANKA

 SUDAN

 SURINAME

 SWAZILAND

 SWEDEN

 SWITZERLAND

 SYRIA

 TAIWAN

 TAJIKISTAN

 TANZANIA

 THAILAND

 TOGO

 TONGA

 TRINIDAD AND TOBAGO

 TUNISIA

 TURKEY

 TURKMENISTAN

 TUVALU

 UGANDA

 UKRAINE

 UNITED ARAB EMIRATES

 UNITED KINGDOM (GREAT BRITAIN)

 UNITED STATES

 URUGUAY

 UZBEKISTAN

 VANUATU

 VATICAN CITY

 VENEZUELA

 VIETNAM

 YEMEN

 ZAMBIA

ZIMBABWE

153

Facts About Nations

There are **193** independent nations in the world. The information for each of them goes across two pages. The left page gives the **name** and **capital** of each nation, its **location**, and its **area**. On the right page, the **population** column tells how many people lived in each country in 2004, according to estimates. The **currency** column shows the name for each nation's money and how much one U.S. dollar was worth there at the start of 2004. The **language** column gives official languages and other common languages.

KEY TO THE **DOTS**

- Africa
- Asia
- Australia
- Europe
- North America
- Pacific Islands
- South America

	NATION	CAPITAL	LOCATION OF NATION	AREA
●	**Afghanistan**	Kabul	Southern Asia, between Iran and Pakistan	250,000 sq. mi. (647,500 sq. km.)
●	**Albania**	Tiranë	Eastern Europe, between Greece and Serbia & Montenegro	11,100 sq. mi. (28,750 sq. km.)
●	**Algeria**	Algiers	North Africa on the Mediterranean Sea, between Libya and Morocco	919,600 sq. mi. (2,381,740 sq. km.)
●	**Andorra**	Andorra la Vella	Europe, in the mountains between France and Spain	174 sq. mi. (450 sq. km.)
●	**Angola**	Luanda	Southern Africa on the Atlantic Ocean, north of Namibia	481,400 sq. mi. (1,246,700 sq. km.)
●	**Antigua & Barbuda**	St. John's	Islands on eastern edge of the Caribbean Sea	174 sq. mi. (440 sq. km.)
●	**Argentina**	Buenos Aires	Fills up most of the southern part of South America	1,068,300 sq. mi. (2,766,890 sq. km.)
●	**Armenia**	Yerevan	Western Asia, north of Turkey and Iran, west of the Caspian Sea	11,500 sq. mi. (29,800 sq. km.)
●	**Australia**	Canberra	Continent south of Asia, between the Indian and Pacific Oceans	2,967,910 sq. mi. (7,686,850 sq. km.)
●	**Austria**	Vienna	Central Europe, north of Italy	32,380 sq. mi. (83,860 sq. km.)
●	**Azerbaijan**	Baku	Western Asia, north of Iran, on the Caspian Sea	33,440 sq. mi. (86,600 sq. km.)
●	**The Bahamas**	Nassau	Islands in the Atlantic Ocean, east of Florida	5,380 sq. mi. (13,940 sq. km.)
●	**Bahrain**	Manama	In the Persian Gulf, near the coast of Qatar	240 sq. mi. (620 sq. km.)

POPULATION	CURRENCY	LANGUAGE	DID YOU KNOW?
29,547,078	$1 = 43 afghanis	Afghan Persian (Dari), Pashtu	In the 1800s, Britain and Russia both sought control of Afghanistan.
3,544,808	$1 = 106.4 leks	Albanian, Greek	Ancient people called Illyrians lived in Albania around A.D. 1000.
33,357,089	$1 = 71.45 dinars	Arabic, French, Berber Dialects	Algeria was a colony of France from 1834 to 1963.
69,865	$1 = .79 euros	Catalan, French, Castilian	This tiny nation has a police force, but no regular army.
10,978,552	$1 = 79.14 kwanzas	Portuguese, African dialects	Decades of civil war, now ended, left Angola with millions of land mines.
68,320	$1 = 2.67. East Carribean dollars	English	Most of the people of these islands trace their roots to West Africa.
39,144,753	$1 = 2.92 pesos	Spanish, English, Italian	Mount Aconcagua (22,834 ft) is the tallest peak in the western hemisphere.
3,325,307	$1 = 558.14 drams	Armenian	Dating to 783 B.C., Yerevan is one of the oldest continuously occupied towns.
19,913,144	$1 = 1.32 Australian dollars	English, aboriginal languages	There are an estimated 50 million kangaroos in Australia.
8,174,762	$1 = .79 euro	German	The Schottengymnasium, a school in Vienna, has been open since 1155.
7,868,385	$1 = 4,913 manats	Azeri, Russian, Armenian	Azerbaijan borders the Caspian Sea, world's largest inland body of water.
299,697	Bahamas dollar Same value as U.S. dollar	English, Creole	Christopher Columbus first landed in the New World on San Salvador, in 1492.
677,886	$1 = .38 dinars	Arabic, English, Farsi, Urdu	Only 1% of this island nation's land can be used for farming.

Facts About Nations

NATION	CAPITAL	LOCATION OF NATION	AREA
Bangladesh	Dhaka	Southern Asia, nearly surrounded by India	56,000 sq. mi. (144,000 sq. km.)
Barbados	Bridgetown	Island in the Atlantic Ocean, north of Trinidad	165 sq. mi. (430 sq. km.)
Belarus	Minsk	Eastern Europe, east of Poland	80,200 sq. mi. (207,600 sq. km.)
Belgium	Brussels	Western Europe, on the North Sea, south of the Netherlands	11,780 sq. mi. (30,510 sq. km.)
Belize	Belmopan	Central America, south of Mexico	8,860 sq. mi. (22,960 sq. km.)
Benin	Porto-Novo	West Africa, on the Gulf of Guinea, west of Nigeria	43,480 sq. mi. (112,620 sq. km.)
Bhutan	Thimphu	Asia, in the Himalaya Mountains, between China and India	18,000 sq. mi. (47,000 sq. km.)
Bolivia	La Paz	South America, in the Andes Mountains, next to Brazil	424,160 sq. mi. (1,098,580 sq. km.)
Bosnia and Herzegovina	Sarajevo	Southern Europe, on the Balkan Peninsula	19,740 sq. mi. (51,130 sq. km.)
Botswana	Gaborone	Southern Africa, between South Africa and Zambia	231,800 sq. mi. (600,370 sq. km.)
Brazil	Brasília	Occupies most of the eastern part of South America	3,286,490 sq. mi. (8,511,970 sq. km.)
Brunei	Bandar Seri Begawan	On the island of Borneo, northwest of Australia in the Pacific Ocean	2,230 sq. mi. (5,770 sq. km.)
Bulgaria	Sofia	Eastern Europe, on the Balkan Peninsula, bordering the Black Sea	42,820 sq. mi. (110,910 sq. km.)
Burkina Faso	Ouagadougou	West Africa, between Mali and Ghana	105,900 sq. mi. (274,200 sq. km.)
Burundi	Bujumbura	Central Africa, northwest of Tanzania	10,750 sq. mi. (27,830 sq. km.)
Cambodia	Phnom Penh	Southeast Asia, between Vietnam and Thailand	69,900 sq. mi. (181,040 sq. km.)
Cameroon	Yaoundé	Central Africa, between Nigeria and Central African Republic	183,570 sq. mi. (475,440 sq. km.)
Canada	Ottawa	Occupies the northern part of North America, north of the United States	3,851,810 sq. mi. (9,976,140 sq. km.)
Cape Verde (not on map)	Praia	Islands off the western tip of Africa	1,560 sq. mi. (4,030 sq. km.)
Central African Republic	Bangui	Central Africa, south of Chad	240,530 sq. mi. (622,984 sq. km.)

POPULATION	CURRENCY	LANGUAGE	DID YOU KNOW?
141,340,476	$1 = 58.6 takas	Bangla, English	A cyclone in Bangladesh in 1970 killed an estimated 300,000 people.
278,289	$1 = 1.99 Barbados dollars	English	It's named for its bearded fig trees (from the Spanish *barbados,* 'bearded ones').
10,310,520	$1 = 2,163 rubles	Byelorussian, Russian	Belarussian bibles were some of the first books printed in Eastern Europe.
10,348,276	$1 = .79 euro	Flemish (Dutch), French, German	Brussels sprouts have been grown near Brussels for some 400 years.
272,945	$1 = 1.97 Belize dollars	English, Spanish, Mayan, Garifuna	Belize is Central America's only country without a Pacific coast.
7,250,033	$1 = 529.22 CFA francs	French, Fon, Yoruba	Sandbanks make access to the coast of Benin difficult.
2,185,569	$1 = 47.6 ngultrums	Dzongkha, Tibetan	Traditional clothing in this Buddhist nation has not changed for centuries.
8,724,156	$1 = 7.8 Bolivianos	Spanish, Quechua, Aymara	The country is named after the independence fighter Simón Bolívar.
4,007,608	$1 = 1.56 convertible marks	Serbo-Croatian	The 1914 assassination of an archduke in Sarajevo triggered World War I.
1,561,973	$1 = 4.42 pulas	English, Setswana	The average baby born in Botswana will live about 35 years.
184,101,109	$1 = 2.88 reals	Portuguese, Spanish, English	Brazil produces about 40% of the world's coffee.
365,251	$1 = 1.70 Brunei dollars	Malay, English, Chinese	This leading oil producer is in the Pacific, not the Middle East.
7,517,973	$1 = 1.55 leva	Bulgarian	In 1989, more than 300,000 Turks fled Bulgaria to escape persecution.
13,574,820	$1 = 529.22. CFA francs	French, tribal languages	This nation won independence from France as Upper Volta, in 1947.
6,231,221	$1 = 1,061 francs	Kirundi, French, Swahili	Tutsi-Hutu ethnic violence killed 200,000 Burundians in the 1990s.
13,363,421	$1 = 3,990 riels	Khmer, French	About 90% of the people in this country are Buddhists.
16,063,678	$1 = 529.22 CFA francs	English, French	Cameroon was a German colony from the 1880s to 1919.
32,507,874	$1 = 1.29 Canadian dollars	English, French	In the War of 1812, U.S. forces tried unsuccessfully to invade Canada.
415,294	$1 = 108.95 escudos	Portuguese, Crioulo	These islands were uninhabited when the Portuguese arrived around 1460.
3,742,482	$1 = 529.22 CFA francs	French, Sangho, Arabic, Hunsa, Swahili	Diamonds are the leading export of this developing nation.

Facts About Nations

NATION	CAPITAL	LOCATION OF NATION	AREA
Chad	N'Djamena	North Africa, south of Libya	496,000 sq. mi. (1,284,000 sq. km.)
Chile	Santiago	Along the western coast of South America	292,260 sq. mi. (756,950 sq. km.)
China	Beijing	Occupies most of the mainland of eastern Asia	3,705,410 sq. mi. (9,596,960 sq. km.)
Colombia	Bogotá	Northwestern South America, southeast of Panama	439,740 sq. mi. (1,138,910 sq. km.)
Comoros	Moroni	Islands between Madagascar and the east coast of Africa	840 sq. mi. (2,170 sq. km.)
Congo, Democratic Republic of the	Kinshasa	Central Africa, north of Angola and Zambia	905,570 sq. mi. (2,345,410 sq. km.)
Congo, Republic of the	Brazzaville	Central Africa, east of Gabon	132,000 sq. mi. (342,000 sq. km.)
Costa Rica	San José	Central America, south of Nicaragua	19,700 sq. mi (51,100 sq. km.)
Côte d'Ivoire (Ivory Coast)	Yamoussoukro	West Africa, on the Gulf of Guinea, west of Ghana	124,500 sq. mi. (322,460 sq. km.)
Croatia	Zagreb	Southern Europe, south of Hungary	21,830 sq. mi. (56,540 sq. km.)
Cuba	Havana	In the Caribbean Sea, south of Florida	42,800 sq. mi. (110,860 sq. km.)
Cyprus	Nicosia	Island in the Mediterranean Sea, off the coast of Turkey	3,570 sq. mi. (9,250 sq. km.)
Czech Republic	Prague	Central Europe, south of Poland, east of Germany	30,350 sq. mi. (78,870 sq. km.)
Denmark	Copenhagen	Northern Europe, between the Baltic Sea and North Sea	16,640 sq. mi. (43,090 sq. km.)
Djibouti	Djibouti	North Africa, on the Gulf of Aden, across from Saudi Arabia	8,500 sq. mi. (22,000 sq. km.)
Dominica	Roseau	Island in the Caribbean Sea	290 sq. mi. (750 sq. km.)
Dominican Republic	Santo Domingo	On an island, along with Haiti, in the Caribbean Sea	18,810 sq. mi. (48,730 sq. km.)
East Timor	Dili	Part of an island in the South Pacific Ocean, north of Australia	5,740 sq. mi. (14,880 sq. km.)
Ecuador	Quito	South America, on the equator, bordering the Pacific Ocean	109,480 sq. mi. (283,560 sq. km.)
Egypt	Cairo	Northeastern Africa, on the Red Sea and Mediterranean Sea	386,660 sq. mi. (1,001,450 sq. km.)

POPULATION	CURRENCY	LANGUAGE	DID YOU KNOW?
9,538,544	$1 = 529.22 CFA francs	French, Arabic, Sara, Sango	Chad has cave paintings that are over 5,000 years old.
15,827,180	$1 = 585.48 pesos	Spanish	This "Shoestring Republic" is 2,650 mi. long but an average of 110 mi. wide.
1,294,629,555	$1 = 8.28 yuan	Mandarin, Yue, Wu, Hakka	The Great Wall of China once extended some 1,500 miles.
42,310,775	$1 = 2,777 pesos	Spanish	This is the only South American country with Caribbean and Pacific coasts.
651,901	$1 = 454.33 francs	Arabic, French, Comorian	Comoros is made up of mountainous islands of volcanic origin.
58,317,930	$1 = 529.22 CFA francs	French	The former "Belgian" Congo lies east of Republic of the Congo.
2,998,040	$1 = 529.22 CFA francs	French, Lingala, Kikongo	Most people live in cities or towns; the rain forests are largely uninhabited.
3,956,507	$1 = 418.67 colones	Spanish	An early Spanish explorer gave Costa Rica its name, which means "rich coast."
17,327,724	$1 = 529.22 CFA francs	French, Dioula	This nation is the world's leading producer of cocoa beans.
4,435,960	$1 = 6.08 kunas	Serbo-Croatian	Croatia was part of Yugoslavia until declaring independence in 1991.
11,308,764	$1 = 1 peso	Spanish	Cuba's 2-inch-long bee hummingbird is the world's smallest bird.
775,927	$1 = .47 pound	Greek, Turkish, English	Cyprus is divided into Greek and Turkish areas.
10,246,178	$1 = 25.65 koruny	Czech, Slovak	Prague is home to Europe's oldest synagogue (c. 1270).
5,413,392	$1 = 5.91 kroner	Danish, Faroese	Legos (from the Danish *Leg Godt*—"play well") come from Denmark.
466,900	$1 = 175 Djibouti francs	French, Arabic, Afar, Somali	French colonizers started building Djibouti City, now the capital, in 1888.
69,278	$1 = 2.67 EC dollars	English, French patois	Banana plantations are vital to Dominica's economy.
8,833,634	$1 = 33.95 pesos	Spanish	U.S. Marines occupied this nation (1916-24) and intervened in 1965.
1,019,252	U.S. dollar	Tetum, Portuguese, Indonesian, English	During Indonesia's 25-year occupation, 25% of the population may have died.
13,971,798	U.S. dollar	Spanish, Quechua	Quito is the oldest capital city in South America.
76,117,421	$1 = 6.18 pounds	Arabic, English, French	About 20,000 ships go through Egypt's Suez Canal each year.

Facts About Nations

NATION	CAPITAL	LOCATION OF NATION	AREA
El Salvador	San Salvador	Central America, southwest of Honduras	8,120 sq. mi. (21,040 sq. km.)
Equatorial Guinea	Malabo	West Africa, on the Gulf of Guinea, off the west coast of Cameroon	10,830 sq. mi. (28,050 sq. km.)
Eritrea	Asmara	Northeast Africa, north of Ethiopia	46,840 sq. mi. (121,320 sq. km.)
Estonia	Tallinn	Northern Europe, on the Baltic Sea, north of Latvia	17,460 sq. mi. (45,230 sq. km.)
Ethiopia	Addis Ababa	East Africa, east of Sudan	435,190 sq. mi. (1,127,130 sq. km.)
Fiji	Suva	Islands in the South Pacific Ocean, east of Australia	7,050 sq. mi. (18,270 sq. km.)
Finland	Helsinki	Northern Europe, between Sweden and Russia	130,130 sq. mi. (337,030 sq. km.)
France	Paris	Western Europe, between Germany and Spain	211,210 sq. mi. (547,030 sq. km.)
Gabon	Libreville	Central Africa, on the Atlantic coast, south of Cameroon	103,350 sq. mi. (267,670 sq. km.)
The Gambia	Banjul	West Africa, on the Atlantic Ocean, surrounded by Senegal	4,400 sq. mi. (11,300 sq. km.)
Georgia	Tbilisi	Western Asia, south of Russia, on the Black Sea	26,900 sq. mi. (69,700 sq. km.)
Germany	Berlin	Central Europe, northeast of France	137,890 sq. mi. (357,020 sq. km.)
Ghana	Accra	West Africa, on the southern coast	92,100 sq. mi. (238,540 sq. km.)
Greece	Athens	Southern Europe, in the southern part of the Balkan Peninsula	50,940 sq. mi. (131,940 sq. km.)
Grenada	Saint George's	Island on the eastern edge of the Caribbean Sea	130 sq. mi. (340 sq. km.)
Guatemala	Guatemala City	Central America, southeast of Mexico	42,040 sq. mi. (108,890 sq. km.)
Guinea	Conakry	West Africa, on the Atlantic Ocean, north of Sierra Leone	94,930 sq. mi. (245,860 sq. km.)
Guinea-Bissau	Bissau	West Africa, on the Atlantic Ocean, south of Senegal	13,950 sq. mi. (36,120 sq. km.)
Guyana	Georgetown	South America, on the northern coast, east of Venezuela	83,000 sq. mi. (214,970 sq. km.)
Haiti	Port-au-Prince	On an island, along with Dominican Republic, in the Caribbean Sea	10,710 sq. mi. (27,750 sq. km.)

POPULATION	CURRENCY	LANGUAGE	DID YOU KNOW?
6,587,541	$1 = 8.75 colones	Spanish	*Casamiento,* a mixture of rice and beans, is a common everyday food.
523,051	$1 = 529.22 CFA francs	Spanish, French, Fang, Bubi	Equatorial Guinea won independence from Spain in 1968.
4,447,307	$1 = 9.24 nakfa	Tigrinya, Tigre, Kunama, Afar	Once an Italian colony, Eritrea was occupied by Britain in World War II.
1,401,945	$1 = 12.42 krooni	Estonian, Russian	Estonia and its Baltic neighbors split from the Soviet Union in 1991.
67,851,281	$1 = 8.55 birr	Amharic, Tigrinya, Orominga	Ethiopian runners have won the Olympic marathon race 4 times.
880,874	$1 = 1.71 Fiji dollars	English, Fijian, Hindustani	Wearing a hat is a sign of disrespect in Fijian culture.
5,214,512	$1 = .79 euro	Finnish, Swedish	Tarja Halonen, Finland's first woman president, took office in 2000.
60,424,213	$1 = .79 euro	French	France produces over 360 kinds of cheese, from cows, goats, and sheep.
1,355,246	$1 = 529.22 CFA francs	French, Bantu dialects	Libreville (French for "freetown") was founded in 1849 for freed slaves.
1,546,848	$1 = 30 dalasi	English, Mandinka, Wolof	This narrow nation lies along both banks of the lower Gambia River.
4,909,633	$1 = 2.03 laris	Georgian, Russian	In 2004, the Georgian parliament adopted a new national flag.
82,424,609	$1 = .79 euro	German	Aside from Russia, Germany is the most populous country in Europe.
20,757,032	$1 = 8,650 cedis	English, Akan, Ewe, Moshi-Dagomba, Ga	Led by Kwame Nkrumah, Ghana won independence in 1957.
10,647,529	$1 = .79 euro	Greek, English, French	Athens is the site of the 2004 Summer Olympics.
89,357	$1 = 2.67 EC dollars	English, French patois	Grenada is the 2nd-largest producer of nutmeg, after Indonesia.
14,280,596	$1 = 8.02 quetzals	Spanish, Mayan languages	There are 23 Amerindian dialects spoken in Guatemala.
9,246,462	$1 = 2,005 francs	French, tribal languages	Common animals in Guinea include parrots, snakes, and crocodiles.
1,388,363	$1 = 529.22 CFA francs	Portuguese, Crioulo	At carnival time people wear masks of sharks, hippos, and bulls.
705,803	$1 = 179 Guyana dollars	English, Amerindian dialects	Dense forest makes up about 75% of this sparsely populated country.
7,656,166	$1 = 40 gourdes	Haitian Creole, French	In 2004, President Aristide left Haiti during an armed rebellion.

Facts About Nations

NATION	CAPITAL	LOCATION OF NATION	AREA
Honduras	Tegucigalpa	Central America, between Guatemala and Nicaragua	43,280 sq. mi. (112,090 sq. km.)
Hungary	Budapest	Central Europe, north of Serbia & Montenegro	35,920 sq. mi. (93,030 sq. km.)
Iceland	Reykjavik	Island off the coast of Europe, in the North Atlantic Ocean	40,000 sq. mi. (103,000 sq. km.)
India	New Delhi	Southern Asia, on a large peninsula on the Indian Ocean	1,269,350 sq. mi. (3,287,590 sq. km.)
Indonesia	Jakarta	Islands south of Southeast Asia, along the equator	705,190 sq. mi. (1,826,440 sq. km.)
Iran	Tehran	Southern Asia, between Iraq and Pakistan	636,000 sq. mi. (1,648,000 sq. km.)
Iraq	Baghdad	In the Middle East, between Syria and Iran	168,750 sq. mi. (437,070 sq. km.)
Ireland	Dublin	Off Europe's coast, in the Atlantic Ocean, west of Great Britain	27,140 sq. mi. (70,280 sq. km.)
Israel	Jerusalem	In the Middle East, between Jordan and the Mediterranean Sea	8,020 sq. mi. (20,770 sq. km.)
Italy	Rome	Southern Europe, jutting out into the Mediterranean Sea	116,310 sq. mi. (301,230 sq. km.)
Jamaica	Kingston	Island in the Caribbean Sea, south of Cuba	4,240 sq. mi. (10,990 sq. km.)
Japan	Tokyo	Four big islands and many small ones, off the east coast of Asia	145,880 sq. mi. (377,840 sq. km.)
Jordan	Amman	In the Middle East, south of Syria, east of Israel	35,300 sq. mi. (91,540 sq. km.)
Kazakhstan	Astana	Central Asia, south of Russia	1,049,200 sq. mi. (2,717,300 sq. km.)
Kenya	Nairobi	East Africa, on the Indian Ocean, south of Ethiopia	224,960 sq. mi. (582,650 sq. km.)
Kiribati	Tarawa	Islands in the middle of the Pacific Ocean, near the equator	280 sq. mi. (720 sq. km.)
Korea, North	Pyongyang	Eastern Asia, in the northern part of the Korean Peninsula	46,540 sq. mi. (120,540 sq. km.)
Korea, South	Seoul	Eastern Asia, south of North Korea, on the Korean Peninsula	38,020 sq. mi. (98,480 sq. km.)
Kuwait	Kuwait City	In the Middle East, on the northern end of the Persian Gulf	6,880 sq. mi. (17,820 sq. km.)
Kyrgyzstan	Bishkek	Western Asia, between Kazakhstan and Tajikistan	76,600 sq. mi. (198,500 sq. km.)

OPULATION	CURRENCY	LANGUAGE	DID YOU KNOW?
6,823,568	$1 = 17.74 lempiras	Spanish	The marimba is Honduras's most popular musical instrument.
10,032,375	$1 = 207.60 forints	Hungarian (Magyar)	Hungary is a little smaller than the state of Indiana
282,151	$1 = 70.94 kronur	Icelandic (Islenska)	85% of Iceland's homes are heated by underground (geothermal) energy.
1,065,070,607	$1 = 45.64 rupees	Hindi, English	India has more people than the next 5 biggest countries combined.
238,452,952	$1 = 8,453 rupiah	Bahasa Indonesian, English, Dutch	Indonesia has 17,000 islands, but only 6,000 are inhabited.
69,018,924	$1 = 8,301 rials	Persian (Farsi), Turkic, Luri	Until the 1930s Iran was known as Persia.
25,374,691	In transition	Arabic, Kurdish	The ancient Sumerians invented cuneiform, an early form of writing.
3,969,558	$1 = .79 euro	English, Gaelic	Ireland is known as the "emerald isle," for its brilliant green grass.
6,199,008	$1 = 4.40 new shekels	Hebrew, Arabic, English	Israel signed a peace treaty with Egypt in 1979, its first with an Arab nation.
58,057,477	$1 = .79 euro	Italian, German, French, Slovene	The Renaissance, the 15th-16th-century revival of learning, began in Italy.
2,713,130	$1 = 59.80 Jamaican dollars	English, Jamaican, Creole	Reggae, a mixture of native, rock, and soul music, is from Jamaica.
127,333,002	$1 = 106.95 yen	Japanese	Japan is in one of earth's most active earthquake zones.
5,611,202	$1 = .71 dinar	Arabic, English	Philadelphia was the ancient name for Amman, Jordan's modern capital.
16,798,552	$1 = 143.26 tenges	Kazakh, Russian	Kazakhstan is the 9th-largest country in land area.
32,021,856	$1 = 76.10 shillings	Swahili, English	The Kenyan Highlands are one of the most productive agricultural regions in Africa.
100,798	$1 = 1.32 Australian dollars	English, Gilbertese	The island of Tarawa was the scene of fierce fighting in World War II.
22,697,553	$1 = 2.2 won	Korean	Settled in 1122 B.C., Pyongyang is the oldest city on the Korean Peninsula.
48,598,175	$1 = 1,195 won	Korean	The Korean language is written in Han'gul, a language script created in the 1400s.
2,257,549	$1 = .29 dinar	Arabic, English	The 1991 Gulf War freed Kuwait from Iraqi forces that had invaded in 1990.
4,965,081	$1 = 40.91 soms	Kyrgyz, Russian	This Central Asian country is almost entirely mountainous.

Facts About Nations

NATION	CAPITAL	LOCATION OF NATION	AREA
Laos	Vientiane	Southeast Asia, between Vietnam and Thailand	91,400 sq. mi. (236,800 sq. km.)
Latvia	Riga	On the Baltic Sea, between Lithuania and Estonia	24,900 sq. mi. (64,590 sq. km.)
Lebanon	Beirut	In the Middle East, between the Mediterranean Sea and Syria	4,000 sq. mi. (10,400 sq. km.)
Lesotho	Maseru	Southern Africa, surrounded by the nation of South Africa	11,720 sq. mi. (30,350 sq. km.)
Liberia	Monrovia	Western Africa, on the Atlantic Ocean, southeast of Sierra Leone	43,000 sq. mi. (111,370 sq. km.)
Libya	Tripoli	North Africa, on the Mediterranean Sea, to the west of Egypt	679,360 sq. mi. (1,759,540 sq. km.)
Liechtenstein	Vaduz	Southern Europe, in the Alps between Austria and Switzerland	60 sq. mi. (160 sq. km.)
Lithuania	Vilnius	Northern Europe, on the Baltic Sea, east of Poland	25,200 sq. mi. (65,200 sq. km.)
Luxembourg	Luxembourg	Western Europe, between France and Germany	1,000 sq. mi. (2,590 sq. km.)
Macedonia	Skopje	Southern Europe, north of Greece	9,780 sq. mi. (25,330 sq. km.)
Madagascar	Antananarivo	Island in the Indian Ocean, off the east coast of Africa	226,660 sq. mi. (587,040 sq. km.)
Malawi	Lilongwe	Southern Africa, south of Tanzania and east of Zambia	45,750 sq. mi. (118,480 sq. km.)
Malaysia	Kuala Lumpur	Southeast tip of Asia and the north coast of the island of Borneo	127,320 sq. mi. (329,750 sq. km.)
Maldives	Male	Islands in the Indian Ocean, south of India	115 sq. mi. (300 sq. km.)
Mali	Bamako	West Africa, between Algeria and Mauritania	480,000 sq. mi. (1,240,000 sq. km.)
Malta	Valletta	Island in the Mediterranean Sea, south of Italy	120 sq. mi. (320 sq. km.)
Marshall Islands	Majuro	Chain of small islands in the middle of the Pacific Ocean	70 sq. mi. (181 sq. km.)
Mauritania	Nouakchott	West Africa, on the Atlantic Ocean, north of Senegal	398,000 sq. mi. (1,030,700 sq. km.)
Mauritius (not on map)	Port Louis	Islands in the Indian Ocean, east of Madagascar	720 sq. mi. (1,860 sq. km.)
Mexico	Mexico City	North America, south of the United States	761,610 sq. mi. (1,972,550 sq. km.)

POPULATION	CURRENCY	LANGUAGE	DID YOU KNOW?
6,068,117	$1 = 7,882 kips	Lao, French, English	In the 1300s, Laos was named the Kingdom of the Million Elephants.
2,332,078	$1 = .53 lat	Lettish, Lithuanian	Riga Castle, now the residence of Latvia's president, dates from 1330.
3,777,218	$1 = 1,514 pounds	Arabic, French, English, Armenian	The Ottoman Turks ruled Lebanon for 400 years until World War I.
1,865,040	$1 = 6.65 maloti	English, Sesotho	Diamonds are Lesotho's chief export.
3,390,635	Same value as U.S. dollar	English, tribal languages	Liberia's capital, Monrovia, is named for U.S. President James Monroe.
5,631,585	$1 = 1.35 dinars	Arabic, Italian, English	In late 2003 Libya agreed to abandon efforts to make atomic weapons.
33,436	$1 = 1.24 Swiss francs	German, Alemanic dialect	The postal system in this tiny country is administered by Switzerland.
3,584,836	$1 = 2.74 litas	Lithuanian, Polish, Russian	Russians are Lithuania's largest ethnic minority.
462,690	$1 = .79 euro	French, German	Four Holy Roman emperors came from this tiny duchy.
2,071,210	$1 = 49.24 denars	Macedonian, Albanian	Skopje was rebuilt after an earthquake in 1963 destroyed over half of the city.
17,501,871	$1 = 5,710 Malagasy francs	Malagasy, French	The island is home to the lemur, one of its many unique wild animals.
11,906,855	$1 = 107.2 kwachas	English, Chichewa	Malawi is one of Africa's most densely populated countries.
23,522,482	$1 = 3.8 ringgits	Malay, English, Chinese dialects	Malaysia's animal life includes elephants, tigers, and orangutans.
339,330	$1 = 12.8 rufiyaa	Maldivian, Divehi, English	The inhabitants were converted to Islam in A.D. 1153.
11,956,788	$1 = 529.22 CFA francs	French, Bambara	Timbuktu was a great learning center in the 15th and 16th centuries.
403,342	$1 = .34 lira	Maltese, English	Valletta is a 16th-century fortress-city built by the Knights of St. John.
57,738	U.S. dollar	English, Marshallese	Bikini Atoll, where the first hydrogen bomb was tested, is here.
2,998,563	$1 = 257 ouguiyas	Hasaniya Arabic, Wolof, Pular	About 40% of Mauritania's land area is covered by sand.
1,220,481	$1 = 26.15 Mauritian rupees	English, French, Creole, Hindi	The dodo became extinct here by 1681, 83 years after the Dutch arrived.
104,959,594	$1 = 11.08 new pesos	Spanish, Mayan dialects	The Aztec capital of Tenochtitlan was destroyed by the Spanish in 1521.

Facts About Nations

NATION	CAPITAL	LOCATION OF NATION	AREA
Micronesia	Palikir	Islands in the western Pacific Ocean	270 sq. mi. (700 sq. km.)
Moldova	Chisinau	Eastern Europe, between Ukraine and Romania	13,000 sq. mi. (33,700 sq. km.)
Monaco	Monaco	Europe, on the Mediterranean Sea, surrounded by France	3/4 of a sq. mi. (2 sq. km.)
Mongolia	Ulaanbaatar	Central Asia between Russia and China	604,000 sq. mi. (1,565,000 sq. km.)
Morocco	Rabat	Northwest Africa, on the Atlantic Ocean and Mediterranean Sea	172,410 sq. mi. (446,550 sq. km.)
Mozambique	Maputo	Southeastern Africa, on the Indian Ocean	309,500 sq. mi. (801,590 sq. km.)
Myanmar (Burma)	Yangon (Rangoon)	Southern Asia, to the east of India and Bangladesh	262,000 sq. mi. (678,500 sq. km.)
Namibia	Windhoek	Southwestern Africa, on the Atlantic Ocean, west of Botswana	318,700 sq. mi. (825,420 sq. km.)
Nauru	Yaren district	Island in the western Pacific Ocean, just below the equator	8 sq. mi. (21 sq. km.)
Nepal	Kathmandu	Asia, in the Himalaya Mountains, between China and India	54,400 sq. mi. (140,800 sq. km.)
Netherlands	Amsterdam	Northern Europe, on the North Sea, to the west of Germany	16,030 sq. mi. (41,530 sq. km.)
New Zealand	Wellington	Islands in the Pacific Ocean east of Australia	103,740 sq. mi. (268,680 sq. km.)
Nicaragua	Managua	Central America, between Honduras and Costa Rica	50,000 sq. mi. (129,490 sq. km.)
Niger	Niamey	North Africa, south of Algeria and Libya	489,000 sq. mi. (1,267,000 sq. km.)
Nigeria	Abuja	West Africa, on the southern coast between Benin and Cameroon	356,670 sq. mi. (923,770 sq. km.)
Norway	Oslo	Northern Europe, on the Scandinavian Peninsula	125,180 sq. mi. (324,220 sq. km.)
Oman	Muscat	On the Arabian Peninsula, southeast of Saudi Arabia	82,030 sq. mi. (212,460 sq. km.)
Pakistan	Islamabad	South Asia, between Iran and India	310,400 sq. mi. (803,940 sq. km.)
Palau	Koror	Islands in North Pacific Ocean, southeast of Philippines	180 sq. mi. (460 sq. km.)
Panama	Panama City	Central America, between Costa Rica and Colombia	30,200 sq. mi. (78,200 sq. km.)

POPULATION	CURRENCY	LANGUAGE	DID YOU KNOW?
108,155	U.S. dollar	English, Trukese, Pohnpeian, Yapese	Micronesia is made up of more than 600 islands and islets.
4,446,455	$1 = 13.1 lei	Moldovan, Russian	Grapes are a major crop, and winemaking is a major industry.
32,270	$1 = .79 euro	French, English, Italian	Monaco is the most densely populated country in the world.
2,751,314	$1 = 1,126 tugriks	Khalkha Mongolian	Mongolia is the most thinly populated country in the world.
32,209,101	$1 = 8.77 dirhams	Arabic, Berber dialects	Casablanca is Morocco's largest city and main seaport.
18,811,731	$1 = 23,120 meticals	Portuguese, native dialects	Decades of civil war have left over a million land mines buried here.
42,720,196	$1 = 6.42 kyats	Burmese	More than 100 native languages are spoken in Myanmar.
1,954,033	$1 = 6.67 dollars	Afrikaans, English, German	Windhoek is situated on a plateau more than a mile above sea level.
12,809	$1 = 1.32 Australian dollars	Nauruan, English	Phosphates, from millions of years of bird droppings, are nearly used up.
27,070,666	$1 = 73 rupees	Nepali, many dialects	Mt. Everest, the world's highest mountain, is partly in Nepal.
16,318,199	$1 = .79 euro	Dutch	Nowadays in the Netherlands, wooden shoes are worn mostly by farmers.
3,993,817	$1 = 1.52 NZ dollars	English, Maori	New Zealand was the first country to grant women full voting rights (1893).
5,232,216	$1 = 15.43 gold cordobas	Spanish	The eastern shore is called Costa de Mosquitos (Mosquito Coast).
11,360,538	$1 = 529.22 CFA francs	French, Hausa, Djerma	Temperatures can exceed 122° F in the hot season, from March to June.
137,253,133	$1 = 139.05 nairas	English, Hausa, Yoruba, Ibo	Nigeria is the biggest oil-producing country in Africa.
4,574,560	$1 = 6.67 kroner	Norwegian	The UN ranks Norway as the world's top country in "quality of life."
2,903,165	$1 = .39 rial Omani	Arabic	Oman has about 13 males for every 10 females.
153,705,278	$1 = 57.24 rupees	Urdu, English, Punjabi, Sindhi	Lahore was capital of the Mughal Empire in India from 1584 to 1598.
20,016	U.S. dollar	English, Palauan	The islands of Palau are old coral reefs that have risen above the sea.
3,000,463	$1 = 1 balboa	Spanish, English	Richard Halliburton swam the Panama Canal in 1928, paying a toll of 36 cents.

Facts About Nations

NATION	CAPITAL	LOCATION OF NATION	AREA
Papua New Guinea	Port Moresby	Part of the island of New Guinea, north of Australia	178,700 sq. mi. (462,840 sq. km.)
Paraguay	Asunción	South America, between Argentina and Brazil	157,050 sq. mi. (406,750 sq. km.)
Peru	Lima	South America, along the Pacific coast, north of Chile	496,230 sq. mi. (1,285,220 sq. km.)
Philippines	Manila	Islands in the Pacific Ocean, off the coast of Southeast Asia	115,830 sq. mi. (300,000 sq. km.)
Poland	Warsaw	Central Europe, on the Baltic Sea, east of Germany	120,730 sq. mi. (312,680 sq. km.)
Portugal	Lisbon	Southern Europe, on the Iberian Peninsula, west of Spain	35,670 sq. mi. (92,390 sq. km.)
Qatar	Doha	Arabian Peninsula, on the Persian Gulf	4,420 sq. mi. (11,440 sq. km.)
Romania	Bucharest	Southern Europe, on the Black Sea, north of Bulgaria	91,700 sq. mi. (237,500 sq. km.)
Russia	Moscow	Stretches from Eastern Europe across northern Asia to the Pacific Ocean	6,592,800 sq. mi. (17,075,200 sq. km.)
Rwanda	Kigali	Central Africa, northwest of Tanzania	10,170 sq. mi. (26,340 sq. km.)
Saint Kitts and Nevis	Basseterre	Islands in the Caribbean Sea, near Puerto Rico	100 sq. mi. (260 sq. km.)
Saint Lucia	Castries	Island on eastern edge of the Caribbean Sea	240 sq. mi. (620 sq. km.)
Saint Vincent and the Grenadines	Kingstown	Islands on eastern edge of the Caribbean Sea, north of Grenada	150 sq. mi. (390 sq. km.)
Samoa (formerly Western Samoa)	Apia	Islands in the South Pacific Ocean	1,100 sq. mi. (2,860 sq. km.)
San Marino	San Marino	Southern Europe, surrounded by Italy	23 sq. mi. (60 sq. km.)
São Tomé and Príncipe	São Tomé	In the Gulf of Guinea, off the coast of West Africa	390 sq. mi. (1,000 sq. km.)
Saudi Arabia	Riyadh	Western Asia, occupying most of the Arabian Peninsula	756,990 sq. mi. (1,960,580 sq. km.)
Senegal	Dakar	West Africa, on the Atlantic Ocean, south of Mauritania	75,750 sq. mi. (196,190 sq. km.)
Serbia and Montenegro	Belgrade, Podgorica	Europe, on Balkan Peninsula, west of Romania and Bulgaria	39,520 sq. mi. (102,350 sq. km.)
Seychelles (not on map)	Victoria	Islands off the coast of Africa, in the Indian Ocean	180 sq. mi. (460 sq. km.)

POPULATION	CURRENCY	LANGUAGE	DID YOU KNOW?
5,420,280	$1 = 3.27 kinas	English, Motu	Wild animals here include the tree kangaroo, wallaby, wild pig, and dingo.
6,191,368	$1 = 5,975 guarani	Spanish, Guarani	The Itaipú dam is the world's biggest hydroelectric plant.
28,863,494	$1 = 3.46 new soles	Spanish, Quechua, Aymara	The warm ocean current known as El Niño appears every few years off Peru.
86,241,697	$1 = 55.49 pesos	Pilipino, English	Most Filipinos live on the 11 largest of the country's 7,100 islands.
38,626,349	$1 = 3.72 zlotys	Polish	Pope John Paul II was born in Poland in 1920.
10,119,250	$1 = .79 euro	Portuguese	Port wine is named for Oporto, Portugal's second largest city.
840,290	$1 = 3.64 riyals	Arabic, English	The government gets 90% of its revenue from selling oil.
22,355,551	$1 = 32,651 lei	Romanian, Hungarian	The Danube Delta is Europe's youngest land geologically.
144,112,353	$1 = 29.24 rubles	Russian, many others	Record lows of −90° F have been recorded in the region of Siberia.
7,954,013	$1 = 556.55 francs	French, English, Kinyarwanda	The source of the Nile River has been located in Rwanda.
38,836	$1 = 2.67 EC dollars	English	St. Kitts was the first island in the West Indies settled by the British, in 1623.
164,213	$1 = 2.67 EC dollars	English, French patois	The island switched hands between the British and French 14 times.
117,193	$1 = 2.67 EC dollars	English, French patois	Black Caribs living here are descended from slaves and native Indians.
177,714	$1 = 2.78 tala	English, Samoan	Most Samoans live in small seashore villages of 100-500 people.
28,503	$1 = .79 euro	Italian	San Marino claims to be Europe's oldest country, founded in A.D. 301.
181,565	$1 = 8,700 dobras	Portuguese	Portugal ruled these islands for nearly 300 years—until 1975.
25,100,425	$1 = 3.75 riyals	Arabic	Mecca, the birthplace of Muhammad, is the holiest city of Islam.
10,852,147	$1 = 529.22 CFA francs	French, Wolof	Senegal is among the world's largest producers of peanuts.
10,663,022	$1 = 54.29 new dinars	Serbo-Croatian, Albanian	Ruins of the Roman town of Singidunum can still be seen in Belgrade.
80,832	$1 = 5.18 rupees	English, French, Creole	This group of about 115 islands is the smallest country in Africa.

Facts About Nations

NATION	CAPITAL	LOCATION OF NATION	AREA
Sierra Leone	Freetown	West Africa, on the Atlantic Ocean, south of Guinea	27,700 sq. mi. (71,740 sq. km.)
Singapore	Singapore	Mostly on one island, off the tip of Southeast Asia	250 sq. mi. (650 sq. km.)
Slovakia	Bratislava	Eastern Europe, between Poland and Hungary	18,860 sq. mi. (48,850 sq. km.)
Slovenia	Ljubljana	Eastern Europe, between Austria and Croatia	7,820 sq. mi. (20,250 sq. km.)
Solomon Islands	Honiara	Western Pacific Ocean	10,980 sq. mi. (28,450 sq. km.)
Somalia	Mogadishu	East Africa, east of Ethiopia	246,200 sq. mi. (637,660 sq. km.)
South Africa	Pretoria (admin.) Cape Town (legisl.)	At the southern tip of Africa	471,010 sq. mi. (1,219,910 sq. km.)
Spain	Madrid	Europe, south of France, on the Iberian Peninsula	194,890 sq. mi. (504,780 sq. km.)
Sri Lanka	Colombo	Island in the Indian Ocean, southeast of India	25,330 sq. mi. (65,610 sq. km.)
Sudan	Khartoum	North Africa, south of Egypt, on the Red Sea	967,500 sq. mi. (2,505,810 sq. km.)
Suriname	Paramaribo	South America, on the northern shore, east of Guyana	63,040 sq. mi. (163,270 sq. km.)
Swaziland	Mbabane	Southern Africa, almost surrounded by South Africa	6,700 sq. mi. (17,360 sq. km.)
Sweden	Stockholm	Northern Europe, on the Scandinavian Peninsula	173,730 sq. mi. (449,960 sq. km.)
Switzerland	Bern (admin.) Lausanne (judicial)	Central Europe, in the Alps, north of Italy	15,940 sq. mi. (41,290 sq. km.)
Syria	Damascus	In the Middle East, north of Jordan and west of Iraq	71,500 sq. mi. (185,180 sq. km.)
Taiwan	Taipei	Island off southeast coast of China	13,890 sq. mi. (35,980 sq. km.)
Tajikistan	Dushanbe	Asia, west of China, south of Kyrgyzstan	55,300 sq. mi. (143,100 sq. km.)
Tanzania	Dar-es-Salaam	East Africa, on the Indian Ocean, south of Kenya	364,900 sq. mi. (945,090 sq. km.)
Thailand	Bangkok	Southeast Asia, south of Laos	198,000 sq. mi. (514,000 sq. km.)
Togo	Lomé	West Africa, between Ghana and Benin	21,930 sq. mi. (56,790 sq. km.)

POPULATION	CURRENCY	LANGUAGE	DID YOU KNOW?
5,883,889	$1 = 2,450 leones	English, Mende, Temne, Krio	Crocodiles and hippos are found in the rivers of Sierra Leone.
4,767,974	$1 = 1.70 Singapore dollars	Chinese, Malay, Tamil, English	Singapore is the world's 2nd most densely populated country.
5,423,567	$1 = 32.68 koruny	Slovak, Hungarian	Bratislava served as the capital of Hungary from 1541 to 1784.
1,938,282	$1 = 188.05 tolars	Slovenian, Serbo-Croatian	Slovenia escaped the violence that affected Yugoslavia in the 1990s.
523,617	$1 = 7.49 Solomon dollars	English, Melanesian	Guadalcanal, one of the islands, was the site of a key World War II battle.
8,304,601	$1 = 2,620 shillings	Somali, Arabic, Italian, English	Thirty U.S. soldiers died here during UN peacekeeping work (1992-94).
42,718,530	$1 = 6.54 rand	Afrikaans, English, Ndebele, Sotho	South Africa has a total of 11 official languages, 9 of them native.
40,280,780	$1 = .79 euro	Castilian Spanish, Catalan, Galician	Spanish rulers grew rich in the 1500s from New World gold and silver.
19,905,165	$1 = 97.2 rupees	Sinhala, Tamil, English	Sri Lanka had the world's first elected female prime minister (1960).
39,148,162	$1 = 260.45 dinars	Arabic, Nubian, Ta Bedawie	Sudan is the largest country in Africa in total area.
436,935	$1 = 2,515 guilders	Dutch, Sranang Tongo	In 1677, Britain "traded" Suriname to the Dutch for New York City.
1,169,241	$1 = 6.64 lilangeni	English, siSwati	4 out of 10 adults in Swaziland have the AIDS virus.
8,986,400	$1 = 7.18 kronor	Swedish	One of the world's oldest parliaments, the Riksdag dates back to 1435.
7,450,867	$1 = 1.24 francs	German, French, Italian, Romansch	Switzerland has not fought in a foreign war since 1515.
18,016,874	$1 = 48.83 pounds	Arabic, Kurdish, Armenian	Damascus may be the world's oldest continuously occupied city.
22,749,838	$1 = 33.93 new Taiwan dollars	Mandarin Chinese, Taiwanese	Anti-Communists founded this "Republic of China" in 1949.
7,011,556	$1 = 2.68 somoni	Tajik, Russian	Dust can take up to 10 days to settle after a strong dust storm here.
36,588,225	$1 = 1,057 shillings	Swahili, English	Tanganyika and Zanzibar joined to form Tanzania in 1964.
64,865,523	$1 = 39.56 bahts	Thai, English	Thailand is the world's largest exporter of rice and farmed shrimp.
5,556,812	$1 = 529.22 CFA francs	French, Ewe, Kabye	About 70% of Togolese people practice traditional African religions.

Facts About Nations

NATION	CAPITAL	LOCATION OF NATION	AREA
Tonga	Nuku'alofa	Islands in the South Pacific Ocean	290 sq. mi. (750 sq. km.)
Trinidad and Tobago	Port-of-Spain	Islands off the north coast of South America	1,980 sq. mi. (5,130 sq. km.)
Tunisia	Tunis	North Africa, on the Mediterranean, between Algeria and Libya	63,170 sq. mi. (163,610 sq. km.)
Turkey	Ankara	On the southern shore of the Black Sea, partly in Europe and partly in Asia	301,380 sq. mi. (780,580 sq. km.)
Turkmenistan	Ashgabat	Western Asia, north of Afghanistan and Iran	188,500 sq. mi. (488,100 sq. km.)
Tuvalu	Funafuti Atoll	Chain of islands in the South Pacific Ocean	10 sq. mi. (26 sq. km.)
Uganda	Kampala	East Africa, south of Sudan	91,140 sq. mi. (236,040 sq. km.)
Ukraine	Kiev	Eastern Europe, south of Belarus and Russia	233,100 sq. mi. (603,700 sq. km.)
United Arab Emirates	Abu Dhabi	Arabian Peninsula, on the Persian Gulf	32,000 sq. mi. (82,880 sq. km.)
United Kingdom (Great Britain)	London	Off the northwest coast of Europe	94,530 sq. mi. (244,820 sq. km.)
United States	Washington, D.C.	In North America; 48 of 50 states between Canada and Mexico	3,717,810 sq. mi. (9,629,090 sq. km.)
Uruguay	Montevideo	South America, on the Atlantic Ocean, south of Brazil	68,040 sq. mi. (176,220 sq. km.)
Uzbekistan	Tashkent	Central Asia, south of Kazakhstan	172,740 sq. mi. (447,400 sq. km.)
Vanuatu	Port-Vila	Islands in the South Pacific Ocean	5,700 sq. mi. (14,760 sq. km.)
Vatican City		Surrounded by the city of Rome, Italy	1/5 sq. mi. (1/2 sq. km.)
Venezuela	Caracas	On the northern coast of South America, east of Colombia	352,140 sq. mi. (912,050 sq. km.)
Vietnam	Hanoi	Southeast Asia, south of China, on the eastern coast	127,240 sq. mi. (329,560 sq. km.)
Yemen	Sanaa	Asia, on the southern coast of the Arabian Peninsula	203,850 sq. mi. (527,970 sq. km.)
Zambia	Lusaka	Southern Africa, east of Angola	290,580 sq. mi. (752,610 sq. km.)
Zimbabwe	Harare	Southern Africa, south of Zambia	150,800 sq. mi. (390,580 sq. km.)

POPULATION	CURRENCY	LANGUAGE	DID YOU KNOW?
110,237	$1 = 2.01 pa'angas	Tongan, English	Tonga is ruled by a King and a prime minister he appoints for life.
1,096,585	$1 = 6.15 Trinidad dollars	English, Hindi, French, Spanish	East Indians, who came here in the 1800s, make up 40% of the population.
10,032,050	$1 = 1.21 dinar	Arabic, French	Pirates from Tunisia roamed the seas until the early 1800s.
68,893,918	$1 = 1,388,889 Turkish liras	Turkish, Kurdish, Arabic	More than 20 of Turkey's mountains are higher than 10,000 ft.
4,863,169	$1 = 4,743.35 manats	Turkmen, Russian, Uzbek	Turkmen are famed for the beautiful carpets they weave from sheep wool.
11,468	$1 = 1.32 Australian dollars	Tuvaluan, English	These low-lying islands are threatened by rising sea levels.
26,404,543	$1 = 1,888 shillings	English, Luganda, Swahili	Bwindi Impenetrable National Park is home to endangered mountain gorillas.
47,732,079	$1 = 5.33 hryvnia	Ukrainian, Russian	In the 1840s, Russian rulers banned the Ukrainian language from schools.
2,523,915	$1 = 3.67 dirhams	Arabic, Persian, English, Hindi	A hereditary ruler, or emir, governs each of the 7 states of this country.
60,270,708	$1 = .56 pound	English	England, Northern Ireland, Scotland, and Wales make up the United Kingdom.
293,027,571	U.S. dollar	English, Spanish	By 1890, the center of the population had moved from Maryland to Indiana.
3,440,205	$1 = 29.07 pesos	Spanish	Uruguay hosted, and won, soccer's first World Cup (1930).
26,410,416	$1 = 948.18 soms	Uzbek, Russian	Alexander the Great and Genghis Khan both conquered this region.
202,609	$1 = 111.6 vatus	French, English, Bislama	Before independence in 1980, Britain and France jointly ruled these islands.
911	$1 = .79 euro	Italian, Latin	The Vatican's Swiss Guards wear a style of uniform that dates from the 1500s.
25,017,387	$1 = 1,597 bolivares	Spanish	Angel Falls, the world's highest waterfall, drops 3,212 ft.
82,689,518	$1 = 15,644 dong	Vietnamese, French, Chinese	France took over Vietnam in 1854 and ruled there until 1954.
20,024,867	$1 = 178.01 rials	Arabic	"Mocha" coffee takes its name from a Yemeni seaport.
10,462,436	$1 = 4,500 kwacha	English, native languages	Fossils show humans inhabited Zambia 100,000 years ago.
12,671,860	$1 = 805 Zimbabwe dollars	English, Shona, Sindebele	The lake behind Kariba Dam is the world's largest-capacity reservoir.

GOVERNMENTS *Around the* WORLD

Among the world's 193 independent nations there are various kinds of governments. In most countries people choose their leaders; in some they don't.

WHAT IS A DEMOCRACY?

The word *democracy* comes from the Greek words *demos* ("people") and *kratia* ("rule"). In a democracy, the *people* rule, rather than an all-powerful individual (dictatorship) or king (monarchy) or small group of people (oligarchy). Since there are too many people to agree on everyday decisions themselves, democracies nowadays are *representative* democracies; this means the people make decisions through the leaders they choose. In the U.S., these include the president and members of Congress. Mexico and some other countries also have a "presidential" system, where voters elect the head of the government. But many democracies use a "parliamentary" system." In these countries—the United Kingdom, Canada, and Japan, for example—voters elect members of a parliament, or legislature, and then the members of parliament pick a cabinet to head the government. The leader of the cabinet is called the prime minister, or premier.

Winston Churchill

In a democracy people can complain about the government and vote it out of office, which they often do. Winston Churchill, one of Britain's greatest prime ministers, probably had this in mind when he said, "Democracy is the worst form of government except for all those others that have been tried."

WHAT IS A MONARCHY?

A country with a king or queen can be called a *monarchy*. Monarchies are almost always hereditary, meaning the throne is passed down in one family. In the United Kingdom and most other nations that still have kings or queens, royal figures have charitable and ceremonial duties but hold little real power—elected officials head the government. These countries are *constitutional* monarchies. But some countries still are *traditional* monarchies, governed by their royal families; Saudi Arabia is an example.

WHAT IS TOTALITARIANISM?

In totalitarian countries the rulers have strong power and the people have little freedom. Germany under Adolf Hitler and Iraq under Saddam Hussein had one all-powerful ruler or dictator. Dictators usually try to put down anyone opposing them. If they hold elections, they may be the only candidate allowed to campaign freely, or the only candidate on the ballot!

There are still some *Communist* nations today, such as Cuba, North Korea, and China (the world's biggest country in population). In these totalitarian countries, the government may run or control the economy. Usually the ruling Communist party is the only party that has power and only loyal Communists can be elected to office.

A *Head of State* is the person with the highest rank or office, such as the queen of the United Kingdom or the president of Italy. That person may often have little or no political power. The *Head of Government*, on the other hand, is the political leader in charge of the government. In many countries, such as Canada or Italy, that would be the prime minister. In the U.S. and some other countries the president is both Head of State and Head of Government.

United Nations

A COMMUNITY OF NATIONS

The United Nations (UN) was started in 1945 after World War II. The first members were 50 nations that met in San Francisco, California. They signed an agreement known as the UN Charter. The UN now has 191 members—including East Timor and Switzerland, which joined in 2002. Only two independent nations—Taiwan and Vatican City—are not members.

HOW THE UN IS ORGANIZED

GENERAL ASSEMBLY What It Does: discusses world problems, admits new members, appoints the secretary-general, decides the UN budget **Members:** All UN members belong to it; each country has one vote.

SECURITY COUNCIL What It Does: handles questions of peace and security **Members:** Five permanent members (China, France, Great Britain, Russia, U.S.), each of whom can veto any proposed action; ten elected by the General Assembly for two-year terms. In early 2004 the ten were Angola, Chile, Germany, Pakistan, and Spain (ending 2004) and Algeria, Benin, Brazil, the Philippines, and Romaina (ending 2005).

ECONOMIC AND SOCIAL COUNCIL What It Does: deals with issues related to trade, economic development, industry, population, children, food, education, health, and human rights **Members:** Fifty-four member countries elected for three-year terms.

INTERNATIONAL COURT OF JUSTICE (WORLD COURT) located at The Hague, Netherlands **What It Does:** highest court for disputes between countries **Members:** Fifteen judges, each from a different country, elected to nine-year terms.

SECRETARIAT What It Does: carries out day-to-day operations of the UN **Members:** UN staff, headed by the secretary-general.

Flags fly at the UN

For more information about the UN, you can write to:
Public Inquiries Unit, United Nations, Room GA-57, New York, NY 10017
Website: www.un.org

Native Americans

What are "Grandfather Rocks"? page 178

Totem pole from the Pacific Northwest

When European explorers first sailed to North America, they thought they had arrived in the East Indies, near the continent of Asia. That's why the explorers called the people they found living on these lands "Indians."

Scientists now believe that these "American Indians," commonly known today as Native Americans, arrived in the Americas more than 20,000 years ago, most likely from Northeast Asia. Many probably came across from Siberia by a "land bridge" that existed when sea levels were lower. Native Americans are not one people, but many different peoples with their own distinct cultures and traditions.

There were about 850,000 Native Americans living in what is now the United States when Columbus arrived. During the 17th, 18th, and 19th centuries, diseases (including many brought by Europeans) and wars with European settlers and soldiers caused the deaths of thousands of American Indians. As more settlers came, and moved westward, the Native peoples were often displaced. The Indian Removal Act of 1830 allowed the government to force all Indians east of the Mississippi to move to Indian Territory (part of what is now Oklahoma). In 1838 and 1839, in what came to be known as the "Trail of Tears," 16,000 Cherokee Indians in Alabama, Georgia, North Carolina, and Tennessee were moved from their homelands to Indian Territory. Nearly a quarter of them died on the way, of hunger, disease, and cold.

By 1910, there were only about 220,000 Native Americans left in the U.S. In 1924, Congress granted native peoples citizenship. Since then, the American Indian population has increased dramatically. According to the U.S. Census Bureau, the total number of American Indians and Alaska Natives in 2002 was about 2.7 million (not counting people who reported belonging to other ethnic groups in addition to Native American).

WHO AM I?

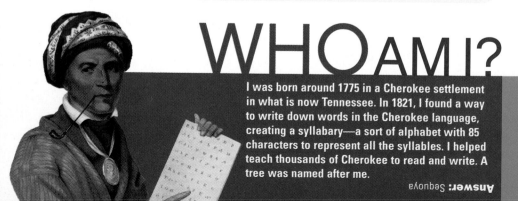

I was born around 1775 in a Cherokee settlement in what is now Tennessee. In 1821, I found a way to write down words in the Cherokee language, creating a syllabary—a sort of alphabet with 85 characters to represent all the syllables. I helped teach thousands of Cherokee to read and write. A tree was named after me.

Answer: Sequoya

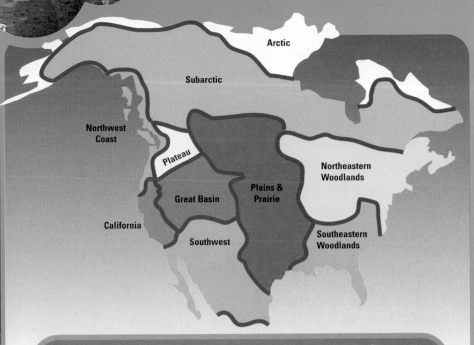

Arctic

Subarctic

Northwest Coast

Plateau

Northeastern Woodlands

Great Basin

Plains & Prairie

California

Southwest

Southeastern Woodlands

MAJOR CULTURAL AREAS of Native North Americans

Climate and geography influenced the culture of the people who lived in these regions. On the plains, for example, people depended on the great herds of buffalo for food. For Aleuts and Eskimos in the far North, seals and whales were an important food source. There are more than 560 tribes officially recognized by the U.S. government today and more than 56 million acres of tribal lands. Below are just a few well-known tribal groups that have lived in these areas.

NORTHEAST WOODLANDS
The Illinois, Iroquois (Mohawk, Onondaga, Cayuga, Oneida, Seneca, and Tuscarora), Lenape, Menominee, Micmac, Narragansett, Potawatomi, Shawnee.

SOUTHEAST WOODLANDS
The Cherokee, Chickasaw, Choctaw, Creek, Seminole.

PLAINS & PRAIRIE
The Arapaho, Blackfoot, Cheyenne, Comanche, Hidatsa, Mandan, Sioux.

SOUTHWEST
The Navajo, Apache, Havasupai, Mojave, Pima, Pueblo (Hopi, Isleta, Laguna, Zuñi).

GREAT BASIN
The Paiute, Shoshoni, Ute.

CALIFORNIA
The Klamath, Maidu, Miwok, Modoc, Patwin, Pomo, Wintun, Yurok.

PLATEAU
The Cayuse, Nez Percé, Okanagon, Salish, Spokan, Umatilla, Walla Walla, Yakima.

NORTHWEST COAST
The Chinook, Haida, Kwakiutl, Makah, Nootka, Salish, Tlinigit, Tsimshian, Tillamook.

SUBARCTIC
The Beaver, Cree, Chipewyan, Chippewa, Ingalik, Kaska, Kutchin, Montagnais, Naskapi, Tanana.

ARCTIC
The Eskimo (Inuit and Yipuk), Aleut.

Inuit girls with sled dogs

Largest U.S. Tribal Groupings*

1. Cherokee, 281,069
2. Navajo, 269,202
3. Sioux, 108,272
4. Chippewa, 105,907
5. Latin American Indian, 104,354

6. Choctaw, 87,349
7. Pueblo, 59,533
8. Apache, 57,060
9. Eskimo, 45,919
10. Iroquois, 45,212

*According to the U.S. Census 2000. Figures are for people reporting only one tribal grouping.

Native American Populations *by State**

Alabama—22,840	Maine—7,291	Oregon—48,341
Alaska—100,494	Maryland—17,379	Pennsylvania—20,900
Arizona—286,680	Massachusetts—18,354	Rhode Island—6,105
Arkansas—18,477	Michigan—60,105	South Carolina—15,069
California—410,501	Minnesota—57,340	South Dakota—63,390
Colorado—51,182	Mississippi—12,431	Tennessee—16,576
Connecticut—11,275	Missouri—25,953	Texas—145,954
Delaware—3,087	Montana—58,048	Utah—32,886
Florida—66,138	Nebraska—16,280	Vermont—2,492
Georgia—25,991	Nevada—31,281	Virginia—23,778
Hawaii—3,863	New Hampshire—3,213	Washington—99,446
Idaho—19,268	New Jersey—25,741	West Virginia—3,686
Illinois—38,815	New Mexico—183,972	Wisconsin—50,042
Indiana—17,249	New York—103,337	Wyoming—11,641
Iowa—10,058	North Carolina—106,454	Wash., D.C.—2,062
Kansas—26,085	North Dakota—31,104	**U.S.—2,752,158**
Kentucky—9,437	Ohio—25,870	
Louisiana—26,073	Oklahoma—278,124	

*2002 U.S. Census estimates. Figures do not include people who reported belonging to other ethnic groups in addition to Native American.

NATIONAL MUSEUM OF THE AMERICAN INDIAN

In September 2004, visitors to the new National Museum of the American Indian (NMAI) in Washington, D.C., will be greeted by the word "welcome" spoken and written in hundreds of different Native American languages. Large boulders known as "Grandfather Rocks" will watch over the entrance. Rocks, as the oldest things on earth, represent ancestors, elders, and history.

The NMAI will be a learning center and showcase for the Smithsonian's collection of more than 800,000 Native objects, including items of artistic, religious, and historical importance, as well as everyday things. The 16th and final Smithsonian museum on the National Mall was designed by American Indian architects and engineers and is meant to reflect the beliefs and principles of many different Native American groups.

▲ *Navajo woman weaving*

What is an octahedron? page 182

NUMERALS *in Ancient Civilization*

People have been counting since the earliest of times. This is what some numerals looked like in different cultures.

Modern	1	2	3	4	5	6	7	8	9	10	20	50	100
Egyptian	I	II	III	IIII	IIIII	IIIIII	IIIIIII	IIIIIIII	IIIIIIIII	∩	∩∩	∩∩∩∩∩	ϑ
Babylonian	Y	YY	YYY	⊻	⊻⊻	⊻⊻⊻	⊻⊻⊻	⊻⊻⊻	⊻⊻⊻	<	«	⋘	⟨«
Greek	A	B	Γ	Δ	E	F	Z	H	θ	I	K	N	P
Mayan	•	••	•••	••••	—	⟐	••	•••	••••	=	⊙	⊡	⊚
Chinese	一	二	三	四	五	六	七	八	九	十	二十	五十	百
Hindu	1	2	3	8	y	ς	)	८	६	10	20	yo	100
Arabic	1	2	3	ʓ	ε	٤	٧	٨	9	1o	2o	٤o	100

ROMAN *NUMERALS*

Roman numerals are still used today. The symbols used for different numbers are the letters I (1), V (5), X (10), L (50), C (100), D (500), and M (1,000). If one Roman numeral is followed by a larger one, the first is subtracted from the second. For example, IX means 10 − 1 = 9. Think of it as "one less than ten." On the other hand, if a Roman numeral is followed by one or more others that are equal or smaller, add them together. Thus, LXI means 50 + 10 + 1 = 61. Can you put the year you were born in Roman numerals?

The Roman Empire fell in A.D. 476. Can you put that number in Roman numerals?

1	I	14	XIV	90	XC
2	II	15	XV	100	C
3	III	16	XVI	200	CC
4	IV	17	XVII	300	CCC
5	V	18	XVIII	400	CD
6	VI	19	XIX	500	D
7	VII	20	XX	600	DC
8	VIII	30	XXX	700	DCC
9	IX	40	XL	800	DCCC
10	X	50	L	900	CM
11	XI	60	LX	1,000	M
12	XII	70	LXX	2,000	MM
13	XIII	80	LXXX	3,000	MMM

▼ *The Colosseum*

ANSWERS ON PAGES 319–322. FOR MORE PUZZLES GO TO WWW.WORLDALMANACFORKIDS.COM

Homework Help
PERCENTS AND FRACTIONS

The term *percent* means *per hundred*. 10 percent (10%) means 10 out of a hundred, or $^{10}/_{100}$, or 10 divided by 100.

Let's say you had 100 marbles, and you gave some to a friend. What percent of the marbles did you give away? If you gave away 10 marbles, that would be 10 out of 100, or 10%. But that is an easy number to use. What if you had 300 marbles, and gave away 72? What percent of the 300 marbles did you give away? What fraction?

To calculate the percentage,
divide 72 by 300.
$72 \div 300 = .24 = 24$ hundredths $= ^{24}/_{100}$.

Since percent means per hundred, "24 per 100" = 24%.

To go from a percentage to a fraction,
divide the percentage by 100 then reduce the fraction.

First rename 24% to $^{24}/_{100}$. Then reduce that fraction to its lowest common denominator. You do this by dividing both the numerator (the top number) and the denominator (the bottom number) by the largest number by which both can be divided. In this case that number is 4. So $^{24}/_{100} = ^{6}/_{25}$.

The PREFIX Tells the Number

After each number are one or more prefixes used to form words that include that number. Knowing what the prefix stands for can help you understand the meaning of the word. For example, four children born at one birth are **quad**ruplets. Seven at once would be **sept**uplets. **Dec**ember gets its name from the calendar used in Roman times, when it was the tenth month (the Roman year began in March). An **oct**opus has eight arms.

▼ A monorail

Number	Prefix	Examples
1	uni-, mon-, mono-	unicycle, unicorn, monarch, monorail
2	bi-	bicycle, binary, binoculars, bifocals
3	tri-	tricycle, triangle, trilogy, trio
4	quadr-, tetr-	quadrangle, quadruplet, tetrahedron
5	pent-, quint-	pentagon, pentathlon, quintuplet
6	hex-, sext-	hexagon, sextuplet, sextet
7	hept-, sept-	heptathlon, septuplet
8	oct-	octave, octet, octopus, octagon
9	non-	nonagon, nonet
10	dec-	decade, decibel, decimal
100	cent-	centipede, century
1000	kilo-	kilogram, kilometer, kilowatt
million	mega-	megabyte, megahertz, megapixel
billion	giga-	gigabyte, gigawatt

Multiplication Table

x	0	1	2	3	4	5	6	7	8	9	10	11	12
0	0	0	0	0	0	0	0	0	0	0	0	0	0
1	0	1	2	3	4	5	6	7	8	9	10	11	12
2	0	2	4	6	8	10	12	14	16	18	20	22	24
3	0	3	6	9	12	15	18	21	24	27	30	33	36
4	0	4	8	12	16	20	24	28	32	36	40	44	48
5	0	5	10	15	20	25	30	35	40	45	50	55	60
6	0	6	12	18	24	30	36	42	48	54	60	66	72
7	0	7	14	21	28	35	42	49	56	63	70	77	84
8	0	8	16	24	32	40	48	56	64	72	80	88	96
9	0	9	18	27	36	45	54	63	72	81	90	99	108
10	0	10	20	30	40	50	60	70	80	90	100	110	120
11	0	11	22	33	44	55	66	77	88	99	110	121	132
12	0	12	24	36	48	60	72	84	96	108	120	132	144

Here's a finger trick that only works for multiplying by 9. Spread your fingers out in front of you. Your left pinky is 1, your left ring finger is 2, and so on. Your right pinky is 10. To find the answer to 9 x 4, fold down your 4th finger (left index finger). Look to the left of the folded finger. You have 3 still sticking out. To the right of the folded finger, you have 6 fingers out (your left thumb, plus the 5 on your right hand). The answer is 36.

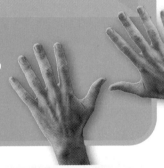

 Homework Help

Here are a few hints to help make this table easier to work with:

▶ First, you can skip half the other numbers! If you know that 4 x 2 = 8, you also know that 2 x 4 = 8. Changing the order of the numbers being multiplied doesn't change the result—that's the commutative property.

▶ You don't have to memorize the row for zero or one. Any time you multiply a number by zero, the answer is zero: 2 x 0 = 0. Multiplying a number by 1 doesn't change its value: 12 x 1 = 12

▶ Now you have only 66 "items" to memorize. You can find them in the triangle in the chart above. And some of them are easy to learn.

▶ Multiplying by 5 and 10 is like *counting* by 5 or 10. Start with 25, for example: 5 x 5 = 25. To multiply 5 by 6, simply add 5 to get 30. Then 35, 40, and so on. All multiplication is really a series of additions: 3 x 5 is the same as 5 + 5 + 5 = 15. To multiply any number by 10, just add a 0 to it: 12 x 10 = 120.

How Many SIDES and FACES Do They Have?

When a figure is flat (two-dimensional), it is a **plane** figure. When a figure takes up space (three-dimensional), it is a **solid** figure. The flat surface of a solid figure is called a **face**. Plane and solid figures come in many different shapes.

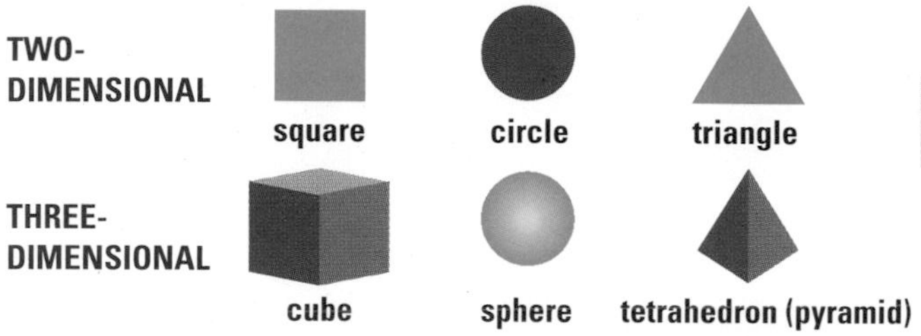

TWO-DIMENSIONAL

square · circle · triangle

THREE-DIMENSIONAL

cube · sphere · tetrahedron (pyramid)

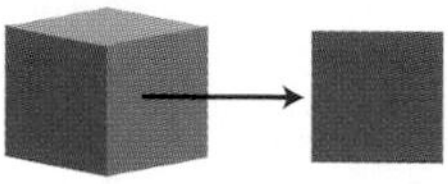

The flat surface of a cube is a square.

What Are POLYGONS?

A polygon is a two-dimensional figure with three or more straight sides (called line segments). A square is a polygon. Polygons have different numbers of sides—and each has a different name. If the sides are all the same length and all the angles between the sides are equal, the polygon is called regular. If the sides are of different lengths or the angles are not equal, the polygon is called irregular. At right are some regular and irregular polygons.

NAME & NUMBER OF SIDES	REGULAR	IRREGULAR
triangle — 3		
quadrilateral or tetragon — 4		
pentagon — 5		
hexagon — 6		
heptagon — 7		
octagon — 8		
nonagon — 9		
decagon — 10		

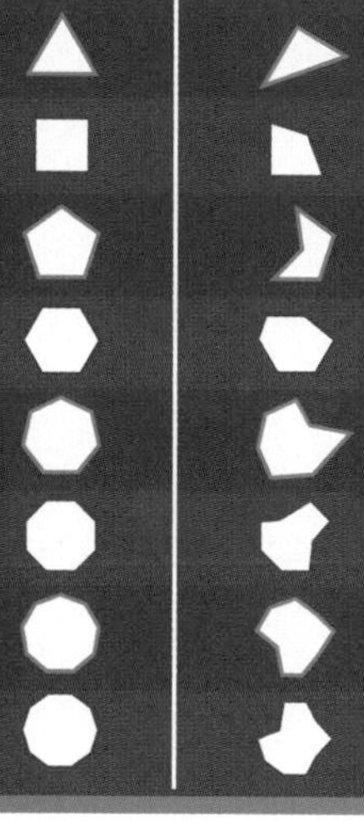

What Are Polyhedrons?

A polyhedron is a three-dimensional figure with four or more faces. Each face on a polyhedron is a polygon. Below are some polyhedrons with many faces.

tetrahedron 4 faces · hexahedron 6 faces · octahedron 8 faces · dodecahedron 12 faces · icosahedron 20 faces

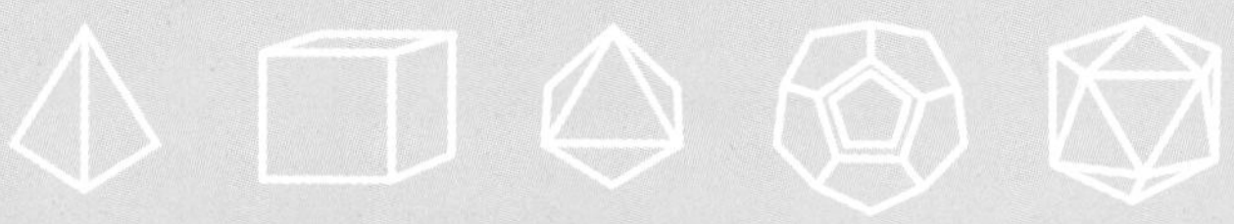

◀ *Great Pyramid of Khefren*

Finding the area of a figure can be easy, if you know the not-so-secret formula.

AREA OF A SQUARE:

A plane figure with four sides is called a **quadrilateral.** A square is a quadrilateral with four right angles and four *equal* sides, like the figure you see here. To find the area for a square, use this formula: **side x side** (**side x side** can also be written as s², pronounced "side squared").

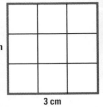

3 cm

The sides of this square are each 3 centimeters long. So the area is 3 x 3, or 9. These are no longer centimeters but **square centimeters**, like the smaller squares inside the big one.

3 cm

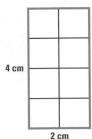

4 cm

2 cm

AREA OF A RECTANGLE:

Rectangles are another type of quadrilateral. They have four right angles, but unlike a square, the sides are not all equal.
To find the area of a rectangle, multiply **BASE x HEIGHT** (length x width).

This rectangle has a base of 4 centimeters and a height of 2 centimeters. Its area is 8 square centimeters.

AREA OF A PARALLELOGRAM:

Parallelograms are quadrilaterals that have parallel opposite sides, but no right angles. The formula for the area of parallelogram is the same as for a rectangle—**BASE X HEIGHT.**

height 2 cm

base 4 cm

AREA OF A TRIANGLE:

A triangle is a three-sided plane figure. The prefix "tri" means three, which refers to the three points where the sides of a triangle meet.

3 cm

To find the area for a triangle use **1/2 x (BASE x HEIGHT)** (first multiply the base by the height, then multiply that number by 1/2).

2 cm

This triangle has a base of 2 centimeters and a height of 3 centimeters. So the area will be 3 square centimeters.

AREA OF A CIRCLE:

The distance around a circle is called its **circumference.** All the points on the circumference are an equal distance from the center. That distance is the **radius.** A **diameter** is any straight line that has both ends on the circle and passes through its center. It's twice as long as the radius.
To find the circle's area you need to use π—a number called **pi** (π) that equals about 3.14. The formula for area is:

3 cm

π x RADIUS x RADIUS (or **π x RADIUS SQUARED**).
For instance, this circle has a radius of 3 centimeters, so its area = π x 3 x 3, or about π x 3²; that is, 3.14 x 9. This comes to 28.26 square centimeters.

What is Pi? *The Greek letter pi (π) stands for the number you get when you divide the circumference of a circle by its diameter. It is always the same, no matter how big the circle is! The Babylonians discovered this in 2000 B.C. Actually, no one can say exactly what the value of π is. When you divide the circumference by the diameter it does not come out even, and you can keep going as many places as you want: 3.14159265…it goes on forever.*

Fractals: Painting by Numbers

Did you know that mathematicians can paint pictures with numbers? The French mathematician Benoit Mandelbrot did this in 1975 when he discovered fractals. Fractals are never-ending patterns of self-repeating shapes created by graphing different algebraic equations. These colorful pictures are made up of patterns of geometric shapes (like circles and squares, but more complex), which can be broken down into smaller sizes, down to a microscopic level. Many things in nature are fractal in structure. That's why scientists can use fractal geometry to make models of coastlines, mountains, and even the shapes of clouds!

Searching for Prime Numbers

Mathematicians have long been interested in prime numbers. A prime number is any number bigger than 1 that can't be divided without a remainder—except by itself and 1.

So 2 would be a prime number. But it's the only even number that's a prime, since every even number can be divided by 2.

3 is another prime number. Can you figure out which other numbers under 10 would be prime numbers? How about from 20 to 30? (If you can't tell right away, try dividing by odd numbers starting with 3. If nothing works, you've got a prime.)

How many prime numbers are there? An infinite number! And mathematicians using computers have figured out prime numbers higher than you could imagine.

Coin Prediction Trick

Ask someone to drop a small handful of coins on a table. Look at the coins, then turn your back and ask the person to flip over pairs of coins at random (as many or as few as he or she likes, but always in pairs). Then ask the person to cover up one coin, so you can't see it. When you turn around, you can tell right away whether the covered coin is a head or a tail.

Turn to the answer pages to see how it's done.

999 999 Using the number 9 6 times, can you represent 100?

If 10 pickers can pick 10 apples in 10 seconds, how many pickers would it take to pick 60 apples in a minute?

ANSWERS ON PAGES 319-322.
FOR MORE PUZZLES GO TO
WWW.WORLDALMANACFORKIDS.COM

Population

Which has more people, New York City or Virginia? page 187

Taking the Census: Everyone Counts

Were you counted during Census 2000?

The United States takes a census every 10 years to try to count all the people and learn some basic things about the population. Census-takers try to track down and count people who did not send back forms, so that the census will be as accurate as possible. Census officials believe the 2000 census was one of the most accurate ever, but that it still missed about 1 out of 100 people. As of April 1, 2000, the total U.S. population was 281,421,906, according to the Census Bureau.

Why is the census needed?

► The census provides a picture of the people. Where do they live? How old are they? What do they do? How much do they earn? How many kids do they have? What is their background?

► The population of a state determines how many representatives it has in the U.S. House and how many electoral votes it gets for presidential elections.

► Census information helps the federal government in Washington, D.C., decide which public services must be provided and where.

When was the first U.S. census taken?

It was in 1790 just after the American Revolution. That year census-takers counted 3,929,214 people living in what was then the United States. Most lived on farms or in small towns. Today, three out of four Americans live in or near cities.

The Growing U.S. Population...

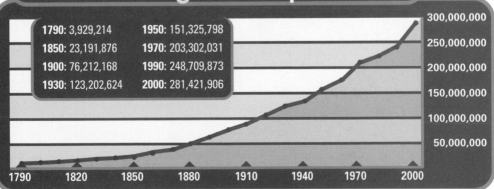

1790: 3,929,214	1950: 151,325,798
1850: 23,191,876	1970: 203,302,031
1900: 76,212,168	1990: 248,709,873
1930: 123,202,624	2000: 281,421,906

300,000,000
250,000,000
200,000,000
150,000,000
100,000,000
50,000,000

1790   1820   1850   1880   1910   1940   1970   2000

WHERE DO PEOPLE LIVE?

In 1959, there were three billion people in the world. In 1999, the number hit six billion. According to the latest estimates by the UN, the world population will reach 6.5 billion by 2005, and is expected to grow to almost nine billion by 2050. This is a lot, but not as much as predicted a few years ago. The UN expects that fewer people will be born and that the deadly AIDS epidemic in many countries will be worse than was once thought.

Smallest Countries*
(Fewest People, mid-2004)

COUNTRY	POPULATION
Vatican City (2003)	911
Tuvalu	11,468
Nauru	12,809
Palau	20,016
San Marino	28,503
Monaco	32,270
Liechtenstein	33,436

* Source: U.S. Census Bureau

Largest Cities in the World

Here are the ten cities that had the most people, according to UN estimates for 2000. Numbers include people from the built-up area around each city (metropolitan area), not just the city. (See page 187 for big U.S. cities by themselves.)

CITY, COUNTRY	POPULATION
Tokyo, Japan	34,450,000
Mexico City, Mexico	18,066,000
New York area, U.S.	17,846,000
São Paulo, Brazil	17,099,000
Mumbai (Bombay), India	16,086,000
Kolkata (Calcutta), India	13,058,000
Shanghai, China	12,887,000
Buenos Aires, Argentina	12,583,000
Delhi, India	12,441,000
Los Angeles area, U.S.	11,814,000

Largest Countries*
(Most People, mid-2004)

COUNTRY	POPULATION
China**	1,294,629,555
India	1,065,070,607
United States	293,027,571
Indonesia	238,452,952
Brazil	184,101,109
Pakistan	153,705,278
Russia	144,112,353
Bangladesh	141,340,476
Nigeria	137,253,133
Japan	127,333,002
Mexico	104,959,594
Philippines	86,241,697
Vietnam	82,689,518
Germany	82,424,609
Egypt	76,117,421
Iran	69,018,924
Turkey	68,893,918
Ethiopia	67,851,281
Thailand	64,865,523
France	60,424,213
United Kingdom	60,270,708
Dem. Rep. of the Congo	58,317,930
Italy	58,057,477
South Korea	48,598,175
Ukraine	47,732,079

* Source: U.S. Census Bureau; ** not including Taiwan

Population of the UNITED STATES, 2003

Estimated U.S. Population on July 1, 2003: 290,809,777.

Rank & State Name	Population	Rank & State Name	Population
1 California	35,484,453	27 Oregon	3,559,596
2 Texas	22,118,509	28 Oklahoma	3,511,532
3 New York	19,190,115	29 Connecticut	3,483,372
4 Florida	17,019,068	30 Iowa	2,944,062
5 Illinois	12,653,544	31 Mississippi	2,881,281
6 Pennsylvania	12,365,455	32 Arkansas	2,725,714
7 Ohio	11,435,798	33 Kansas	2,723,507
8 Michigan	10,079,985	34 Utah	2,351,467
9 Georgia	8,684,715	35 Nevada	2,241,154
10 New Jersey	8,638,396	36 New Mexico	1,874,614
11 North Carolina	8,407,248	37 West Virginia	1,810,354
12 Virginia	7,386,330	38 Nebraska	1,739,291
13 Massachusetts	6,433,422	39 Idaho	1,366,332
14 Indiana	6,195,643	40 Maine	1,305,728
15 Washington	6,131,445	41 New Hampshire	1,287,687
16 Tennessee	5,841,748	42 Hawaii	1,257,608
17 Missouri	5,704,484	43 Rhode Island	1,076,164
18 Arizona	5,580,811	44 Montana	917,621
19 Maryland	5,508,909	45 Delaware	817,491
20 Wisconsin	5,472,299	46 South Dakota	764,309
21 Minnesota	5,059,375	47 Alaska	648,818
22 Colorado	4,550,688	48 North Dakota	633,837
23 Alabama	4,500,752	49 Vermont	619,107
24 Louisiana	4,496,334	50 District of Columbia	563,384
25 South Carolina	4,147,152	51 Wyoming	501,242
26 Kentucky	4,117,827		

Largest Cities in the United States

Cities grow and shrink in population. At right is a list of the largest cities in the United States in 2002 compared with their populations in 1950. Which seven cities increased in population? Which three decreased?

Rank & City	2002	1950
1 New York, NY	8,084,316	7,891,957
2 Los Angeles, CA	3,798,981	1,970,358
3 Chicago, IL	2,886,251	3,620,962
4 Houston, TX	2,009,834	596,163
5 Philadelphia, PA	1,492,231	2,071,605
6 Phoenix, AZ	1,371,960	106,818
7 San Diego, CA	1,259,532	334,387
8 Dallas, TX	1,211,467	434,462
9 San Antonio, TX	1,194,222	408,442
10 Detroit, MI	925,051	1,849,568

did you know?

In 2002, there were 72 million children (18 years old and younger) in the U.S., representing 26% of the population. In 1960, kids made up 36% of the population.

The Many Faces of America:
IMMIGRATION

▼ Immigrants entering the U.S. at Ellis Island, early 1900s

The number of people in the U.S. who were born in another country (foreign-born) reached 32.5 million in 2002, or 11.5 percent of the population. This percent has been rising since 1970, when it was down to 4.7 percent, and is the highest since 1930. In the early 1900s, most immigrants came from Europe; in 2002, 52% of the foreign-born population were from Latin America, and 26% were born in Asia.

Immigrants come for various reasons, such as to live in freedom, to escape poverty or oppression, and to make better lives for themselves and their children. The figures below, from U.S. Citizenship and Immigration Services, part of the Department of Homeland Security, cover legal immigrants only. In addition, the U.S. government estimates that in the 1990s about 350,000 people each year came across the border illegally or overstayed their temporary visa. There were an estimated 7 million unauthorized immigrants in the U.S. in 2000; about 70% of these were from Mexico.

What Countries Do Immigrants Come From?

Below are some of the countries immigrants came from in 2002. Immigration from all countries to the U.S. totaled 1,063,732 in 2002.

	Number	Percent of total
Mexico	219,380	20.6
India	71,105	6.7
China	61,282	5.8
Philippines	51,308	4.8
Vietnam	33,627	3.2
El Salvador	31,168	2.9
Cuba	28,272	2.7
Bosnia-Herzegovina	25,373	2.4
Dominican Republic	22,604	2.1
Ukraine	21,217	2.0
Korea	21,021	2.0
Russia	20,833	2.0
Haiti	20,268	1.9
Canada	19,519	1.8
Colombia	18,845	1.8

Where Do Immigrants Settle?

In 2002, about 65% of all immigrants to the U.S. moved to the states below. California received almost 50% of the immigrants from Mexico, 43% of those from the Philippines, and about one-third of those from China, India, Korea, and Vietnam. Florida received 79% of the immigrants from Cuba, 54% of those from Haiti, and about one-third of those from Colombia. Half of the immigrants from the Dominican Republic chose New York.

California
291,216

New York
114,827

Florida
90,819

Texas
88,365

New Jersey
57,721

Illinois
47,235

This bar chart shows the states that received the highest number of immigrants in 2002.

To go to Goa, where would you go? **page 190**

NOBEL PRIZES

The Nobel Prizes are named after Alfred B. Nobel (1833-1896), a Swedish scientist who invented dynamite, and left money for these prizes. They are given every year for promoting peace, and for physics, chemistry, medicine-physiology, literature, and economics.

In 2003, the Peace Prize went to Iranian activist Shirin Ebadi for "her efforts for democracy and human rights." The rights of women and children have been her main concern. She is the first Iranian and first woman from an Islamic country to win it.

Shirin Ebadi

PAST WINNERS OF THE NOBEL PEACE PRIZE INCLUDE:

◄ **2002 JIMMY CARTER,** former U.S. president and peace negotiator

2001 UNITED NATIONS (UN); KOFI ANNAN, UN secretary-general

1999 MÉDECINS SANS FRONTIÈRES (DOCTORS WITHOUT BORDERS), an organization that gives medical help to disaster and war victims

1997 JODY WILLIAMS and the **INTERNATIONAL CAMPAIGN TO BAN LANDMINES**

1994 YASIR ARAFAT, Palestinian leader; **SHIMON PERES,** foreign minister of Israel; **YITZHAK RABIN,** prime minister of Israel

1993 NELSON MANDELA, leader of South African blacks; **F. W. DE KLERK,** president of South Africa

1992 RIGOBERTA MENCHÚ TUM, activist for Indian peasant rights in Guatemala

1989 DALAI LAMA, Tibetan Buddhist leader, forced into exile in 1959

1986 ELIE WIESEL, Holocaust survivor and author

1981 OFFICE OF THE UN HIGH COMMISSIONER FOR REFUGEES

1965 UNICEF (UN Children's Fund)

1964 MARTIN LUTHER KING JR., civil rights leader

1961 DAG HAMMARSKJÖLD, UN sectretary-general

1919 WOODROW WILSON, U.S. president who played the key role in founding the League of Nations

1906 THEODORE ROOSEVELT, U.S. president who helped settle the Russo-Japanese War

Bee a Winner

IF YOU HAVE A KNACK FOR SPELLING OR AN INTEREST IN WORLD GEOGRAPHY, THEN THESE TWO NATIONAL CONTESTS MAY BE FOR YOU.

NATIONAL SPELLING BEE

The National Spelling Bee was started in Louisville, Kentucky, by the Courier-Journal in 1925. Newspapers across the U.S. run spelling bees for kids 15 and under. Winners may qualify for the Scripps Howard National Spelling Bee held in Washington, D.C., in late May or early June. If interested, ask your school principal to contact your local newspaper. (For a behind-the-scenes look at the National Spelling Bee, try the 2002 film *Spellbound*.)

Practice makes . . . a winner! **Sai Gunturi**, a 13-year-old eighth grader from Dallas, Texas, won his first local spelling bee in the third grade. He went to the nationals three times getting as high as 7th place. On his fourth try, in May 2003, he became the national champion over 250 other kids when he correctly spelled **pococurante**. (It means "a careless or indifferent person.")

WEB SITE *http://www.spellingbee.com*

Here are the words Sai spelled on his way to the top. Some of them are just a little bit difficult!

1. sanguine
2. *(written round)*
3. insalubrious
4. Veracruzano
5. marmoraceous
6. mistassini
7. solfeggio
8. piezochemistry
9. voussoir
10. halogeton
11. dipnoous
12. gadarene
13. peirastic
14. rhathymia
15. pococurante

National Geographic Bee

Each year thousands of schools in the U.S. participate in the National Geographic Bee using materials prepared by the National Geographic Society. Since it started in 1989, millions of students have competed in this contest for a $25,000 college scholarship and the honor of being a national champion.

James Williams, a 14-year-old from Vancouver, Washington, won first place in the 2003 National Geographic Bee in May 2003. James is in the eighth grade and is homeschooled. He has also competed in the National Science Olympiad and the National Science Bowl. Second place went to Dallas Simons, a 13-year-old from Nashville, Tennessee, and in third place was Sean Rao, a 14-year-old from Hubertus, Wisconsin.

WINNING QUESTION: *Goa, a state in southwestern India, was a possession of which country until 1961?*
ANSWER: *Portugal*

To enter, you must be in grades 4 through 8. School-level bees are followed by state-level bees and then the nationals. For more information, ask your principal to write to:
National Geographic Bee; National Geographic Society; 1145 17th Street NW; Washington, D.C. 20036-4688. The registration deadline each year is October 15.

WEB SITE *http://www.nationalgeographic.com*

ENTERTAINMENT AWARDS

The Oscar ceremonies are watched on TV by hundreds of millions of people around the world. Among other entertainment awards are the Grammys and the MTV Video Music Awards.

Academy Awards

The Oscars are awarded by the Academy of Motion Picture Arts and Sciences for the best in movies. Here are some winners for 2003:

Best Picture: *The Lord of the Rings: The Return of the King*

Best Actor: Sean Penn, *Mystic River*

Best Actress: Charlize Theron, *Monster*

Best Supporting Actor: Tim Robbins, *Mystic River*

Best Supporting Actress: Renée Zellweger, *Cold Mountain*

Best Director: Peter Jackson, *The Lord of the Rings: The Return of the King*

Best Original Screenplay: Sofia Coppola, *Lost in Translation*

Best Animated Film: *Finding Nemo*

MTV Video Music Awards

The MTV Video Music Awards are presented each year in a variety of music video categories. Here are some winners for 2003:

Best Video of the Year: Missy Elliott, "Work It"

Best New Artist: 50 Cent, "In Da Club"

Best Male Video: Justin Timberlake, "Cry Me a River"

Best Female Video: : Beyoncé Knowles, featuring Jay-Z, "Crazy in Love"

Best Group Video: Coldplay, "The Scientist"

Best Pop Video: Justin Timberlake, "Cry Me a River"

Best Rock Video: Linkin Park, "Somewhere I Belong"

Best Hip Hop Video: Missy Elliott, "Work It"

Grammy Awards

Grammys are given out each year by the National Academy of Recording Arts and Sciences. Some of the winners for 2003 were:

Record of the Year (single): "Clocks," Coldplay

Album of the Year: *Speakerboxxx/The Love Below*, OutKast

Song of the Year: "Dance With My Father," Richard Marx & Luther Vandross

New Artist: Evanescence

Pop Vocal Album: *Justified*, Justin Timberlake

Pop Female Performance: "Beautiful," Christina Aguilera

Pop Male Performance: "Cry Me a River," Justin Timberlake

Pop Duo or Group: "Underneath It All," No Doubt

Traditional R&B Album: *Dance With My Father*, Luther Vandross

Contemporary R&B Album: *Dangerously in Love*, Beyoncé

Rock Album: *One by One*, Foo Fighters

Rock Song: "Seven Nation Army," written by Jack White (of The White Stripes)

Rap Album: *Speakerboxxx/The Love Below*, OutKast

Female Rap Soloist: "Work It", Missy Elliott

Male Rap Soloist: "Lose Yourself," Eminem

Country Album: *Livin', Lovin', Losin'—Songs of the Louvin Brothers,* Various Artists

Country Song: "It's Five O'Clock Somewhere," written by Alan Jackson & Jimmy Buffett

Spoken Word Album for Children: *Prokofiev: Peter and the Wolf/Beintus: Wolf Tracks,* Bill Clinton, Mikhail Gorbachev, & Sophia Loren

Musical Album for Children: *Bon Appétit!,* Cathy Fink & Marcy Marxer

Film or TV Song: "A Mighty Wind," written by Christopher Guest, Eugene Levy, & Michael McKean

Contests, Contests EVERYWHERE!

It just seems to be part of human nature to find out who is the best at something, no matter what it is! There are state, national, and international competitions in a wild variety of events. Many are held as part of a festival or fair. Here are some contests that are a strain on your brain, some that are just fun—and some that are both. Contests like these, and many others, may take place near you.

NATIONAL SCHOOL SCRABBLE TOURNAMENT Held in Boston every April, this contest is open to kids in grades 5 through 8. Qualifying tournaments, with six 44-minute rounds, can be held within clubs, classrooms, schools, districts, regions, or states.
WEB SITE http://school.scrabble-assoc.com/documents/national.aps

NATIONAL GEOGRAPHIC WORLD CHAMPIONSHIP Every two years, student teams from all over the world compete in this event. The U.S. took home the gold in Tampa, Florida, in the 2003 championship. The first round is a written test, followed by an outdoor map-reading contest. The final round is like a quiz show.
WEB SITE http://www.nationalgeographic.com/geographybee/olympiad.html

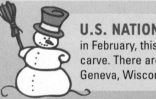

U.S. NATIONAL SNOW SCULPTING COMPETITION Usually held in February, this contest gives each team a 7-foot-by-9-foot block of snow to carve. There are special events for kids. The 2004 contest was held in Lake Geneva, Wisconsin.

THE SMITHSONIAN KITE FESTIVAL Open to kite builders of all ages in many categories, this contest is held at cherry blossom time (late March to early April) on the National Mall in Washington, D.C.
WEB SITE http://kitefestival.org

INTERNATIONAL CHERRY PIT SPITTING CHAMPIONSHIP Open to spitters of all ages, this competition is held every year in Eau Claire, Michigan, in July. The world record is nearly 96 feet! (Watermelon seeds are often used in other spitting contests. And every April at Purdue University's "Bug Bowl" there is a cricket spitting contest!)

WORLD COW CHIP THROWING CONTEST Held every April in Beaver, Oklahoma.  The object is to throw a hunk of dried cow dung (a "cow chip") as far as you can. The record is over 185 feet. This is one of many throwing contests. Eggs, fish, squid, pumpkins, and fruitcake are just a few of the other things people may throw.

Religion

What is "nirvana?" see below

How did the universe begin? Why are we here on Earth? What happens to us after we die? For most people, religion is a way of answering questions like these. Believing in a God or gods, or in a higher power, is one way of making sense of the world around us. Religions can also help guide people's lives. About six billion people all over the world are religious believers.

Different religions have different beliefs. For example, Christians, Jews, and Muslims all believe in one God, while Hindus believe in many gods. On this page and the next are some facts about the world's major religions.

Buddhism

WHO STARTED BUDDHISM? Gautama Siddhartha (the Buddha), around 525 B.C.

WHAT WRITINGS ARE THERE? The three main collections of Buddhist writings are called the **Tripitaka**, or "Three Baskets." Many of these writings are called **sutras** or "teachings."

WHAT DO BUDDHISTS BELIEVE? Buddha taught that life is filled with suffering. In order to be free of that suffering, believers have to give up worldly possessions and worldly goals and try to achieve a state of perfect peace known as *nirvana*.

HOW MANY ARE THERE? In 2003, there were nearly 373 million Buddhists in the world, 98% of them in Asia.

WHAT KINDS ARE THERE? There are two main kinds of Buddhists. **Theravada** ("Path of the Elders") **Buddhism**, the older kind, is more common in the southern part of Asia. **Mahayana** ("Great Vessel") **Buddhism** is more common in northern Asia.

Christianity

WHO STARTED CHRISTIANITY? Jesus Christ, in the first century. He was born in Bethlehem between 8 B.C. and 4 B.C. and died about A.D. 29.

WHAT WRITINGS ARE THERE? The **Bible**, including the Old Testament and New Testament, is the main religious writing of Christianity.

WHAT DO CHRISTIANS BELIEVE? That there is one God. That Jesus Christ is the Son of God, who came on Earth, died to save humankind, and rose from the dead.

HOW MANY ARE THERE? Christianity is the world's biggest religion. In 2003, there were more than two billion Christians, in nearly all parts of the world. More than one billion of the Christians were **Roman Catholics**, who follow the leadership of the pope in Rome. Other groups of Christians include **Orthodox Christians**, who accept most of the same teachings as Roman Catholics but follow different leadership, and **Protestants**, who often disagree with Catholic teachings. Protestants rely especially on the Bible itself. They belong to many different group or "denominations."

Hinduism

WHO STARTED HINDUISM? Aryan beliefs spread into India, around 1500 B.C. These beliefs were mixed with the beliefs of the people who already lived there.

WHAT WRITINGS ARE THERE? The **Vedas** are the most important writings in Hinduism. They include ancient hymns and rules for religious ceremonies. Other writings include the teachings of the **Upanishads** and a long poem about war, the **Bhagavad Gita**.

WHAT DO HINDUS BELIEVE? Hindus believe there are many gods and many ways of worshipping and that people die and are reborn many times as other living things. They also believe there is a universal soul, known as *Brahman*. The goal of life is to escape the cycle of birth and death and become part of the *Brahman*. This is done by leading a good life.

HOW MANY ARE THERE? In 2003, there were about 837 million Hindus, mainly in India and places where people from India have gone to live.

WHAT KINDS ARE THERE? There are many kinds of Hindus, who worship different gods or goddesses.

Islam

WHO STARTED ISLAM? Muhammad, the Prophet, in A.D. 610.

WHAT WRITINGS ARE THERE? The **Koran** (al-Qur'an in Arabic) sets out the main beliefs and practices of Islam, the religion of Muslims.

WHAT DO MUSLIMS BELIEVE? People who believe in Islam are known as Muslims. The word **"Islam"** means submission to God. Muslims believe that there is no other god than the one God; that Muhammad is the prophet and lawgiver of his community; that they should pray five times a day, fast during the month of **Ramadan**, give to the poor, and once during their life make a pilgrimage to Mecca in Saudi Arabia *(hajj)* if they can afford it.

HOW MANY ARE THERE? In 2003, there were more than 1.2 billion Muslims, mostly in parts of Africa and Asia. The two main branches are: **Sunni Muslims**, who make up 83% of all Muslims today, and **Shiite Muslims**, who broke away in a dispute over leadership after Muhammad died in 632.

Judaism

WHO STARTED JUDAISM? Abraham is considered to be the founder of Judaism. He lived around 1300 B.C.

WHAT WRITINGS ARE THERE? The most important is the **Torah**, the first five books of the Old Testament of the Bible.

WHAT DO JEWS BELIEVE? Jews believe that there is one God who created the universe and rules over it, and that they should be faithful to God and carry out God's commandments.

HOW MANY ARE THERE? In 2003, there were about 14.6 million Jews living around the world. Many live in Israel and the United States.

WHAT KINDS ARE THERE? In the United States and Europe there are three main forms: **Orthodox**, **Conservative**, and **Reform**. Orthodox Jews are the most traditional. They follow strict laws about how they dress, what they can eat, and how they conduct their lives. Conservative Jews follow many of the traditions. Reform Jews are the least traditional.

Major Holy Days for
CHRISTIANS, JEWS, AND MUSLIMS

CHRISTIAN HOLY DAYS

	2004	2005	2006
Ash Wednesday	February 25	February 9	March 1
Good Friday	April 9	March 25	April 14
Easter Sunday	April 11	March 27	April 16
Easter for Orthodox Churches	April 11	May 1	April 23
Christmas	December 25	December 25	December 25

*Some Orthodox churches celebrate Christmas on January 6.

JEWISH HOLY DAYS

The Jewish holy days begin at sundown the night before the first full day of the observance. The dates of first full days are listed below.

	2004-5 (5765)	2005-6 (5766)	2006-7 (5767)
Rosh Hashanah (New Year)	September 16	October 4	September 23
Yom Kippur (Day of Atonement)	September 25	October 13	October 2
Hanukkah (Festival of Lights)	December 8	December 26	December 16
Passover	April 24	April 13	April 3

ISLAMIC (MUSLIM) HOLY DAYS

The Islamic holy days begin at sundown the night before the first full day of the observance. The dates of first full days are listed below.

	2004-5 (1425)	2005-6 (1426)	2006 (1427)
Muharram 1 (New Year)	February 21	February 10	January 30
Mawlid (Birthday of Muhammad)	May 1	April 21	April 10
Ramadan 1	October 15	October 4	September 23
Eid al-Fitr (Shawwal 1)	November 13	November 3	October 23
Eid al-Adha (Dhûl-Hijjah 10)	January 20	January 10	December 30

Major Holy Days for
BUDDHISTS AND HINDUS

BUDDHIST HOLY DAYS
Not all Buddhists use the same calendar to determine holidays and festivals. Here are some well-known Buddhist observances and the months in which they may fall:

Nirvana Day, mid-February: marks the death of Siddhartha Gautama (the Buddha).

Vesak or Visakah Puja (Buddha Day), April/May: the most important holiday. Celebrates the birth, enlightenment, and death of the Buddha.

Asalha Puja (Dharma Day), July: commemorates the Buddha's first teaching, in which he revealed the Four Noble Truths.

Magha Puja or Sangha Day, February: commemorates the day when 1,250 of Buddha's disciples (sangha) visited him without being called.

Vassa (Rains Retreat), July-October: a 3-month period during Asia's rainy season, when monks stay inside and study. Other people try to live simply and give up bad habits. Sometimes called "Buddhist Lent."

The Dalai Lama

HINDU HOLY DAYS
Different Hindu groups use different calendars. Here are a few of the many Hindu festivals and the months in which they may fall:

Maha Shivaratri, February/March: festival dedicated to Shiva, creator and destroyer.

Holi, March/April: festival of spring.

Ramanavami, March/April: anniversary of the birth of Rama, who is Vishnu in human form.

Diwali, October/November: Hindu New Year, the "Festival of Lights."

RELIGIOUS MEMBERSHIP
in the UNITED STATES

The two largest religious groups in the U.S. are Protestants followed by Roman Catholics. The pie chart below shows about how many people belong to these and other religious groups. These numbers are only estimates; no one knows exactly how many people belong to each group.

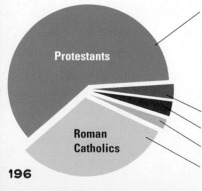

Protestants

Roman Catholics

More than 80 million
Including:

Baptists....................30 million	Methodists..........12 million
Pentecostals............11 million	Lutherans..............8 million
Mormon....................5 million	Presbyterians........4 million
Episcopalians............2 million	Reformed Churches...............2 million

Muslims.........................5-6 million

Jews............................6 million

Orthodox Christians.....4 million

63 million

There were also an estimated 2.5 million Buddhists and 1 million Hindus.

Science

Is there really such a thing as krypton? page 198

THE WORLD OF Science

The Latin root of the word "science" is *scire*, meaning "to know." There are many kinds of knowledge, but when people use the word *science* they usually mean a kind of knowledge that can be discovered and backed up by observation or experiments.

The branches of scientific study can be loosely grouped into the four main areas shown below. Each branch of science has more specific areas of study within them than can be listed here. For example **zoology** includes *entomology* (study of insects), which in turn includes *lepidopterology*, the study of butterflies and moths!

It's important to remember that in answering questions about our lives, our world, and our universe, scientists must often draw from more than one discipline. **Biochemists**, for example, deal with the chemistry that happens inside living things. **Paleontologists** study fossil remains of ancient plants and animals. **Astrophysicists** study matter and energy in outer space. And mathematics, considered by many to be an art and a science by itself, is used by all scientists.

Physical Science

ASTRONOMY—stars, planets, outer space
CHEMISTRY—properties and behaviors of substances
PHYSICS—matter and energy

Life Science (Biology)

ANATOMY—structure of the human body
BOTANY—plants
ECOLOGY—living things in relation to their environment
GENETICS—heredity
PATHOLOGY—diseases and their effects on the human body
PHYSIOLOGY—the body's biological processes
ZOOLOGY—animals

Earth Science

GEOGRAPHY—Earth's surface and its relationship to humans
GEOLOGY—Earth's structure
    MINERALOGY—minerals
    PETROLOGY—rocks
    SEISMOLOGY—earthquakes
    VOLCANOLOGY—volcanoes
HYDROLOGY—water
METEOROLOGY—Earth's atmosphere and weather
OCEANOGRAPHY—the sea, including currents and tides

Social Science

ANTHROPOLOGY—human cultures and physical characteristics
ECONOMICS—production and distribution of goods and services
POLITICAL SCIENCE—governments
PSYCHOLOGY—mental processes and behavior
SOCIOLOGY—human society and community life

WHAT EVERYTHING *IS* MADE OF

Everything we see and use is made up of basic ingredients called elements. There are more than 100 elements. Most have been found in nature. Some are created by scientists in labs.

Elements in Earth's Crust
(percent by weight)

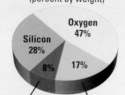

Oxygen 47%
Silicon 28%
8%
17%
Aluminum
Iron, Calcium, Sodium, Potassium, Others

Elements in the Atmosphere
(percent by volume)

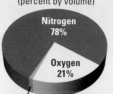

Nitrogen 78%
Oxygen 21%
1% Argon, Carbon Dioxide, Others

How Elements are Named
How many of these elements have you heard of?

Elements are named after places, scientists, figures in mythology, or properties of the element. But no element gets a name until the International Union of Pure and Applied Chemistry (IUPAC) accepts it. In all, 110 elements have been named. Several others have been reported, but not named and not yet confirmed.

NAME	SYMBOL	WHAT IT IS	WHEN FOUND	NAMED FOR
Aluminum	Al	metal	1825	*alumen,* Latin word for "alum"
Helium	He	gas	1868	the Greek work *helios,* meaning sun
Iodine	I	nonmetallic solid	1811	the Greek word *iodes,* meaning violet
Iridium	Ir	transitional metal	1804	the Latin word *iridis,* meaning rainbow
Krypton	Kr	gas	1898	the Greek word *kryptos,* meaning hidden
Mercury	Hg	transitional metal	B.C.	the Roman god Mercury
Neon	Ne	gas	1898	the Greek word *neon,* meaning new
Polonium	Po	metal	1898	Poland, native land of chemist Marie Curie; she and her husband discovered it.
Uranium	U	radioactive metal	1789	the planet Uranus

All About...
Compounds

Carbon, hydrogen, nitrogen, and oxygen are the most common chemical elements in the human body. Many other elements may be found in small amounts. These include calcium, iron, phosphorous, potassium, and sodium.

When elements join together, they form compounds. Water is a compound made up of hydrogen and oxygen. Salt is a compound made up of sodium and chlorine.

COMMON NAME	CONTAINS THE COMPOUND	CONTAINS THE ELEMENTS
Baking soda	sodium bicarbonate	sodium, hydrogen, carbon, oxygen
Chalk	calcium carbonate	calcium, carbon, oxygen
Hydrogen peroxide	hydrogen peroxide	hydrogen, oxygen
Rust	iron oxide	iron, oxygen
Sugar	sucrose	carbon, hydrogen, oxygen
Toothpaste	sodium fluoride	sodium, fluorine
Vinegar	acetic acid	carbon, hydrogen, oxygen

CHEMICAL SYMBOLS ARE SCIENTIFIC SHORTHAND

When scientists write the names of elements, they often use a symbol instead of spelling out the full name. The symbol for each element is one or two letters. Scientists write O for oxygen and He for helium. The symbols usually come from the English name for the element (C for carbon). The symbols for some of the elements come from the element's Latin name. For example, the symbol for gold is Au, which is short for *Aurum*, the Latin word for gold.

Homework Help

It All Starts With an Atom

The smallest possible piece of an element that has all the properties of the original element is called an **atom**. Each tiny atom is made up of even smaller particles called **protons, neutrons,** and **electrons**. These are made up of even smaller particles called **quarks**.

To tell one element from another, scientists count the number of protons in an atom. The total number of protons is called the element's **atomic number**. All of the atoms of an element have the same number of protons and electrons, but some atoms have a different number of neutrons. For example, carbon-12 has six protons and six neutrons, and carbon-13 has six protons and seven neutrons.

We call the amount of matter in an atom its **atomic mass.** Carbon-13 has a greater atomic mass than carbon-12. The average atomic mass of all of the different atoms of the same element is called the element's **atomic weight**. Every element has a different atomic number and a different atomic weight.

199

Some FAMOUS Scientists

ARCHIMEDES (about 287 B.C.–212 B.C.), Greek mathematician and inventor who discovered that heavy objects could be moved using pulleys and levers. He was one of the first to test his ideas with experiments. He also is said to have shouted "Eureka!" ("I have found it!").

NICOLAUS COPERNICUS (1473–1543), Polish scientist who is known as the founder of modern astronomy. He came up with the theory that Earth and other planets revolve around the Sun. But most thinkers continued to believe that Earth was the center of the universe.

GALILEO GALILEI (1564–1642), Italian astronomer and physicist who established basic principles of physics. Using a telescope he built, he observed the moons of Jupiter and craters on our Moon. He agreed with Copernicus that the Earth moves around the Sun.

Galileo Galilei

SIR ISAAC NEWTON (1642–1727), a British scientist who worked out the basic laws of motion and gravity. He also showed that sunlight is made up of all the colors of the rainbow. He invented the branch of mathematics called calculus, but he kept this discovery quiet. Soon after, the German philosopher Gottfried von Leibniz (1646–1716) also worked out a system of calculus, and made it widely known.

CHARLES DARWIN (1809–1882), British scientist who is best known for his theory of evolution by natural selection. According to this theory, living creatures, by gradually changing so as to have the best chances of survival, slowly developed over millions of years into the forms they have today.

GEORGE WASHINGTON CARVER (1864–1943), born in Missouri of slave parents, became world-famous for his agricultural research. He found many new and nutritious uses for peanuts and sweet potatoes, and taught farmers in the South to rotate their crops in order to increase their yield.

ALBERT EINSTEIN (1879–1955), German-American physicist who developed a revolutionary theory about the relationships between time, space, matter, and energy. He won a Nobel Prize in 1921.

Albert Einstein

MARGARET MEAD (1901–1978), U.S. anthropologist whose groundbreaking study of Samoan culture, *Coming of Age in Samoa*, was a best-seller in 1928. In it, she concluded that culture had a big influence on human behavior.

LEAKEY, a family of British paleontologists—Louis (1903–1972), Mary (1913–1996), and Richard (born 1944)—who discovered and studied fossil remains of early human ancestors in Africa. Mary's discovery in 1959 of a skull 1.7 million years old brought them worldwide fame. She continued her work after her husband Louis's death, and their son, Richard, followed in their footsteps.

RACHEL CARSON (1907–1964), U.S. biologist and leading environmentalist whose 1962 book *Silent Spring* warned that chemicals used to kill pests were killing harmless wildlife. Eventually DDT and certain other pesticides were banned in the U.S.

GERTRUDE ELION (1918–1999), U.S. chemist who played a key role in developing drugs to treat leukemia and viral diseases. She never earned a Ph.D., but she received many honorary degrees and, in 1988, won the Nobel Prize in Physiology or Medicine.

SCIENCE MUSEUMS

If you like exhibits you can touch interact with, here are a few museums that you might like to visit:

EXPLORATORIUM, San Francisco, California. Since 1969 this museum has been famous for all of its "hands-on" exhibits, which help visitors learn about animal behavior, electricity, hearing, heat and temperature, color, light, motion, sound and music, weather, and more.
WEB SITE *http://www.exploratorium.edu*

FRANKLIN INSTITUTE SCIENCE MUSEUM, Philadelphia, Pennsylvania. Benjamin Franklin has his own exhibit hall where visitors can experiment with some of his inventions. The bioscience exhibit invites people to listen to their own heartbeats and experience what it's like inside a human heart. "It's All in the Brain" helps visitors experience how the brain reacts to the outside world.
WEB SITE *http://www.fi.edu*

THE SCIENCE PLACE & TI FOUNDERS IMAX THEATER, Dallas, Texas. Opened in 1946, this museum has over 250 hands-on activities. It's also home to the only public planetarium in Dallas. Check out the Spider Maze exhibit, which has an interactive crawl-through web. The overnight "camp-in" is a popular event at this museum.
WEB SITE *http://www.scienceplace.org*

THE MUSEUM OF SCIENCE, Boston, Massachusetts, invites visitors to become explorers in the world of natural mysteries: check out the action on the Science Live! Stage, get wired in at the Cahners Computer Place, take a dip in the Virtual Fish Tank, and find out why "Seeing is Deceiving" at the Light House in the Investigate activity center.
WEB SITE *http://www.mos.org*

THE MUSEUM OF SCIENCE AND INDUSTRY, Chicago, Illinois, is the largest science museum in a single building in the Western Hemisphere. It has more than 800 exhibits. Among these is the Great Train Story, a 3,500-sq.-ft. model train display, elaborately depicting a journey from Seattle to Chicago.
WEB SITE *http://www.msichicago.org*

THE ONTARIO SCIENCE CENTRE, Toronto, Ontario, Canada, has scads of informative and occasionally wacky exhibits. The "Amazing Aging Machine," a computer with special imaging software, shows how you may look when you're 30 or 60 years older. The Van de Graaf generator—a giant silver ball—demonstrates electrical effects by making your hair stand up.
WEB SITE *http://www.ontariosciencecentre.ca*

Foucault Pendulum at the Museum of Science and Industry in Chicago

SCIENCE q&a

WHY DO PLANTS NEED SUNLIGHT? Sunlight—along with water and carbon dioxide, a gas found in the air—is necessary for **photosynthesis**. That's the process by which plants make their food. In fact, the word *photosynthesis* means putting together (*synthesis*) with light (*photo*). Leaves are the food factories in plants, where photosynthesis takes place. Chlorophyll, a chemical that gives leaves their green color, plays a key role in the process. Photosynthesis also releases oxygen into the atmosphere—a good thing, since that's what people breathe! In winter when there is less sunlight, photosynthesis slows down and then stops, and plants live off the food they have stored. When the green chlorophyll goes out of the leaves, they take on the color of other chemicals in them—that's how trees get their beautiful autumn leaves.

WHAT ARE CLOUDS MADE OF? Clouds are made up of a great many tiny droplets of water. The droplets are small enough that they don't fall to the ground, but there are enough of them that they can be seen. Clouds also contain dust, which the droplets stick to. Sometimes people "seed" clouds with dust, to help large drops of water form so that it will rain.

WHY DOES ICE FLOAT? Ice floats because it is less dense—its molecules are less tightly packed—than the water around it. The atoms of most substances are more tightly packed in the solid state than in the gas or liquid states. Water is special. It exists on Earth in all three states: gas (steam), liquid (water), and solid (ice). At 212° F (100° C) or higher, water is a gas. Below 212°F, it becomes a liquid. As water cools down, the atoms squeeze together-up to a point. At 39°F, the atoms spread out to link in a special way. At 32°F (0°C), water freezes and the atoms spread even farther apart to form a rigid crystal structure called "ice."

WHY DOES SHAKING A CAN OF SODA MAKE IT SPRAY? A can of soda contains *carbon dioxide* gas under pressure. The pressure makes it dissolve in the soda. Molecules in a liquid have a strong attraction for each other (called *surface tension*). It takes energy to separate them, so it is hard for the carbon dioxide inside the can to form bubbles. Once a bubble is formed, it takes less energy for the gas molecules to join the existing bubble. When you open a soda can, the gas escapes slowly and the soda takes a long time to go flat. But if you shake the can first, the little bit of gas above the soda seeps into the liquid as small bubbles. This gives the gas many "starting points" to get out—in a hurry.

HOW DO FISH BREATHE? Like humans and other animals, fish need to take in oxygen. But they get it in a different way—through their *gills*, which are located on either side of the fish, just behind the mouth. When fish open their mouths, water comes in; when they close their mouths the water is pumped over the gills. (This is how it works for most fish; sharks and some other species don't have as good a pumping system and so they need to keep swimming to force water over the gills.) The gills have surfaces with many tiny blood vessels—capillaries—and when the water passes over these surfaces, the oxygen in the water passes into the blood of the fish (as it does in people's lungs). The gills are delicate structures, held up by the water. When a fish is taken out of water, the gills collapse and the fish suffocates.

WHAT IS AN ECHO? An *echo* is a reflection of a sound. Sound travels in waves, which can bounce off another surface. The speed of sound is slow enough so that you can hear a repeat of the sound after a slight delay when the sound waves bounce back to you. When sound waves bounce off many surfaces, such as in a cave or a canyon, you might hear several echoes.

WHY IS THE SKY BLUE? *Sunlight* makes the sky blue. Light from the Sun is actually white until it reaches Earth's atmosphere. Then it hits water vapor, dust, and other particles in the air and scatters in different directions. White light is made up of all the colors of the spectrum. Since blue is scattered much more than any other color, blue is what we see when we look up at a clear sky. During sunrises and sunsets, we see red and orange because, with the Sun closer to the horizon, the light has to travel through much more of the atmosphere, and the blue is scattered before it gets to us, so that what's left is primarily red and orange light.

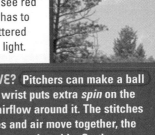

CAN A BASEBALL PITCHER REALLY MAKE A BALL CURVE? Pitchers can make a ball curve as much as 17½ inches from its path. A snap of the wrist puts extra *spin* on the ball. As it spins, the stitches on one side move with the airflow around it. The stitches on the other side move against the airflow. When stitches and air move together, the flow is faster. The increased speed reduces the air pressure on that side. On the opposite side, the air pressure is increased. The ball moves—curves—toward the side of the ball with the lower pressure.

WHAT CAUSES RAINBOWS? The light we usually see (visible light) is made up of different frequencies, or colors, in a certain range, called the *spectrum*. The colors of the visible spectrum are red, orange, yellow, green, blue, indigo, and violet. White light is a mixture of all these colors. A *prism* can separate the frequencies mixed in a beam of white light. When you see a rainbow, the tiny water droplets in the air act as many tiny prisms, separating the Sun's white light into the colors of the spectrum.

HOW DOES OIL MAKE "RAINBOWS" ON A WET STREET? Just like a soap bubble, a thin layer of oil on water creates interference effects. Light is reflected from two surfaces: from the top of the oil, and from the water surface beneath it. Light that passes through the oil gets slightly out of sync with the light reflected off the top. Scientists call this being "out of phase." The two sets of light waves can interfere with one another, increasing or decreasing the original frequency, which changes the color your eye sees. The colors you see in the oil layer depend on how thick it is and on the angle you view it from.

Here's a useful way to remember the order of the colors of the spectrum. Remember the name ROY G. BIV
R = red, O = orange, Y = yellow, G = green, B = blue, I = indigo, V = violet

WHAT IS DNA?

Every cell in every living thing (or organism) has **DNA**, a molecule that holds all the information about that organism. The structure of DNA was discovered in 1953 by the British scientist Francis Crick and the American scientist James Watson, building on research by others before them.

Lengths of connected DNA molecules, called **genes**, are like tiny pieces of a secret code. They determine what each organism is like in great detail. Almost all the DNA and genes come packaged in rod-like structures called **chromosomes**—humans have 46. There are 22 almost identical pairs, plus the X and Y chromosomes, which determine whether a human is male (one X chromosome and one Y chromosome) or female (two X chromosomes).

Genes are passed on from parents to children, and no two organisms (except clones or identical twins) have the same DNA. Many things—the color of our eyes or hair, whether we're tall or short, our chances of getting certain diseases—depend on our genes.

What Makes Us *Human*

The human genome is the DNA code for our species—it's what makes us human beings. In 2000, the U.S. Human Genome Project identified the 3.1 billion separate codes in human DNA. In 2003, researchers succeeded in mapping out all the human chromosomes. The human genome contains 30,000 to 40,000 genes. That's not many more genes than a roundworm—about 20,000—and it's fewer than the 50,000-plus genes of a rice plant! But unlike most other genes, human genes can produce more than one kind of protein. Proteins perform most life functions and make up a large part of cellular structures.

By studying human genes, scientists can learn more about hereditary diseases and get a better idea of how humans evolved.

Quick Quiz

1. **The most common element in the human body is**
   A hydrogen   B carbon   C oxygen   D nitrogen

2. **The last Ice Age occurred about how many years ago?**
   A last December   B 500-700   C 10,000   D 3 million

3. **Tree rings can help scientists study**
   A birds   B dinosaurs   C climate   D fruit

4. **Seismology is the study of**
   A earthquakes   B measurements   C monkeys   D caves

5. **The layers of gases that surround most planets are known as the**
   A biosphere   B hydrosphere   C atmosphere   D lithosphere

6. **The Greek mathematician, Euclid, is known as the father of**
   A Archimedes   B geometry   C algebra   D astronomy

7. **Plants usually breathe through small openings in their leaves called:**
   A gills   B stomata   C veins   D pupils

8. **Animals and plants are classified with words from which language?**
   A French   B English   C German   D Latin

9. **Which animal is the closest relative to human beings?**
   A orangutan   B chimpanzee   C mountain gorilla   D lemur

10. **Our organs are made up of millions of microscopic building blocks called**
    A H_2O B keys   C cells   D muscles

Answers on Pages 319–322. For more puzzles go to WWW.WORLDALMANACFORKIDS.COM

Build a **Volcano!**

A **stratovolcano** is kind we usually picture in our minds when we think of a volcano. It's a composite volcano, which means it's built up of lava flows mixed with layers of pyroclastic material—rock and ash that has erupted out of it (see page 87). A stratovolcano usually has steep sides and is fairly symmetrical. Alternating explosive and quiet eruptions of thick lava create these tall cones. After making its basic form, you can let this volcano build itself by mixing mini-batches of "lava" and letting them drip down the sides.

This can get messy, so wear old clothes, and be sure to have an adult around!

WHAT YOU NEED:

- ▶ Cardboard, newspaper, paper towels, cardboard tube
- ▶ White glue, masking tape, small paper cups
- ▶ Paint: red and black (any kind of water-based paint)
- ▶ Small paintbrush or sticks
- ▶ Small container (film container, shampoo bottle cap, etc.)
- ▶ Baking soda, white vinegar, water, liquid soap
- ▶ Sand, pebbles, red food coloring, flour, coffee grounds.

BUILDING THE VOLCANO:

▶ Use a square of cardboard as the base. Tape the cardboard tube upright in the center.

▶ Make loose paper balls of different sizes and tape them so they keep their shape. Put them around the tube to build up the basic cone shape of your volcano. Tape them in place.

▶ Cover the volcano with paper towels dipped in a water and glue mix. Two layers should do it. This will be the surface of your volcano (aluminum foil will work too). Make sure you leave a hole at the top for your film container to fit down into.

▶ In a paper cup, mix some black paint with a little flour and coffee grounds (or sand). You want it to flow, but not too fast. With a brush or stick, try letting a few drops of the mix drip onto the lip of the volcano. Let the drops fall in the same spot until it begins to flow down the side of the volcano. Keep mixing and dripping batches down the sides until most of your volcano is covered. When you get the hang of it, you can pour it right from the cup onto the volcano lip. Watch it ooze slowly down the mountain!

▶ The black represents old flows that have cooled. To make flows that haven't quite cooled all the way, mix a little red into the black.

▶ Sprinkle sand (or brown sugar) and even small rocks onto the wet flows to represent pyroclastic material.

▶ To make fresh lava flows that are "hot," make your mix with just red paint. These can be slightly runnier than your black flows.

▶ To make an "eruption," mix a little water, red food coloring, and baking soda in the small container. Put it in the top of your volcano. Pour a little vinegar into it and watch the pink fizz flow over the sides like a lava flow.

Space

What are "Spirit" and "Opportunity"? page 213

The SOLAR SYSTEM

Earth and the planets travel around the Sun. Together with the Sun, they are part of the solar system.

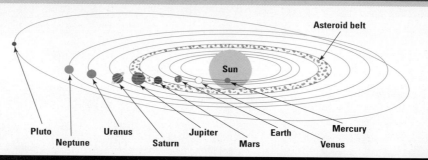

Asteroid belt

Sun

Pluto
Neptune
Uranus
Saturn
Jupiter
Mars
Earth
Venus
Mercury

The SUN is a STAR

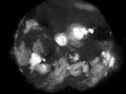

Did you know that the Sun is a star, like the other stars you see at night? It is a typical, medium-size star. But because the Sun is much closer to our planet than any other star, we can study it in great detail. The diameter of the Sun is 864,000 miles—more than 100 times Earth's diameter. The gravity of the Sun is nearly 28 times the gravity of Earth.

How Hot Is the Sun? The surface temperature of the sun is close to 10,000°F, and it is believed that the Sun's inner core may reach temperatures around 30 million degrees! The Sun provides enough light and heat energy to support all forms of life on our planet.

The Planets are in Motion

The planets move around the Sun along elliptical paths called **orbits**. One complete path around the Sun is called a **revolution**. Earth takes one year, or 365 1/4 days, to make one revolution around the Sun. Planets that are farther away from the Sun take longer. Some planets have one or more **moons**. A moon orbits a planet in much the same way that the planets orbit the Sun. Each planet also spins (or rotates) on its **axis**. An axis is an imaginary line running through the center of a planet. The time it takes Earth to rotate on its axis equals one day.

Here's a useful way to remember the names of planets in order of their usual distance from the Sun. Think of this sentence: **M**y **V**ery **E**xcellent **M**other **J**ust **S**ent **U**s **N**ine **P**izzas

M = Mercury, **V** = Venus, **E** = Earth, **M** = Mars, **J** = Jupiter, **S** = Saturn, **U** = Uranus, **N** = Neptune, **P** = Pluto.

WHAT'S OUT THERE?

What is in the Universe besides planets?

GALAXY is the name of a group of billions of stars held together by gravity. Galaxies also contain interstellar gas and dust. The universe may have about 50 billion galaxies. The one we live in is called the **Milky Way**. The Sun and most stars we see are just a few of the more than 200 billion stars in the Milky Way.

NEBULA is the name historically given to any fuzzy patch in the sky, even galaxies and star clusters. **Planetary nebulas** come from the late stages of some stars, while star clusters and galaxies are star groupings. **Emission nebulas,** reflection nebulas, and dark dust clouds are regions of interstellar gas and dust that may be hundreds of light-years wide and are often birthplaces of stars. Emission nebulas give off a reddish glow, caused when their hydrogen gas is heated by newly formed, hot stars in the vicinity. Dust particles in some areas reflect hot blue starlight and appear as reflection nebulas. Dark dust clouds, though still mainly gas, contain enough dust to absorb starlight and appear as **dark nebulas**.

Great Nebula in Orion

BLACK HOLE is the name given to a region in space with gravity so strong that nothing can get out—not even light. Black holes are most likely formed when giant stars at least 20 times as massive as our Sun burn up their fuel and collapse, creating very dense cores. Scientists also think bigger, "supermassive" black holes may form from the collapse of many stars in the centers of galaxies. Astronomers can't see black holes, since they do not give off light. They watch for signs, such as effects on the orbits of nearby stars, or X-ray bursts from matter being sucked into the black hole.

SATELLITES are objects that move in an orbit around a planet. Moons are natural satellites. Artificial satellites, launched into orbit by humans, are used as space stations and observatories. They are also used to take pictures of Earth's surface and to transmit communications signals.

Comet Hale-Bopp

ASTEROIDS (or minor planets) are solid chunks of rock or metal that range in size from small boulders to hundreds of miles across. Ceres, the largest, is about 600 miles in diameter. Thousands of asteroids orbit the Sun between Mars and Jupiter in what we call the Asteroid Belt.

COMETS are moving chunks of ice, dust, and rock that form huge gaseous heads as they move nearer to the Sun. One of the most well-known is Halley's Comet. It can be seen about every 76 years and will appear in the sky again in the year 2061.

METEOROIDS are small pieces of stone or metal traveling in space. Most meteoroids are fragments from comets or asteroids that broke off from crashes in space with other objects. A few are actually chunks that blew off the Moon or Mars after an asteroid hit. When a meteoroid enters the Earth's atmosphere, it usually burns up completely. This streak of light is called a meteor, or "shooting star." If a piece of a meteoroid survives its trip through our atmosphere and lands on Earth, it is called a **meteorite**.

THE PLANETS

1 MERCURY

Average distance from the Sun: 36 million miles
Diameter: 3,032 miles
Average temp.: 333° F
Surface: silicate rock
Time to revolve around the Sun: 88 days
Time to rotate on its axis: 58 days, 15 hours, 36 minutes
Number of moons: 0

didyouknow? *Scientists believe that the Caloris Basin—a crater over 800 miles wide and big enough to hold Texas—was created by the impact of an asteroid slamming into Mercury 4 billion years ago.*

2 VENUS

Average distance from the Sun: 67 million miles
Diameter: 7,521 miles
Average temp.: 867° F
Surface: silicate rock
Time to revolve around the Sun: 224.7 days
Time to rotate on its axis: 243 days
Number of moons: 0

didyouknow? *Venus has more volcanoes than any other planet in the solar system— perhaps 100,000, or even more. Volcanic plains—plains where lava has flowed— cover much of the planet's surface.*

3 EARTH

Average distance from the Sun: 93 million miles
Diameter: 7,926 miles
Average temp.: 59° F
Surface: water, basalt and granite rock
Time to revolve around the Sun: 365 ¼ days
Time to rotate on its axis: 23 hours, 56 minutes, 4.2 seconds
Number of moons: 1

didyouknow? *The temperature inside the Earth goes up about 1 degree F for every 100-200 feet in depth; the temperature at the center is thought to be about 8,000-9,000 degrees F.*

4 MARS

Average distance from the Sun: 142 million miles
Diameter: 4,213 miles
Average temp.: −81° F
Surface: iron-rich basaltic rock
Time to revolve around the Sun: 687 days
Time to rotate on its axis: 24 hours, 37 minutes, 22 seconds
Number of moons: 2

didyouknow? *In 1877, Italian astronomer Giovanni Schiaparelli thought he saw lines on Mars, which he called "channels," or "canali" in Italian. This was mistranslated into English as "canals," making people think there were intelligent canal-building Martians.*

5 JUPITER

Average distance from the Sun: 484 million miles
Diameter: 88,732 miles
Average temp.: −162° F
Surface: liquid hydrogen
Time to revolve around the Sun: 11.9 years
Time to rotate on its axis: 9 hours, 55 minutes, 30 seconds
Number of moons: 61

didyouknow? *The 4 largest moons were discovered by Galileo in 1610; 21 others were not found until 2003.*

6 SATURN

Average distance from the Sun: 888 million miles
Diameter: 74,975 miles
Average temp.: −218° F
Surface: liquid hydrogen
Time to revolve around the Sun: 29.5 years
Time to rotate on its axis: 10 hours, 39 minutes, 22 seconds
Number of moons: 31

didyouknow? *Saturn's rings—which are made up of millions of particles—are more than 100,000 miles wide, but only about 700 feet thick.*

7 URANUS

Average distance from the Sun:
1.8 billion miles
Diameter: 31,763 miles
Average temp.: −323° F
Surface: liquid hydrogen and helium
Time to revolve around the Sun: 84 years
Time to rotate on its axis: 17 hours, 14 minutes
Number of moons: 26

did you know? *Because Uranus is tipped 98 degrees on its axis, its seasons are far more extreme than those of Earth: the north pole is dark for 42 years at a time.*

8 NEPTUNE

Average distance from the Sun:
2.8 billion miles
Diameter: 30,603 miles
Average temp.: −330° F
Surface: liquid hydrogen and helium
Time to revolve around the Sun: 164.8 years
Time to rotate on its axis: 16 hours, 6 minutes
Number of moons: 13

did you know? *Neptune was discovered in 1846, after British astronomer John Adams and French mathematician Urbain Le Verrier independently predicted where it would be, based on its effect on Uranus's orbit.*

9 PLUTO

Average distance from the Sun:
3.6 billion miles
Diameter: 1,413 miles
Average temp.: −369° F
Surface: rock and frozen gases
Time to revolve around the Sun: 247.7 years
Time to rotate on its axis: 6 days, 9 hours, 18 minutes
Number of moons: 1

did you know? *Some scientists do not consider Pluto a planet, but rather one of many large objects orbiting the Sun outside Neptune's orbit.*

In November 2003, astronomers discovered the **most far-away** object ever found in our solar system. It's currently over 8 billion miles from Earth and takes 10,500 Earth years to complete one orbit around the Sun. The temperature there never goes above −400° F, so the scientists proposed naming it **Sedna**, after the Inuit goddess who lived in an icy cave at the bottom of the ocean. If Pluto is called a planet, this may be called a planet too. It would be the **smallest** planet, after Pluto, and the **coldest**!

More Planet Facts

Largest planet: JUPITER
Fastest-moving planet: MERCURY (107,000 MPH)
Warmest planet: VENUS
Shortest day: MERCURY

Longest day: JUPITER
Planet closest to the Sun: MERCURY
Planet closest to Earth: VENUS (Every 19 months, Venus gets closer to Earth than any other planet ever does.)

The MOON

The moon is about 238,900 miles from Earth. It is 2,160 miles in diameter and has no atmosphere. The dusty surface is covered with deep craters. It takes the same time for the moon to rotate on its axis as it does to orbit Earth (27 days, 7 hours, 43 minutes). This is why one side of the moon is always facing Earth. The moon has no light of its own, but reflects light from the Sun. The fraction of the lighted part of the moon that we see at a certain time is called a phase. It takes the moon about 29½ days to go through all its phases. This is called a **lunar month.**

PHASES of the MOON

| New Moon | Crescent Moon | First Quarter | Full Moon | Last Quarter | Crescent Moon | New Moon |

What is an ECLIPSE?

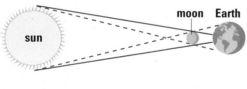

During a **solar eclipse,** the moon casts a shadow on Earth. A total solar eclipse is when the Sun is completely blocked out. When this happens, the halo of gas around the Sun called the **corona** can be seen.

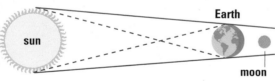

Sometimes Earth casts a shadow on the moon. During a total **lunar eclipse,** the moon remains visible, but it looks dark, often with a reddish tinge (from sunlight bent through Earth's atmosphere).

Upcoming total Solar Eclipses

TOTAL SOLAR ECLIPSES
March 29, 2006
Will be seen across the Atlantic Ocean, Africa, and part of Asia.
August 1, 2008
Will be seen in northern Canada, Greenland, and Asia.
July 22, 2009
Will be seen in eastern Asia and the central Pacific Ocean.

Upcoming total Lunar Eclipses

TOTAL LUNAR ECLIPSES
October 28, 2004
Will be seen in North and South America, Europe, and Africa.
March 3, 2007
Will be seen in the Americas, Europe, Africa, and Asia.
August 28, 2007
Will be seen in eastern Asia, Australia, the Pacific Ocean, and the Americas.

CONSTELLATIONS

Ancient cultures used myths to explain how constellations came to be. The constellation of Cassiopeia looks like the letter "W" in the sky. In Greek mythology, Cassiopeia was an Ethiopian queen. She was the wife of Cepheus and the mother of Andromeda. According to tradition, when she died she was changed into the constellation that is named after her.

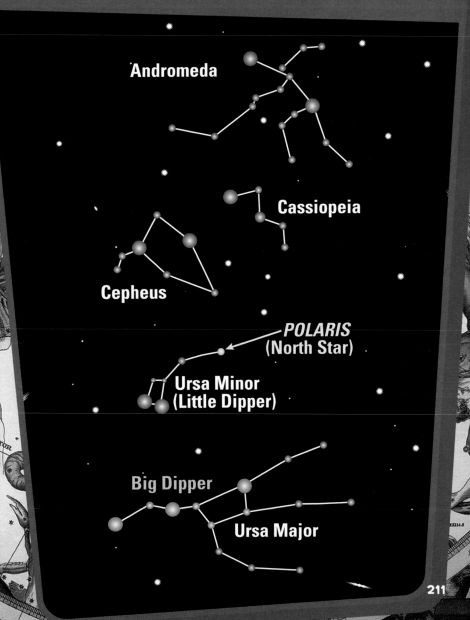

Andromeda

Cassiopeia

Cepheus

POLARIS
(North Star)

Ursa Minor
(Little Dipper)

Big Dipper

Ursa Major

211

American space exploration began in 1958, when the Explorer I satellite was launched into orbit and NASA (the National Aeronautics and Space Administration) was formed.

SEARCHING for LIFE

For years scientists have tried to discover whether there is life on other planets in our solar system or elsewhere. They look for signs of what is needed for life on Earth—basics like water and proper temperature.

NASA is searching for signs of life on Mars. This search will continue until at least 2013. Some spacecraft will fly around Mars taking pictures. Others will land there to study soil and rocks and look for living things. Scientists have already found evidence that there was water on Mars at least in the past.

NASA has a new telescope mission planned for 2005 called the Terrestrial Planet Finder. It will look for planets similar to Earth in other solar systems through a giant, space-based telescope.

Outside of NASA, another program is looking for life on other worlds. It is called SETI (Search for Extraterrestrial Intelligence). Most often it uses powerful radio telescopes to detect signs of life. Recently, however, astronomers began searching for light signals as signs of extraterrestrial life.

UNMANNED MISSIONS
in the Solar System

LAUNCH DATE

1962	**Mariner 2** First successful flyby of Venus.	
1964	**Mariner 4** First probe to reach Mars, 1965.	
1972	**Pioneer 10** First probe to reach Jupiter, 1973.	
1973	**Mariner 10** Only U.S. probe to reach Mercury, 1974.	
1975	**Viking 1 and 2** Landed on Mars in 1976.	
1977	**Voyager 1** Reached Jupiter in 1979 and Saturn in 1980.	
1977	**Voyager 2** Reached Jupiter in 1979, Saturn in 1981, Uranus in 1986, Neptune in 1989.	
1989	**Magellan** Orbited Venus and mapped its surface.	
1989	**Galileo** Reached Jupiter, 1995.	
1996	**Mars Global Surveyor** Began mapping surface in 1999.	
1996	**Mars Pathfinder** Landed on Mars, sent a roving vehicle (Sojourner) to explore the surface in 1997.	
1996	**Near Shoemaker** First to land on an asteroid (Eros), early 2001.	
1997	**Cassini** Expected to reach Saturn in July 2004.	
2001	**Mars Odyssey** Began mapping and studying Mars in early 2002.	
2004	**Rosetta** Expected to land on a far-away comet in 2014.	
2004	**Deep Impact** Set to launch in December, should reach a nearer comet in July 2005.	

MARS ROVERS

On January 3, 2004, the NASA mission control crew at the Jet Propulsion Laboratory in California celebrated when *Spirit*, the first of its two Mars Exploration Rovers, landed safely on the surface of Mars. A few weeks later, on January 24, a second rover, *Opportunity*, successfully touched down on the opposite side of the red planet.

Within hours of landing, both of these robot geologists immediately beamed breathtaking images of Mars back to Earth, revealing a reddish rocky surface near *Spirit*, and a powdery dark red soil with outcroppings of bedrock near *Opportunity*. Over the next 90 "sols" (Martian days), equal to 92 days on Earth, NASA sent remote commands over millions of miles to the rovers, instructing them to move across the Martian surface. The rovers took hundreds of pictures and analyzed Martian rocks. One of the main goals of the mission was to search for signs of water, and help scientists answer the questions about whether or not Mars once supported life.

WATER ON MARS

On March 2, NASA scientists announced that data returned by *Opportunity* showed beyond a doubt that liquid water once flowed on the surface of Mars. Scientists don't know how long or when exactly the water was there. But the presence of water means there may well have been some form of life on Mars, at least in the past. Some scientists believe there may still be liquid water flowing deep under the planet's surface, and that some form of life may thrive there even now.

WHO AM I?

I was born in Decatur, Alabama, and grew up in Chicago, Illinois. I have degrees in chemical engineering and African and Afro-American studies. I am also a medical doctor. I was selected for the NASA astronaut program in 1987, and flew on the space shuttle *Endeavour* in 1992 as a Science Mission Specialist. My spaceflight on *Endeavour* made me the first African-American woman in space.

Answer: Dr. Mae Jemison

First Astronauts in SPACE

The start of the U.S. space program in 1958 was a response to the Soviet Union's launching of its satellite Sputnik I into orbit on October 4, 1957. In 1961, three years after NASA was formed, President John F. Kennedy promised Americans that the United States would land a person on the moon by the end of the 1960s. NASA landed men on the moon in July 1969. Since then, more than 400 astronauts have made trips into outer space. This time line shows some of their early flights.

1961 On April 12, Soviet cosmonaut Yuri Gagarin, in *Vostok 1,* became the **first human to orbit Earth**. On May 5, U.S. astronaut Alan B. Shepard Jr. of the *Mercury 3* mission became the first American in space.

1962 On February 20, U.S. astronaut John H. Glenn Jr. of *Mercury 6* became the **first American to orbit Earth**.

1963 From June 16 to 19, the Soviet spacecraft *Vostok 6* carried the **first woman in space**, Valentina V. Tereshkova.

1965 On March 18, Soviet cosmonaut Aleksei A. Leonov became the **first person to walk in space**. He spent 10 minutes outside the spaceship. On December 15, *U.S. Gemini 6A* and *7* (with astronauts) became the **first vehicles to rendezvous** (approach and see each other) **in space**.

1966 On March 16, *U.S. Gemini 8* became the **first craft to dock with** (become attached to) **another vehicle** (an unmanned *Agena* rocket).

1967 On January 27, a fire in a U.S. *Apollo* spacecraft on the ground killed astronauts Virgil I. Grissom, Edward H. White, and Roger B. Chaffee. On April 24, *Soyuz 1* crashed on Earth, killing Soviet cosmonaut Vladimir Komarov.

1969 On July 20, after successful flights of *Apollo 8, 9,* and *10*, U.S. *Apollo 11*'s **lunar module** *Eagle* **landed on the moon's surface** in the area known as the Sea of Tranquility. Neil Armstrong became the **first person ever to walk on the moon**.

1970 In April, *Apollo 13* astronauts returned safely to Earth after an explosion damaged their spacecraft and prevented them from landing on the moon.

1971 In July and August, U.S. *Apollo 15* astronauts tested the **Lunar Rover** on the moon.

1972 In December, *Apollo 17* was the sixth and **final U.S. space mission to land successfully on the moon**.

1973 On May 14, the U.S. put its **first space station, Skylab**, into orbit. The last Skylab crew left in January 1974.

1975 On July 15, the U.S. launched an *Apollo* spacecraft and the U.S.S.R. launched a *Soyuz* spacecraft. Two days later, the **American and Soviet crafts docked**, and for several days their crews worked and spent time together in space. This was NASA's last space mission with astronauts until the space shuttle.

In the 1970s, NASA developed the space shuttle program. Earlier space capsules could not be used again after returning to Earth. In 1986, the Soviet Union launched its MIR space station. By the mid-1990s, the U.S. and Russia were sharing projects in space.

1977	The first shuttle, **Enterprise**, took off from the back of a 747 jet airliner.
1981	**Columbia** was launched and became the first shuttle to reach Earth's orbit.
1983	In April, NASA began using a third shuttle, **Challenger**.
1984	In August, the shuttle **Discovery** was launched for the first time.
1985	In October, the shuttle **Atlantis** was launched for the first time.
1986	On January 28, after 24 successful missions, **Challenger** exploded 73 seconds after takeoff. All seven astronauts, including teacher Christa McAuliffe, died. In February, the Soviet space station **Mir** was launched into orbit.
1988	In September new safety procedures led to a successful launch of **Discovery**.
1990	On April 24, the **Hubble Space Telescope** was launched from **Discovery**.
1992	In May, NASA launched a new shuttle, **Endeavour**.
1995	In June, **Atlantis** docked with **Mir** for the first time.
1998	In December, **Endeavour** was launched with **Unity**, a U.S.-built part of the International Space Station (ISS). The crew attached it to the Russian-built **Zarya** control module.
2000	The first crew arrived at the ISS in November.
2001	In February, **Atlantis** carried the lab module **Destiny** to the ISS. **Mir** parts splashed down in the Pacific in March, ending the 15-year Russian program.
2002	In March, **Columbia** astronauts carried out the fourth repair/upgrade of the **Hubble Space Telescope**.
2003	On February 1, 2003, after a 16-day scientific mission, space shuttle **Columbia** disintegrated during its reentry into the Earth's atmosphere, killing the seven-member crew.

The **International Space Station** (ISS) is being built by 16 countries, including the U.S. and Russia. When it's finished, the ISS will weigh over 1 million pounds. It will be about a hundred yards square (356 feet wide and 290 feet long). That's four times bigger than the Russian *Mir* space station. There will be almost an acre of solar panels to supply electricity to the 52 computers and six scientific laboratories on board. The ISS is orbiting the Earth at an average altitude of 240 miles.

Since the February 2003 *Columbia* disaster, U.S. space shuttles have been grounded. The next U.S. launch was not expected until 2005. Since the space shuttles are the only vehicles that can carry the big parts needed to finish the ISS, the date for completing work on the space station has been pushed from 2006 to 2008. In the meantime, astronauts continue to travel to the ISS on Russian *Soyuz* rockets.

The ZODIAC

The **zodiac** is an imaginary belt that goes around the sky. The orbits of the Sun, the moon, and planets known to ancient peoples are within it. The zodiac is divided into 12 sections, which are called **signs of the zodiac**. The ancient Babylonians named each of the sections for a constellation that could be seen within its limits during ancient times. Astrologers believe that your personality and fortune are influenced by the sign under which you were born. But this belief has no scientific basis.

ARIES (Ram)
March 21–April 19

TAURUS (Bull)
April 20–May 20

GEMINI (Twins)
May 21–June 21

CANCER (Crab)
June 22–July 22

LEO (Lion)
July 23–August 22

VIRGO (Maiden)
August 23–Sept. 22

LIBRA (Balance)
Sept. 23–Oct. 23

SCORPIO (Scorpion)
Oct. 24–Nov. 21

SAGITTARIUS
(Archer)
Nov. 22–Dec. 21

CAPRICORN (Goat)
Dec. 22–Jan. 19

AQUARIUS
(Water Bearer)
Jan. 20–Feb. 18

PISCES (Fishes)
Feb. 19–March 20

The Riddle of Mars

Years ago, people believed there were canals filled with water on Mars. Today, scientists know that isn't true. But they do have evidence that water once flowed on Mars and that there is still frozen water on the planet.

Imagine that Mars really did have canals connecting these outposts marked with letters. Starting at the outpost marked with a red T, can you go to each station only once, in order to form a sentence?

ANSWERS ON PAGES 319-322.
FOR MORE PUZZLES GO TO
WWW.WORLDALMANACFORKIDS.COM

Sports

Who invented basketball? page 219

BASEBALL

In the 2003 World Series, marking the 100th aniversary of baseball's fall classic, the Florida Marlins defeated the New York Yankees, 4 games to 2, to win their 2nd Series in 7 years. The Marlins, an expansion team that joined the league in 1993, had become the 1st wild-card team to win a World Series in 1997. The only other wild-card team to win it all were the Anaheim Angels in 2002.

Behind pitcher Josh Beckett's complete-game, 5-hit shutout, the Marlins beat the heavily favored Yankees, 2-0, in the decisive Game 6 on Oct. 25, 2003, at Yankee Stadium in New York City. Pitching on only 3 days rest, the 23-year-old right-hander struck out 9 and allowed no runners past 2nd base. Beckett, who in 2 starts gave up only 2 runs in 16 ⅓ innings, was named MVP of the World Series.

2003 MAJOR LEAGUE LEADERS

MVP AWARD
NL: Barry Bonds, San Francisco
AL: Alex Rodriguez, Texas

CY YOUNG AWARD (top pitcher)
NL: Eric Gagne, Los Angeles
AL: Roy Halladay, Toronto

ROOKIE OF THE YEAR
NL: Dontrell Willis, Florida
AL: Angel Berroa, Kansas City

BATTING CHAMPS
NL: Albert Pujols, St. Louis, .359
AL: Bill Mueller, Boston, .326

HOME RUN LEADERS
NL: Jim Thome, Philadelphia, 47
AL: Alex Rodriguez, Texas, 47

EARNED RUN AVERAGE LEADERS
NL: Jason Schmidt, San Francisco, 2.34
AL: Pedro Martinez, Boston, 2.22

Rodriguez

COOL FEATS, FACTS, & FIRSTS

▶ On July 29, 2003, Boston's switch-hitter Bill Mueller became the only player in Major League history to hit a grand slam from both sides of the plate in the same game (and in consecutive at bats) in the Red Sox 14-7 win over the Texas Rangers.

▶ Deion Sanders is the only athlete ever to play in both the World Series and the Super Bowl. He played in the 1992 Series with the Atlanta Braves and in the Super Bowl for the San Francisco 49ers (1995) and Dallas Cowboys (1996).

▶ Wes Ferrell hit more home runs in his career (38) than any pitcher in history. His 9 homers in 1931 are still a single season record for his position.

▶ Ed Vosberg holds a special place in baseball history. He's the only athlete to play in the World Series in Little League (1973), in college (University of Arizona, champions, 1980), and also in the Major Leagues (Florida Marlins, champions, 1997).

Some Major League Records*

BATTERS

Most home runs
Career: 755, Hank Aaron (1954-76)
Season: 73, **Barry Bonds** (2001)
Game: 4, by 12 different players

Most hits
Career: 4,256, Pete Rose (1963-86)
Season: 257, George Sisler (1920)
Game: 7, Rennie Stennett (1975)

Most stolen bases
Career: 1,406, **Rickey Henderson** (1979-)
Season: 130, **Rickey Henderson** (1982)
Game: 6, Wilbert Robinson (1892);
        Eddie Collins (1912)

PITCHERS

Most strikeouts
Career: 5,714, Nolan Ryan (1966-93)
Season: 383, Nolan Ryan (1973)
Game: 20, **Roger Clemens** (1986, 1996);
        Kerry Wood (1998)

Most wins
Career: 511, Cy Young (1890-1911)
Season: 41, Jack Chesbro (1904)

Most saves
Career: 478, Lee Smith (1980-97)
Season: 57, Bobby Thigpen (1990)

*Through the 2003 season. Players in bold played in 2003. Game stats are for nine-inning games only.

WHO AM I?

I was born in Georgia on January 31, 1919. I went to college at UCLA, in California, where I lettered in baseball, basketball, football, and track. But I'm most remembered for playing baseball for the Brooklyn Dodgers in 1947. I was named Rookie of the Year then and two years later, I was the National League MVP. I was elected to the Baseball Hall of Fame in 1962.

Answer: Jackie Robinson, first black major leaguer

BASEBALL HALL of FAME

The National Baseball Hall of Fame and Museum opened in 1939, in Cooperstown, New York. To be eligible for membership, players must be retired from baseball for five years. In 2004, Dennis Eckersley and Paul Molitor were headed to Cooperstown.

WEB SITE http://www.baseballhalloffame.org

Hall of Fame plaque for Hank Aaron, the all-time leader in home runs ▶

LITTLE LEAGUE

little League Baseball is the largest youth sports program in the world. It began in 1939 in Williamsport, Pennsylvania, with 45 boys playing on three teams. Now nearly three million boys and girls ages 5 to 18 play on 200,000 Little League teams in more than 80 countries.

WEB SITE http://www.littleleague.org

BASKETBALL

Basketball began in 1891 in Springfield, Massachusetts, when Dr. James Naismith invented it, using peach baskets as hoops. At first, each team had nine players instead of five. Big-time pro basketball started in 1949, when the National Basketball Association (NBA) was formed. The Women's National Basketball Association (WNBA) began play in 1997.

HIGHLIGHTS OF THE 2002–2003 NBA SEASON

SCORING LEADER:
Tracy McGrady,
Orlando Magic

Games: 67
Points: 1,878
Average: 28.0

REBOUNDING LEADER:
Kevin Garnett ▶
Minnesota Timberwolves

Games: 82
Rebounds: 1,139
Average: 13.9

BLOCKED SHOTS LEADER:
Theo Ratliff,
Portland
Trailblazerss

Games: 82
Blocks: 307
Average: 3.61

ASSISTS LEADER:
Jason Kidd,
New Jersey Nets

Games: 67
Assists: 618
Average: 9.2

STEALS LEADER:
Baron Davis,
New Orleans Hornets

Games: 67
Steals: 158
Average: 2.36

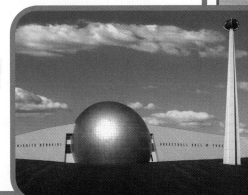

Hall of Fame

The Naismith Memorial Basketball Hall of Fame in Springfield, Massachusetts, was founded in 1959 to honor great basketball players, coaches, referees, and others important to the history of the game. The new Basketball Hall of Fame opened in 2002, with a 120-foot diameter "basketball" as part of the building. The newest class, headed for the Hall of Fame, in September 2004 includes Clyde Drexler, Maurice Stokes, first female Globetrotter Lynette Woodard, coach Bill Sharman, and international star Drazen Dalipagic.

WEB SITE http://www.hoophall.com

The NBA record for most three-pointers in a game without a miss is held by Latrell Sprewell. He set the record playing for the New York Knicks when he hit 9 out of 9 three-point shots in a game against the Los Angeles Clippers on February 4, 2003.

Some All-Time NBA Records*

POINTS

Career: 38,387, Kareem Abdul Jabbar (1969-89)

Season: 4,029, Wilt Chamberlain (1961-62)

Game: 100, Wilt Chamberlain (1962)

ASSISTS

Career: 15,806, **John Stockton** (1984-2003)

Season: 1,164 **John Stockton** (1990-91)

Game: 30, Scott Skiles (1990)

REBOUNDS

Career: 23,924, Wilt Chamberlain (1959-73)

Season: 2,149, Wilt Chamberlain (1960-61)

Game: 55, Wilt Chamberlain (1960)

3-POINTERS

Career: 2,330, **Reggie Miller** (1987-)

Season: 267, Dennis Scott (1996-97)

Game: 12, **Kobe Bryant** (2003)

Through the 2003 season. Players in bold played in 2003.

HIGHLIGHTS
of the
2003
WNBA
SEASON

A year after posting the worst record in the WNBA (9-23), the Detroit Shock denied the Los Angeles Sparks a third straight WNBA Championship. Detroit defeated Los Angeles, 83-78, in Game 3 of the WNBA Finals, Sept. 16 at the Palace of Auburn Hills in Michigan. Detroit center Ruth Riley scored a career-high 27 points and was named MVP of the Finals. The Shock became only the 3rd champion in WNBA history, after Los Angeles and 4-time winners Houston.

WNBA STATISTICAL LEADERS AND AWARDS IN 2003

Most Valuable Player: Ruth Riley, Detroit
Defensive Player of the Year: Sheryl Swoopes, Houston
Coach of the Year: Bill Laimbeer, Detroit
Most Improved Player of the Year: Michelle Snow, Houston
Scoring Leader: Lauren Jackson, Seattle
Games: 33   Points: 698   Average: 21.2
Rebounding Leader: Chamique Holdsclaw, Washington
Games: 27   Rebounds: 294   Average: 10.9
Assists Leader: Ticha Penicheiro, Sacramento
Games: 34   Assists: 229   Average: 6.7

◄ *Ruth Riley*

College Basketball

The men's National Collegiate Athletic Association (NCAA) Tournament began in 1939. Today, it is a spectacular 65-team extravaganza. The Final Four weekend, when the semi-finals and finals are played, is one of the most-watched sports competitions in the U.S. The Women's NCAA Tournament began in 1982. Since then, the popularity of the women's game has grown by leaps and (re)bounds.

THE 2004 NCAA TOURNAMENT RESULTS

MEN'S FINAL FOUR
SEMI-FINALS:
Georgia Tech 67, Oklahoma St. 65
Connecticut 79, Duke 78
FINALS:
Connecticut 82, Georgia Tech 73
MOST OUTSTANDING PLAYER:
Emeka Okafor

WOMEN'S FINAL FOUR
SEMI-FINALS:
Tennessee 52, LSU 50
Connecticut 67, Minnesota 58
FINALS:
Connecticut 70, Tennessee 61
MOST OUTSTANDING PLAYER:
Diana Taurasi, Connecticut

THE JOHN R. WOODEN AWARD
Awarded to the nation's outstanding male college basketball player by the Los Angeles Athletic Club.

2004 winner: Jameer Nelson, St. Joseph

THE WADE TROPHY
Awarded to the nation's outstanding female college basketball player by the National Association for Girls and Women in Sport.

2003 winner: Alana Beard, Duke

CYCLING

The "modern" bicycle, with two wheels the same size, pedals, and a chain drive, appeared at the end of the 1800s. In fact, it was not until 1869 that the name *bicycle* came into use. Before that, the various two-wheeled inventions were known as "velocipedes." Clubs were formed and races held, but cycling was mostly a sport for the upper classes; bicycles were too expensive for most people. The world's best known cycling race, the Tour de France, was first held in 1903.

Tour De Lance!

In July of 2003, Lance Armstrong became the first American — and only the second cyclist ever—to win the Tour de France race 5 times in a row. He finished the 3-week, 2,032-mile tour in 2003 with an overall time of 83 hours, 41 minutes, 12 seconds.

Lance's first win, in 1999, was very special. In 1996, he had been diagnosed with cancer. He had two operations and went through chemotherapy. This didn't stop him. In May 1998, he came back to win a race in Austin, Texas. That same year he signed with the U.S. Postal Service Team and set his sights on the Tour de France. After his fourth win in 2002, Lance said he would try to break the record of five straight wins (1991-1995) he shares with Spain's Miguel Indurain.

Lance was born September 18, 1971, and raised by his mother in Plano, Texas. When he was 13, he won the first Iron Kids Triathlon (1985), beating lots of bigger kids. The cycling part was his favorite. By 1991, he was the U.S. Amateur National Champion.

FOOTBALL

American football began as a college sport. The first game that was like today's football took place between Yale and Harvard in New Haven, Connecticut, on November 13, 1875. The National Football League started in 1922. The rival American Football League began in 1960. The two leagues played the first Super Bowl in 1967. In 1970, the leagues merged. In 2002, the Houston Texans join the NFL, and the AFC and NFC were realigned into four divisions of four teams.

Pats Top Panthers

At Super Bowl XXXVIII in Houston, the AFC's New England Patriots beat the NFC Carolina Panthers, 32-29, in one of the most exciting NFL Championships ever. The Carolina Panthers, who had a record of 1-15 two years before, were in the Super Bowl for the first time. They were facing the New England Patriots, who had won 14 games in a row and the 2002 Super Bowl.

Patriot quarterback Tom Brady, who completed a record 32 passes, won his second Super Bowl MVP Award. Brady drove his team downfield for a 41-yard field goal attempt, with 4 seconds left. Kicker Adam Vinatieri won the game on the last play—just as he did in Super Bowl XXXVI!

2003 NFL LEADERS & AWARDS

◄ **Steve McNair**

RUSHING YARDS: Jamal Lewis, Baltimore Ravens • 2,066
RUSHING TDS: Priest Holmes, Kansas City Chiefs • 27
RECEPTIONS: Torry Holt, St. Louis Rams • 117
RECEIVING YARDS: Torry Holt, St. Louis Rams • 1,696
RECEIVING TDS: Randy Moss, Minnesota Vikings • 17
PASSING YARDS: Peyton Manning, Indianapolis Colts • 4,267
PASSER RATING: Steve McNair, Tennessee Titans • 100.4
PASSING TDS: Brett Favre, Green Bay Packers • 32
PASS INTERCEPTIONS: Brian Russell, Minnesota Vikings;
Tony Parrish, San Francisco 49ers • 9
SACKS: Michael Strahan, NY Giants • 18.5

2003 ASSOCIATED PRESS AWARDS

Most Valuable Player:
Peyton Manning, Indianapolis Colts
& Steve McNair, Tennessee Titans
Offensive Player of the Year:
Jamal Lewis, Baltimore Ravens
Defensive Player of the Year:
Ray Lewis, Baltimore Ravens

Coach of the Year:
Bill Belichick, New England Patrio
Offensive Rookie of the Year:
Anquan Boldin, Arizona Cardinals
Defensive Rookie of the Year:
Terrell Suggs, Baltimore Ravens
Comeback Player of the Year:
Jon Kitna, Cincinnati Bengals

Peyton Manning ▲

FAMOUS NFL GAMES

"THE ICE BOWL" December 31, 1967, NFL Championship, Green Bay, Wisconsin: **Green Bay Packers 21, Dallas Cowboys 17**. At kickoff, it was 13 degrees below zero, with a windchill of –46. Incredibly, 50,000 fans had come to see the Packers go for their third NFL title in a row. With 16 seconds to play, Green Bay was behind 17-14. After two running plays from the Dallas 1-yard line went nowhere, Green Bay was out of time-outs. Everyone thought quarterback Bart Starr would throw. If it failed, the clock would stop, and they could kick a field goal to tie. But Starr took the snap and made his now-famous dive for the touchdown, and the win.

"THE GUARANTEE" January 12, 1969, Super Bowl III, Miami: **New York Jets 16, Baltimore Colts 7**. Three days before the game, Jets quarterback Joe Namath said, "I think we'll win it; in fact I'll guarantee it." The Jets were thought to be a weaker team because they were from the American Football League, which had just started playing in 1960. The NFL's Colts had lost only once all season and were favored to win by 18 points. But Namath became a legend — and a Super Bowl MVP—when the Jets did win, giving the AFL the credibility it deserved. The next year the two leagues merged.

"THE CATCH" January 10, 1982, NFC Championship Game, San Francisco: **San Francisco 49ers 28, Dallas Cowboys 27**. The 49ers and Cowboys traded the lead six times. With under five minutes to go and behind 27-21, the 49ers started at their own 11-yard line. Led by quarterback Joe Montana, the Niners were able to move the ball to the Cowboys' 6-yard line with 58 seconds left. Montana hit receiver Dwight Clark, whose leaping catch (now frequently replayed) for the winning TD sent the 49ers to their first Super Bowl.

"THE MUSIC CITY MIRACLE" January 8, 2000, AFC Wildcard Playoff, Nashville, Tennessee: **Tennessee 22, Buffalo Bills 16**. After a field goal gave them a 16-15 lead, the Bills kicked off to the Titans with just 16 seconds left in the game. Lorenzo Neal fielded the kick at the Titan 24-yard line, took a step, then handed off to Frank Wycheck. Wycheck ran to his right, stopped, and threw the ball back across the field to a wide open Kevin Dyson. Dyson caught the lateral and with a wall of blockers in front of him, raced 75 yards for a TD and a "miracle" win in the "Music City."

Joe Namath

NFL All-Time Record Holders*

RUSHING YARDS
Career: 17,418, **Emmit Smith** (1990-)
Season: 2,105, Eric Dickerson (1984)
Game: 295, **Jamal Lewis** (2003)

RECEIVING YARDS
Career: 22,466, **Jerry Rice** (1985-)
Season: 1,848, **Jerry Rice** (1995)
Game: 309, Stephone Paige (1985)

PASSING YARDS
Career: 61,361, Dan Marino (1983-99)
Season: 5,084, Dan Marino (1984)
Game: 554, Norm Van Brocklin (1951)

POINTS SCORED
Career: 2,346, **Gary Anderson** (1982-2003)
Season: 176, Paul Hornung (1960)
Game: 40, Ernie Nevers (1929)

*Through the 2003 season. Players in bold played in 2003. Game stats don't include overtime games.

Pro Football HALL of FAME

Football's Hall of Fame in Canton, Ohio, was founded in 1963 by the National Football League to honor outstanding players, coaches, and contributors.

Four players—tackle Bob Brown, defensive end Carl Eller, quarterback John Elway, and running back Barry Sanders—were to be inducted into the hall in August 2004.

WEB SITE http://www.profootballhof.com

College Football

College football is one of America's most colorful and exciting sports. The National Collegiate Athletic Association (NCAA), founded in 1906, oversees the sport today.

In 2004, the University of Southern California (USC) and Louisiana State University (LSU) shared the national championship. LSU defeated Oklahoma, 21-14, in the Sugar Bowl in New Orleans on January 4. USC beat Michigan, 28-14, in the Rose Bowl on January 1.

Unlike in college basketball, there is no playoff in football to determine a single champion. Since each of these two teams was ranked at the top of a major poll (*see box*), they can claim to be co-champions.

2003 *TOP 5* COLLEGE TEAMS

Chosen by the Associated Press Poll and the USA Today/ESPN Poll

Rank	AP	USA Today/ESPN
1	USC	LSU (13-1)
2	LSU	USC (12-1)
3	Oklahoma	Oklahoma (12-2)
4	Ohio St.	Ohio St. (11-2)
5	Miami (FL)	Miami (FL) (11-2)

HEISMAN TROPHY

Oklahoma University quarterback Jason White was the 2003 winner. The 23-year-old senior threw 40 TD passes and led the nation in passing efficiency, completing 64% of his passes for 3,744 yards and only 8 interceptions. After he had missed most of two seasons with knee injuries, the NCAA granted him one more year of eligibility. He planned to return to Oklahoma for the 2004 season.

ALL-TIME DIVISION I NCAA LEADERS

RUSHING YARDS
1. 6,397, Ron Dayne, Wisconsin
2. 6,297, Ricky Williams, Texas
3. 6,082, Tony Dorsett, Pittsburgh
4. 5,598, Charles White, USC
5. 5,596, Travis Prentice, Miami (OH)

PASSING YARDS
1. 15,031, Ty Detmer, Brigham Young
2. 12,746, Tim Rattay, Louisiana Tech
3. 12,541, Chris Redman, Louisville
4. 12,429, Kliff Kingsbury, Texas Tech
5. 11,425, Todd Santos, San Diego St.

Great Moment in College Football

JANUARY 2, 1984, ORANGE BOWL: MIAMI 31, NEBRASKA 30. The underdog Miami Hurricanes led the top-ranked, undefeated Nebraska Cornhuskers, 17-0. But the 'Huskers didn't give up—they even scored a TD on a trick play known as the "fumblerooski." The quarterback put the ball on the ground, where it was picked up by a lineman who ran it into the end zone. Miami still led, 31-17, in the fourth quarter, but Nebraska scored two more TDs to pull within a point of the 'Canes. After their final score, Nebraska tried a two-point conversion that would have given them the win. But quarterback Turner Gill's pass was blocked, and Miami got the victory and a national championship.

GOLF

Golf began in Scotland as early as the 1400s. The first golf course in the U.S. opened in 1888 in Yonkers, NY. The sport has grown to include both men's and women's professional tours. And millions play golf just for fun.

The men's tour in the U.S. is run by the Professional Golf Association (PGA). The four major championships (with the year first played) are:

British Open (1860)
United States Open (1895)
PGA Championship (1916)
Masters Tournament (1934)

The women's tour in the U.S. is guided by the Ladies Professional Golf Association (LPGA). The four major championships are:

United States Women's Open (1946)
McDonalds LPGA Championship (1955)
Nabisco Championship (1972)
Women's British Open* (1976)
*Replaced the du Maurier Classic as a major in 2001.

The All-Time "Major" Players

Here is a list of the pro golfers who've won the most major championships.

MEN

1. Jack Nicklaus, 18
2. Walter Hagan, 11
3. Ben Hogan, 9
   Gary Player, 9
5. Tom Watson, 8
   Tiger Woods, 8

WOMEN

1. Patty Berg, 15
2. Mickey Wright, 13
3. Louise Suggs, 11
4. Babe Didrikson Zaharias, 10
5. Betsy Rawls, 8

did you know?

Michelle Wie is a major sensation. The 6-foot-tall ninth grader from Hawaii has made the finals of the Hawaii Pearl Open, a men's tournament, the past two years. Michelle is taller than a lot of the people she meets and can hit a ball farther than a lot of the best players in golf—about 300 yards!

GYMNASTICS

It takes strength, coordination, and grace to become a top gymnast. Although the sport goes back to ancient Greece, modern-day gymnastics began in Sweden in the early 1800s. The sport has been part of the Olympics since 1896.The first World Gymnastic Championships were held in Antwerp, Belgium, in 1903.

Men today compete in the All-Around, High Bar, Parallel Bars, Rings, Vault, Pommel Horse, Floor Exercises, and Team Combined. The women's events are the All-Around, Uneven Parallel Bars, Balance Beam, Floor Exercises, and Team Combined. In rhythmic gymnastics, women compete in All-Around, Rope, Hoop, Ball, Clubs, and Ribbon.

The 100th anniversary World Gymnastic Championships was held in Anaheim, California, August 16-24, 2003. The U.S. women won their first-ever team gold medal. Americans Chellsie Memmel and Hollie Vise tied for the gold in the uneven bars. The U.S. men took the team silver behind China. For the U.S., Paul Hamm won the all-around title and tied for the gold in the floor excercise.

ICE HOCKEY

I ce hockey began in Canada in the mid-1800s. The National Hockey League (NHL) was formed in 1916. In 2003, the NHL had 30 teams—24 in the U.S. and 6 in Canada.

HIGHLIGHTS

In 2003, the New Jersey Devils won their third Stanley Cup championship in nine seasons, defeating the Anaheim Mighty Ducks, four games to three. New Jersey goalie Martin Brodeur had three shutouts in the finals and an NHL-record seven in the postseason. Anaheim Goalie Jean-Sebastien Giguere became only the 5th player on a losing team to win the Conn Smythe Trophy as playoff MVP.

SEASON	WINNER	RUNNER-UP
1990-91	Pittsburgh Penguins	Minnesota North Stars
1991-92	Pittsburgh Penguins	Chicago Black Hawks
1992-93	Montreal Canadiens	Los Angeles Kings
1993-94	New York Rangers	Vancouver Canucks
1994-95	New Jersey Devils	Detroit Red Wings
1995-96	Colorado Avalanche	Florida Panthers
1996-97	Detroit Red Wings	Philadelphia Flyers
1997-98	Detroit Red WIngs	Washington Capitals
1998-99	Dallas Stars	Buffalo Sabres
1999-2000	New Jersey Devils	Dallas Stars
2000-2001	Colorado Avalanche	New Jersey Devils
2001-2002	Detroit Red Wings	Carolina Hurricanes
2002-2003	New Jersey Devils	Anaheim Mighty Ducks

did you know?

At the end of the 2002-2003 season, Colorado goalie Patrick Roy retired as the NHL's winningest goalie (551). Roy ended his 18-year career with many records, including games played (1,029), playoff victories (151), playoff games (247), and playoff shutouts (23). He won the Stanley Cup 4 times, twice each with Montreal and Colorado, and is the only 3-time Conn Smythe winner in hockey history.

Some All-time NHL Records*

GOALS SCORED
Career: 894, Wayne Gretzky (1979-99)
Season: 92, Wayne Gretzky (1981-82)
Game: 7, Joe Malone (1920)

GOALIE WINS
Career: 551, Patrick Roy (1984-2003)
Season: 47, Bernie Parent (1973-74)

POINTS SCORED
Career: 2,857, Wayne Gretzky (1979-99)
Season: 215, Wayne Gretzky (1985-86)
Game: 10, Darryl Sittler (1976)

GOALIE SHUTOUTS
Career: 103, Terry Sawchuk (1949-70)
Season: 22, George Hainsworth (1928-29)

*Through the 2002-2003 season; of these players, only Patrick Roy played in that season.

HOCKEY HALL of FAME

The Hockey Hall of Fame in Toronto, Ontario, Canada, was opened in 1961 to honor hockey greats. **WEB SITE** *http://www.hhof.com*

The OLYMPIC GAMES

The first Olympics were held in Greece more than 2,500 years ago. In 776 B.C. they featured just one event—a footrace. Boxing, wrestling, chariot racing, and the pentathlon (which consists of five different events) came later. The Olympic Games were held every four years for more than 1,000 years, until A.D. 393, when a Roman emperor stopped them.

2004 SUMMER OLYMPICS: *ATHENS, GREECE*

The Olympic Games were born in ancient Greece, and the first modern Games were held in Athens in 1896. In 2004, some 10,500 athletes and 3,000 officials representing 202 teams were expected to attend the 28th Olympiad from August 13 through the 29th. There will be 301 events in 28 sports. The mascots are Phevos and Athena, who are brother and sister. They are named after two ancient Greek gods: Phevos or Phoebus (a name for Apollo), god of light and music, and Athena, goddess of wisdom and patron of the city of Athens. The emblem of the Athens Olympics is an olive wreath, or *kotinos*, which was the award given to winners in the ancient games. The following Olympics will be held in Turin, Italy (Winter 2006) and in Beijing, China (Summer 2008).

2004 *SUMMER* OLYMPIC SPORTS

Archery
Badminton
Baseball
Basketball
Boxing
Canoe/Kayak
 (slalom, sprint)
Cycling (road, mountain bike, track)
Diving
Equestrian (dressage, jumping, 3-day event)
Fencing
Field Hockey

Football (Soccer)
Gymnastics (artistic, rhythmic, trampoline)
Handball
Judo
Modern Pentathlon
 (show jumping, running, fencing, pistol shooting, swimming—one event per day for 5 days)
Rowing
Sailing
Shooting

Softball
Swimming
Synchronized
 Swimming
Table Tennis
 (Ping-Pong)
Taekwondo
Tennis
Track and
 Field
Triathlon
Volleyball
 (beach, indoor)
Water Polo
Weightlifting
Wrestling

227

1896	The first modern Olympic Games were held in Athens, Greece. A total of 312 athletes from 13 nations participated in nine sports.
1900	Women competed in the Olympic Games for the first time.
1908	For the first time, medals were awarded to the first three people to finish each event—a gold for first, a silver for second, and a bronze for third.
1920	The Olympic flag was raised for the first time, and the Olympic oath was introduced. The five interlaced rings of the flag represent: Africa, America, Europe, Asia, and Australia.
1924	The first Winter Olympics, featuring skiing and skating events, were held.
	The Olympic flame was introduced at the Olympic Games. A relay of runners carries a torch with the flame from Olympia, Greece, to the site of each Olympics.
1994	Starting with the 1994 Winter Olympics, the winter and summer Games have alternated every two years, instead of being held in the same year, every fourth year.

SWIMMING

When the modern Olympic Games began in Athens, Greece, in 1896, the only racing stroke was the breaststroke. Today, men and women at the Olympics swim the backstroke, breaststroke, butterfly, and freestyle, in events ranging from 50 meters to 1,500 meters.

Some Great U.S. Olympic Swimmers

Mark Spitz made history by winning seven gold medals at the 1972 Games in Munich. He won 11 medals—nine gold—in his Olympic career.

Matt Biondi won seven medals—five gold—at the 1988 Olympics in Seoul. He won eight gold medals, 11 overall, in his Olympic career from 1984 to 1992.

Janet Evans, at age 17, won three golds at the 1988 Olympics in Seoul. In 1992 she won another gold and a silver at Barcelona.

Dara Torres won five golds at the 2000 Games in Sydney, the most by a U.S. woman at one Olympiad. Seven years after retiring, she returned to become the first American to swim in four Olympics (1984, 1988, 1992, 2000).

WHO AM I?

I was born on March 23, 1929, in England. I studied medicine at Oxford University, where I also ran track. I went on to become a doctor, but most people remember me for doing something many thought was impossible at the time: running a mile in under four minutes. It was hard to work at the hospital all day and still find time to train, but I did. On May, 6, 1954, I ran a mile in 3 minutes, 59.4 seconds. Lots of runners followed in my footsteps, and today the record is 3:43.13, set in 1999.

Answer: Roger Bannister

Soccer, also called football outside the U.S., is the number one sport worldwide, played by the most people, and in almost every country. More than 240 million people play organized soccer, according to a 2000 survey done by FIFA (Fédération Internationale de Football Association), the sport's international governing body. That's one out of every 25 people on the planet. The survey also found that more than 20 million women play soccer. The United States was the country with the highest number of regular adult soccer players, with about 18 million, followed by Indonesia (10 million), Mexico (7.4 million), China (7.2 million), Brazil (7 million), and Germany (6.3 million).

THE WORLD CUP

The final of the 2003 **Women's World Cup** was held October 12, 2003, at the Home Depot Center in Carson, California. Germany defeated Sweden, 2-1, in overtime. Germany's best previous finishes had been second in 1995 and third in 1991.

In the third-place game on October 11, the U.S. defeated Canada, 3-1. Shannon Boxx, Kristine Lilly, and Tiffeny Milbrett each scored for the U.S. In the semifinals, Germany beat the U.S., 3-0. The loss was a surprise for the U.S. team, which had won two World Cup titles and finished third twice.

Shannon Boxx

FIFA, soccer's world governing body, moved the Women's World Cup from China to the U.S. over concerns about the epidemic of SARS (Severe Acute Respiratory Syndrome), which had started there. The 2007 Women's World Cup was then scheduled for China.

Held every four years, the **Men's World Cup** is the biggest soccer tournament in the world. The first World Cup was held in Uruguay in 1930. The next men's World Cup is scheduled to be held in 12 cities in Germany in 2006. The final will be held in Berlin.

WUSA *WOMEN'S UNITED SOCCER ASSOCIATION*

In the 2003 WUSA Founder's Cup championship game in San Diego, California, the Washington Freedom defeated the Atlanta Beat in overtime, 2-1. Abby Wambach was the MVP. She scored both goals for Washington, the second coming six minutes into overtime.

On September 15, 2003, WUSA announced that it would fold. Though some top players had taken pay cuts, the league was about $16 million in debt. Low TV ratings and sponsorship spelled doom for the league. Game attendance fell from more than 8,000 per game in its first year (2001) to 6,700 in 2003. **WEB SITE** *http://www.wusa.com*

MLS *MAJOR LEAGUE SOCCER*

The San Jose Earthquakes defeated the Chicago Fire, 4-2, in the 2003 MLS Cup Championship match November 23, 2003, at the Home Depot Center in Carson, California. Landon Donovan, who scored 2 goals in the match, was named MVP of the game. It was the 2nd MLS Cup for the Earthquakes, who also won the title in 2001. **WEB SITE** *http://www.mlsnet.com*

SPECIAL OLYMPICS

The Special Olympics is the world's largest program of sports training and athletic competition for children and adults with intellectual disabilities. Founded in 1968, Special Olympics International has offices in all 50 U.S. states and Washington, D.C., and throughout the world. The organization offers training and competition to 1.5 million athletes in 150 countries. The Special Olympics International holds World Games every two years. These alternate between summer and winter sports. Nagano, Japan, will host the 2005 World Winter Games February 26-March 5. The 2003 World Summer Games were held in Dublin, Ireland.

SPECIAL OLYMPICS **OFFICIAL SPORTS**

► **Winter:** alpine and cross-country skiing, figure and speed skating, floor hockey, snowshoeing, snowboarding

► **Summer:** aquatics (swimming and diving), athletics (track and field), basketball, bowling, cycling, equestrian, golf, gymnastics, powerlifting, roller skating, soccer, softball, tennis, volleyball

► **Demonstration sports:** badminton, bocce, sailing

WEB SITE http://www.specialolympics.org

Tennis

Modern tennis began in 1873. It was based on court tennis. In 1877 the first championships were held in Wimbledon, near London. In 1881 the first official U.S. men's championships were held at Newport, Rhode Island. Six years later, the first women's championships took place, in Philadelphia. The four most important ("grand slam") tournaments today are the Australian Open, the French Open, the All-England (Wimbledon) Championships, and the U.S. Open.

Grand Slam Tournaments

ALL-TIME **GRAND SLAM** SINGLES WINNERS

MEN	Australian	French	Wimbledon	U.S.	Total
Pete Sampras (b. 1971)	2	0	7	5	14
Roy Emerson (b. 1936)	6	2	2	2	12
Bjorn Borg (b. 1956)	0	6	5	0	11
Rod Laver (b. 1938)	3	2	4	2	11
Bill Tilden (1893-1953)	*	0	3	7	10
WOMEN					
Margaret Smith Court (b. 1942)	11	5	3	5	24
Steffi Graf (b. 1969)	4	6	7	5	22
Helen Wills Moody (1905-1998)	*	4	8	7	19
Chris Evert (b. 1954)	2	7	3	6	18
Martina Navratilova (b. 1956)	3	2	9	4	18

*Never played in tournament.

XGAMES

The X Games, founded by ESPN television executive Ron Semiao, were first held in June 1995 in Newport, Rhode Island. They originally featured skateboarding and BMX biking events. Considered the Olympics of action sports, the X Games include both summer and winter competitions, each held annually in the United States. Star athletes include skateboarder Tony Hawk, street luger Biker Sherlock, and BMX (bicycle) freestyler Dave Mirra.

2004 WINTER X GAMES
About 250 athletes from all over the world competed at the eighth annual Winter X Games, held January 24-27 in Aspen, Colorado. Events included Snowboarding, Skiing, Snowmobiling, and the Moto-X (off-road motorcycling). Among the highlights: Olympic silver medalist Danny Kass scooped up two more silver medals in the Men's Slopestyle and SuperPipe snowboarding; he was named Most Outstanding Athlete of Winter X Games VIII. Sixteen-year-old Hannah Teeter won gold in the Women's Snowboarding SuperPipe.

SUMMER X GAMES
The Summer X Games, held every year since 1995, feature competitions in such events as In-line Skating, Bike Stunt, Downhill BMX, Moto X (off-road motorcycling), Skateboard, Surfing, and Wakeboard. Surfing became an official event at X Games IX, held in Los Angeles in August 2003.

The 10th X Games were set to be held in August 2004 in Los Angeles, California.
WEB SITE http://expn.go.com

X GAMES GLOBAL CHAMPIONSHIP
The first-ever Global X Games were held in May 2003. This team event featured six world regions competing against each other in both summer and winter action sports. The summer sports were contested in San Antonio, Texas. The winter events were held in Whistler Blackcomb, British Columbia, Canada. In all, six sports and 11 events were featured, with a total of 126 athletes competing (21 per team). Team USA took home the gold with a total of 196 points, beating Team Europe (167 points) and Team Australia (142).

Tony Hawk

X-Fact-ors

X Skateboarder Tony Hawk and BMX rider Dave Mirra share the record for most X Games medals, with 16 each.

X At the 2003 Summer X Games, 13-year-old Ryan Sheckler became the youngest winner ever, taking home the gold in the Skateboard Park event.

X Tony Hawk landed the first-ever 900 (2.5 times around) in X Games history at the 2003 games, winning gold in the Best Vert Trick skateboard event.

X In 2003, 16-year-old Shaun White became the first athlete to compete in different sports at the Summer and Winter X Games.

Transportation

What was the "Tom Thumb"?   page 234

Getting from There to Here
A SHORT HISTORY OF TRANSPORTATION

5000 B.C.
People harness animal-muscle power. Oxen and donkeys carry heavy loads.

3500 B.C.
Egyptians create the first sailboat. Before this, people made rafts or canoes and paddled them with poles or their hands.

1450s
Portuguese build fast ships with three masts. These plus the compass usher in an age of exploration.

1730s
Stagecoach service begins in the U.S.

1783
In Paris, the Montgolfier brothers fly the first hot air balloon.

1825
The Erie Canal connects the Hudson River with Lake Erie, opening up water passage to what was then the West.

5000 B.C.

3500 B.C.
In Mesopotamia (modern-day Iraq), people invent vehicles with wheels. But the first wheels are made of heavy wood, and the roads are terrible.

Around 1000
Using magnetic compasses, Chinese are able to sail long distances in flat-bottomed ships called junks.

1660s
Horse-drawn stagecoaches begin running in France. They stop at stages to switch horses and passengers—the first mass transit system.

1769
James Watt patents the first successful steam engine.

1807
Robert Fulton patents a highly efficient steamboat.

1830
Passenger rail service begins in England with the *Rocket*, a steam engine built by George Stephenson. It goes about 24 miles an hour.

1869
Transcontinental railroad is completed at Promontory Point, Utah. The Suez Canal opens, saving ships a long trip around Africa.

1903
At Kitty Hawk, North Carolina, the Wright brothers fly the first powered heavier-than-air machine.

1964
Shinkansen "bullet train" service (124 mph) begins in Japan.

1839
Kirkpatrick Macmillan of Scotland invents the first pedaled bicycle.

1873
San Francisco's cable car system begins service.

1939
The first practical helicopter and first jet plane are invented. The jet flies up to 434 mph. Jet passenger service began in 1958.

1994
Cars and trains cross under the English Channel in the new Channel Tunnel or "Chunnel."

NOW!

1860s
Paddle-wheel steamboats dominate U.S. river travel.

1897
The first U.S. subway service begins in Boston. New York City follows in 1904.

1908
Henry Ford builds the first Model T, a practical car for the general public.

1969
U.S. astronauts aboard *Apollo 11* land on the Moon.

1862
Étienne Lenoir of Belgium builds the first car with an internal-combustion engine.

TRAINS

▲ *TGV in France*

The first successful steam locomotive was built in England in 1804. Richard Trevithick's engine pulled 24,000 pounds of iron, 70 men, and 5 wagons along a 9.5-mile track. In 1830 the Baltimore and Ohio introduced America's first steam locomotive, the **"Tom Thumb,"** to haul both passengers and freight. America's first transcontinental railroad was built from 1862 to 1869. Other railroad lines soon followed. In 1893, the first electrified rail line went into service, in Baltimore. Diesel engines were introduced in 1928, and streamlined trains began to appear in 1934.

The most famous modern high-speed trains are the **Shinkansen (Bullet Train)**, introduced in Japan in 1964, and France's **Train à Grande Vitesse (TGV)**, which started service in 1981. Both have a top speed of 186 mph. In the U.S. in 2000, Amtrak introduced **Acela Express** 150-mph high-speed service between Boston and Washington, D.C. Japan Railway is testing **Maglev** (MAGnetic LEVitation) trains. These use huge magnetic forces to lift trains above the track and send them forward on electrical currents. The lack of friction helps them cruise at speeds of around 280 mph, with a record speed of 348 mph set in 2003.

Autos

In 1886 Gottlieb Daimler patented a three-wheeled motor carriage in Germany. That same year, Karl Benz produced his **first successful gasoline-powered vehicle**. John W. Lambert of Ohio made the first gas-powered automobile in the U.S. in 1891. Five years later, the Duryea Brothers of Springfield, Massachusetts, started the first car manufacturing company in the U.S. Henry Ford came soon after. His production of the **Model T** using an assembly line in 1913 revolutionized the automobile industry, making cars affordable for large numbers of people, including his own workers.

▲ *1911 Ford Model T*

Today, some developers are seeking fuel efficiency. The most fuel-efficient cars sold today are **gas-electric hybrids**. These can get up to 60 miles per gallon, using both a gas and an electric engine. When the gas engine runs, it charges batteries for the electric engine, which is used for slow speeds or to boost the gas engine. A computer decides which engine to use.

SOLAR RACING

In July 2003, 30 odd-looking cars drove 2,300 miles from Chicago to Los Angeles along historic Route 66 (see page 238). This is the University of Missouri-Rolla's Solar *Miner IV*, winner of the U.S. Department of Energy's American Solar Challenge in a record of 51 hours—an average of 43.3 mph. These electric cars are powered by the sun. The black area is covered with *photovoltaic*, or solar, cells—small wafer-like units that change sunlight into electricity. The cars work best in full sunlight, but can use power stored in their batteries on cloudy days or to go uphill. They can go up to 75 mph! Like Indy racecars, solar cars are not practical for everyday use. But events like this one, and the World Solar Challenge in Australia, help improve solar and electric vehicle technology.

AIR

▲ *Boeing 747*

EARLY AIRCRAFT In 1783, the Montgolfier brothers flew the first **hot air balloon** over Paris. Another Frenchman, Henri Giffard, flew the first dirigible, or **blimp,** in 1852. It was powered by steam. The first heavier-than-air flying machine was also steam-powered. Samuel P. Langley of the Smithsonian Institution in Washington, D.C., built a model plane with just a 12-foot wingspan that flew nearly a mile in 1896. Wilbur and Orville Wright had also been experimenting with manned heavier-than-air machines. In 1903 they traveled from their bicycle shop in Dayton, Ohio, to Kitty Hawk, North Carolina. Here they made 4 successful manned flights on December 17, launching the air age.

MILESTONES IN AVIATION Airlines were first developed in the U.S. to carry mail. **Transcontinental service** was launched in 1921, **bringing mail** from San Francisco to New York in 33 hours, compared to the record of 89 hours set by a train, in 1876. By 1926, regular airmail service was in place, and a pilot named Charles A. Lindbergh was flying the Chicago-to-St. Louis route. **Passenger service** was well under way by 1930.

Aircraft continued to get bigger and faster. In 1936, the DC-3 set a record flying from Los Angeles to Newark, New Jersey, in 13 hours and 4 minutes. In 1959 the **Boeing 707** debuted. It was the first successful passenger jet. The **Boeing 707** could carry 180 passengers at 550 miles per hour—about 225 mph faster than propeller-powered airliners. One of the most famous airliners to be developed was the **Boeing 747** "jumbo jet," introduced in 1969. Cruising at 566 mph, it can carry about 500 passengers.

SEA

Ships are used for many activities, from fishing, to vacationing, to exploration, to war. But their most important job has always been carrying cargo. The Egyptians were building reed and wooden sailboats 5,000 years ago. They also built wooden **barges** over 200 feet long that could carry close to 2,000,000 pounds of cargo.

By the 1500s, huge sailing ships called **galleons** were hauling cargo around the world. Spanish galleons carried gold, spices, and other riches back to Europe from South America. These ships had to be big and needed cannons to defend themselves from pirates. Later cargo ships did without cannons (though modern-day pirates still raid ships). **Packet ships** began regularly scheduled passenger service across the Atlantic in 1818. In the 1840s, the U.S. built the first **clipper ships**. With a slender hull and many sails, they were the fastest ships of the pre-steam era.

The **world's biggest ship** today is the supertanker *Jahre Viking*. It's 1,502 feet long. That's longer than the Empire State building is tall. The *Jahre Viking* can carry 4.2 million barrels of oil. The *Queen Mary 2*, which was launched in January 2004, is the largest passenger ship ever. It's 23 stories high and 1,132 feet long.

The Queen Mary 2

WHY IS IT 4 A.M. IN LOS ANGELES WHEN IT'S 7 A.M. IN NEW YORK?

When the sun rises on the east coast, it's still dark in the central states, and the farther west you go, the farther away you are from daybreak. Before the mid-1800s, traveling east or west was so slow that it was possible to use the local time set by each city. But when the railroads came, people could travel hundreds of miles in a day. Organizing a schedule using many different times was nearly impossible. No one could ever agree what time it was! Railroads had to have a system of **standard time** and **time zones**. The familiar time zones of Eastern, Central, Mountain, and Pacific were adopted by railroads in the U.S. and Canada in 1883.

The next year, 24 international time zones—one for each hour of the day—were established. These begin at the **prime meridian,** the longitude line passing through Greenwich, England. Halfway around the world, in the Pacific Ocean, is the **International Date Line,** which roughly follows the 180th meridian and is in the 12th time zone. Cross the line going west, and it's tomorrow. Going east, the date is one day earlier.

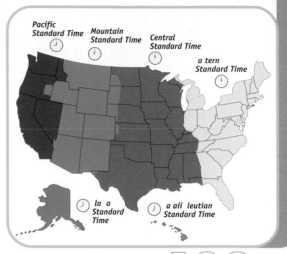

NEW YORK CITY SUBWAY TURNS 100

On October 27, 2004, New York City will celebrate the centennial (100th anniversary) of its subway system. When construction of the subway began in 1900, New York was the second-biggest city in the world, and many of its 3.4 million citizens were packed into small neighborhoods in Manhattan. Streets were crowded with carriages, people, trolley cars, vendors—even horse-drawn buses. Now, there would be a new fast and reliable way to get around town.

The first subway line was 9.1 miles long, with 28 stations. It ran in Manhattan from City Hall to Harlem. Today, there are 468 stations in four boroughs, and nearly 850 miles of track, making this one of the longest subway systems in the world. Placed end to end, the tracks would run from New York City to Chicago!

The subway carried 150,000 people the first day it opened, with a 5-cent fare. The record for the most riders in one day is 8,872,244, on December 23, 1946. Although it costs $2 per ride now, the average number of passengers in one day (2003) was 4.5 million. There are more than 6,400 cars, the world's largest subway fleet, and they made 1,721,115 trips in 2003 for a total distance of 347,188,000 miles!

"America on the Move," the Smithsonian Museum of American History's largest-ever exhibit, opened in November 2003. It shows the role of transportation in U.S. history. You can visit it in Washington, DC, or online at **WEB SITE** *http://americanhistory.si.edu/onthemove/*

On the Job

Riverboat Captain

You could say that riverboating flows in Dale Lozier's veins. She grew up on the boats her father, Capt. Tom, built and ran for his Memphis Queen Riverboats company. Now she is a riverboat captain herself, and owner of the fleet of nine vessels operating out of Memphis, Tennessee. Her top priority: to make sure things run smoothly for all aboard as they cruise the mighty Mississippi!

Q: How long have you been with the company?
I started work at the Memphis Queen Line literally from the first day my dad bought it in October 1960. "Working the boats" was a family affair. Dad began building boats, most in the backyard. A day has not passed since that I have not been close to the boats. From concessions, deck swabbing, and taking out the garbage I moved through sales and management to getting my captain's license, and then to taking over full ownership and operation.

Q. What skills or personality traits should a riverboat captain have?
Above all, any boat captain should be extremely conscious of safety, for passengers, crew, and the vessel. A captain must be mature—absolutely not a risk taker and most certainly avoid the "Not my boat" attitude. Obviously a captain should know how boats work, both mechanically and in operation. No captain can truly master a boat until they understand both its limitations and capacities and the waters they cruise. A captain is first and finally in the hot seat for every part of the cruise. A love of people of all ages is necessary in this business because of its tourism aspect.

Q: What kind of training did you need?
Experience was the most important part of getting my captains' license. Of course, there were formal tests required by the Coast Guard. I virtually aced the written tests without any classroom instruction. I had to pass a physical and repeat that every five years for my license renewal. Every aspiring captain has to have letters from other captains to certify their competence in all the seaman skills a captain needs.

Q: Are passengers surprised to learn that their captain is female?
A female captain still seems a bit of an oddity, but there is a long history of women captains. Quite a few are on the river today, including one who is also a nun! A pioneer woman captain in the early-to mid-part of the last century was "Ma Greene" of the Greene Line. She piloted regularly but kept it secret so the passengers wouldn't worry. Her family ran the famous *Delta Queen* and other magnificent boats. When I pilot and describe how I came to be a captain, most comments are very favorable. Young women in particular seem intrigued and encouraged.

Travel

Where is "The Forbidden City"? page 239

ROAD TRIP

Wherever you are, there is likely to be a festival, an amusement park, a national park, or historic site just a short drive away (see pages 240-242). A road trip—short or long—can be lots of fun, with plenty of interesting sights along the way.

The first cross-country drive was made in 1903. H. Nelson Jackson and Sewall K. Crocker (and a bulldog named Bud) drove from California to New York in an early car known as a Winton. There were few roads or bridges in the West, and lots of mud everywhere. The whole trip took 63 days and cost $8,000, including the price of the car. In 1909, Alice Huyler Ramsey became the first woman to drive across the U.S. Her trip from New York to San Francisco took 59 days.

By 1930, there were 23 million cars on the road. More than half of American families owned one. Today in the U.S. there are more cars than licensed drivers. People wanted to see things and go places—especially west. The first coast-to-coast highway was the Lincoln Highway, finished by 1930. U.S. Highway 1, completed in 1926, ran from Ft. Kent, Maine, to Miami, Florida. But the most famous highway was Route 66, completed in 1926, connecting Chicago to Los Angeles. Now called "Historic Route 66," it still has billboards and giant statues advertising its famous hotels, attractions, and restaurants.

A ROADSIDE SAMPLER:
Just a few of the millions of sights across the U.S.!

San Jose, California The spooky, sprawling **Winchester Mystery House** has 160 rooms, 950 doors, and 10,000 windows. Staircases lead into ceilings, windows cut into floors, and one door opens onto an eight-foot drop into a kitchen sink!

Silver Springs, Florida Silver Springs is called **"Florida's first tourist attraction."** Its clear water and glass-bottom boats have delighted visitors since 1878.

Cawker City, Kansas If wacky is your thing, check out this string. More than 7 million feet of it! At nearly 18,000 pounds it's the **World's Largest Ball of Twine**.

Margate, New Jersey You won't soon forget **Lucy the Elephant**. Built in 1881, she's made of wood and stands 65 feet tall.

Hayward, Wisconsin Pretend you're the bait in the toothy mouth of the 143-foot-long fiberglass fish at **The National Freshwater Fishing Hall of Fame & Museum**.

Look in your local newspaper or check your state or town website for interesting events and places to visit in your area. Sometimes there's more to do than you think!

UN-NATURAL WONDERS: *Big City Destinations*

You can have fun and learn about different cultures by visiting cities in other countries, or even your own! Each one has its own flavor of food, art, architecture, history, and more.

ATHENS The Acropolis, a 500-foot-tall sandstone hill, towers over the city. On it are the ruins of the Parthenon and the Temple of Athena Nike, both built nearly 2,500 years ago. In 2004, the Summer Olympics return to this ancient city.

LONDON

See the Tower of London, a royal fortress that has stood on the banks of the Thames River for over 900 years. It houses the crown jewels, and there is a museum of arms and armor.

BEIJING Dog statues guard the entrance to "The Forbidden City." For 500 years only the emperors were allowed inside. It's the Palace Museum now, open to all. In 2008, the Summer Olympics will be held in China for the first time.

ROME

Along with the famous Trevi Fountain, you'll want to see the Colosseum and other historic Roman ruins. At the Vatican, don't miss the Sistine Chapel, painted by Michelangelo from 1508 to 1512.

CHICAGO The Buckingham Fountain is a landmark on Chicago's Lake Michigan waterfront. The tallest building in the U.S., the Sears Tower, overlooks the city. Try some deep-dish pizza.

PHILADELPHIA

Visit Independence Hall, where the Declaration of Independence was adopted and the U.S. Constitution was drafted. Spend time in the Franklin Institute Science Museum. And don't forget to have a "Philly Cheesesteak" sandwich.

NEW ORLEANS Settled by the French in 1718, this city on the Mississippi became part of the U.S. with the Louisiana Purchase of 1803. It's world-famous for jazz music, Mardi Gras, and foods like jambalaya and shrimp gumbo.

SAN FRANCISCO

Ride the famous cable cars. See Alcatraz and the Golden Gate Bridge. And maybe visit the Ghirardelli Chocolate Factory! Enjoy the street performers at Fisherman's Wharf. You can also eat great seafood there and watch the boats on the bay.

NATIONAL PARKS

AND THE LIKE

The world's first national park was Yellowstone, established in 1872. Today, there are 57 national parks, including one in the Virgin Islands and one in American Samoa. The National Park Service oversees 388 areas in all, also including national monuments, battlefields, military parks, historical parks, historic sites, lakeshores, seashores, recreation areas, scenic rivers and trails, and the White House—84.4 million acres all told! For more information, you can write the National Park Service, Department of the Interior, 1849 C Street NW, Washington, D.C. 20240.

WEB SITE For information on-line, go to http://www.nps.gov/parks.html

YOSEMITE NATIONAL PARK

This park, established in 1890, covers 761,266 acres in east-central California. It has the world's largest concentration of granite domes—mountain-like rocks that were created by glaciers millions of years ago. You can see many of them rising thousands of feet above the valley floor. Two of the most famous are Half-Dome, which looks smooth and rounded, and El Capitan, which is the biggest single granite rock on earth. Skilled climbers come from all over the world to scale this 4,000-foot-high wall of rock. Yosemite Falls, which drops 2,425 feet, is the highest waterfall in North America, and the fifth highest in the world. It is actually two waterfalls, called the upper and lower falls, connected by a series of smaller waterfalls. Yosemite also features lakes, meadows, and giant sequoia trees, and is home to bighorn sheep and bears.

GRAND CANYON NATIONAL PARK

This national park, established in 1919, has one of the world's most spectacular landscapes, covering more than 1 million acres in northwestern Arizona. The canyon is 6,000 feet deep at its deepest point and 15 miles wide at its widest. The walls display a cross-section of the earth's crust from as far back as two billion years ago. Most of the 40 identified rock layers that form the canyon's 277-mile-long wall are exposed, offering a detailed look at the earth's geologic history. The Colorado River—which carved out the giant canyon—still runs through the park, which is a valuable wildlife preserve with many rare, endangered animals. The pine and fir forests, painted deserts, plateaus, caves, and sandstone canyons offer a wide range of habitats.

MAMMOTH CAVE NATIONAL PARK

Mammoth Cave in southwestern Kentucky is part of the biggest known cave system in the world. The cave was discovered by pioneers in 1798 and became part of a national park in 1941. There are more than 360 known miles of passageways, with more being discovered each year. The network of caves was created millions of years ago as water dissolved its way through rock. There are narrow tunnels, broad caverns, and giant vertical shafts.

The caves are decorated with icicle-shaped mineral formations that hang from the ceiling (*stalactites*) and grow up from the floor (*stalagmites*). Blindfish, eyeless crayfish, colorless spiders, and other rare creatures have adapted to the blackness and isolation of cave life.

ASSATEAGUE ISLAND NATIONAL SEASHORE

This 37-mile-long barrier island, partly in Maryland and partly in Virginia, became a National Seashore in 1965. The island is known for its sandy beaches and migrating birds. But the most popular attraction is the wild horses, made famous by Marguerite Henry's book, *Misty of Chincoteague*. They're split into two herds—one on the Virginia side and one in Maryland—separated at the state line by a fence. Each herd is limited to 150 horses to protect the natural resources of the island. On the last Wednesday and Thursday of July each year, the Chincoteague Volunteer Fire Department holds the "Pony Penning" for the Virginia herd. Since 1924, the ponies have been herded across the channel (less than a 10 minute swim) to Chincoteague Island, where a carnival is held and the young horses (foals) are auctioned off to good homes.

ALCATRAZ ISLAND NATIONAL HISTORIC LANDMARK

The island of Alcatraz is part of the Golden Gate National Recreation Area in San Francisco. The area, established in 1972, is the largest urban national park (75,000 acres) in the world. While the island is noted for its beautiful view, it's more famous for its prison, which housed such gangsters as Al Capone and George "Machine Gun" Kelly. It was a military prison from 1868 to 1933. It was a maximum-security penitentiary from then until it closed in 1963. The cold water and rough currents of San Francisco Bay made Alcatraz hard to escape from. Thirty-six prisoners tried to get away over the years; two succeeded in escaping from the island in 1962, but their survival is questionable.

The first amusement parks appeared in Europe over 400 years ago. Attractions included flower gardens, bowling, music, and a few simple rides.

The first real roller coaster in the U.S. was the Switchback Gravity Pleasure Railway. It opened in Brooklyn's Coney Island in 1884 and went all of 6 miles per hour! In 1893, the **George Ferris Great Wheel** was introduced in Chicago. The "Ferris" Wheel weighed over 4 million pounds and stood 264 feet high. It had 36 cars that could hold 60 people each! It revolved about 4 times per hour. The wheel was taken down and rebuilt in St. Louis for the 1904 Exposition. In 1894, Chutes Park opened in Chicago—the first park to charge admission.

In the 1920s, some of the best **roller coasters** of all time were built—reaching speeds of 60 mph. Some large cities had as many as six amusement parks. But the stock market crash and Great Depression in the 1930s caused many to close.

In 1955, **Disneyland** opened in Anaheim, California. Sections of the park, such as Tomorrowland and the Magic Kingdom, had their own themes, making it the country's first theme park.

WORLD'S FASTEST ROLLER COASTERS*

1. **Top Thrill Dragster:** 120 mph, Sandusky, Ohio
2. **Dodonpa:** 107 mph, FujiYoshida-shi, Japan
3. **Superman: The Escape:** 100 mph, Valencia, California
   Tower of Terror: 100 mph, Gold Coast, Australia
4. **Steel Dragon 2000:** 95 mph, Mie, Japan
5. **Millennium Force:** 92 mph, Sandusky, Ohio

WORLD'S TALLEST ROLLER COASTERS*

1. **Top Thrill Dragster:** 420 ft, Sandusky, Ohio
2. **Superman: The Escape:** 415 ft, Valencia, California
3. **Tower of Terror:** 377 ft, Gold Coast, Australia
4. **Steel Dragon 2000:** 318 ft, Mie, Japan
5. **Millennium Force:** 310 ft, Sandusky, Ohio

WORLD'S LONGEST ROLLER COASTERS*

1. **Steel Dragon 2000:** 8,133 ft, Mie, Japan
2. **The Ultimate:** 7,450 ft, North Yorkshire, England
3. **The Beast:** 7,400 ft, Cincinnati, Ohio
4. **Son of Beast:** 7,032 ft, Cincinnati, Ohio
5. **Millennium Force:** 6,595 ft, Sandusky, Ohio

*Rankings as of mid-2004. For more information check out www.ultimaterollercoaster.com

Fabulous Facts

Biggest park: Walt Disney World, Lake Buena Vista, Florida, 28,000 acres

Most rides: 68, Cedar Point, Sandusky, Ohio

Most roller coasters: 16, Cedar Point, Sandusky, Ohio, and Six Flags Magic Mountain, Valencia, California

Oldest Ferris wheel: Wonderland, Gaultier, Mississippi (It opened at Palace Amusements in New Jersey in 1895 and moved to Wonderland in 1990.)

Tallest observation wheel: 443 feet, London Eye (also known as the Millennium Wheel), London, England

Top Thrill Dragster ▶

United States

What First Lady spoke Chinese? page 256

FACTS & FIGURES

AREA	LAND	WATER	TOTAL
50 states and Washington, D.C.	3,537,440 square miles	256,648 square miles	3,794,085 square miles

POPULATION (MID-2004): 293,027,571 CAPITAL: Washington, D.C.

LARGEST, HIGHEST, AND OTHER STATISTICS

Sears Tower

Largest state: Alaska (663,267 square miles)
Smallest state: Rhode Island (1,545 square miles)
Northernmost city: Barrow, Alaska (71°17' north latitude)
Southernmost city: Hilo, Hawaii (19°44' north latitude)
Easternmost city: Eastport, Maine (66°59'05" west longitude)
Westernmost city: Atka, Alaska (174°12' west longitude)
Highest settlement: Climax, Colorado (11,360 feet)
Lowest settlement: Calipatria, California (184 feet below sea level)
Oldest national park: Yellowstone National Park (Idaho, Montana, Wyoming), 2,219,791 acres, established 1872
Largest national park: Wrangell-St. Elias, Alaska (8,323,148 acres)
Longest river system: Mississippi-Missouri-Red Rock (3,710 miles)
Deepest lake: Crater Lake, Oregon (1,932 feet)
Highest mountain: Mount McKinley, Alaska (20,320 feet)
Lowest point: Death Valley, California (282 feet below sea level)
Tallest building: Sears Tower, Chicago, Illinois (1,450 feet)
Tallest structure: TV tower, Blanchard, North Dakota (2,063 feet)
Longest bridge span: Verrazano-Narrows Bridge, New York (4,260 feet)
Highest bridge: Royal Gorge, Colorado (1,053 feet above water)

INTERNATIONAL BOUNDARY LINES OF THE U.S.

U.S.-Canadian border .... 3,987 miles
(excluding Alaska)
Alaska-Canadian border ..... 1,538 miles
U.S.-Mexican border .... 1,933 miles
(Gulf of Mexico to Pacific Ocean)

Atlantic coast .... 2,069 miles
Gulf of Mexico coast .... 1,631 miles
Pacific coast............... 7,623 miles
Arctic coast, Alaska......... 1,060 miles

A PLACE TO SHOP At 4.2 million square feet, the Mall of America in Bloomington, Minnesota, is so big you could put 32 Boeing 747s, 258 Statues of Liberty, or 24,336 school buses inside it. But the biggest mall in the U.S. doesn't need to be heated even in the cold Minnesota winter! The miles of lights inside and the nearly 1 million visitors per week keep the building plenty warm.

THE U.S. CONSTITUTION

The Foundation of American Government

The Constitution is the document that created the present government of the United States. It was written in 1787 and went into effect in 1789. It establishes the three branches of the U.S. government, which are the executive (headed by the president), the legislative (the Congress), and the judicial (the Supreme Court and other federal courts). The first 10 amendments to the Constitution (the **Bill of Rights**) explain the basic rights of all American citizens.

You can find the constitution on-line at:

WEB SITE http://www.house.gov/
Constitution/Constitution.html

The **Preamble** to the **Constitution**

The Constitution begins with a short statement called the Preamble. The Preamble states that the government of the United States was established by the people.

"We the people of the United States, in order to form a more perfect union, establish justice, insure domestic tranquility, provide for the common defense, promote the general welfare, and secure the blessings of liberty to ourselves and our posterity, do ordain and establish this Constitution for the United States of America."

THE ARTICLES

The original Constitution contained seven articles. The first three articles of the Constitution establish the three branches of the U.S. government.

Article 1, Legislative Branch Creates the Senate and House of Representatives and describes their functions and powers.

Article 2, Executive Branch Creates the office of the President and the Electoral College and lists their powers and responsibilities.

Article 3, Judicial Branch Creates the Supreme Court and gives Congress the power to create lower courts. The powers of the courts and certain crimes are defined.

Article 4, The States Discusses the relationship of the states to one another and to the citizens. Defines the states' powers.

Article 5, Amending the Constitution Describes how the Constitution can be amended (changed).

Article 6, Federal Law Makes the Constitution the supreme law of the land over state laws and constitutions.

Article 7, Ratifying the Constitution Establishes how to ratify (approve) the Constitution.

Amendments *to the* Constitution

The writers of the Constitution understood that it might need to be amended, or changed, in the future, but they wanted to be careful and made it hard to change. Article 5 describes how the Constitution can be amended.

In order to take effect, an amendment must be approved by a two-thirds majority in both the House of Representatives and the Senate. It must then be approved (ratified) by three-fourths of the states (38 states). So far, there have been 27 amendments. One of them (the 18th, ratified in 1919) banned the manufacture or sale of liquor. It was cancelled by the 21st Amendment, in 1933.

The Bill of Rights: *The First Ten Amendments*

The first ten amendments were adopted in 1791 and contain the basic freedoms Americans enjoy as a people. These amendments are known as the Bill of Rights.

1 Guarantees freedom of religion, speech, and the press.

2 Guarantees the right to have firearms.

3 Guarantees that soldiers cannot be lodged in private homes unless the owner agrees.

4 Protects people from being searched or having property searched or taken away by the government without reason.

5 Protects rights of people on trial for crimes.

6 Guarantees people accused of crimes the right to a speedy public trial by jury.

7 Guarantees the right to a trial by jury for other kinds of cases.

8 Prohibits "cruel and unusual punishments."

9 Says specific rights listed in the Constitution do not take away rights that may not be listed.

10 Establishes that any powers not given specifically to the federal government belong to states or the people.

Other Important Amendments

13 (1865): Ends slavery in the United States.

14 (1868): Bars states from denying rights to citizens; guarantees equal protection under the law for all citizens.

15 (1870): Guarantees that a person cannot be denied the right to vote because of race or color.

19 (1920): Gives women the right to vote.

22 (1951): Limits the president to two four-year terms of office.

24 (1964): Outlaws the poll tax (a tax people had to pay before they could vote) in federal elections. (The poll tax had been used to keep African Americans in the South from voting.)

25 (1967): Specifies presidential succession; also gives the president the power to appoint a new vice president, if one dies or leaves office in the middle of a term.

26 (1971): Lowers the voting age to 18 from 21.

SYMBOLS of the United States

The Great Seal

The Great Seal of the United States shows an American bald eagle with a ribbon in its mouth bearing the Latin words *e pluribus unum* (out of many, one). In its talons are the arrows of war and an olive branch of peace. On the back of the Great Seal is an unfinished pyramid with an eye (the eye of Providence) above it. The seal was approved by Congress on June 20, 1782.

THE FLAG

The flag of the United States has 50 stars (one for each state) and 13 stripes (one for each of the original 13 states). It is called unofficially the "Stars and Stripes."

The first U.S. flag was commissioned by the Second Continental Congress in 1777 but did not exist until 1783, after the American Revolution. Historians are not certain who designed the Stars and Stripes. Many different flags are believed to have been used during the American Revolution.

The flag of 1777 was used until 1795. In that year Congress passed an act ordering that a new flag have 15 stripes, alternate red and white, and 15 stars on a blue field. In 1818, Congress directed that the flag have 13 stripes and that a new star be added for each new state of the Union. The last star was added in 1960 for the state of Hawaii.

1777   **1795**   **1818**

There are many customs for flying the flag and treating it with respect. For example, it should not touch the floor and no other flag should be flown above it, except for the UN flag at UN headquarters. When the flag is raised or lowered, or passes in a parade, or during the Pledge of Allegiance, people should face it and stand at attention. Those in military uniform should salute. Others should put their right hand over their heart. The flag is flown at half staff as a sign of mourning.

Pledge of Allegiance to the Flag

"I pledge allegiance to the flag of the United States of America and to the republic for which it stands, one nation under God, indivisible, with liberty and justice for all."

THE NATIONAL ANTHEM

"The Star-Spangled Banner" was a poem written in 1814 by Francis Scott Key as he watched British ships bombard Fort McHenry, Maryland, during the War of 1812. It became the National Anthem by an act of Congress in 1931. The music to "The Star-Spangled Banner" was originally a tune called "Anacreon in Heaven."

The **Executive** Branch

The **executive branch** of the federal government is headed by the president, who enforces the laws passed by Congress and is commander in chief of U.S. armed forces. It also includes the vice president, people who work for the president or vice president, the major departments of the government, and special agencies. The **cabinet** is made up of the vice president, heads of major departments, and other officials. It meets when the president chooses. The chart at right shows cabinet departments in the order in which they were created. The Department of Homeland Security was created by a law signed in November 2002.

PRESIDENT

VICE PRESIDENT

CABINET DEPARTMENTS

1. State
2. Treasury
3. Defense
4. Justice
5. Interior
6. Agriculture
7. Commerce
8. Labor
9. Housing and Urban Development
10. Transportation
11. Energy
12. Education
13. Health and Human Services
14. Veterans Affairs
15. Homeland Security

HOW LONG DOES THE **PRESIDENT SERVE**?

The president serves a four-year term, starting on January 20. No president can be elected more than twice, or more than once if he or she had served two years as president filling out the term of a president who left office.

WHAT HAPPENS IF THE **PRESIDENT DIES?**

If the president dies in office or cannot complete the term, the vice president becomes president. If the president is disabled, the vice president can become acting president. The next person to become president after the vice president would be the Speaker of the House of Representatives.

The White House has an address on the World Wide Web especially for kids. It is:
WEB SITE http://www.whitehousekids.gov

You can send e-mail to the president at:
EMAIL president@whitehouse.gov

The White House, home of the U.S. president

Elections Electing a President

Every four years on the first Tuesday after the first Monday in November, American voters go to the polls and elect a president and vice president. Right? Well, sort of. The president and vice president are are not actually elected by a direct vote of the people. They are really elected by the 538 members of the Electoral College.

The Electoral College is not really a college, but a group of people chosen in each state. The writers of the Constitution did not agree on how a president should be selected. Some did not trust ordinary people to make a good choice. So they compromised and agreed to have the Electoral College do it.

In the early days electors voted for whomever they wanted. In modern times the political parties hold primary elections and conventions to choose candidates for president and vice president. When voters pick candidates of a particular party, they are actually choosing electors from that party. But these electors have agreed to vote for their party's candidate, and except in very rare cases this is what they do.

In the map below, the numbers not in parentheses show how many electoral votes each state has in the 2004 election. If the number was different in the 2000 election it is shown in parentheses. The colors show which states were won by each candidate in 2000. When you read this, you may also know what happened in the 2004 presidential election!

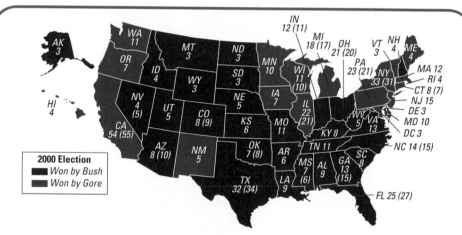

2000 Election
■ Won by Bush
■ Won by Gore

The **Electoral College** *State by State*

The number of electors for each state is equal to the total number of senators (2), plus the U.S. House members each state has in Congress. In addition the District of Columbia has 3 electoral votes. The numbers of representatives for some states changed in 2002, because of 2000 Census results. So the numbers of electoral votes for the 2004 presidential elections are also new. The electors chosen in November meet in state capitals in December. In almost all states, the party that gets the most votes in November wins ALL the electoral votes for the state. In January the electors' votes are officially opened during a special session of Congress. If no presidential candidate wins a majority of these votes, the House of Representatives chooses the president. This happened in 1800, 1824, and 1877.

Can a candidate who didn't win the most popular votes still win a majority of electoral votes?
Yes. That's what happened in 1876, 1888, and again in 2000.

PRESIDENTS AND VICE PRESIDENTS OF THE UNITED STATES

PRESIDENT / VICE PRESIDENT	YEARS IN OFFICE
1 George Washington	**1789–1797**
John Adams	1789–1797
2 John Adams	**1797–1801**
Thomas Jefferson	1797–1801
3 Thomas Jefferson	**1801–1809**
Aaron Burr	1801–1805
George Clinton	1805–1809
4 James Madison	**1809–1817**
George Clinton	1809–1812
Elbridge Gerry	1813–1814
5 James Monroe	**1817–1825**
Daniel D. Tompkins	1817–1825
6 John Quincy Adams	**1825–1829**
John C. Calhoun	1825–1829
7 Andrew Jackson	**1829–1837**
John C. Calhoun	1829–1832
Martin Van Buren	1833–1837
8 Martin Van Buren	**1837–1841**
Richard M. Johnson	1837–1841
9 William H. Harrison	**1841**
John Tyler	1841
10 John Tyler	**1841–1845**
No Vice President	
11 James Knox Polk	**1845–1849**
George M. Dallas	1845–1849
12 Zachary Taylor	**1849–1850**
Millard Fillmore	1849–1850
13 Millard Fillmore	**1850–1853**
No Vice President	
14 Franklin Pierce	**1853–1857**
William R. King	1853
15 James Buchanan	**1857–1861**
John C. Breckinridge	1857–1861
16 Abraham Lincoln	**1861–1865**
Hannibal Hamlin	1861–1865
Andrew Johnson	1865
17 Andrew Johnson	**1865–1869**
No Vice President	
18 Ulysses S. Grant	**1869–1877**
Schuyler Colfax	1869–1873
Henry Wilson	1873–1875
19 Rutherford B. Hayes	**1877–1881**
William A. Wheeler	1877–1881
20 James A. Garfield	**1881**
Chester A. Arthur	1881
21 Chester A. Arthur	**1881–1885**
No Vice President	
22 Grover Cleveland	**1885–1889**
Thomas A. Hendricks	1885
23 Benjamin Harrison	**1889–1893**
Levi P. Morton	1889–1893
24 Grover Cleveland	**1893–1897**
Adlai E. Stevenson	1893–1897
25 William McKinley	**1897–1901**
Garret A. Hobart	1897–1899
Theodore Roosevelt	1901
26 Theodore Roosevelt	**1901–1909**
Charles W. Fairbanks	1905–1909
27 William Howard Taft	**1909–1913**
James S. Sherman	1909–1912
28 Woodrow Wilson	**1913–1921**
Thomas R. Marshall	1913–1921
29 Warren G. Harding	**1921–1923**
Calvin Coolidge	1921–1923
30 Calvin Coolidge	**1923–1929**
Charles G. Dawes	1925–1929
31 Herbert Hoover	**1929–1933**
Charles Curtis	1929–1933
32 Franklin D. Roosevelt	**1933–1945**
John Nance Garner	1933–1941
Henry A. Wallace	1941–1945
Harry S. Truman	1945
33 Harry S. Truman	**1945–1953**
Alben W. Barkley	1949–1953
34 Dwight D. Eisenhower	**1953–1961**
Richard M. Nixon	1953–1961
35 John F. Kennedy	**1961–1963**
Lyndon B. Johnson	1961–1963
36 Lyndon B. Johnson	**1963–1969**
Hubert H. Humphrey	1965–1969
37 Richard M. Nixon	**1969–1974**
Spiro T. Agnew	1969–1973
Gerald R. Ford	1973–1974
38 Gerald R. Ford	**1974–1977**
Nelson A. Rockefeller	1974–1977
39 Jimmy Carter	**1977–1981**
Walter F. Mondale	1977–1981
40 Ronald Reagan	**1981–1989**
George H. W. Bush	1981–1989
41 George H. W. Bush	**1989–1993**
Dan Quayle	1989–1993
42 Bill Clinton	**1993–2001**
Al Gore	1993–2001
43 George W. Bush	**2001–**
Richard B. Cheney	2001–

PRESIDENTS of the United States

1 **GEORGE WASHINGTON** Federalist Party   **1789–1797**
BORN: Feb. 22, 1732, at Wakefield, Westmoreland County, Virginia
MARRIED: Martha Dandridge Custis (1731-1802); no children
DIED: Dec. 14, 1799; buried at Mount Vernon, Fairfax County, Virginia
EARLY CAREER: Soldier; head of the Virginia militia; commander of the
Continental Army; chairman of Constitutional Convention (1787)

2 **JOHN ADAMS** Federalist Party   **1797–1801**
BORN: Oct. 30, 1735, in Braintree (now Quincy), Massachusetts
MARRIED: Abigail Smith (1744-1818); 3 sons, 2 daughters
DIED: July 4, 1826; buried in Quincy, Massachusetts
EARLY CAREER: Lawyer; delegate to Continental Congress; signer of the
Declaration of Independence; first vice president

3 **THOMAS JEFFERSON** Democratic-Republican Party   **1801–1809**
BORN: Apr. 13, 1743, at Shadwell, Albemarle County, Virginia
MARRIED: Martha Wayles Skelton (1748-1782); 1 son, 5 daughters
DIED: July 4, 1826; buried at Monticello, Albemarle County, Virginia
EARLY CAREER: Lawyer; member of the Continental Congress; author of the
Declaration of Independence; governor of Virginia; first secretary of
state; author of the Virginia Statute on Religious Freedom

4 **JAMES MADISON** Democratic-Republican Party   **1809-1817**
BORN: Mar. 16, 1751, at Port Conway, King George County, Virginia
MARRIED: Dolley Payne Todd (1768-1849); no children
DIED: June 28, 1836; buried at Montpelier Station, Virginia
EARLY CAREER: Member of the Virginia Constitutional Convention (1776);
member of the Continental Congress; major contributor to the U.S.
Constitution; writer of the *Federalist Papers*; secretary of state

5 **JAMES MONROE** Democratic-Republican Party   **1817–1825**
BORN: Apr. 28, 1758, in Westmoreland County, Virginia
MARRIED: Elizabeth Kortright (1768-1830); 2 daughters
DIED: July 4, 1831; buried in Richmond, Virginia
EARLY CAREER: Soldier; lawyer; U.S. senator; governor of Virginia;
secretary of state

6 **JOHN QUINCY ADAMS** Democratic-Republican Party   **1825–1829**
BORN: July 11, 1767, in Braintree (now Quincy), Massachusetts
MARRIED: Louisa Catherine Johnson (1775-1852); 3 sons, 1 daughter
DIED: Feb. 23, 1848; buried in Quincy, Massachusetts
EARLY CAREER: Diplomat; U.S. senator; secretary of state

ANDREW JACKSON Democratic Party   **1829–1837**
BORN: Mar. 15, 1767, in Waxhaw, South Carolina
MARRIED: Rachel Donelson Robards (1767-1828); 1 son
DIED: June 8, 1845; buried in Nashville, Tennessee
EARLY CAREER: Lawyer; U.S. representative and senator; soldier in the
    U.S. Army

MARTIN VAN BUREN Democratic Party   **1837–1841**
BORN: Dec. 5, 1782, at Kinderhook, New York
MARRIED: Hannah Hoes (1783-1819); 4 sons
DIED: July 24, 1862; buried at Kinderhook, New York
EARLY CAREER: Governor of New York; secretary of state; vice president

WILLIAM HENRY HARRISON Whig Party   **1841**
BORN: Feb. 9, 1773, at Berkeley, Charles City County, Virginia
MARRIED: Anna Symmes (1775-1864); 6 sons, 4 daughters
DIED: Apr. 4, 1841; buried in North Bend, Ohio
EARLY CAREER: First governor of Indiana Territory; superintendent of
    Indian affairs; U.S. representative and senator

JOHN TYLER Whig Party   **1841–1845**
BORN: Mar. 29, 1790, in Greenway, Charles City County, Virginia
MARRIED: Letitia Christian (1790-1842); 3 sons, 5 daughters
    Julia Gardiner (1820-1889); 5 sons, 2 daughters
DIED: Jan. 18, 1862; buried in Richmond, Virginia
EARLY CAREER: U.S. representative and senator; vice president

JAMES KNOX POLK Democratic Party   **1845–1849**
BORN: Nov. 2, 1795, in Mecklenburg County, North Carolina
MARRIED: Sarah Childress (1803-1891); no children
DIED: June 15, 1849; buried in Nashville, Tennessee
EARLY CAREER: U.S. representative; Speaker of the House; governor
    of Tennessee

ZACHARY TAYLOR Whig Party   **1849–1850**
BORN: Nov. 24, 1784, in Orange County, Virginia
MARRIED: Margaret Smith (1788-1852); 1 son, 5 daughters
DIED: July 9, 1850; buried in Louisville, Kentucky
EARLY CAREER: Indian fighter; general in the U.S. Army

MILLARD FILLMORE Whig Party   **1850–1853**
BORN: Jan. 7, 1800, in Cayuga County, New York
MARRIED: Abigail Powers (1798-1853); 1 son, 1 daughter
    Caroline Carmichael McIntosh (1813-1881); no children
DIED: Mar. 8, 1874; buried in Buffalo, New York
EARLY CAREER: Farmer; lawyer; U.S. representative; vice president

FRANKLIN PIERCE Democratic Party   **1853–1857**
BORN: Nov. 23, 1804, in Hillsboro, New Hampshire
MARRIED: Jane Means Appleton (1806-1863); 3 sons
DIED: Oct. 8, 1869; buried in Concord, New Hampshire
EARLY CAREER: U.S. representative, senator

JAMES BUCHANAN Democratic Party   **1857–1861**
BORN: Apr. 23, 1791, Cove Gap, near Mercersburg, Pennsylvania
MARRIED: Never
DIED: June 1, 1868, buried in Lancaster, Pennsylvania
EARLY CAREER: U.S. representative; secretary of state

ABRAHAM LINCOLN Republican Party   **1861-1865**
BORN: Feb. 12, 1809, in Hardin County, Kentucky
MARRIED: Mary Todd (1818-1882); 4 sons
DIED: Apr. 15, 1865; buried in Springfield, Illinois
EARLY CAREER: Lawyer; U.S. representative

ANDREW JOHNSON Democratic Party   **1865–1869**
BORN: Dec. 29, 1808, in Raleigh, North Carolina
MARRIED: Eliza McCardle (1810-1876); 3 sons, 2 daughters
DIED: July 31, 1875; buried in Greeneville, Tennessee
EARLY CAREER: Tailor; member of state legislature; U.S. representative;
    governor of Tennessee; U.S. senator; vice president

ULYSSES S. GRANT Republican Party   **1869–1877**
BORN: Apr. 27, 1822, in Point Pleasant, Ohio
MARRIED: Julia Dent (1826-1902); 3 sons, 1 daughter
DIED: July 23, 1885; buried in New York City
EARLY CAREER: Army officer; commander of Union forces during
    Civil War

RUTHERFORD B. HAYES Republican Party   **1877–1881**
BORN: Oct. 4, 1822, in Delaware, Ohio
MARRIED: Lucy Ware Webb (1831-1889); 5 sons, 2 daughters
DIED: Jan. 17, 1893; buried in Fremont, Ohio
EARLY CAREER: Lawyer; general in Union Army; U.S. representative;
    governor of Ohio

JAMES A. GARFIELD Republican Party   **1881**
BORN: Nov. 19, 1831, in Orange, Cuyahoga County, Ohio
MARRIED: Lucretia Rudolph (1832-1918); 5 sons, 2 daughters
DIED: Sept. 19, 1881; buried in Cleveland, Ohio
EARLY CAREER: Teacher; Ohio state senator; general in Union Army;
    U.S. representative

CHESTER A. ARTHUR Republican Party   **1881–1885**
BORN: Oct. 5, 1829, in Fairfield, Vermont
MARRIED: Ellen Lewis Herndon (1837-1880); 2 sons, 1 daughter
DIED: Nov. 18, 1886; buried in Albany, New York
EARLY CAREER: Teacher; lawyer; vice president

GROVER CLEVELAND Democratic Party   **1885–1889**
BORN: Mar. 18, 1837, in Caldwell, New Jersey
MARRIED: Frances Folsom (1864-1947); 2 sons, 3 daughters
DIED: June 24, 1908; buried in Princeton, New Jersey
EARLY CAREER: Lawyer; mayor of Buffalo; governor of New York

BENJAMIN HARRISON Republican Party   **1889-1893**
BORN: Aug. 20, 1833, in North Bend, Ohio
MARRIED: Caroline Lavinia Scott (1832-1892); 1 son, 1 daughter
    Mary Scott Lord Dimmick (1858-1948); 1 daughter
DIED: Mar. 13, 1901; buried in Indianapolis, Indiana
EARLY CAREER: Lawyer; general in Union Army; U.S. senator

GROVER CLEVELAND   **1893–1897**
SEE 22, ABOVE

WILLIAM MCKINLEY Republican Party   **1897–1901**
BORN: Jan. 29, 1843, in Niles, Ohio
MARRIED: Ida Saxton (1847-1907); 2 daughters
DIED: Sept. 14, 1901; buried in Canton, Ohio
EARLY CAREER: Lawyer; U.S. representative; governor of Ohio

THEODORE ROOSEVELT Republican Party   **1901–1909**
BORN: Oct. 27, 1858, in New York City
MARRIED: Alice Hathaway Lee (1861-1884); 1 daughter
    Edith Kermit Carow (1861-1948); 4 sons, 1 daughter
DIED: Jan. 6, 1919; buried in Oyster Bay, New York
EARLY CAREER: Assistant secretary of the Navy; cavalry leader in
    Spanish-American War; governor of New York; vice president

WILLIAM HOWARD TAFT Republican Party   **1909–1913**
BORN: Sept. 15, 1857, in Cincinnati, Ohio
MARRIED: Helen Herron (1861-1943); 2 sons, 1 daughter
DIED: Mar. 8, 1930; buried in Arlington National Cemetery, Virginia
EARLY CAREER: Reporter; lawyer; judge; secretary of war

WOODROW WILSON Democratic Party   **1913–1921**
BORN: Dec. 28, 1856, in Staunton, Virginia
MARRIED: Ellen Louise Axson (1860-1914); 3 daughters
    Edith Bolling Galt (1872-1961); no children
DIED: Feb. 3, 1924; buried in Washington, D.C.
EARLY CAREER: College professor and president; governor of New Jersey

WARREN G. HARDING Republican Party   1921–1923
BORN: Nov. 2, 1865, near Corsica (now Blooming Grove), Ohio
MARRIED: Florence Kling De Wolfe (1860-1924); 1 daughter
DIED: Aug. 2, 1923; buried in Marion, Ohio
EARLY CAREER: Ohio state senator; U.S. senator

29

CALVIN COOLIDGE Republican Party   1923–1929
BORN: July 4, 1872, in Plymouth, Vermont
MARRIED: Grace Anna Goodhue (1879-1957); 2 sons
DIED: Jan. 5, 1933; buried in Plymouth, Vermont
EARLY CAREER: Massachusetts state legislator; lieutenant governor and
    governor; vice president

30

HERBERT HOOVER Republican Party   1929-1933
BORN: Aug. 10, 1874, in West Branch, Iowa
MARRIED: Lou Henry (1875-1944); 2 sons
DIED: Oct. 20, 1964; buried in West Branch, Iowa
EARLY CAREER: Mining engineer; secretary of commerce

31

FRANKLIN DELANO ROOSEVELT Democratic Party   1933–1945
BORN: Jan. 30, 1882, in Hyde Park, New York
MARRIED: Anna Eleanor Roosevelt (1884-1962); 4 sons, 1 daughter
DIED: Apr. 12, 1945; buried in Hyde Park, New York
EARLY CAREER: Lawyer; New York state senator; assistant secretary of
    the Navy; governor of New York

32

HARRY S. TRUMAN Democratic Party   1945–1953
BORN: May 8, 1884, in Lamar, Missouri
MARRIED: Elizabeth Virginia "Bess" Wallace (1885-1982); 1 daughter
DIED: Dec. 26, 1972; buried in Independence, Missouri
EARLY CAREER: Farmer; haberdasher (ran men's clothing store); judge;
    U.S. senator; vice president

33

DWIGHT D. EISENHOWER Republican Party   1953–1961
BORN: Oct. 14, 1890, in Denison, Texas
MARRIED: Mary "Mamie" Geneva Doud (1896-1979); 2 sons
DIED: Mar. 28, 1969; buried in Abilene, Kansas
EARLY CAREER: Commander, Allied landing in North Africa and later
    Supreme Allied Commander in Europe during World War II;
    president of Columbia University

34

JOHN FITZGERALD KENNEDY Democratic Party   1961–1963
BORN: May 29, 1917, in Brookline, Massachusetts
MARRIED: Jacqueline Lee Bouvier (1929-1994); 2 sons, 1 daughter
DIED: Nov. 22, 1963; buried in Arlington National Cemetery, Virginia
EARLY CAREER: U.S. naval commander; U.S. representative and senator

35

36 **LYNDON BAINES JOHNSON** Democratic Party **1963–1969**
BORN: Aug. 27, 1908, near Stonewall, Texas
MARRIED: Claudia "Lady Bird" Alta Taylor (b. 1912); 2 daughters
DIED: Jan. 22, 1973; buried in Johnson City, Texas
EARLY CAREER: U.S. representative and senator; vice president

37 **RICHARD MILHOUS NIXON** Republican Party **1969–1974**
BORN: Jan. 9, 1913, in Yorba Linda, California
MARRIED: Thelma "Pat" Ryan (1912-1993); 2 daughters
DIED: Apr. 22, 1994; buried in Yorba Linda, California
EARLY CAREER: Lawyer; U.S. representative and senator; vice president

38 **GERALD R. FORD** Republican Party **1974-1977**
BORN: July 14, 1913, in Omaha, Nebraska
MARRIED: Elizabeth "Betty" Bloomer (b. 1918); 3 sons, 1 daughter
EARLY CAREER: Lawyer; U.S. representative; vice president

39 **JIMMY (JAMES EARL) CARTER** Democratic Party **1977-1981**
BORN: Oct. 1, 1924, in Plains, Georgia
MARRIED: Rosalynn Smith (b. 1927); 3 sons, 1 daughter
EARLY CAREER: Peanut farmer; Georgia state senator; governor
of Georgia

40 **RONALD REAGAN** Republican Party **1981–1989**
BORN: Feb. 6, 1911, in Tampico, Illinois
MARRIED: Jane Wyman (b. 1914); 1 son, 1 daughter
Nancy Davis (b. 1923); 1 son, 1 daughter
EARLY CAREER: Film and television actor; governor of California

41 **GEORGE H.W. BUSH** Republican Party **1989–1993**
BORN: June 12, 1924, in Milton, Massachusetts
MARRIED: Barbara Pierce (b. 1925); 4 sons, 2 daughters
EARLY CAREER: U.S. Navy pilot; businessman; U.S. representative; U.S.
ambassador to the UN; CIA director, vice president

42 **BILL (WILLIAM JEFFERSON) CLINTON** Democratic Party **1993–2001**
BORN: Aug. 19, 1946, in Hope, Arkansas
MARRIED: Hillary Rodham (b. 1947); 1 daughter
EARLY CAREER: College professor; Arkansas state attorney general;
governor of Arkansas

43 **GEORGE W. BUSH** Republican Party **2001-**
BORN: July 6, 1946, in New Haven, Connecticut
MARRIED: Laura Welch (b. 1946); 2 daughters
EARLY CAREER: Political adviser; businessman; governor of Texas

Presidential Facts

Tallest president: Abraham Lincoln. He was 6 feet, 4 inches.

Shortest president: James Madison. He was 5 feet, 4 inches.

Sons of presidents to be president: John Quincy Adams (6th president), son of John Adams (2nd president); George W. Bush (43rd), son of George H.W. Bush (41st).

Grandson of a president to be president: Benjamin Harrison (23rd president), grandson of William Henry Harrison (9th president).

First president to attend a major league baseball game: Benjamin Harrison, June 6, 1892 (Cincinnati defeated Washington, 7-4).

Only president to be married in the White House: Grover Cleveland, in 1886.

President with the most children: John Tyler, who had 15 children with two wives.

Only unmarried president: James Buchanan

First president to leave the U.S. while in office: Theodore Roosevelt, who visited the Panama Canal in 1906.

First president to cross the Atlantic Ocean while in office: Woodrow Wilson, in 1918.

Meet *the* First Ladies

SARAH POLK, wife of James K. Polk, was well-educated, a rarity for a woman in the early 1800s. She had studied Greek and Roman literature and often helped her husband with speeches.

LOU HENRY HOOVER, wife of Herbert Hoover, spoke several languages, including Chinese, and had a degree in geology. As First Lady she worked to involve all children in sports.

LUCY HAYES, wife of Rutherford B. Hayes, was the first president's wife who had a college degree. When she and her husband went to the West Coast in 1880, she became the first First Lady to travel across North America.

HILLARY RODHAM CLINTON, wife of Bill Clinton, was a successful lawyer and an active First Lady with a special interest in children's rights. In 2000, she became the first First Lady to be elected to office, as a U.S. senator from New York.

HELEN TAFT, wife of William H. Taft, who had frequently visited Japan when her husband was the top U.S. official in the Philippines, accepted Washington, D.C.'s first 3,000 Japanese cherry trees as a gift from the city of Tokyo.

LAURA BUSH, wife of George W. Bush, was a librarian and teacher. She is interested in books, history, art, and the well-being of children. She and her husband have twin daughters, both college students.

The **Legislative** Branch

CONGRESS

The Congress of the United States is the legislative branch of the federal government. Congress's major responsibility is to pass the laws that govern the country and determine how money collected in taxes is spent. It is the president's responsibility to enforce the laws. Congress consists of two parts—the Senate and the House of Representatives.

THE SENATE

The Senate has 100 members, two from each state. The Constitution says ▲ *The Senate*
that the Senate will have equal representation (the same number of representatives) from each state. Thus, small states have the same number of senators as large states. Senators are elected for six-year terms. There is no limit on the number of terms a senator can serve.

The Senate also has the responsibility of approving people the president appoints for certain jobs: for example, cabinet members and Supreme Court justices. The Senate must approve all treaties by at least a two-thirds vote. It also has the responsibility under the Constitution of putting on trial high-ranking federal officials who have been impeached by the House of Representatives.

WEB SITE www.senate.gov

THE HOUSE OF REPRESENTATIVES

The number of members of the House of Representatives for each state depends on its population according to a recent census. But each state has at least one representative, no matter how small its population. A term lasts two years.

▼ *The Capitol, where Congress meets*

The first House of Representatives in 1789 had 65 members. As the country's population grew, the number of representatives increased. Since the 1910 census, however, the total membership has been kept at 435. After the results of Census 2000 were added up, 8 states gained seats and 10 states lost seats.

WEB SITE www.house.gov

Here are the numbers of representatives each state will has in 2004, compared with 10 years earlier and 30 years earlier:

State	2004	1994	1974
Alabama	7	7	7
Alaska	1	1	1
Arizona	8	6	4
Arkansas	4	4	4
California	53	52	43
Colorado	7	6	5
Connecticut	5	6	6
Delaware	1	1	1
Florida	25	23	15
Georgia	13	11	10
Hawaii	2	2	2
Idaho	2	2	2
Illinois	19	20	24
Indiana	9	10	11
Iowa	5	5	6
Kansas	4	4	5
Kentucky	6	6	7
Louisiana	7	7	8
Maine	2	2	2
Maryland	8	8	8
Massachusetts	10	10	12
Michigan	15	16	19
Minnesota	8	8	8
Mississippi	4	5	5
Missouri	9	9	10
Montana	1	1	2
Nebraska	3	3	3
Nevada	3	2	1
New Hampshire	2	2	2
New Jersey	13	13	15
New Mexico	3	3	2
New York	29	31	39
North Carolina	13	12	11
North Dakota	1	1	1
Ohio	18	19	23
Oklahoma	5	6	6
Oregon	5	5	4
Pennsylvania	19	21	25
Rhode Island	2	2	2
South Carolina	6	6	6
South Dakota	1	1	2
Tennessee	9	9	9
Texas	32	30	24
Utah	3	3	2
Vermont	1	1	1
Virginia	11	11	10
Washington	9	9	7
West Virginia	3	3	4
Wisconsin	8	9	9
Wyoming	1	1	1

Washington, D.C., Puerto Rico, American Samoa, Guam, and the Virgin Islands each have one nonvoting member of the House of Representatives.

Women in Congress

As of January 2004, there were 62 women serving in the U.S. House of Representatives and 14 in the U.S. Senate. All together, 193 women have served in the House and 33 in the Senate.

The first woman elected to the House was Jeannette Rankin (Montana) in 1916. In 1932, Hattie Caraway (Arkansas) was the first woman to be elected to the Senate. Margaret Chase Smith, of Maine, was the first woman elected to both houses of Congress (House in 1940, Senate in 1948).

New York's Shirley Chisholm became the first African-American woman in Congress after being elected to the House in 1968. In 1992, Carol Moseley Braun of Illinois became the first African-American woman elected to the Senate.

In November, 2002, California Representative Nancy Pelosi was selected by her fellow Democrats as their leader in the House of Representatives. This was the highest position in Congress ever held by a woman.

Carol Moseley Braun ▶

HOW A **BILL** BECOMES A **LAW**

STEP 1 SENATORS AND REPRESENTATIVES PROPOSE BILL.

A proposed law is called a **bill**. Any member of Congress may propose (introduce) a bill. A bill is introduced in each house of Congress. The House of Representatives and the Senate consider a bill separately. A member of Congress who introduces a bill is known as the bill's **sponsor**. Bills to raise money always begin in the House of Representatives.

STEP 2 HOUSE AND SENATE COMMITTEES CONSIDER THE BILL.

The bill is then sent to appropriate committees for consideration. A bill relating to agriculture, for example, would be sent to the agriculture committees in the House and in the Senate. A committee is made up of a small number of members of the House or Senate. Whichever party has a majority in the House or Senate has a majority on each committee. When committees are considering a bill, they hold **hearings** at which people can speak for or against it.

STEP 3 COMMITTEES VOTE ON THE BILL.

The committees can change the bill as they see fit. Then they vote on it.

STEP 4 THE BILL IS DEBATED IN THE HOUSE AND SENATE.

If the committees vote in favor of the bill, it goes to the full House and Senate, where it is debated and may be changed further. The House and Senate can then vote on it.

STEP 5 FROM HOUSE AND SENATE TO CONFERENCE COMMITTEE.

If the House and the Senate pass different versions of the same bill, the bill must go to a **conference committee,** where differences between the two versions must be worked out. A conference committee is a special committee made up of both Senate and House members.

STEP 6 FINAL VOTE IN THE HOUSE AND SENATE.

The House and the Senate then vote on the conference committee version. In order for this version to become a law, it must be approved by a majority of members of both houses of Congress and signed by the president.

STEP 7 THE PRESIDENT SIGNS THE BILL INTO LAW.

If the bill passes both houses of Congress, it goes to the president for his signature. Once the president signs a bill, it becomes law.

STEP 8 WHAT IF THE PRESIDENT DOESN'T SIGN IT?

Sometimes the president does not approve of a bill and decides not to sign it. This is called **vetoing** it. A bill that has been vetoed goes back to Congress, where the members can vote again. If the House and the Senate pass the bill with a two-thirds majority vote, it becomes law. This is called **overriding** the veto.

President Lyndon B. Johnson, signing the Civil Rights Act, 1964. ▶

The SUPREME COURT

Above are the nine justices who were on the Supreme Court at the start of its 2003–2004 session. **Back row** *(from left to right): Ruth Bader Ginsburg, David H. Souter, Clarence Thomas, Stephen Breyer.* **Front row** *(from left to right): Antonin Scalia, John Paul Stevens, Chief Justice William H. Rehnquist, Sandra Day O'Connor, Anthony M. Kennedy.*

The highest court in the United States is the Supreme Court. It has nine justices who are appointed for life by the president with the approval of the Senate. Eight of the nine members are called associate justices. The ninth is the chief justice, who presides over the Court's meetings.

WHAT DOES THE SUPREME COURT DO?

The Supreme Court's major responsibilities are to judge cases that involve reviewing federal laws, actions of the president, treaties of the United States, and laws passed by state governments to be sure they do not conflict with the U.S. Constitution. If the Supreme Court finds that a law or action violates the Constitution, the law is struck down.

THE SUPREME COURT'S DECISION IS FINAL.

Most cases must go through other state courts or federal courts before they reach the Supreme Court. The Supreme Court is the final court for a case, and the justices decide which cases they will review. After the Supreme Court hears a case, it may agree or disagree with the decision by a lower court. Each justice has one vote, and the majority rules. When the Supreme Court makes a ruling, its decision is final, so each of the justices has a very important job.

did you know?

The youngest person ever appointed to the Supreme Court was Joseph Story, age 32, in 1811. The oldest justice to be appointed was Horace Lurton, age 65 in 1909. Oliver Wendell Holmes reached the highest age on the Court; he retired in 1932 at the age of 90. William O. Douglas, who became a justice at the age of 40 in 1939, served on the Court for 36 years, 209 days, longer than any other justice in history.

United States History
TIME LINE

THE FIRST PEOPLE IN NORTH AMERICA: BEFORE 1492

14,000 B.C.— 11,000 B.C.
Paleo-Indians use stone points attached to spears to hunt big **mammoths** in northern parts of North America.

11,000 B.C.
Big mammoths disappear and Paleo-Indians begin to gather **plants** for food.

After A.D. 500
Anasazi peoples in the Southwestern United States live in homes on cliffs, called **cliff dwellings**. Anasazi pottery and dishes are well known for their beautiful patterns.

After A.D. 700
Mississippian Indian people in the Southeastern United States develop farms and build **burial mounds**.

0,000 B.C.

30,000 B.C. — 11,000 B.C.
First people (called **Paleo-Indians**) cross from Siberia to Alaska and begin to move into North America.

9500 B.C. — 1000 B.C.
North American Indians begin using **stone** to grind food and to hunt bison and smaller animals.

1000 B.C.— A.D. 500
Woodland Indians, who lived east of the Mississippi River, bury their dead under large **mounds** of earth (which can still be seen today).

700–1492
Many **different Indian cultures** develop throughout North America.

COLONIAL AMERICA AND THE AMERICAN REVOLUTION: 1492–1783

1492

1492
Christopher **Columbus** sails across the Atlantic Ocean and reaches an island in the Bahamas in the Caribbean Sea.

1513
Juan **Ponce de León** explores the Florida coast.

1524
Giovanni da **Verrazano** explores the coast from Carolina north to Nova Scotia, enters New York harbor.

1540
Francisco Vásquez de **Coronado** explores the Southwest.

1565
St. Augustine, Florida, the **first town** established by Europeans in the United States, is founded by the Spanish. Later burned by the English in 1586.

BENJAMIN FRANKLIN (1706–1790)

was a great American leader, printer, scientist, and writer. In 1732, he began publishing a magazine called *Poor Richard's Almanack*. Poor Richard was a make-believe person who gave advice about common sense and honesty. Many of Poor Richard's sayings are still known today. Among the most famous are "God helps them that help themselves" and "Early to bed, early to rise, makes a man healthy, wealthy, and wise."

1634

1634
Maryland is founded as a Catholic colony, with religious freedom for all granted in 1649.

1664
The English seize **New Amsterdam** from the Dutch. The city is renamed New York.

1699
French settlers move into Mississippi and Louisiana.

1732
Benjamin Franklin begins publishing *Poor Richard's Almanack.*

1754– 1763
French and Indian War between England and France. The French are defeated and lose their lands in Canada and the American Midwest.

1764–1766
England places taxes on sugar that comes from their North American colonies. England also requires colonists to buy stamps to help pay for royal troops. Colonists protest, and the **Stamp Act** is repealed in 1766.

1607
Jamestown, Virginia, the first English settlement in North America, is founded by Captain John Smith.

1609
Henry Hudson sails into **New York Harbor**, explores the Hudson River. Spaniards settle Santa Fe, New Mexico.

1619
The first African **slaves** are brought to Jamestown. (Slavery is made legal in 1650.)

1620
Pilgrims from England arrive at Plymouth, Massachusetts on the *Mayflower*.

1626
Peter Minuit buys **Manhattan** island for the Dutch from Man-a-hat-a Indians for goods worth $24. The island is renamed New Amsterdam.

1630
Boston is founded by Massachusetts colonists led by John Winthrop.

FAMOUS WORDS FROM THE DECLARATION OF INDEPENDENCE, JULY 4, 1776

"We hold these truths to be self-evident, that all men are created equal, that they are endowed by their Creator with certain unalienable rights, that among these are life, liberty, and the pursuit of happiness."

1770
Boston Massacre: English troops fire on a group of people protesting English taxes.

1773
Boston Tea Party: English tea is thrown into the harbor to protest a tax on tea.

1775
Fighting at **Lexington and Concord**, Massachusetts, marks the beginning of the American Revolution.

1776
The Declaration of Independence is approved July 4 by the Continental Congress (made up of representatives from the American colonies).

1781
British General **Cornwallis surrenders** to the Americans at Yorktown, Virginia, ending the fighting in the Revolutionary War.

THE NEW NATION: 1783–1900

WHO ATTENDED THE CONVENTION?

The **Constitutional Convention** met in Philadelphia in the hot summer of 1787. Most of the great founders of America attended. Among those present were George Washington, James Madison, and John Adams. They met to form a new government that would be strong and, at the same time, protect the liberties that were fought for in the American Revolution. The Constitution they created is still the law of the United States.

THE LOUISIANA PURCHASE (1803)

1784

1784
The first successful daily **newspaper,** the *Pennsylvania Packet & General Advertiser,* is published.

1787
The **Constitutional Convention** meets to write a Constitution for the U.S.

1789
The new **Constitution** is approved by the states. George Washington is chosen as the first president.

1800
The federal government moves to a new capital, **Washington, D.C.**

1803
The U.S. makes the **Louisiana Purchase** from France. The Purchase doubles the area of the U.S.

The Trail of Tears

"THE TRAIL OF TEARS"

The **Cherokee Indians** living in Georgia were forced by the government to leave in 1838. They were sent to Oklahoma. On the long march, thousands died because of disease and the cold weather.

UNCLE TOM'S CABIN

Harriet Beecher Stowe's novel about the **suffering of slaves** was an instant bestseller in the North and banned in most of the South. When President Abraham Lincoln met Stowe, he called her "the little lady who started this war" (the Civil War).

1836

1836
Texans fighting for independence from Mexico are defeated at the **Alamo.**

1838
Cherokee Indians are forced to move to Oklahoma, along "The **Trail of Tears**."

1844
The **first telegraph** line connects Washington, D.C., and Baltimore.

1846—1848
U.S. war with Mexico: Mexico is defeated, and the United States takes control of the Republic of Texas and of Mexican territories in the West.

1848
The discovery of **gold** in California leads to a "rush" of 80,000 people to the West in search of gold.

1852
Uncle Tom's Cabin is published.

1831
The Liberator, a newspaper opposing slavery, is published in Boston.

1804
Lewis and Clark, with their guide Sacagawea, explore what is now the northwestern United States.

1812–1814
War of 1812 with Great Britain: British forces burn the Capitol and White House. Francis Scott Key writes the words to "The Star-Spangled Banner."

1820
The **Missouri Compromise** bans slavery west of the Mississippi River and north of 36°30' latitude, except in Missouri.

1823
The **Monroe Doctrine** warns European countries not to interfere in the Americas.

1825
The **Erie Canal** opens linking New York City with the Great Lakes.

CIVIL WAR DEAD AND WOUNDED

The U.S. **Civil War** between the North and South lasted four years (1861-1865) and resulted in the death or wounding of more than 600,000 people. Little was known at the time about the spread of diseases. As a result, many casualties were also the result of illnesses such as influenza, measles, and infections from battle wounds.

1869
The **first railroad** connecting the East and West coasts is completed.

1898
Spanish-American War: The U.S. defeats Spain, gains control of the Philippines, Puerto Rico, and Guam.

1858
Abraham Lincoln and Stephen Douglas **debate** about slavery during their Senate campaign in Illinois.

1860
Abraham **Lincoln** is elected president.

1861
The **Civil War** begins.

1863
President Lincoln issues the **Emancipation Proclamation**, freeing most slaves.

1865
The **Civil War ends** as the South surrenders. President Lincoln is assassinated.

1890
Battle of Wounded Knee is fought in South Dakota—the last major battle between Indians and U.S. troops.

265

UNITED STATES SINCE 1900

WORLD WAR I

In **World War I** the United States fought with Great Britain, France, and Russia (the Allies) against Germany and Austria-Hungary. The Allies won the war in 1918.

1900

1903
The United States begins digging the **Panama Canal**. The canal opens in 1914, connecting the Atlantic and Pacific oceans.

1908
Henry Ford introduces the **Model T** car, priced at $850.

1916
Jeannette Rankin of Montana becomes the first woman elected to Congress.

1917–1918
The United States joins **World War I** on the side of the Allies against Germany.

1927
Charles A. **Lindbergh** becomes the first person to fly alone nonstop across the Atlantic Ocean.

1954
The U.S. Supreme Court **forbids racial segregation** in public schools.

SCHOOL SEGREGATION

The U.S. Supreme Court ruled that **separate schools** for black students and white students were **not equal.** The Court said such schools were against the U.S. Constitution. The ruling also applied to other forms of segregation—separation of the races supported by some states.

1954

1963
President John **Kennedy** is assassinated.

1964
Congress passes the **Civil Rights Act,** which outlaws discrimination in voting and jobs.

1965
The United States sends large numbers of soldiers to fight in the **Vietnam War.**

1968
Civil rights leader **Martin Luther King Jr.** is assassinated in Memphis. Senator **Robert F. Kennedy** is assassinated in Los Angeles.

1969
U.S. Astronaut Neil Armstrong becomes the **first person** to walk **on the moon.**

1973
U.S. participation in the **Vietnam War ends.**

THE GREAT DEPRESSION

The stock market crash of October 1929 led to a period of severe hardship for the American people—the **Great Depression**. As many as 25 percent of all workers could not find jobs. The Depression lasted until the early 1940s. The Depression also led to a great change in politics. In 1932, Franklin D. Roosevelt, a Democrat, was elected president. He served as president for 12 years, longer than any other president.

1929
A stock market crash marks the beginning of the **Great Depression.**

1933
President Franklin D. Roosevelt's **New Deal** increases government help to people hurt by the Depression.

1941
Japan attacks **Pearl Harbor,** Hawaii. The United States enters World War II.

1945
Germany and Japan surrender, **ending World War II.** Japan surrenders after the U.S. drops atomic bombs on Hiroshima and Nagasaki.

1947
Jackie Robinson becomes the **first black baseball player** in the major leagues when he joins the Brooklyn Dodgers.

1950–1953
U.S. armed forces fight in the **Korean War.**

WATERGATE

In June 1972, five men were arrested in the **Watergate** building in Washington, D.C., for trying to bug telephones in the offices of the Democratic National Committee. Some of those arrested worked for the committee to reelect President Richard Nixon. Later it was discovered that Nixon was helping to hide information about the break-in.

1985
U.S. President Ronald Reagan and Soviet leader Mikhail Gorbachev begin working together to **improve relations** between their countries.

1991
The **Persian Gulf War:** The United States and its allies defeat Iraq.

2000
George W. Bush narrowly defeats Al Gore in a closely fought battle for the presidency.

NOW!

1974
President Richard **Nixon resigns** because of the Watergate scandal.

1979
U.S. **hostages** are taken **in Iran**, beginning a 444-day crisis that ends with their release in 1981.

1981
Sandra Day O'Connor becomes the **first woman** on the U.S. Supreme Court.

1999
After an **impeachment** trial, the Senate finds President Bill Clinton not guilty.

2001
Hijacked jets crashed into the **World Trade Center** and the Pentagon, September 11, killing about 3,000 people.

2003
U.S.-led forces invade Iraq and remove dictator **Saddam Hussein.**

African Americans
Work for Change

Would you like to learn more about the history of African Americans from the era of slavery to the present? These events and personalities can be a starting point. Can you add some more?

Rev. Dr. Martin Luther King Jr. ▶

1619 — First Africans are brought to Virginia as **slaves.**

1831 — Nat Turner starts a **slave revolt** in Virginia that is promptly put down.

1856–57 — **Dred Scott,** a slave, sues to be freed because he had left slave territory, but the Supreme Court denies his claim.

1861–65 — The North defeats the South in the brutal Civil War; the **13th Amendment** ends nearly 250 years of slavery. The Ku Klux Klan is founded.

1865–77 — Southern blacks play leadership roles in government under **Reconstruction;** the 15th Amendment (1870) gives black men the right to vote.

1896 — Supreme Court rules in a case called *Plessy versus Ferguson* that segregation is legal when facilities are "**separate but equal.**" Discrimination and violence against blacks are increasing.

1910 — W. E. B. Du Bois (1868–1963) founds National Association for the Advancement of Colored People (**NAACP**), fighting for equality for blacks.

1920s — African American culture (jazz music, dance, literature) flourishes during the "**Harlem Renaissance.**"

1954 — Supreme Court rules in a case called ***Brown versus Board of Education*** of *Topeka* that school segregation is unconstitutional.

1957 — Black students, backed by federal troops, enter segregated **Little Rock** Central High School.

1955–65 — **Malcolm X** (1925–65) emerges as key spokesman for black nationalism.

1963 — **Rev. Dr. Martin Luther King Jr.** (1929–68) gives his "I Have a Dream" speech at a March that inspired more than 200,000 people in Washington, D.C.— and throughout the nation.

1964 — Sweeping **civil rights bill** banning racial discrimination is signed by President Lyndon Johnson.

1965 — King leads protest march in **Selma,** Alabama; blacks riot in **Watts** section of Los Angeles.

1967 — Gary, Indiana, and Cleveland, Ohio, are first major U.S. cities to elect **black mayors;** Thurgood Marshall (1908–93) becomes first black on the **Supreme Court.**

1995 — Hundreds of thousands of black men in take part in "**Million Man March**" rally in Washington, D.C., urging responsibility for families and communities.

2001 — Retired Gen. **Colin Powell** becomes first African American secretary of state, filling the top foreign policy position in President George W. Bush's cabinet.

They Made History

These African-Americans fought racial barriers to achieve their goals.

GUION S. BLUFORD (born 1942) was the first African-American U.S. astronaut. An Air Force pilot with a degree in aerospace engineering, he went on four Shuttle missions and logged 688 hours in space.

◀ *Guion S. Bluford*

ALTHEA GIBSON (1927-2003) was the first African-American tennis player to compete at the U.S. championship (in 1950) and at Wimbledon (in 1951). In 1957 and 1958, she won both tournaments.

ROBERT L. JOHNSON (born 1946) founded BET (Black Entertainment Television) in 1980, the leading African American-owned media company in the U.S. In 2002, he became the first black owner of a major professional sports franchise—a new NBA team to play in Charlotte, North Carolina.

REV. MARTIN LUTHER KING JR. (1929–1968) used stirring words, strong leadership, and commitment to nonviolence to help change U.S. history. From the mid-1950s to his assassination in 1968, he was the most influential leader of the U.S. civil rights movement. In 1964 he received the Nobel Peace Prize. His birthday was named a national holiday.

JACOB LAWRENCE (1917-2000), one of the greatest painters of the 20th century, was known for his colorful paintings of everyday life in the black community. His series of 60 panels, called "Migration,"

▲ *Jacob Lawrence*

showed the movement of African-Americans from the rural South to the urban North after World War I.

MALCOLM X (1925–1965) was a forceful Black Muslim leader who spoke against injustices toward blacks and called for blacks to keep separate from whites. He was assassinated by rivals in 1965. His life story, *The Autobiography of Malcolm X,* became a best-seller and helped make him a hero to many people.

ROSA PARKS (born 1913) is known as the mother of America's civil rights movement. When she refused to give up her bus seat to a white man in 1955, blacks in Montgomery, Alabama, started a year-long boycott of the bus system, which led to desegregation of the city's buses.

Rosa Parks

FRANK ROBINSON (born 1935), an aggressive outfielder and base runner, was the only baseball player ever named MVP in both the National League and the American League. He became the first black field manager in the majors in 1975. He was elected to the Baseball Hall of Fame in 1982.

CLARENCE THOMAS (born 1948), an outspoken black conservative, he was nominated to the Supreme Court in 1991, and confirmed after controversial hearings. He was the second African-American to reach that position and replaced Thurgood Marshall, who was the first.

HARRIET TUBMAN (1821-1913) escaped slavery when she was in her twenties. Before the Civil War, she repeatedly risked her life to lead hundreds of slaves to freedom by way of a network of homes and churches called the "Underground Railroad."

Harriet Tubman

PHILLIS WHEATLEY (c. 1754-1784) was America's first black poet. Sold into slavery to a wealthy Boston family, she wrote her first poem at the age of 13. Most of her poems reflect her religious New England upbringing. She was eventually freed, but died in poverty.

1. **Which state has the smallest population?**
   A Vermont   B Rhode Island   C Wyoming   D Colorado

2. **The Civil War began with the bombardment of Fort Sumter in which state?**
   A South Carolina   B Pennsylvania   C Massachusetts   D Virginia

3. **How many justices on the U.S. Supreme Court are women (as of April 2004)?**
   A 7   B 2   C 4   D 1

4. **Which president served 12 years, the longest term in office of any president?**
   A George Washington   B Ronald Reagan   C Franklin Roosevelt   D Theodore Roosevelt

5. **How many amendments are in the Bill of Rights?**
   A 5   B 15   C 10   D 7

6. **Which president is NOT on Mount Rushmore in South Dakota?**
   A George Washington   B John Adams   C Theodore Roosevelt   D Abraham Lincoln

7. **Benjamin Franklin founded which university?**
   A Pennsylvania State University   B Princeton University   C Columbia University
   D University of Pennsylvania

8. **Which city was occupied by the British during the entire Revolutionary War?**
   A Philadelphia   B Boston   C New York City   D Baltimore

9. **Which was the first national park in the U.S.?**
   A Yosemite   B Great Smoky Mountains   C Yellowstone   D Disney World

10. **Which is the southernmost city in the U.S.?**
    A New Orleans, LA   B Hilo, HI   C Key West, FL   D San Diego, CA

11. **Geronimo was chief of which Native American tribe?**
    A Mohawk   B Sioux   C Apache   D Shawnee

12. **Which astronaut was also a U.S. senator?**
    A John Glenn   B Alan Shepard   C Jim Lovell   D Neil Armstrong

13. **In which state is Mount McKinley, the tallest mountain in the U.S.?**
    A California   B Washington   C Alaska   D New Hampshire

14. **What First Lady spoke Chinese?**
    A Abigail Adams   B Dolley Madison   C Lou Hoover   D Eleanor Roosevelt

Answers on Pages 319–322. For more puzzles go to
WWW.WORLDALMANACFORKIDS.COM

WHO AM I?

I was born in Boston, Massachusetts, in 1882 and raised in nearby Worcester. I graduated from Mount Holyoke College and earned a masters degree in Sociology at Columbia University. I spent the next 25 years fighting for improved living and working conditions for the poor. After many years as a social worker, I served as industrial commissioner of New York State. In 1933, I was appointed U.S. secretary of labor, making me the first woman ever to hold a cabinet position. I held this post for 12 years during President Franklin Roosevelt's entire administration.

Answer: Frances Perkins

Firefighter

What's it like to rush into a burning building when everyone else is trying to escape? To find out, *The World Almanac for Kids* asked New York City firefighter James Dillon. For two decades, he has been battling blazes and saving lives. Today, as a lieutenant, he also oversees the firefighters who work at his firehouse, Engine 312, in Queens.

Q: When and how did you decide to become a firefighter?

My father was a deputy chief for the fire department. When I was about seven I used to go to work with him. It was a thrill to ride in his car and see lights and sirens, hoses and ladders.

Q: What is a typical day on the job like?

Every day we make sure all the equipment is working. Then we clean up the firehouse. We also shop for and cook our own meals. We inspect buildings and check hydrants. Every time we are here we're ready to jump up, get on the rig, and go out the door for some type of an emergency, even if it's not necessarily a fire. Engine companies also handle medical emergencies until the Emergency Medical Service (EMS) can arrive.

Q: What is the hardest part of the job?

Dealing with other people's misfortunes, especially when it involves little kids.

Q: Does any experience especially stand out?

Obviously, September 11, 2001. I was working in Brooklyn at the time, at Ladder 105. Everybody who was working that day was killed: all seven guys from the house (one from the engine and six from the truck). I got to Ground Zero about 11:00 A.M. The whole time frame after that kind of melds together. If we weren't digging or actually on duty, then we were attending funerals.

Q: What do you like best about being a firefighter?

Just knowing that not a lot of people would like to do this job, and we do it. We take a lot of pride in it, and we try to do it well every time we come to work.

Q: Any advice you would give to a kid about becoming a firefighter?

Stay in shape, stay in school. It's a great job, but it's more of a vocation than an occupation. It's not a job that you can do halfway.

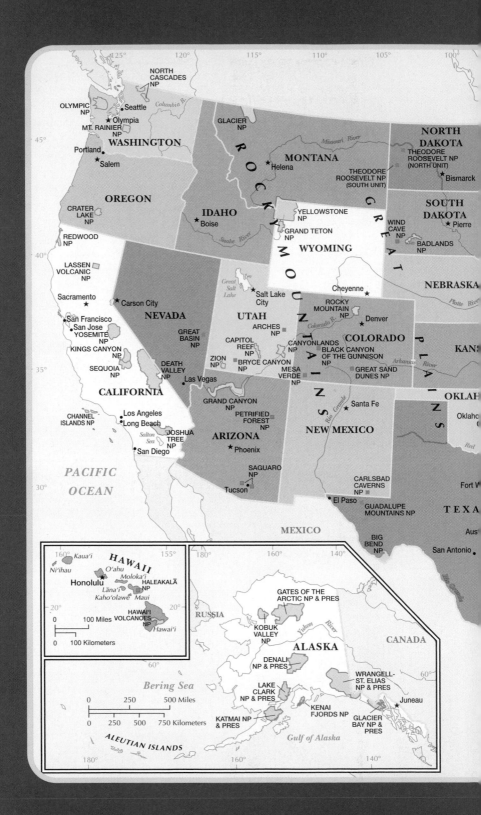

NORTH
CASCADES
NP

OLYMPIC
NP
• Seattle
Columbia R.
★ Olympia
MT. RAINIER
NP

GLACIER
NP

R
O
C
K
Y

Missouri River

NORTH
DAKOTA
THEODORE
ROOSEVELT NP
(NORTH UNIT)

45°

WASHINGTON

MONTANA

Portland •
★ Helena

Salem ★

THEODORE
ROOSEVELT NP
(SOUTH UNIT)

• Bismarck

OREGON

IDAHO

YELLOWSTONE
NP

SOUTH
DAKOTA

• Pierre

CRATER
LAKE
NP

• Boise

Snake River

GRAND TETON
NP

G
R
E
A
T

WIND
CAVE
NP

BADLANDS
NP

REDWOOD
NP

40°

WYOMING

M
O
U
N
T
A
I
N
S

NEBRASKA

LASSEN
VOLCANIC
NP

Great
Salt
Lake

• Salt Lake
City

Cheyenne •

Platte River

Sacramento
★

ROCKY
MOUNTAIN
NP

★ Carson City

NEVADA

UTAH

ARCHES
NP

• Denver

KAN:

San Francisco •
San Jose •
YOSEMITE
NP
KINGS CANYON
NP

GREAT
BASIN
NP

CAPITOL
REEF
NP

CANYONLANDS
NP

COLORADO

BLACK CANYON
OF THE GUNNISON

Arkansas
River

35°

ZION
NP

BRYCE CANYON
NP

MESA
VERDE
NP

GREAT SAND
DUNES NP

SEQUOIA
NP

DEATH
VALLEY
NP

• Las Vegas

CALIFORNIA

CHANNEL
ISLANDS NP

Los Angeles •
Long Beach •

GRAND CANYON
NP

PETRIFIED
FOREST
NP

Santa Fe •

OKLA

Salton
Sea

JOSHUA
TREE
NP

Oklaho

San Diego •

ARIZONA

NEW MEXICO

• Phoenix

N

PACIFIC
OCEAN

30°

SAGUARO
NP

Tucson •

CARLSBAD
CAVERNS
NP

Fort W

• El Paso

GUADALUPE
MOUNTAINS NP

TEXA

MEXICO

BIG
BEND
NP

Aus•

• San Antonio

HAWAII

160°   Kaua'i   155°
Ni'ihau   O'ahu   Moloka'i
Honolulu
Lāna'i   HALEAKALĀ
Kaho'olawe Maui   NP

20°   20°
0   100 Miles
HAWAI'I
VOLCANOES
0   100 Kilometers   NP
Hawai'i

180°   160°   140°

GATES OF THE
ARCTIC NP & PRES

RUSSIA

KOBUK
VALLEY
NP

Yukon River

ALASKA

CANADA

60°

Bering Sea

DENALI
NP & PRES

WRANGELL-
ST. ELIAS
NP & PRES

60°

0   250   500 Miles

LAKE
CLARK
NP & PRES

KENAI
FJORDS NP

• Juneau

0   250   500   750 Kilometers

KATMAI NP
& PRES

GLACIER
BAY NP &
PRES

ALEUTIAN ISLANDS

180°   160°   140°

Gulf of Alaska

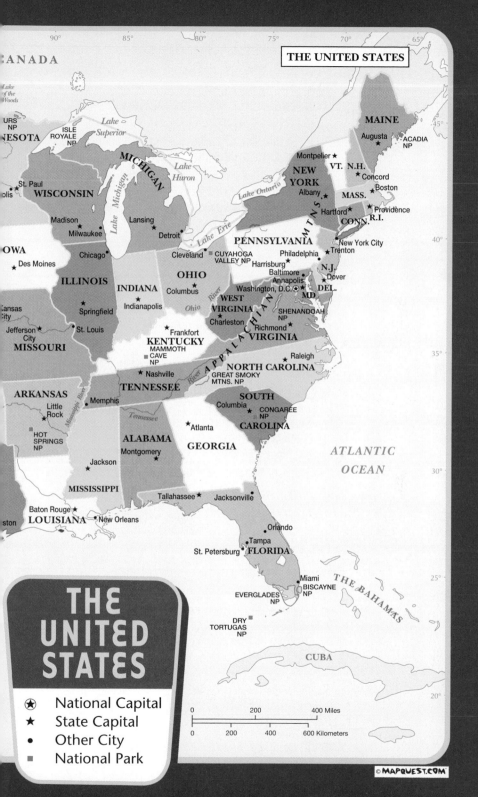

THE UNITED STATES

CANADA

90°   85°   80°   75°   70°   65°

Lake of the Woods

URS NP

NESOTA

MINNESOTA

St. Paul ★
olis

Lake Superior

ISLE ROYALE NP

MICHIGAN

Lake Michigan

Lake Huron

45°

MAINE

Augusta ★

Montpelier ★

VT.   N.H.

Concord ★

ACADIA NP

WISCONSIN

Madison ★

Milwaukee •

Lansing ★

Detroit •

Lake Ontario

NEW YORK

Albany ★

Boston ★

MASS.

Hartford ★   Providence ★

CONN.   R.I.

OWA

IOWA

Des Moines ★

Chicago •

Lake Erie

Cleveland •

PENNSYLVANIA

CUYAHOGA VALLEY NP

New York City •

Trenton ★

40°

ILLINOIS

Springfield ★

INDIANA

Indianapolis ★

OHIO

Columbus ★

Harrisburg ★

Baltimore •

Philadelphia •

N.J.

Dover ★

DEL.

Kansas City ★

St. Louis •

Ohio River

WEST VIRGINIA

Charleston ★

Annapolis ★

Washington, D.C. ⊛

MD

SHENANDOAH NP

Jefferson City ★

MISSOURI

Frankfort ★

KENTUCKY

MAMMOTH CAVE NP

VIRGINIA

Richmond ★

Raleigh ★

35°

Nashville ★

TENNESSEE

Tennessee River

GREAT SMOKY MTNS. NP

NORTH CAROLINA

ARKANSAS

Little Rock ★

Memphis •

Mississippi River

Columbia ★

SOUTH

CONGAREE NP

CAROLINA

ATLANTIC OCEAN

HOT SPRINGS NP

Atlanta ★

ALABAMA

Montgomery ★

GEORGIA

Jackson ★

MISSISSIPPI

30°

Baton Rouge ★

LOUISIANA

ston

New Orleans •

Tallahassee ★

Jacksonville •

Orlando •

Tampa •

St. Petersburg •

FLORIDA

Miami •

BISCAYNE NP

THE BAHAMAS

25°

EVERGLADES NP

DRY TORTUGAS NP

CUBA

20°

THE UNITED STATES

⊛ National Capital
★ State Capital
• Other City
■ National Park

APPALACHIAN MTNS.

0   200   400 Miles

0   200   400   600 Kilometers

© MAPQUEST.COM

273

FACTS About the STATES

After every state name is the postal abbreviation. The Area includes both land and water; it is given in square miles (sq. mi.) and square kilometers (sq. km.). Numbers in parentheses after Population, Area, and Entered Union show the state's rank compared with other states. City populations are for mid-2002.

ALABAMA (AL) *Heart of Dixie, Camellia State*

POPULATION (2003): 4,500,752 (23rd) **AREA:** 52,419 sq. mi. (30th) (135,765 sq. km.) 🌼 Camellia 🐦 Yellowhammer 🌲 Southern longleaf pine 🎵 "Alabama" **ENTERED UNION:** December 14, 1819 (22nd) ⭐ Montgomery **LARGEST CITIES (WITH POP.):** Birmingham, 239,416; Montgomery, 201,425; Mobile, 194,862; Huntsville, 162,536

⚙️ clothing and textiles, metal products, transportation equipment, paper, industrial machinery, food products, lumber, coal, oil, natural gas, livestock, peanuts, cotton

WEB SITE *http://www.alabama.gov • http://www.touralabama.org*

did you know? *From 1940 to 1946, about 1,000 of the first African-American pilots were trained at the Tuskegee Institute. The unit known as the "Tuskegee Airmen" flew over 200 missions in World War II without losing a single plane to enemy fire.*

ALASKA (AK) *The Last Frontier*

POPULATION (2003): 648,818 (47th) **AREA:** 663,267 sq. mi. (1st) (1,717,854 sq. km.) 🌼 Forget-me-not 🐦 Willow ptarmigan 🌲 Sitka spruce 🎵 "Alaska's Flag" **ENTERED UNION:** January 3, 1959 (49th) ⭐ Juneau **LARGEST CITIES (WITH POP.):** Anchorage, 268,983; Fairbanks, 30,780; Juneau, 30,751

⚙️ oil, natural gas, fish, food products, lumber and wood products, fur

WEB SITE *http://www.state.ak.us • http://www.travelalaska.com*

did you know? *Three types of bears live in Alaska: black, grizzly, and polar. Seventeen of the 20 highest U.S. mountains are here, including Mt. McKinley, highest peak in North America.*

ARIZONA (AZ) *Grand Canyon State*

POPULATION (2003): 5,580,811 (18th) **AREA:** 113,998 sq. mi. (6th) (295,253 sq. km.) 🌼 Blossom of the Saguaro cactus 🐦 Cactus wren 🌲 Paloverde 🎵 "Arizona" **ENTERED UNION:** February 14, 1912 (48th) ⭐ Phoenix **LARGEST CITIES (WITH POP.):** Phoenix, 1,371,960; Tucson, 503,151; Mesa, 426,841; Glendale, 230,564; Scottsdale, 215,779; Chandler, 202,016

⚙️ electronic equipment, transportation and industrial equipment, instruments, printing and publishing, copper and other metals

WEB SITE *http://www.az.gov • http://www.arizonaguide.com*

did you know? *Every year huge numbers of tourists travel on foot or by mule to the bottom of the Grand Canyon—the world's largest gorge.*

ARKANSAS (AR) *Natural State, Razorback State*

POPULATION (2003): 2,725,714 (32nd) **AREA:** 53,179 sq. mi. (29th) (137,733 sq. km.) 🌸Apple blossom 🐦Mockingbird 🌲Pine 🎵"Arkansas" **ENTERED UNION:** June 15, 1836 (25th) ⭐Little Rock **LARGEST CITIES (WITH POP.):** Little Rock, 184,055; Fort Smith, 81,519; Fayetteville 60,732; North Little Rock, 60,007

⚙food products, paper, electronic equipment, industrial machinery, metal products, lumber and wood products, livestock, soybeans, rice, cotton, natural gas

WEB SITE *http://www.arkansas.gov • http://www.arkansas.com*

did you know? *Almost 1 million gallons of water flow out of the springs at Hot Springs every day. When Bill Clinton became governor in 1979 at the age of 32, he was the youngest in the nation.*

Little Rock ⭐

CALIFORNIA (CA) *Golden State*

POPULATION (2003): 35,484,453 (1st) **AREA:** 163,696 sq. mi. (3rd) (423,971 sq. km.) 🌸Golden poppy 🐦California valley quail 🌲California redwood 🎵"I Love You, California" **ENTERED UNION:** September 9, 1850 (31st) ⭐Sacramento **LARGEST CITIES (WITH POP.):** Los Angeles, 3,798,981; San Diego, 1,259,532; San Jose, 900,443; San Francisco, 764,049; Long Beach, 472,412; Fresno, 445,227; Sacramento, 435,245; Oakland, 402,777

⚙transportation and industrial equipment, electronic equipment, oil, natural gas, motion pictures, milk, cattle, fruit, vegetables

WEB SITE *http://www.ca.gov • http://www.gocalif.ca.gov*

did you know? *In Death Valley, the hottest and driest place in the U.S., summer temperatures soar above 115° F. The oldest known living tree on Earth is a bristlecone pine tree called "Methuselah." It has stood in California's White Mountains for nearly 5,000 years!*

⭐Sacramento
San Francisco
Los Angeles
San Diego

COLORADO (CO) *Centennial State*

POPULATION (2003): 4,550,688 (22nd) **AREA:** 104,094 sq. mi. (8th) (269,602 sq. km.) 🌸Rocky Mountain columbine 🐦Lark bunting 🌲Colorado blue spruce 🎵"Where the Columbines Grow" **ENTERED UNION:** August 1, 1876 (38th) ⭐Denver **LARGEST CITIES (WITH POP.):** Denver, 560,415; Colorado Springs, 371,182; Aurora, 286,028; Lakewood, 143,754; Fort Collins 124,665

⚙instruments and industrial machinery, food products, printing and publishing, metal products, electronic equipment, oil, coal, cattle

WEB SITE *http://www.colorado.gov • http://www.colorado.com*

did you know? *Colorado's Rocky Mountain National Park, which covers about 450 square miles on the Continental Divide, is one of the most popular national parks in the U.S.*

Denver ⭐
Colorado Springs

Key: 🌸Flower 🐦Bird 🌲Tree 🎵Song ⭐Capital ⚙Important Products

CONNECTICUT (CT) *Constitution State, Nutmeg State*

Hartford

POPULATION (2003): 3,483,372 (29th) **AREA:** 5,543 sq. mi. (48th) (14,356 sq. km.) Mountain laurel American robin White oak "Yankee Doodle" **ENTERED UNION:** January 9, 1788 (5th) Hartford **LARGEST CITIES (WITH POP.):** Bridgeport, 140,104; Hartford, 124,558; New Haven, 124,176; Stamford, 119,850; Waterbury, 107,883

aircraft parts, helicopters, industrial machinery, metals and metal products, electronic equipment, printing and publishing, medical instruments, chemicals, dairy products, stone

WEB SITE http://www.ct.gov • http://www.ctbound.org

didyouknow? *The Hartford Courant is the country's oldest newspaper in continuous publication. It started as a weekly in 1764. George Washington placed an ad in the paper to rent out some of his land in Mount Vernon.*

DELAWARE (DE) *First State, Diamond State*

Dover

POPULATION (2003): 817,491 (45th) **AREA:** 2,489 sq. mi. (49th) (6,446 sq. km.) Peach blossom Blue hen chicken American holly "Our Delaware" **ENTERED UNION:** December 7, 1787 (1st) Dover **LARGEST CITIES (WITH POP.):** Wilmington, 72,503; Dover, 32,581; Newark, 29,798

chemicals, transportation equipment, food products, chickens

WEB SITE http://www.delaware.gov • http://www.visitdelaware.net

didyouknow? *People from Sweden settled in Delaware, at Fort Christina (present-day Wilmington) in 1638.*

FLORIDA (FL) *Sunshine State*

Tallahassee

Jacksonville

Miami

POPULATION (2003): 17,019,068 (4th) **AREA:** 65,755 sq. mi. (22nd) (170,305 sq. km.) Orange blossom Mockingbird Sabal palmetto palm "Old Folks at Home" **ENTERED UNION:** March 3, 1845 (27th) Tallahassee (population, 155,171) **LARGEST CITIES (WITH POP.):** Jacksonville, 762,461; Miami, 374,791; Tampa, 315,140; St. Petersburg, 248,546; Hialeah, 228,149; Orlando, 193,722; Ft. Lauderdale, 158,194

electronic and transportation equipment, industrial machinery, printing and publishing, food products, citrus fruits, vegetables, livestock, phosphates, fish

WEB SITE http://www.myflorida.com • http://www.flausa.com

didyouknow? *NASA's main launch site, the Kennedy Space Center, is located on Cape Canaveral. Since 1962, many famous spaceflights have launched there, including the Apollo missions to the Moon, the Space Shuttle flights, and the recent Mars Rovers.*

GEORGIA **(GA)** *Empire State of the South, Peach State*

★ **Atlanta**

POPULATION (2003): 8,684,715 (9th) **AREA:** 59,425 sq. mi. (24th) (153,910 sq. km.) 🌸Cherokee rose 🐦Brown thrasher 🌳Live oak 🎵"Georgia on My Mind" **ENTERED UNION:** January 2, 1788 (4th) ★Atlanta **LARGEST CITIES (WITH POP.):** Atlanta, 424,868; Augusta, 193,101; Columbus, 185,948; Savannah, 127,691; Athens, 102,663

⚙clothing and textiles, transportation equipment, food products, paper, chickens, peanuts, peaches, clay

WEB SITE *http://www.georgia.gov • http://www.georgia.org*

did you know? *Rev. Martin Luther King Jr., former President Jimmy Carter, and baseball legend Jackie Robinson were all born in Georgia. In 1912, Juliette Gordon Low founded the Girl Scouts of America in Savannah.*

HAWAII **(HI)** *Aloha State*

★ **Honolulu**

POPULATION (2003): 1,257,608 (42nd) **AREA:** 10,931 sq. mi. (43rd) (28,311 sq. km.) 🌸Yellow hibiscus 🐦Hawaiian goose 🌳Kukui 🎵"Hawaii Ponoi" **ENTERED UNION**: August 21, 1959 (50th) ★Honolulu **LARGEST CITIES (WITH POP.):** Honolulu, 378,155; Hilo, 40,759; Kailua, 36,513; Kaneohe, 34,970

⚙food products, pineapples, sugar, printing and publishing, fish, flowers

WEB SITE *http://www.ehawaiigov.org • http://www.gohawaii.com*

did you know? *Hawaii has eight main islands: Hawaii, Maui, Oahu, Kauai, Molokai, Lanai, Niihau, and Kahoolawe. Kilauea, a volcano on "the Big Island" of Hawaii, has been erupting continuously since 1983.*

IDAHO **(ID)** *Gem State*

POPULATION (2003): 1,366,332 (39th) **AREA:** 83,570 sq. mi. (14th) (216,445 sq. km.) 🌸Syringa 🐦Mountain bluebird 🌳White pine 🎵"Here We Have Idaho" **ENTERED UNION:** July 3, 1890 (43rd) ★Boise **LARGEST CITIES (WITH POP.):** Boise, 189,847; Nampa, 60,259; Pocatello, 51,242; Idaho Falls, 51,096

⚙potatoes, hay, wheat, cattle, milk, lumber and wood products, food products

WEB SITE *http://www.idaho.gov • http://www.visitid.org*

★ **Boise**

did you know? *Boise has the only state capitol building that is kept warm by geothermal energy—heat from underground. In fact, Idaho has more than 1,500 hot springs or geothermal wells. These heat thousands of buildings, saving more than 200,000 barrels of oil a year!*

Key: 🌸Flower 🐦Bird 🌳Tree 🎵Song ★Capital ⚙Important Products

ILLINOIS (IL) *Prairie State*

Chicago

Springfield ⭐

POPULATION (2003): 12,653,544 (5th) **AREA:** 57,914 sq. mi. (25th) (149,997 sq. km.) 🌸Native violet 🐦Cardinal 🌳White oak 🎵"Illinois" **ENTERED UNION:** December 3, 1818 (21st) ⭐ Springfield **LARGEST CITIES (WITH POP.):** Chicago, 2,886,251; Aurora, 156,974; Rockford, 151,068; Naperville, 135,389; Joliet, 118,423; Peoria, 112,670; Springfield, 111,834

⚙️industrial machinery, metals and metal products, printing and publishing, electronic equipment, food products, corn, soybeans, hogs

WEB SITE *http://www.illinois.gov • http://www.enjoyillinois.com*

didyouknow? *Abraham Lincoln moved from Indiana to Illinois in 1831. He served in the state legislature, and later represented Illinois in Congress. Illinois was his home until he became president in 1861. No wonder the state adopted the slogan, "Land of Lincoln."*

INDIANA (IN) *Hoosier State*

Indianapolis ⭐

POPULATION (2003): 6,195,643 (14th) **AREA:** 36,418 sq. mi. (38th) (94,322 sq. km.) 🌸Peony 🐦Cardinal 🌳Tulip poplar 🎵"On the Banks of the Wabash, Far Away" **ENTERED UNION:** December 11, 1816 (19th) ⭐Indianapolis **LARGEST CITIES (WITH POP.):** Indianapolis, 783,612; Fort Wayne, 210,070; Evansville, 119,081; South Bend, 106,558; Gary, 100,945

⚙️transportation equipment, electronic equipment, industrial machinery, iron and steel, metal products, corn, soybeans, livestock, coal

WEB SITE *http://www.in.gov • http://www.enjoyindiana.com*

didyouknow? *True to its motto, "Crossroads of America," Indiana has more miles of interstate highway per square mile than any other state.*

IOWA (IA) *Hawkeye State*

Des Moines ⭐

POPULATION (2003): 2,944,062 (30th) **AREA:** 56,272 sq. mi. (26th) (145,744 sq. km.) 🌸Wild rose 🐦Eastern goldfinch 🌳Oak 🎵"The Song of Iowa" **ENTERED UNION:** December 28, 1846 (29th) ⭐Des Moines **LARGEST CITIES (WITH POP.):** Des Moines, 198,076; Cedar Rapids, 122,514; Davenport, 97,777; Sioux City, 84,131

⚙️corn, soybeans, hogs, cattle, industrial machinery, food products

WEB SITE *http://www.iowa.gov • http://www.traveliowa.com*

didyouknow? *About 91% of the land in Iowa is used for agriculture, the highest percentage of any state. Iowa has about 15.4 million hogs—about 5 for each person in the state. The average Iowa farm family grows enough food to feed 279 people.*

KANSAS (KS) *Sunflower State*

POPULATION (2003): 2,723,507 (33rd) **AREA:** 82,277 sq. mi. (15th) (213,096 sq. km.) ✿Native sunflower ⦿Western meadowlark ✿Cottonwood ♪"Home on the Range" **ENTERED UNION:** January 29, 1861 (34th) ★Topeka **LARGEST CITIES (WITH POP.):** Wichita, 355,126; Overland Park, 158,430; Kansas City, 146,978; Topeka, 122,103

Topeka ★

Wichita ●

✿cattle, aircraft and other transportation equipment, industrial machinery, food products, wheat, corn, hay, oil, natural gas

WEB SITE *http:// www.accesskansas.org • http://www.travelks.org*

didyouknow? *The Chisholm Trail, used by cowboys to drive cattle from Texas through Indian Territory (now Oklahoma), ended in Abilene. Wyatt Earp, marshall of Dodge City, was among the legendary lawmen who kept the peace in rowdy frontier towns along the way.*

KENTUCKY (KY) *Bluegrass State*

POPULATION (2003): 4,117,827 (26th) **AREA:** 40,409 sq. mi. (37th) (104,659 sq. km.) ✿Goldenrod ⦿Cardinal ✿Tulip poplar ♪"My Old Kentucky Home" **ENTERED UNION:** June 1, 1792 (15th) ★Frankfort (population, 27,660) **LARGEST CITIES (WITH POP.):** Lexington 263,618; Louisville, 251,399

★ **Frankfort**

Louisville

✿coal, industrial machinery, electronic equipment, transportation equipment, metals, tobacco, cattle

WEB SITE *http:// www.kentucky.gov • http://www.kentuckytourism.com*

didyouknow? *With over 350 miles of underground passageways, Kentucky's Mammoth Cave is the largest known cave system in the world. President Abraham Lincoln was born near Hodgenville in 1809. The Kentucky Derby horse race began in Louisville in 1875.*

LOUISIANA (LA) *Pelican State*

POPULATION (2003): 4,496,334 (24th) **AREA:** 51,840 sq. mi. (31st) (134,265 sq. km.) ✿Magnolia ⦿Eastern brown pelican ✿Cypress ♪"Give Me Louisiana" **ENTERED UNION:** April 30, 1812 (18th) ★Baton Rouge **LARGEST CITIES (WITH POP.):** New Orleans, 473,681; Baton Rouge, 225,702; Shreveport, 199,033; Lafayette, 111,272

✿natural gas, oil, chemicals, transportation equipment, paper, food products, cotton, fish

WEB SITE *http://www.louisiana.gov • http://www.louisianatravel.com*

Baton Rouge ★

New Orleans ●

didyouknow? *In 1803 the U.S. paid France $15 million for the Louisiana Territory, which included most of present-day Louisiana and 12 more states. The purchase nearly doubled the size of the country. Thousands visit the world-famous Mardi Gras festival in New Orleans each year.*

Key: ✿Flower ⦿Bird ✿Tree ♪Song ★Capital ✿Important Products

MAINE (ME) Pine Tree State

POPULATION (2003): 1,305,728 (40th) **AREA:** 35,385 sq. mi. (39th) (91,647 sq. km.) ⚙️White pine cone and tassel 🐦Chickadee 🌲Eastern white pine 🎵"State of Maine Song" **ENTERED UNION:** March 15, 1820 (23rd) ⭐ Augusta (population, 18,551) **LARGEST CITIES (WITH POP.):** Portland, 63,882; Lewiston, 35,648; Bangor, 31,541

⚙️paper, transportation equipment, wood and wood products, electronic equipment, footwear, clothing, potatoes, milk, eggs, fish, and seafood

Augusta
⭐

WEB SITE *http://www.maine.gov • http://www.visitmaine.com*

didyouknow? *Maine is nearly as big as the other 5 New England states (Connecticut, Massachusetts, New Hampshire, Rhode Island, Vermont) combined. Maine harvests about 90% of all U.S. lobsters and blueberries.*

MARYLAND (MD) Old Line State, Free State

Baltimore •
Annapolis ⭐
⭐
Washington, D.C.

POPULATION (2003): 5,508,909 (19th) **AREA:** 12,407 sq. mi. (42nd) (32,134 sq. km.) ⚙️Black-eyed susan 🐦Baltimore oriole 🌳White oak 🎵"Maryland, My Maryland" **ENTERED UNION:** April 28, 1788 (7th) ⭐Annapolis (population, 36,196) **LARGEST CITIES (WITH POP.):** Baltimore, 638,614; Gaithersburg, 56,300; Frederick, 56,063; Rockville, 52,573; Bowie, 52,123

⚙️printing and publishing, food products, transportation equipment, electronic equipment, chickens, soybeans, corn, stone

WEB SITE *http://www.maryland.gov • http://www.mdisfun.org*

didyouknow? *Francis Scott Key wrote "The Star-Spangled Banner," inspired by the flag flying during the bombardment of Baltimore's Fort McHenry in the War of 1812. Annapolis was the nation's capital in 1783-84. The U.S. Naval Academy was founded there in 1845.*

MASSACHUSETTS (MA) Bay State, Old Colony

Boston ⭐

POPULATION (2003): 6,433,422 (13th) **AREA:** 10,555 sq. mi. (44th) (27,337 sq. km.) ⚙️Mayflower 🐦Chickadee 🌳American elm 🎵"All Hail to Massachusetts" **ENTERED UNION:** February 6, 1788 (6th) ⭐Boston **LARGEST CITIES (WITH POP.):** Boston, 589,281; Worcester, 174,962; Springfield, 151,915; Lowell, 104,901; Cambridge, 101,807

⚙️ industrial machinery, electronic equipment, instruments, printing and publishing, metal products, fish, flowers and shrubs, cranberries

WEB SITE *http://www.mass.gov • http://www.massvacation.com*

didyouknow? *On April 18, 1775, Paul Revere began his famous midnight ride from Boston to Lexington to warn Samuel Adams and John Hancock that British troops were on their way to arrest them. In 1891, James Naismith created the game of basketball in Springfield. The Basketball Hall of Fame, now in a new state-of-the-art facility, is also in Springfield.*

MICHIGAN (MI) Great Lakes State, Wolverine State

POPULATION (2003): 10,079,985 (8th) **AREA:** 96,716 sq. mi. (11th) (250,493 sq. km.) 🌼Apple blossom 🐦Robin 🌲White pine 🎵"Michigan, My Michigan" **ENTERED UNION:** January 26, 1837 (26th) ⭐Lansing **LARGEST CITIES (WITH POP.):** Detroit, 925,051; Grand Rapids, 196,595; Warren, 137,672; Sterling Heights, 126,146; Flint, 121,763; Lansing 118,588

⚙️automobiles, industrial machinery, metal products, office furniture, plastic products, chemicals, food products, milk, corn, natural gas, iron ore, blueberries

WEB SITE http://www.michigan.gov • http://www.travel.michigan.org

Lansing ⭐ Detroit

did you know? Battle Creek, the headquarters for Kellogg's, Ralston Foods, and the Post cereal division of Kraft Foods, is known as the Cereal Capital of the World. The Mackinac Bridge, which connects Michigan's Lower and Upper Peninsulas, is one of the world's longest suspension bridges (main span, 3,800 feet).

MINNESOTA (MN) North Star State, Gopher State

POPULATION (2003): 5,059,375 (21st) **AREA:** 86,939 sq. mi. (12th) (225,171 sq. km.) 🌼Pink and white lady's-slipper 🐦Common loon 🌲Red pine 🎵"Hail! Minnesota" **ENTERED UNION:** May 11, 1858 (32nd) ⭐St. Paul **LARGEST CITIES (WITH POP.):** Minneapolis, 375,635; St. Paul, 284,037; Rochester, 90,515; Duluth, 86,419

⚙️industrial machinery, printing and publishing, computers, food products, scientific and medical instruments, milk, hogs, cattle, corn, soybeans, iron ore

WEB SITE http://www.state.mn.us • http://www.exploreminnesota.com

Minneapolis St. Paul ⭐

did you know? Minnesota's 11,000 lakes make boating a popular activity. The first TONKA truck was made near Lake Minnetonka, which it was named after. The Mall of America in Bloomington is the largest U.S. shopping mall, big enough to hold 32 Boeing 747 airplanes.

MISSISSIPPI (MS) Magnolia State

POPULATION (2003): 2,881,281 (31st) **AREA:** 48,430 sq. mi. (32nd) (125,433 sq. km.) 🌼Magnolia 🐦Mockingbird 🌲Magnolia 🎵"Go, Mississippi!" **ENTERED UNION:** December 10, 1817 (20th) ⭐Jackson **LARGEST CITIES (WITH POP.):** Jackson, 180,881; Gulfport, 72,511; Biloxi, 49,809

⚙️transportation equipment, furniture, electrical machinery, lumber and wood products, cotton, rice, chickens, cattle

WEB SITE http://www.mississippi.gov • http://www.visitmississippi.org

⭐ Jackson

did you know? Stretching for 26 miles, the Mississippi Gulf Coast is the longest man-made sand beach in the world. Elvis Presley, the "King" of rock and roll, was born in Tupelo on Jan. 8, 1935.

Key: Flower Bird Tree Song Capital 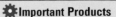Important Products

MISSOURI (MO) Show Me State

POPULATION (2003): 5,704,484 (17th) **AREA:** 69,704 sq. mi. (21st) (180,533 sq. km.) 🌸Hawthorn 🐦Bluebird 🌳Dogwood 🎵"Missouri Waltz" **ENTERED UNION:** August 10, 1821 (24th) ⭐Jefferson City (population 39, 079) **LARGEST CITIES (WITH POP.):** Kansas City, 443,471; St. Louis, 338,353; Springfield, 151,010; Independence, 113,027

⚙️transportation equipment, electrical and electronic equipment, printing and publishing, food products, cattle, hogs, milk, soybeans, corn, hay, lead

WEB SITE http://www.missouri.gov • http://www.missouritourism.org

did you know? *Gateway Arch in St. Louis, which honors the spirit of the Western pioneers, is the tallest monument (630 feet high) in the U.S. In 1811-12, New Madrid was struck by three of the most powerful earthquakes in U.S. history, one of which was felt 1,000 miles away.*

MONTANA (MT) Treasure State

POPULATION (2003): 917,621 (44th) **AREA:** 147,042 sq. mi. (4th) (380,837 sq. km.) 🌸Bitterroot 🐦Western meadowlark 🌳Ponderosa pine 🎵"Montana" **ENTERED UNION:** November 8, 1889 (41st) ⭐Helena (population, 26,353) **LARGEST CITIES (WITH POP.):** Billings, 92,008; Missoula, 59,518; Great Falls, 56,046; Butte, 32,716

⚙️cattle, copper, gold, wheat, barley, wood and paper products

WEB SITE http://www.discoveringmontana.com • http://visitmt.com

did you know? *The world's first International Peace Park was established in 1932 as a symbol of U.S.-Canadian friendship. It consists of Canada's Waterton Lakes National Park in Alberta and Glacier National Park in Montana. In 1917, Montana elected Jeannette Rankin as the first woman to serve in the U.S. House of Representatives.*

NEBRASKA (NE) Cornhusker State

POPULATION (2003): 1,739,291 (38th) **AREA:** 77,354 sq. mi. (16th) (200,346 sq. km.) 🌸Goldenrod 🐦Western meadowlark 🌳Cottonwood 🎵"Beautiful Nebraska" **ENTERED UNION:** March 1, 1867 (37th) ⭐Lincoln **LARGEST CITIES (WITH POP.):** Omaha, 399,357; Lincoln, 232,362; Bellevue, 46,217; Grand Island, 43,010

⚙️cattle, hogs, milk, corn, soybeans, hay, wheat, sorghum, food products, industrial machinery

WEB SITE http://www.nebraska.gov • http://www.visitnebraska.org

did you know? *Nebraska is the only state with a unicameral (one-house) legislature. Nebraska's Chimney Rock (a 500-foot-high natural rock formation) was the most famous landmark for travelers on the Oregon Trail.*

NEVADA (NV) *Sagebrush State, Battle Born State, Silver State*

POPULATION (2003): 2,241,154 (35th) **AREA:** 110,561 sq. mi. (7th) (286,352 sq. km.) 🌼Sagebrush 🐦Mountain bluebird 🌲Single-leaf piñon, bristlecone pine 🎵"Home Means Nevada" **ENTERED UNION:** October 31, 1864 (36th) ⭐Carson City (population, 54,311) **LARGEST CITIES (WITH POP.):** Las Vegas, 508,604; Henderson, 206,153; Reno, 190,248

⚙gold, silver, cattle, hay, food products, plastics, chemicals

WEB SITE *http://www.nv.gov • http://www.travelnevada.com*

did you know? *The state's name is taken from the Sierra Nevada mountain range (nevada is Spanish for "snow covered"). Nevada produces 40% of all the silver mined in the United States.*

⭐ Carson City

Las Vegas

NEW HAMPSHIRE (NH) *Granite State*

POPULATION (2003): 1,287,687 (41st) **AREA:** 9,350 sq. mi. (46th) (24,216 sq. km.) 🌼Purple lilac 🐦Purple finch 🌲White birch 🎵"Old New Hampshire" **ENTERED UNION:** June 21, 1788 (9th) ⭐Concord **LARGEST CITIES (WITH POP.):** Manchester, 108,398; Nashua, 87,705; Concord, 41,404

⚙industrial machinery, electric and electronic equipment, metal products, plastic products, dairy products, maple syrup and maple sugar

WEB SITE *http://www.nh.gov • http://www.visitnh.gov*

did you know? *New Hampshire was the first colony to declare its independence from England and start its own government—six months before the Declaration of Independence. Christa McAuliffe, who died in the 1986 explosion of the space shuttle* Challenger, *was a schoolteacher from Concord.*

Concord ⭐

NEW JERSEY (NJ) *Garden State*

POPULATION (2003): 8,638,396 (10th) **AREA:** 8,721 sq. mi. (47th) (22,587 sq. km.) 🌼Purple violet 🐦Eastern goldfinch 🌲Red oak 🎵none **ENTERED UNION:** December 18, 1787 (3rd) ⭐Trenton **LARGEST CITIES (WITH POP.):** Newark, 277,000; Jersey City, 240,100; Paterson, 150,750; Elizabeth, 123,279; Trenton, 85,650

⚙chemicals, pharmaceuticals/drugs, electronic equipment, nursery and greenhouse products, food products, tomatoes, blueberries, and peaches

WEB SITE *http://www.newjersey.gov • http://www.visitnj.org*

did you know? *The city of Paterson is one of the birthplaces of the Industrial Revolution in America. In the 1790s, the Society for Establishing Useful Manufactures built a factory on the Passaic River. Until the early 20th century, Paterson produced many types of goods, including large amounts of silk fabric, inspiring the name "Silk City."*

Newark •

⭐ Trenton

Key: 🌼Flower 🐦Bird 🌲Tree 🎵Song ⭐Capital ⚙Important Products

283

NEW MEXICO (NM) *Land of Enchantment*

Santa Fe
⭐
● **Albuquerque**

POPULATION (2003): 1,874,614 (36th) **AREA:** 121,589 sq. mi. (5th) (314,914 sq. km.) 🌼Yucca 🐦Roadrunner 🌲Piñon 🎵"O, Fair New Mexico" **ENTERED UNION:** January 6, 1912 (47th) ⭐Santa Fe **LARGEST CITIES (WITH POP.):** Albuquerque, 463,874; Las Cruces, 75,015; Santa Fe, 65,127; Rio Rancho, 56,614

⚙️electronic equipment, foods, machinery, clothing, lumber, transportation equipment, hay, onions, chiles

WEB SITE *http://www.state.nm.us • http://www.newmexico.org*

did you know? *Carlsbad Caverns National Park contains Lechuguilla Cave, the deepest cave in the U.S. at over 1,570 feet deep. Hundreds of thousands of bats swarm out of the caverns every night to feed on insects.*

NEW YORK (NY) *Empire State*

Albany
⭐
●● **Buffalo**

New York City

POPULATION (2003): 19,190,115 (3rd) **AREA:** 54,556 sq. mi. (27th) (141,299 sq. km.) 🌼Rose 🐦Bluebird 🌲Sugar maple 🎵"I Love New York" **ENTERED UNION:** July 26, 1788 (11th) ⭐Albany (population, 93,779) **LARGEST CITIES (WITH POP.):** New York, 8,084,316; Buffalo, 287,698; Rochester, 217,158; Yonkers, 197,234; Syracuse, 145,164

⚙️books and magazines, automobile and aircraft parts, toys and sporting goods, electronic equipment, machinery, clothing and textiles, metal products, milk, cattle, hay, apples

WEB SITE *http://www.state.ny.us • http://www.iloveny.com*

did you know? *Cooperstown is home to the Baseball Hall of Fame, which first opened in 1939. Created in 1892, Adirondack State Park covers about 6 million acres of land, and is larger than the Yellowstone, Yosemite, Grand Canyon, Glacier, and Olympic national parks combined.*

NORTH CAROLINA (NC) *Tar Heel State, Old North State*

Raleigh ⭐
● **Charlotte**

POPULATION (2003): 8,407,248 (11th) **AREA:** 53,819 sq. mi. (28th) (139,391 sq. km.) 🌼Dogwood 🐦Cardinal 🌲Pine 🎵"The Old North State" **ENTERED UNION:** November 21, 1789 (12th) ⭐Raleigh **LARGEST CITIES (WITH POP.):** Charlotte, 580,597; Raleigh, 306,944; Greensboro, 228,217; Durham, 195,914; Winston-Salem, 188,934

⚙️clothing and textiles, tobacco and tobacco products, industrial machinery, electronic equipment, furniture, cotton, soybeans, peanuts

WEB SITE *http://www.ncgov.com • http://www.visitnc.com*

did you know? *In 1903 the Wright Brothers made the first successful flight in a powered airplane near Kitty Hawk.*

NORTH DAKOTA (ND) *Peace Garden State*

POPULATION (2003): 633,837 (48th) **AREA:** 70,700 sq. mi. (19th) (183,112 sq. km.) 🌹Wild prairie rose 🐦Western meadowlark 🌳American elm 🎵"North Dakota Hymn"
ENTERED UNION: November 2, 1889 (39th) ⭐Bismarck
LARGEST CITIES (WITH POP.): Fargo, 91,204; Bismarck, 56,234; Grand Forks, 48,546; Minot, 35,617

⚙wheat, barley, hay, sunflowers, sugar beets, cattle, sand and gravel, food products, farm equipment, high-tech electronics

⭐ **Bismarck**

WEB SITE *http://www.discovernd.com • http://www.ndtourism.com*

did you know? *The state's nickname is taken from the International Peace Garden, which straddles the boundary between North Dakota and Manitoba in Canada.*

OHIO (OH) *Buckeye State*

POPULATION (2003): 11,435,798 (7th) **AREA:** 44,825 sq. mi. (34th) (116,096 sq. km.) 🌹Scarlet carnation 🐦Cardinal 🌳Buckeye 🎵"Beautiful Ohio"
ENTERED UNION: March 1, 1803 (17th) ⭐Columbus **LARGEST CITIES (WITH POP.):** Columbus, 725,228; Cleveland, 467,851; Cincinnati, 323,885; Toledo, 309,106; Akron, 214,349; Dayton, 162,669

⚙metal and metal products, transportation equipment, industrial machinery, rubber and plastic products, electronic equipment, printing and publishing, chemicals, food products, corn, soybeans, livestock, milk

Cleveland
Columbus
⭐
• **Cincinnati**

WEB SITE *http://www.ohio.gov • http://www.ohiotourism.com*

did you know? *The Rock and Roll Hall of Fame is in Cleveland, and the Pro Football Hall of Fame is in Canton. Ohio Senator John Glenn, in 1962 the first American to orbit Earth, returned to space in 1998 at the age of 77, the oldest person to fly in space.*

OKLAHOMA (OK) *Sooner State*

POPULATION (2003): 3,511,532 (28th) **AREA:** 69,898 sq. mi. (20th) (181,035 sq. km.) 🌹Mistletoe 🐦Scissor-tailed flycatcher 🌳Redbud 🎵"Oklahoma!" **ENTERED UNION:** November 16, 1907 (46th) ⭐Oklahoma City **LARGEST CITIES (WITH POP.):** Oklahoma City, 519,034; Tulsa, 391,908; Norman, 97,831; Lawton, 91,333; Broken Arrow, 83,088

⚙natural gas, oil, cattle, nonelectrical machinery, transportation equipment, metal products, wheat, hay

Tulsa•
⭐
Oklahoma City

WEB SITE *http://www.youroklahoma.com • http://www.travelok.com*

did you know? *Oklahoma has the largest Native American population of any state in the United States and is tribal headquarters for 39 tribes. Oklahoma City lies above an oil field, and derricks pump oil right on the Capitol grounds.*

Key: 🌹Flower 🐦Bird 🌳Tree 🎵Song ⭐Capital ⚙Important Products

OREGON (OR) *Beaver State*

Portland

⭐ **Salem**

POPULATION (2003): 3,559,596 (27th) **AREA:** 98,381 sq. mi. (9th) (254,806 sq. km.) 🌼 Oregon grape 🐦 Western meadowlark 🌲 Douglas fir 🎵 "Oregon, My Oregon" **ENTERED UNION:** February 14, 1859 (33rd) ⭐ Salem **LARGEST CITIES (WITH POP.):** Portland, 539,438; Salem, 140,977; Eugene, 140,395; Gresham, 94,706

⚙️ lumber and wood products, electronics and semiconductors, food products, paper, cattle, hay, vegetables, Christmas trees

WEB SITE *http://www.oregon.gov • http://www.traveloregon.com*

did you know? *The caves in Oregon Caves National Monument, discovered in 1874, are carved out of solid marble. Oregon has the only state flag with different pictures on each side—it has the state seal on the front and a beaver, the state animal, on the back.*

PENNSYLVANIA (PA) *Keystone State*

Harrisburg

Pittsburgh ⭐

Philadelphia

POPULATION (2003): 12,365,455 (6th) **AREA:** 46,055 sq. mi. (33rd) (119,282 sq. km.) 🌼 Mountain laurel 🐦 Ruffed grouse 🌲 Hemlock 🎵 "Pennsylvania" **ENTERED UNION:** December 12, 1787 (2nd) ⭐ Harrisburg (population, 48,540) **LARGEST CITIES (WITH POP.):** Philadelphia, 1,492,231; Pittsburgh, 327,898; Allentown, 106,105; Erie, 102,122

⚙️ iron and steel, coal, industrial machinery, printing and publishing, food products, electronic equipment, transportation equipment, stone, clay and glass products

WEB SITE *http://www.state.pa.us • http://www.experiencepa.com*

did you know? *A turning point in the Civil War, the battle at Gettysburg stopped the second, and last, major Confederate invasion of the North. In 1777-78, George Washington and the Continental Army endured a harsh winter at Valley Forge, where one in ten soldiers died from cold and disease. Valley Forge is now a National Historical Park.*

RHODE ISLAND (RI) *Little Rhody, Ocean State*

Providence

⭐

POPULATION (2003): 1,076,164 (43rd) **AREA:** 1,545 sq. mi. (50th) (4,002 sq. km.) 🌼 Violet 🐦 Rhode Island red 🌲 Red maple 🎵 "Rhode Island" **ENTERED UNION:** May 29, 1790 (13th) ⭐ Providence **LARGEST CITIES (WITH POP.):** Providence, 175,901; Warwick, 87,039; Cranston, 81,113; Pawtucket, 74,033

⚙️ costume jewelry, toys, textiles, machinery, electronic equipment, fish

WEB SITE *http://www.ri.gov • http://www.visitrhodeisland.com*

did you know? *Rhode Island is the smallest state in the U.S. Although Rhode Island was the first colony to declare its independence from England in 1776, it was the last of the original 13 colonies to ratify the Constitution (in 1790).*

SOUTH CAROLINA (SC) *Palmetto State*

POPULATION (2003): 4,147,152 (25th) **AREA:** 32,020 sq. mi. (40th) (82,931 sq. km.) ✿Yellow jessamine ◗Carolina wren ✿Palmetto ♪"Carolina" **ENTERED UNION:** May 23, 1788 (8th) ✪Columbia **LARGEST CITIES (WITH POP.):** Columbia, 117,394; Charleston, 98,795; North Charleston, 80,691; Greenville, 56,181

✿clothing and textiles, chemicals, industrial machinery, metal products, livestock, tobacco, Portland cement

WEB SITE *http://www.myscgov.com • http://www.discoversouthcarolina.com*

didyouknow? *The Civil War began in Charleston harbor with the first shots fired on Fort Sumter, in 1861.*

Columbia ✪

SOUTH DAKOTA (SD) *Mt. Rushmore State, Coyote State*

POPULATION (2003): 764,309 (46th) **AREA:** 77,116 sq. mi. (17th) (199,730 sq. km.) ✿Pasqueflower ◗Chinese ring-necked pheasant ✿Black Hills spruce ♪"Hail, South Dakota" **ENTERED UNION:** November 2, 1889 (40th) ✪Pierre (population, 14,012) **LARGEST CITIES (WITH POP.):** Sioux Falls, 130,491; Rapid City, 60,262; Aberdeen, 24,312

✿food and food products, machinery, electric and electronic equipment, corn, soybeans

WEB SITE *http://www.state.sd.us • http://www.travelsd.com*

didyouknow? *Massive sculptures in the Black Hills include the presidents' faces on Mt. Rushmore and the still-unfinished Crazy Horse Memorial, a mountain carved into the image of the Oglala Sioux chief seated on his horse.*

✪Pierre

TENNESSEE (TN) *Volunteer State*

POPULATION (2003): 5,841,748 (16th) **AREA:** 42,143 sq. mi. (36th) (109,150 sq. km.) ✿Iris ◗Mockingbird ✿Tulip poplar ♪"My Homeland, Tennessee"; "When It's Iris Time in Tennessee"; "My Tennessee"; "Tennessee Waltz"; "Rocky Top" **ENTERED UNION:** June 1, 1796 (16th) ✪Nashville **LARGEST CITIES (WITH POP.):** Memphis, 648,882; Nashville, 545,915; Knoxville, 173,661; Chattanooga, 155,404

✪Nashville

•Memphis

✿chemicals, machinery, vehicles, food products, metal products, publishing, electronic equipment, paper products, rubber and plastic products, tobacco

WEB SITE *http://www.tennessee.gov • http://www.tnvacation.com*

didyouknow? *The Grand Ole Opry, the world's longest-running live radio program, is broadcast from Nashville, the country-music capital of the world. Elvis Presley's home, Graceland, is located in Memphis. Great Smoky Mountains National Park is the most visited national park in the U.S.*

Key: ✿Flower ◗Bird ✿Tree ♪Song ✪Capital ✿Important Products

287

TEXAS (TX) Lone Star State

POPULATION (2003): 22,118,509 (2nd) **AREA:** 268,581 sq. mi. (2nd) (695,622 sq. km.) Bluebonnet Mockingbird Pecan "Texas, Our Texas" **ENTERED UNION:** December 29, 1845 (28th) Austin **LARGEST CITIES (WITH POP.):** Houston, 2,009,834; Dallas, 1,211,467; San Antonio, 1,194,222; Austin, 671,873; El Paso, 577,415; Fort Worth, 567,516; Arlington, 349,944; Corpus Christi, 278,520

oil, natural gas, cattle, milk, eggs, transportation equipment, chemicals, clothing, industrial machinery, electrical and electronic equipment, cotton, grains

WEB SITE http://www.texasonline.com • http://www.traveltex.com

did you know? The Alamo, where in 1836 Texans fought against Mexico for independence, is considered the cradle of Texas liberty. The state was an independent nation from 1836 to 1845. Texas produces more oil and more cotton than any other state.

UTAH (UT) Beehive State

POPULATION (2003): 2,351,467 (34th) **AREA:** 84,899 sq. mi. (13th) (219,887 sq. km.) Sego lily Seagull Blue spruce "Utah, We Love Thee" **ENTERED UNION:** January 4, 1896 (45th) Salt Lake City **LARGEST CITIES (WITH POP.):** Salt Lake City, 181,266; West Valley City, 111,254; Provo, 105,170

transportation equipment, medical instruments, electronic parts, food products, steel, copper, cattle, corn, hay, wheat, barley

WEB SITE http://www.utah.gov • http://www.utah.com

did you know? The last rails of the transcontinental railroad, connecting the tracks laid by the Union Pacific and Central Pacific railroad companies, were laid at Promontory Summit, Utah, in 1869. Utah's Great Salt Lake covers about 2,100 square miles, with an average depth of 13 feet.

VERMONT (VT) Green Mountain State

POPULATION (2003): 619,107 (49th) **AREA:** 9,614 sq. mi. (45th) (24,900 sq. km.) Red clover Hermit thrush Sugar maple "These Green Mountains" **ENTERED UNION:** March 4, 1791 (14th) Montpelier (population, 8,026) **LARGEST CITIES (WITH POP.):** Burlington, 39,466; Rutland, 17,098; South Burlington, 15,870

machine tools, furniture, scales, books, computer parts, foods, dairy products, apples, maple syrup

WEB SITE http://www.vermont.gov • http://www.vermontvacation.com

did you know? Vermont's 1777 constitution was the first to both prohibit slavery and give all men the right to vote. An independent republic from 1777 to 1791, Vermont joined the Union as the 14th state. Until then, its territory had been claimed by both New York and New Hampshire.

VIRGINIA (VA) *Old Dominion*

POPULATION (2003): 7,386,330 (12th) **AREA:** 42,774 sq. mi. (35th) (110,784 sq. km.) ⚘Dogwood 🐦Cardinal 🌳Dogwood 🎵"Carry Me Back to Old Virginia" **ENTERED UNION:** June 25, 1788 (10th) ⭐Richmond **LARGEST CITIES (WITH POP.):** Virginia Beach, 433,934; Norfolk, 239,036; Chesapeake, 206,665; Richmond, 197,456; Arlington, 189,927; Newport News, 180,272

Alexandria •

Richmond ⭐

Norfolk

🔧transportation equipment, textiles, chemicals, printing, machinery, electronic equipment, food products, coal, livestock, tobacco, wood products, furniture

WEB SITE *http://www.virginia.gov • http://www.virginia.org*

didyouknow? *Founded in 1607, Jamestown was the first permanent English settlement in America and Virginia's first capital. Richmond was the capital of the Confederacy. The Pentagon in Arlington, one of the world's largest buildings, has 284 restrooms and 4,200 clocks.*

WASHINGTON (WA) *Evergreen State*

POPULATION (2003): 6,131,445 (15th) **AREA:** 71,300 sq. mi. (18th) (184,666 sq. km.) ⚘Western rhododendron 🐦Willow goldfinch 🌳Western hemlock 🎵"Washington, My Home" **ENTERED UNION:** November 11, 1889 (42nd) ⭐Olympia (population, 43,519) **LARGEST CITIES (WITH POP.):** Seattle, 570,426; Tacoma, 197,553; Spokane, 196,305; Vancouver, 149,811; Bellevue, 112,894

• Seattle
⭐ Olympia

🔧aircraft, lumber, pulp and paper, machinery, electronics, computer software, aluminum, processed fruits and vegetables

WEB SITE *http://www.access.wa.gov • http://www.experiencewashington.com*

didyouknow? *Mount Rainier is the tallest volcano in the lower 48 states. On May 18, 1980, Mt. Saint Helens erupted. The eruption lasted 9 hours and destroyed 230 square miles of woods.*

WEST VIRGINIA (WV) *Mountain State*

POPULATION (2003): 1,810,354 (37th) **AREA:** 24,230 sq. mi. (41st) (62,755 sq. km.) ⚘Big rhododendron 🐦Cardinal 🌳Sugar maple 🎵"The West Virginia Hills"; "This Is My West Virginia"; "West Virginia, My Home Sweet Home" **ENTERED UNION:** June 20, 1863 (35th) ⭐Charleston **LARGEST CITIES (WITH POP.):** Charleston, 51,702; Huntington, 49,910; Parkersburg, 32,299; Wheeling, 30,367

⭐ Charleston

🔧coal, natural gas, fabricated metal products, chemicals, automobile parts, aluminum, steel, machinery, cattle, hay, apples, peaches, tobacco

WEB SITE *http://www.wv.gov • http://www.callwva.com*

didyouknow? *On Oct. 16, 1859, abolitionist leader John Brown and 18 others seized the federal arsenal in Harpers Ferry in an attempt to end slavery by force. Federal troops captured him and he was put to death in Charlestown later that year.*

Key: ⚘Flower 🐦Bird 🌳Tree 🎵Song ⭐Capital 🔧Important Products

WISCONSIN (WI) *Badger State*

POPULATION (2003): 5,472,299 (20th) **AREA:** 65,498 sq. mi. (23rd) (169,639 sq. km.) 🌸Wood violet 🐦Robin 🌳Sugar maple 🎵"On, Wisconsin!" **ENTERED UNION:** May 29, 1848 (30th) ⭐Madison **LARGEST CITIES (WITH POP.):** Milwaukee, 590,895; Madison, 215,211; Green Bay, 101,515; Kenosha, 92,513; Racine, 80,712

⚙️paper products, printing, milk, butter, cheese, foods, food products, motor vehicles and equipment, medical instruments and supplies, plastics, corn, hay, vegetables

WEB SITE http://www.wisconsin.gov • http://www.travelwisconsin.com

didyouknow? *Wisconsin, the dairy capital of the U.S., produces more milk than any other state. One of the world's largest air shows takes place every year at the end of July in Oshkosh.*

WYOMING (WY) *Cowboy State*

POPULATION (2003): 501,242 (50th) **AREA:** 97,814 sq. mi. (10th) (253,337 sq. km.) 🌸Indian paintbrush 🐦Western meadowlark 🌳Plains cottonwood 🎵"Wyoming" **ENTERED UNION:** July 10, 1890 (44th) ⭐Cheyenne **LARGEST CITIES (WITH POP.):** Cheyenne, 53,658; Casper, 50,024; Laramie, 26,885

⚙️ oil, natural gas, petroleum (oil) products, cattle, wheat, beans

WEB SITE http://www.state.wy.us • http://www.wyomingtourism.org

didyouknow? *Wyoming boasts the first official national park, Yellowstone, the first national forest, Shoshone, and the first national monument, Devils Tower.*

COMMONWEALTH OF PUERTO RICO (PR)

San Juan

HISTORY: Christopher Columbus landed in Puerto Rico in 1493. Puerto Rico was a Spanish colony for centuries, then was ceded (given) to the United States in 1898 after the Spanish-American War. In 1952, still associated with the United States, Puerto Rico became a commonwealth with its own constitution. **POPULATION (2003):** 3,878,532 **AREA:** 5,324 sq. mi. (13,789 sq. km.) 🌸Maga 🐦Reinita 🌳Ceiba **NATIONAL ANTHEM:** "La Borinqueña" ⭐San Juan **LARGEST CITIES (WITH POP.):** San Juan, 433,412; Bayamón, 224,670; Carolina, 187,468; Ponce, 186,112

⚙️chemicals, food products, electronic equipment, clothing and textiles, industrial machinery, coffee, sugarcane, fruit, hogs

WEB SITE http://www.gobierno.pr • http://www.gotopuertorico.com

didyouknow? *Puerto Rico is one of the world's most densely populated islands. La Fortaleza, dating from 1533, is the official residence of the governor, the oldest executive mansion in continuous use in the New World.*

WASHINGTON, D.C.
The Capital of the United States

LAND AREA: 61 square miles **POPULATION (2003):** 563,384
FLOWER: American beauty rose **BIRD:** Wood thrush

WEB SITE http://www.dc.gov • http://www.washington.org

HISTORY Washington, D.C., became the capital of the United States in 1800, when the federal government moved there from Philadelphia. The city of Washington was designed and built to be the capital. It was named after George Washington. Many of its major sights are on the Mall, an open grassy area that runs from the Capitol to the Potomac River. open grassy area that runs from the Capitol to the Potomac River.

CAPITOL, which houses the U.S. Congress, is at the east end of the Mall, on Capitol Hill. Its dome can be seen from far away.

FRANKLIN DELANO ROOSEVELT MEMORIAL, honoring the 32nd president of the United States, and his wife, Eleanor, was dedicated in 1997. It is outdoors in a parklike setting.

JEFFERSON MEMORIAL, a circular marble building located near the Potomac River. Its design is partly based on one by Thomas Jefferson for the University of Virginia.

KOREAN WAR VETERANS MEMORIAL, dedicated in 1995, is at the west end of the Mall. It shows troops ready for combat.

LINCOLN MEMORIAL, at the west end of the Mall, is built of white marble and styled like a Greek temple. Inside is a large, seated statue of Abraham Lincoln. His Gettysburg Address is carved on a nearby wall.

NATIONAL ARCHIVES, on Constitution Avenue, holds the Declaration of Independence, Constitution, and Bill of Rights.

NATIONAL GALLERY OF ART, on the Mall, is one of the world's great art museums.

NATIONAL WORLD WAR II MEMORIAL, located between the Lincoln Memorial and the Washington Monument at the Mall, honors the 16 million Americans who served during the war. Its dedication was scheduled for May 2004.

SMITHSONIAN INSTITUTION has 14 museums, including the National Air and Space Museum and the Museum of Natural History. The National Zoo is part of the Smithsonian.

U.S. HOLOCAUST MEMORIAL MUSEUM presents the history of the Nazis' murder of more than six million Jews and millions of other people from 1933 to 1945. The exhibit *Daniel's Story* tells the story of the Holocaust from a child's point of view.

VIETNAM VETERANS MEMORIAL has a black-granite wall shaped like a V. Names of the Americans killed or missing in the Vietnam War are inscribed on the wall.

WASHINGTON MONUMENT, a white marble pillar, or obelisk, standing on the Mall and rising to over 555 feet. From the top, there are wonderful views of the city.

WHITE HOUSE, at 1600 Pennsylvania Avenue, has been the home of every U.S. president except George Washington.

WOMEN IN MILITARY SERVICE FOR AMERICA MEMORIAL, near the entrance to Arlington National Cemetery. It honors the 1.8 million women who have served in the U.S. armed forces.

◀ *Jefferson Memorial*

HOW THE STATES

ALABAMA comes from an Indian word for "tribal town."

ALASKA comes from *alakshak*, the Aleutian (Eskimo) word meaning "peninsula" or "land that is not an island."

ARIZONA comes from a Pima Indian word meaning "little spring place," or the Aztec word *arizuma*, meaning "silver-bearing."

ARKANSAS is a variation of *Quapaw*, the name of an Indian tribe. *Quapaw* means "south wind."

CALIFORNIA is the name of an imaginary island in a Spanish story. It was named by Spanish explorers of Baja California, a part of Mexico.

COLORADO comes from a Spanish word meaning "red." It was first given to the Colorado River because of its reddish color.

Colorado

CONNECTICUT comes from an Algonquin Indian word meaning "long river place."

DELAWARE is named after Lord De La Warr, the English governor of Virginia in colonial times.

FLORIDA, which means "flowery" in Spanish, was named by the explorer Ponce de León, who landed there during Easter.

GEORGIA was named after King George II of England, who granted the right to create a colony there in 1732.

HAWAII probably comes from *Hawaiki*, or *Owhyhee*, the native Polynesian word for "homeland."

IDAHO's name is of uncertain origin, but it may come from a Kiowa Apache name for the Comanche Indians.

Idaho

ILLINOIS is the French version of *Illini*, an Algonquin Indian word meaning "men" or "warriors."

INDIANA means "land of the Indians."

IOWA comes from the name of an American Indian tribe that lived on the land that is now the state.

KANSAS comes from a Sioux Indian word that possibly meant "people of the south wind."

KENTUCKY comes from an Iroquois Indian word, possibly meaning "meadowland."

LOUISIANA, which was first settled by French explorers, was named after King Louis XIV of France.

MAINE means "the mainland." English explorers called it that to distinguish it from islands nearby.

MARYLAND was named after Queen Henrietta Maria, wife of King Charles I of England, who granted the right to establish an English colony there.

MASSACHUSETTS comes from an Indian word meaning "large hill place."

MICHIGAN comes from the Chippewa Indian words *mici gama*, meaning "great water" (referring to Lake Michigan).

Michigan

MINNESOTA got its name from a Dakota Sioux Indian word meaning "cloudy water" or "sky-tinted water."

MISSISSIPPI is probably from Chippewa Indian words meaning "great river" or "gathering of all the waters," or from an Algonquin word, *messipi*.

MISSOURI comes from an Algonquin Indian term meaning "river of the big canoes."

GOT THEIR NAMES

MONTANA comes from a Latin or Spanish word meaning "mountainous."

Nebraska

NEBRASKA comes from "flat river" or "broad water," an Omaha or Otos Indian name for the Platte River.

NEVADA means "snow-clad" in Spanish. Spanish explorers gave the name to the Sierra Nevada Mountains.

NEW HAMPSHIRE was named by an early settler after his home county of Hampshire, in England.

NEW JERSEY was named for the English Channel island of Jersey.

NEW MEXICO was given its name by 16th-century Spaniards in Mexico.

NEW YORK, first called New Netherland, was renamed for the Duke of York and Albany after the English took it from Dutch settlers.

NORTH CAROLINA, the northern part of the English colony of Carolana, was named for King Charles I.

NORTH DAKOTA comes from a Sioux Indian word meaning "friend" or "ally."

OHIO is the Iroquois Indian word for "fine or good river."

OKLAHOMA comes from a Choctaw Indian word meaning "red man."

OREGON may have come from *Ouaricon-sint,* a name on an old French map that was once given to what is now called the Columbia River. That river runs between Oregon and Washington.

PENNSYLVANIA meaning "Penn's woods," was the name given to the colony founded by William Penn.

RHODE ISLAND may have come from the Dutch "Roode Eylandt" (red island) or may have been named after the Greek island of Rhodes.

SOUTH CAROLINA, the southern part of the English colony of Carolana, was named for King Charles I.

South Dakota

SOUTH DAKOTA comes from a Sioux Indian word meaning "friend" or "ally."

TENNESSEE comes from "Tanasi," the name of Cherokee Indian villages on what is now the Little Tennessee River.

TEXAS comes from a word meaning "friends" or "allies," used by the Spanish to describe some of the American Indians living there.

UTAH comes from a Navajo word meaning "upper" or "higher up."

Utah

VERMONT comes from two French words, *vert* meaning "green" and *mont* "mountain."

VIRGINIA was named in honor of Queen Elizabeth I of England, who was known as the Virgin Queen because she was never married.

WASHINGTON was named after George Washington, the first president of the United States. It is the only state named after a president.

WEST VIRGINIA got its name from the people of western Virginia, who formed their own government during the Civil War.

WISCONSIN comes from a Chippewa name that is believed to mean "grassy place." It was once spelled *Ouisconsin* and *Mesconsing.*

Wyoming

WYOMING comes from Algonquin Indian words that are said to mean "at the big plains," "large prairie place," or "on the great plain."

Weather

Which state has the highest record low (12° F)? page 296

WEATHER WORDS

barometer An instrument that measures atmospheric pressure. Falling pressure means stormy weather, while rising pressure means calm weather.

blizzard A heavy snowstorm with strong winds that, with blowing snow, make it hard to see.

freezing rain Water that freezes as it hits the ground.

fog Tiny water droplets that float in the air. It's like a cloud formed at ground level.

front Boundary between two air masses.

frost Ice crystals that form on surfaces.

hail Frozen water droplets that keep getting coated with ice until heavy enough to fall to the ground as hailstones.

humidity Amount of water vapor (water in the form of a gas) in the air.

meteorologist A person who studies the atmosphere, weather, and weather forecasting.

precipitation Water that falls from clouds as rain, snow, hail, or sleet.

tornado A violently rotating column of air (wind) that forms a funnel. A tornado can suck up and destroy anything in its path, and also cause severe damage from flying debris.

typhoon A hurricane (see below) that forms in the northern Pacific Ocean, west of the International Date Line.

wind chill A measure of how cold it feels when there is a wind. When it is 35°F and the wind is 15 miles an hour, it will feel like 25°F.

WHAT IS A HURRICANE?

Hurricanes are the largest storms. They form over warm, usually tropical, oceans. As the warm seawater evaporates into the air, the pressure drops and winds begin to circulate, creating a huge wall of clouds and rain, wrapped around a calm center. As warm, moist air continues to feed the storm, it gets stronger and can spread out to an area 300 miles wide. Winds up to 250 miles an hour can rip trees out by their roots and tear roofs off buildings. Torrential rains and giant waves caused by the fierce wind can cause flooding and massive damage.

HURRICANE NAMES IN THE NORTH ATLANTIC

Until the 20th century, people named storms after saints. In 1953, the U.S. government began to use women's names for hurricanes. Men's names were added in 1978.

2004: Alex, Bonnie, Charley, Danielle, Earl, Frances, Gaston, Hermine, Ivan, Jeanne, Karl, Lisa, Matthew, Nicole, Otto, Paula, Richard, Shary, Tomas, Virginie, Walter

2005: Arlene, Bret, Cindy, Dennis, Emily, Franklin, Gert, Harvey, Irene, Jose, Katrina, Lee, Maria, Nate, Ophelia, Philippe, Rita, Stan, Tammy, Vince, Wilma

Let it Snow!

It's cold and white. It's fun to slide on, but no fun to shovel. Snow seems like simple stuff, but it's pretty complicated. When the temperature up in the clouds is below 32° F (0° C) water droplets can freeze into crystals of ice. But there has to be some dust or other tiny particles in the air for the ice to form around. Once there are some ice crystals in the cloud, water vapor can turn directly into ice instead of condensing into water and then freezing (raindrops that freeze on the way down to earth are called ice pellets, or sleet).

Water molecules are made up of one oxygen and two hydrogen molecules. When water starts to freeze, the hydrogen molecules hook together in ways that form six-sided (hexagonal) crystals of ice called "snow crystals." What we think of as snowflakes are really many snow crystals stuck together. Snowflakes are usually less than half an inch across, but can be as big as the palm of your hand. The shape snow crystals take depends on the temperature at which they form as they fall through the air. Sometimes they melt a little then refreeze. A difference of just one degree can change how one looks. Next time it snows, try to catch a snowflake and see what shape it is.

did you know?

• *The snowfall record for one day in the U.S. is 62 inches—at Thompson Pass in Alaska on Dec. 29, 1955. It kept snowing until New Year's Eve, for a total of 175 inches—or more than 14 feet of snow.*

• *The U.S. record for snowfall in a single season was set in Mt. Baker, Washington, in 1998-99, where 1,140 inches fell. That's 95 feet of snow!*

WEB SITE For more information, check out the National Snow and Ice Data Center web site: http://www.nsidc.org

Mt. Baker ▶

What is El Niño?

El Niño describes a change in the normal pattern of warm currents in the tropical Pacific Ocean that happens every 2 to 7 years. It is called "El Niño"—a Spanish phrase referring to the Christ child—because fishermen from Peru noticed that the warm waters in their area, indicating the current change, usually came around Christmas. In a normal year, warm water collects in the western Pacific and cold water rises near South America. But during El Niño, a large zone of warm water—2 to 10 degrees warmer than the the ocean around it—collects off the coast of South America (see orange on map). A change in wind patterns is one of the reasons this happens, but scientists still aren't sure of the exact causes. Other possible causes include changes in air pressure, global warming, and even undersea earthquakes.

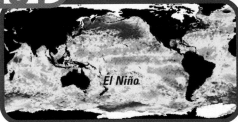

El Niño

Scientists use satellites as well as a network of buoys in the ocean to measure temperature, currents, and winds in the tropical Pacific Ocean. It is important to study El Niño because it leads to big changes in weather around the world. During El Niño, Australia often has droughts and terrible brushfires. The eastern U.S. gets colder (it snowed in Miami, Florida, in 1977). And in California, coastal storms cause a lot of damage.

Taking Temperatures

Two systems for measuring temperature are used in weather forecasting. One is **Fahrenheit** (abbreviated F). The other is **Celsius** (abbreviated C). Another word for Celsius is Centigrade. Zero degrees (0°) Celsius is equal to 32 degrees (32°) Fahrenheit.

To convert from Celsius to Fahrenheit:
Multiply by 1.8 and add 32. (°F = 1.8 x °C + 32)
Example: 20° C x 1.8 = 36; 36 + 32 = 68° F

To convert from Fahrenheit to Celsius, reverse the process:
Subtract 32 and divide by 1.8.
Example: 68° F − 32 = 36; 36/1.8= 20° C

didyouknow? *Hawaii has the warmest record low temperature of any state. The low of 12°F was reached on May 17, 1979, at the top of 13,770-foot Mauna Kea.*

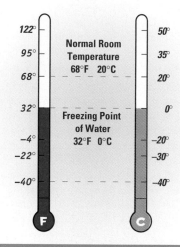

Normal Room Temperature
68°F   20°C

Freezing Point of Water
32°F   0°C

F   C

HOTTEST and COLDEST Places in the World

Continent	Highest Temperature	Lowest Temperature
Africa	El Azizia, Libya, 136°F (58°C)	Ifrane, Morocco, −11°F (−24°C)
Antarctica	Vanda Station, 59°F (15°C)	Vostok, −129°F (−89°C)
Asia	Tirat Tsvi, Israel, 129°F (54°C)	Verkhoyansk, Russia, and Oimekon, Russia, −90°F (−68°C)
Australia	Cloncurry, Queensland, 128°F (53°C)	Charlotte Pass, New South Wales, −9°F (−23°C)
Europe	Seville, Spain, 122°F (50°C)	Ust'Shchugor, Russia, −67°F (−55°C)
North America	Death Valley, California, 134°F (57°C)	Snag, Yukon Territory, Canada −81°F (−63°C)
South America	Rivadavia, Argentina, 120°F (49°C)	Sarmiento, Argentina, −27°F (−33°C)

HOTTEST PLACES IN THE U.S.

State	Temperature	Year
California	134°F	1913
Arizona	128°F	1994*
Nevada	125°F	1994*

* Tied with a record set earlier

COLDEST PLACES IN THE U.S.

State	Temperature	Year
Alaska	−80°F	1971
Montana	−70°F	1954
Utah	−69°F	1985

Clouds

Clouds come from moisture in the atmosphere that cools and forms into tiny water droplets or ice crystals. The science of clouds is called **nephology**. The names we still use for clouds come from a lecture given in December 1802 by the English meteorologist Luke Howard. Here are some of the cloud types that he named using Latin words. They fall into three main categories:

▶ **HIGH CLOUDS** Cirrus clouds and other clouds that start with the prefix "cirro-" are generally found above 20,000 feet. (*Cirrus* in Latin means "lock of hair.")

❶ **Cirrus clouds** are thin, wispy high-altitude clouds made of ice crystals. They often appear in nice weather.

❷ **Cirrocumulus clouds** are small rounded white puffs that sometimes form in long rows. Sunlight can make them look like fish scales, which makes for a "mackerel sky."

Other clouds at this level are cirrostratus and contrails. Contrails (**con**densation **trails**) are man-made clouds formed when the hot humid jet exhaust hits very cold high altitude air.

▶ **MID-LEVEL CLOUDS** Clouds that begin with the prefix "alto-" ("high") are usually found between 6,500 and 23,000 feet. They are high, though not the highest.

Altostratus clouds form a smooth gray or bluish sheet high up in the sky. The sun or moon can usually be seen faintly. (*Stratus* in Latin means "spread out.")

Altocumulus clouds are puffy gray blobs that appear in rows or waves. Part of the cloud is usually a little darker, distinguishing it from cirrocumulus.

▶ **LOW CLOUDS** These clouds have no prefix and are generally found below 6,500 feet.

❸ **Cumulus clouds** are puffy white vertical clouds that get biggest during mid-afternoon. They form in many different shapes. (*Cumulus* means "heap" or "pile.")

❹ **Cumulonimbus clouds**, also known as storm clouds, are darkish and ominous-looking. They can bring heavy storms, often with thunder and lightning. (*Nimbus* means "storm cloud.")

Nimbostratus clouds form a shapeless dark layer across the sky blocking out the sun and moon. They often bring a long period of snow or rain.

To read more about the weather try the Weather Channel at *http://www.weather.com* or try the government's National Oceanic and Atmospheric Administration at *http://www.noaa.gov*

HURRICANE HUNTER

His job is no breeze! Captain Chad Gibson is a "Hurricane Hunter," a member of a U.S. Air Force Reserve unit in Biloxi, Mississippi, that fearlessly flies into hurricanes and other storms. He and other crew members help Florida's National Hurricane Center track hurricanes. Gibson's job: Aerial Reconnaissance Weather Officer, or flight meteorologist. He observes and records meteorological data at flight level using a computer that encodes weather data every 30 seconds.

Q: Why is there a need for Hurricane Hunters?
The bottom line is we save lives. According to the Hurricane Center, the data that we collect in every storm increases the accuracy of forecasters by 25 to 30 percent. We've increased the accuracy so people will believe the forecast and actually evacuate.

Q: What do you see when you fly through the eye of a storm?
Once you get to the center of a very strong storm it's like standing on the 50-yard line of a huge football stadium. You look around and you see a wall of clouds all the way around you. If you tilt your head and look up, it's clear blue.

Q: What's the biggest misconception people have about your job?
A lot of people think we fly above the storm and then fly down into the eye, which is completely erroneous. We're flying no higher than 10,000 feet. We do avoid really severe weather— severe turbulence and any tornadic activity— but we fly through alot. We've been thrown around a lot. It's a pilot roller coaster ride.

Q: What's the most challenging part of your job?
The ability to multi-task because you are working with five other personalities and you're under stress. You're in this aluminum can for 10 hours. Everybody knows what you're doing and why. You must be sure your directions are clear and you're making the right decision. There's a lot to do in a short amount of time.

Q: How did you decide to go into this line of work?
I loved flying ever since I was a little kid. I had a pilot's license since I was 17. When I was in college they asked us to fill out dream sheets. I figured becoming a Hurricane Hunter would be awesome. It is a unique position. For someone who loves aviation and weather, you won't find a better job than this!

Weights & Measures

What is your height measured in hands? see below

Metrology isn't the study of weather. (That's *meteorology*.) It is the science of measurement. Almost everything you use every day is measured—either when it is made or when it's sold. Materials for buildings and parts for machines must be measured carefully so they will fit together. Clothes have sizes so you'll know which to choose. Many items sold in a supermarket are priced by weight or by volume.

EARLIEST MEASUREMENTS

The human body was the first ruler. An "inch" was the width of a thumb; a "hand" was five fingers wide; a "foot" was—you guessed it—the length of a foot! A "cubit" ran from the elbow to the tip of the middle finger (about 20 inches), and a "yard" was the length of a whole arm.

Later, measurements came from daily activities, like plowing. A "furlong" was the distance an ox team could plow before stopping to rest (now we say it is about 220 yards). The trouble with these units was that they were different from person to person, place to place, and ox to ox.

ANCIENT MEASURE

1 foot =	**1 yard =**	**1 acre =**
length of a person's foot	from nose to fingertip	land an ox could plow in a day

MODERN MEASURE

12 inches	3 feet or 36 inches	4,840 square yards

MEASUREMENTS *WE USE* TODAY

The official system in the U.S. is the customary system (sometimes called the imperial or English system). Scientists and most other countries use the International System of Units (metric system). The Weights and Measures Division of the U.S. National Institute of Standards and Technology (NIST) makes sure that a gallon of milk in California is the same as one in New York. When the NIST was founded in 1901, there were as many as eight different "standard" gallons in the U.S., and four different legal measures of a "foot" in Brooklyn, New York, alone.

One old measure still used today is the "hand," which equals 4 inches. Hands are used to record the height of horses, which is measured from the withers, or shoulders, to the ground. The average racehorse is about 16 hands (hh) tall. A five-foot girl is 15 hands tall.

LENGTH

The basic unit of **length** in the U.S. system is the **inch**. Length, width, and thickness all use the inch or larger related units.

1 foot (ft.) = 12 inches (in.)
1 yard (yd.) = 3 feet = 36 inches
1 rod (rd.) = 5½ yards
1 furlong (fur.) = 40 rods = 220 yards
 = 660 feet
1 mile (mi.) (also called statute mile) =
 8 furlongs = 1,760 yards = 5,280 feet
1 nautical mile = 6,076.1 feet = 1.15 statute miles
1 league = 3 miles

AREA

Area is used to measure a section of a two-dimensional surface like the floor or a piece of paper. Most area measurements are given in **square units**. Land is measured in **acres**.

1 square foot (sq. ft.) = 144 square inches
 (sq. in.)
1 square yard (sq. yd.) = 9 square feet =
 1,296 square inches
1 square rod (sq. rd.) = 30¼ square yards
1 acre = 160 square rods = 4,840 square
 yards = 43,560 square feet
1 square mile (sq. mi.) = 640 acres

CAPACITY

Units of **capacity** are used to measure how much of something will fit into a container. **Liquid measure** is used to measure liquids, such as water or gasoline. **Dry measure** is used with large amounts of solid materials, like grain or fruit. Although both liquid and dry measures use the terms "pint" and "quart," they mean different amounts and should not be confused.

Dry Measure
1 quart (qt.) = 2 pints (pt.)
1 peck (pk.) = 8 quarts
1 bushel (bu.) = 4 pecks

Liquid Measure
1 gill = 4 fluid ounces
1 pint (pt.) = 4 gills = 16 ounces
1 quart (qt.) = 2 pints = 32 ounces
1 gallon (gal.) = 4 quarts = 128 ounces

For measuring most U.S. liquids,
 1 barrel (bbl.) = 31½ gallons

For measuring oil, 1 barrel (bbl.) = 42 gallons

Cooking Measurements
The measurements used in cooking are based on the **fluid ounce**.
1 teaspoon (tsp.) = ⅙ fluid ounce (fl. oz.)
1 tablespoon (tbsp.) = 3 teaspoons
 = ½ fluid ounce
1 cup = 16 tablespoons = 8 fluid ounces
1 pint = 2 cups
1 quart = 2 pints
1 gallon = 4 quarts

VOLUME

The amount of space taken up by an object (or the amount of space available within an object) is measured in **volume**. Volume is usually expressed in **cubic units**. If you wanted to buy a room air conditioner and needed to know how much space there was to be cooled, you could measure the room in cubic feet.

1 cubic foot (cu. ft.) = 12 inches x 12 inches
 x 12 inches = 1,728
 cubic inches (cu. in.)
1 cubic yard (cu. yd.) = 27 cubic feet

DEPTH

Some measurements of length are used to measure ocean depth and distance.

1 fathom = 6 feet
1 cable = 120 fathoms = 720 feet

WEIGHT

Although 1 cubic foot of popcorn and 1 cubic foot of rock take up the same amount of space, it wouldn't feel the same if you tried to lift them. We measure heaviness as **weight**. Most objects are measured in **avoirdupois weight** (pronounced a-ver-de-POIZ):

1 dram (dr.) = 27.344 grains (gr.)
1 ounce (oz.) = 16 drams = 437.5 grains
1 pound (lb.) = 16 ounces
1 hundredweight (cwt.) = 100 pounds
1 ton = 2,000 pounds (also called short ton)

The METRIC System

The metric system was created in France in 1795. Standardized in 1960 and given the name International System of Units, it is now used in most countries. The system is based on 10, like the decimal counting system. The basic unit for length is the **meter**. The **liter** is a basic unit of volume or capacity, and the **gram** is a basic unit of mass. Related units are made by adding a prefix to the basic unit. The prefixes and their meanings are:

milli- = 1/1,000   deci- = 1/10   hecto- = 100
centi- = 1/100   deka- = 10   kilo- = 1,000

for Example

millimeter (mm)	= 1/1,000 of a meter	milligram (mg)	= 1/1,000 of a gram
kilometer (km)	= 1,000 meters	kilogram (kg)	= 1,000 grams

To get a rough idea of measurements in the metric system, it helps to know that a **liter** is a little more than a quart. A **meter** is a little over a yard. A **kilogram** is a little over 2 pounds. And a **kilometer** is just over half a mile.

Homework Help Converting Measurements

From:	Multiply by:	To get:	From:	Multiply by:	To get:
inches	2.5400	centimeters	centimeters	.3937	inches
inches	.0254	meters	centimeters	.0328	feet
feet	30.4800	centimeters	meters	39.3701	inches
feet	.3048	meters	meters	3.2808	feet
yards	.9144	meters	meters	1.0936	yards
miles	1.6093	kilometers	kilometers	.621	miles
square inches	6.4516	square centimeters	square centimeters	.1550	square inches
square feet	.0929	square meters	square meters	10.7639	square feet
square yards	.8361	square meters	square meters	1.1960	square yards
acres	.4047	hectares	hectares	2.4710	acres
cubic inches	16.3871	cubic centimeters	cubic centimeters	.0610	cubic inches
cubic feet	.0283	cubic meters	cubic meters	35.3147	cubic feet
cubic yards	.7646	cubic meters	cubic meters	1.3080	cubic yards
quarts (liquid)	.9464	liters	liters	1.0567	quarts (liquid)
ounces	28.3495	grams	grams	.0353	ounces
pounds	.4536	kilograms	kilograms	2.2046	pounds

World History

Where were the 1904 Olympics held? page 315

Each of the five sections in this chapter tells the history of a major region of the world: the Middle East, Africa, Asia, Europe, and the Americas. Major events from ancient times to the present are described under the headings for each region.

THE ANCIENT MIDDLE EAST 4000 B.C.–1 B.C.

4000–3000 B.C.
► The world's first cities are built by the Sumerian peoples in Mesopotamia, now southern Iraq.
► Sumerians develop a kind of writing called cuneiform.
► Egyptians develop a kind of writing called hieroglyphics.

2700 B.C. Egyptians begin building the great pyramids in the desert. The pharaohs' (kings') bodies are buried in them.

1792 B.C. Some of the first written laws are created in Babylonia. They are called the Code of Hammurabi.

◄ *Hieroglyphics*
ACHIEVEMENTS OF THE ANCIENT MIDDLE EAST
Early peoples of the Middle East:
❶ Studied the stars (astronomy).
❷ Invented the wheel.
❸ Created written language from picture drawings (hiero-glyphics and cuneiform).
  ❹ Established the 24-hour day.
   ❺ Studied medicine and mathematics.

1200 B.C. Hebrew people settle in Canaan in Palestine after escaping from slavery in Egypt. They are led by the prophet Moses.

THE TEN COMMANDMENTS
Unlike most early peoples in the Middle East, the Hebrews believed in only one God (monotheism). They believed that God gave Moses the Ten Commandments on Mount Sinai when they fled Egypt.

1000 B.C. King David unites the Hebrews in one strong kingdom.

ANCIENT PALESTINE Palestine was invaded by many different peoples after 1000 B.C., including the Babylonians, the Egyptians, the Persians, and the Romans. It came under Arab Muslim control in the 600s and remained mainly under Muslim control until the 1900s.

336 B.C. Alexander the Great, King of Macedonia, builds an empire from Egypt to India.

63 B.C. Romans conquer Palestine and make it part of their empire.

Around 4 B.C. Jesus Christ, the founder of the Christian religion, is born in Bethlehem. He is crucified about A.D. 29.

◄ *The pyramids and sphinx at Giza*

THE MIDDLE EAST A.D. 1–1940s

ISLAM: A RELIGION GROWS IN THE MIDDLE EAST 570–632 Muhammad is born in Mecca in Arabia. Around 610, as a prophet, he starts to proclaim and teach Islam, a religion which spreads from Arabia to all the neighboring regions in the Middle East and North Africa. His followers are called Muslims.

THE KORAN

▲ *The Koran*

The holy book of Islam is the Koran. It was related by Muhammad beginning in 611. The Koran gives Muslims a program they must follow. For example, it gives rules about how one should treat one's parents and neighbors.

632 Muhammad dies. By now, Islam is accepted in Arabia as a religion.

641 Arab Muslims conquer the Persians.

LATE 600s Islam begins to spread to the west into Africa and Spain.

711–732 Umayyads invade Europe but are defeated by Frankish leader Charles Martel in France. This defeat halts the spread of Islam into Western Europe.

1071 Muslim Turks conquer Jerusalem.

1095–1291 Europeans try to take back Jerusalem and other parts of the Middle East for Christians during the Crusades.

THE SPREAD OF ISLAM

The Arab armies that went across North Africa brought great change:
1. The people who lived there were converted to Islam.
2. The Arabic language replaced many local languages as an official language. North Africa is still an Arabic-speaking region today, and Islam is the major faith.

ACHIEVEMENTS OF THE UMAYYAD AND ABBASID DYNASTIES The Umayyads (661–750) and the Abbasids (750–1256) were the first two Muslim-led dynasties. Both empires stretched across northern Africa, across the Middle East, and into Asia. Both were known for great achievements. They:
1. Studied math and medicine.
2. Translated the works of other peoples, including Greeks and Persians.
3. Spread news of Chinese inventions like paper and gunpowder.
4. Wrote great works on religion and philosophy.

1300–1900s The Ottoman Turks, who are Muslims, create a huge empire, covering the Middle East, North Africa, and part of Eastern Europe. The Ottoman Empire falls apart gradually, and European countries take over portions of it beginning in the 1800s.

1914–1918 World War I begins in 1914. The Ottoman Empire has now broken apart. Most of the Middle East falls under British or French control.

1921 Two new Arab kingdoms are created: Transjordan and Iraq. The French take control of Syria and Lebanon.

1922 Egypt becomes independent from Britain.

JEWS MIGRATE TO PALESTINE Jewish settlers from Europe began migrating to Palestine in the 1880s. They wanted to return to the historic homeland of the Hebrew people. In 1945, after World War II, many Jews who survived the Holocaust migrated to Palestine. Arabs living in the region opposed the Jewish immigration. In 1948, after the British left, war broke out between the Jews and the Arabs.

Dome of the Rock and the Western Wall, Jerusalem ▼

THE MIDDLE EAST 1940s–2000s

1948 The state of Israel is created.

THE ARAB-ISRAELI WARS Arab countries near Israel (Egypt, Iraq, Jordan, Lebanon, and Syria) attack the new country in 1948 but fail to destroy it. Israel and its neighbors fight wars again in 1956, 1967, and 1973. Israel wins each war. In the 1967 war, Israel captures the Sinai Desert from Egypt, the Golan Heights from Syria, and the area known as the West Bank from Jordan.

1979 Egypt and Israel sign a peace treaty, providing for Israel to return the Sinai to Egypt.

THE MIDDLE EAST AND OIL
Much of the oil we use to drive our cars, heat our homes, and run our machines comes from the Arabian peninsula in the Middle East. For a brief time in 1973-1974, Arab nations would not let their oil be sold to the United States because of its support of Israel. The United States still relies heavily on oil imports from the region.

THE 1990s AND 2000s

▶ In 1991, the U.S. and its allies go to war with Iraq after Iraq invades Kuwait. Iraq is defeated and signs a peace agreement but is accused of violating it. In 2003, the U.S. and Britain invade Iraq and remove the regime of Saddam Hussein.

▶ Tensions between Israel and the Palestinians increase, fueled by suicide bombings by Palestinians, and Israeli military actions in the occupied territories.

Oil pumping station in Iraq

ANCIENT AFRICA 3500 B.C.–A.D. 900

ANCIENT AFRICA In ancient times, northern Africa was dominated, for the most part, by the Egyptians, Greeks, and Romans. However, we know very little about the lives of ancient people in Africa south of the Sahara Desert (sub-Saharan Africa). The people of Africa south of the Sahara did not have written languages in ancient times. What we learn about them comes from such things as weapons, tools, and other items from their civilization that have been found in the earth.

2000 B.C. The Kingdom of Kush arises just south of Egypt. It becomes a major center of art, learning, and trade. Kush dies out around A.D. 350.

500 B.C. The Nok culture becomes strong in Nigeria, in West Africa. The Nok use iron for tools and weapons. They are also known for their fine terra-cotta sculptures of heads. ▶

AROUND A.D. 1 Bantu-speaking peoples in West Africa begin to move into eastern and southern Africa.

50 The Kingdom of Axum in northern Ethiopia, founded by traders from Arabia, becomes a wealthy trading center for ivory.

300s Ghana, the first known African state south of the Sahara Desert, takes power in the upper Senegal and Niger river region. It controls the trade in gold that is being sent from the southern parts of Africa north to the Mediterranean Sea.

660s–900 The Islamic religion spreads across North Africa and into Spain.

Niger River, Mali

AFRICA 900s–2000s

900 Arab Muslims begin to settle along the coast of East Africa. Their contact with Bantu people produces the Swahili language, which is still spoken today.

1050 The Almoravid Kingdom in Morocco, North Africa, is powerful from Ghana to as far north as Spain.

1230 The Mali Kingdom begins in North Africa. Timbuktu, a center for trade and learning, is its main city.

1464 The Songhay Empire becomes strong in West Africa. By around 1500, it has destroyed Mali. The Songhay are remembered for their bronze sculptures.

1505–1575 Portuguese settlement begins in Africa. Portuguese people settle in Angola, Mozambique, and other areas.

THE AFRICAN SLAVE TRADE

Once Europeans began settling in the New World, they needed people to harvest their sugar. The first African slaves were taken to the Caribbean. Later, slaves were taken to South America and the United States. The slaves were crowded onto ships and many died during the long journey. Shipping of African slaves to the United States lasted until the early 1800s.

1652–1835

1. Dutch settlers arrive in southern Africa. They are known as the Boers.
2. Shaka the Great forms a Zulu Empire in eastern Africa. The Zulus are warriors.
3. The "Great Trek" (march) of the Boers north takes place. They defeat the Zulus at the Battle of Bloody River.

1899: BOER WAR The South African War between Great Britain and the Boers begins. It is also called the Boer War. The Boers accept British rule but are allowed a role in government.

1948 The white South African government creates the policy of apartheid, the total separation of blacks and whites. Blacks are banned from restaurants, theaters, schools, and jobs considered "white." Apartheid sparked protests, many of which ended in bloodshed.

1983 Droughts (water shortages) lead to starvation over much of Africa.

THE 1990s AND 2000s
Apartheid ends in South Africa. In 1994, Nelson Mandela becomes South Africa's first black president. Also in 1994, civil war in Rwanda leads to the massacre of 500,000 civilians. Meanwhile, the disease AIDS kills several million people each year. Africa accounts for 70 percent of AIDS cases worldwide. In Zimbabwe, for example, one out of every four adults has HIV/AIDS.

▲ Nelson Mandela

COLONIES win their FREEDOM

Most of the countries on the African continent and nearby islands were once colonies of a European nation such as Britain, France, or Portugal, but later became independent. Here are some major African countries that achieved independence in the 1900s.

Country	Became Independent	From
Egypt	1952	Britain
Morocco	1956	France
Sudan	1956	Britain
Ghana	1957	Britain
Burkina Faso	1960	France
Cameroon	1960	France
Congo, Dem. Rep. of	1960	Belgium
Côte d'Ivoire	1960	France
Mali	1960	France
Niger	1960	France
Nigeria	1960	Britain
Zimbabwe	1960	Britain
South Africa	1961	Britain
Tanzania	1961	Britain
Algeria	1962	France
Uganda	1962	Britain
Kenya	1963	Britain
Malawi	1964	Britain
Angola	1975	Portugal
Mozambique	1975	Portugal

305

3500 B.C. Communities of people settle in the Indus River Valley of India and Pakistan and the Yellow River Valley of China.

2500 B.C. Cities of Mohenjo-Daro and Harappa in Pakistan become centers of trade and farming.

AROUND 1523 B.C. Shang peoples in China build walled towns and use a kind of writing based on pictures. This writing develops into the writing Chinese people use today.

衣貽夷

1500 B.C. The Hindu religion (Hinduism) begins to spread throughout India.

AROUND 1050 B.C. Chou peoples in China overthrow the Shang and control large territories.

700 B.C. In China, a 500-year period begins in which many warring states fight one another.

563 B.C. Siddhartha Gautama is born in India. He becomes known as the Buddha—which means the "Enlightened One"—and is the founder of the Buddhist religion (Buddhism).

551 B.C. The Chinese philosopher Confucius is born. His teachings— especially the rules about how people should treat each other—spread throughout China and are still followed today. ▶

TWO IMPORTANT ASIAN RELIGIONS Many of the world's religions began in Asia. Two of the most important were:

1. **Hinduism.** Hinduism began in India and has spread to other parts of southern Asia and to parts of the Pacific region.
2. **Buddhism.** Buddhism also began in India and spread to China, Japan, and Southeast Asia. Today, both religions have millions of followers all over the world.

320–232 B.C.: INDIA

1. Northern India is united under the emperor Chandragupta Maurya.
2. Asoka, emperor of India, sends Buddhist missionaries throughout southern Asia to spread the Buddhist religion.

221 B.C. The Chinese ruler Shih Huang Ti makes the Chinese language the same throughout the country. Around the same time, the Chinese begin building the Great Wall of China. Its main section is more than 2,000 miles long and is meant to keep invading peoples from the north out of China.

202 B.C. The Han people of China win control of all of China.

ACHIEVEMENTS OF THE ANCIENT CHINESE

1. Invented paper.
2. Invented gunpowder.
3. Studied astronomy.
4. Studied engineering.
5. Invented acupuncture to treat illnesses.

The Great Wall of China

ANCIENT ASIA A.D. 1–1700s

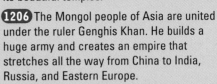

320 The Gupta Empire controls northern India. The Guptas are Hindus. They drive the Buddhist religion out of India. The Guptas are well known for their many advances in the study of mathematics and medicine.

618 The Tang dynasty begins in China. The Tang dynasty is well known for music, poetry, and painting. They export silk and porcelains as far away as Africa.

THE SILK ROAD ▶

Around 100 B.C., only the Chinese knew how to make silk. Europeans were willing to pay high prices for the light, comfortable material. To get it, they sent fortunes in glass, gold, jade, and other items to China. The exchanges between Europeans and Chinese created one of the greatest trading routes in history—the Silk Road. Chinese inventions such as paper and gunpowder were also spread over the Silk Road. Europeans found out how to make silk around A.D. 500, but trade continued until about 1400.

960 The Northern Sung dynasty in China makes advances in banking and paper money. China's population of 50 million doubles over 200 years, thanks to improved ways of farming that lead to greater food production.

▼ *Statues from Angkor Wat temple, Cambodia*

1000 The Samurai, a warrior people, become powerful in Japan. They live by a code of honor known as Bushido. ▶

1180 The Khmer Empire based in Angkor is powerful in Cambodia. The empire became widely known for its beautiful temples.

1206 The Mongol people of Asia are united under the ruler Genghis Khan. He builds a huge army and creates an empire that stretches all the way from China to India, Russia, and Eastern Europe.

1264 Kublai Khan, the grandson of Genghis Khan, rules China as emperor from his new capital at Beijing.

1368 The Ming dynasty comes to power in China. The Ming drive the Mongols out of the country.

1467–1603 WAR AND PEACE IN JAPAN

❶ Civil war breaks out in Japan. The conflicts last more than 100 years.

❷ Peace comes to Japan under the military leader Hideyoshi.

❸ The Shogun period reaches its peak in Japan (it lasts until 1868). Europeans are driven out of the country and Christians are persecuted.

1526 THE MUGHALS IN INDIA

❶ The Mughal Empire in India begins under Babur. The Mughals are Muslims who invade and conquer India.

❷ Akbar, the grandson of Babur, becomes Mughal emperor of India. He attempts to unite Hindus and Muslims but does not succeed.

1644 The Ming dynasty in China is overthrown by the Manchu peoples. They allow more Europeans to trade in China.

1739 Nadir Shah, a Persian warrior, conquers parts of western India and captures the city of Delhi.

1839 The Opium War takes place in China between the Chinese and the British. The British and other Western powers want to control trade in Asia. The Chinese want the British to stop selling opium to the Chinese. Britain wins the war in 1842.

1858 The French begin to take control of Indochina (Southeast Asia).

1868 The Shogunate dynasty ends in Japan. The new ruler is Emperor Meiji. Western ideas begin to influence the Japanese.

THE JAPANESE IN ASIA Japan became a powerful country during the early 20th century. It was a small country with few raw materials of its own. For example, Japan had to buy oil from other countries. The Japanese army and navy took control of the government during the 1930s. Japan soon began to invade some of its neighbors. In 1941, the United States and Japan went to war after Japan attacked the U.S. Navy at Pearl Harbor, Hawaii.

1945 Japan is defeated in World War II after the U.S. drops atomic bombs on the Japanese cities of Hiroshima and Nagasaki.

1947 India and Pakistan become independent from Great Britain, which had ruled them as colonies since the mid-1800s.

1949 China comes under the rule of the Communists led by Mao Zedong. ▶

CHINA UNDER THE COMMUNISTS The Communists brought many changes to China. Private property was abolished, and the government took over all businesses and farms. Religions were persecuted. Many people were put in jail or executed.

1950–1953 THE KOREAN WAR North Korea, a Communist country, invades South Korea. The U.S. and other nations join to fight the invasion. China joins North Korea. The Korean War ends in 1953. Neither side wins.

1954–1975 THE VIETNAM WAR The French are defeated in Indochina in 1954 by Vietnamese Communists. The U.S. sends troops in 1965 to fight on the side of South Vietnam against the Communists in the North. The U.S. withdraws in 1973. In 1975, South Vietnam is taken over by North Vietnam.

1972 President Richard Nixon visits China to improve relations.

1989 Chinese students protest for democracy, but the protests are crushed by the army in Beijing's Tiananmen Square.

THE 1990s Japan, South Korea, Taiwan, and some other countries show great strength in the early 1990s, but then have serious financial trouble. Iraq invades Kuwait but is driven back (1991) in a war with the U.S. and its allies. Britain returns Hong Kong to China (1997). China builds its economy, but is accused of widespread human rights abuses.

THE 2000s U.S.-led military action overthrows the Taliban regime in Afghanistan (2001) and seeks to root out terrorists there. North Korea admits it has been developing nuclear weapons. The U.S. and Britain (2003) go to war against Iraq and drive out the regime of Saddam Hussein.

Tokyo, Japan ▶

ANCIENT EUROPE 4000 B.C.—300s B.C.

4000 B.C. People in many parts of Europe start building monuments out of large stones called megaliths. Examples can still be seen today, including Stonehenge in England.

2500 B.C.—1200 B.C.
THE MINOANS AND THE MYCENAEANS

1. People on the island of Crete (Minoans) in the Mediterranean Sea built great palaces and became sailors and traders.
2. People in the city of Mycenae in Greece built stone walls and a great palace.
3. Mycenaean people invaded Crete and destroyed the power of the Minoans.

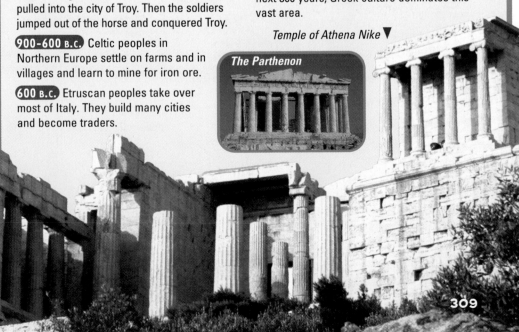

Treasury of Atreus at Mycenae

THE TROJAN WAR The Trojan War was a conflict between invading Greeks and the people of Troas (Troy) in Southwestern Turkey around 1200 B.C. Although little is known today about the real war, it has become a part of Greek poetry and mythology (see pages 134-135). According to a famous legend, a group of Greek soldiers hid inside a huge wooden horse. The horse was pulled into the city of Troy. Then the soldiers jumped out of the horse and conquered Troy.

900-600 B.C. Celtic peoples in Northern Europe settle on farms and in villages and learn to mine for iron ore.

600 B.C. Etruscan peoples take over most of Italy. They build many cities and become traders.

SOME ACHIEVEMENTS OF THE GREEKS
The early Greeks were responsible for:

1. The first governments that were elected by people. Greeks invented democratic government.
2. Great poets such as Homer, who composed the *Iliad*, a long poem about the Trojan War, and the *Odyssey*, an epic poem about the travels of Odysseus.
3. Great thinkers such as Socrates, Plato, and Aristotle.
4. Great architecture, like the Parthenon and the Temple of Athena Nike on the Acropolis in Athens (*see below*).

431 B.C. The Peloponnesian Wars begin between the Greek cities of Athens and Sparta. The wars end in 404 B.C. when Sparta wins.

338 B.C. King Philip II of Macedonia in northern Greece conquers all the cities of Greece.

336 B.C. Philip's son Alexander becomes king. He conquers lands and makes an empire from the Mediterranean Sea to India. He is known as Alexander the Great. For the next 300 years, Greek culture dominates this vast area.

Temple of Athena Nike ▼

The Parthenon

309

264 B.C.–A.D. 476
ROMAN EMPIRE The city of Rome in Italy begins to expand and captures surrounding lands. The Romans gradually build a great empire and control all of the Mediterranean region. At its height, the Roman Empire includes Western Europe, Greece, Egypt, and much of the Middle East. The Roman Empire lasts until A.D. 476.

ROMAN ACHIEVEMENTS
1. Roman law. Many of our laws are based on Roman law.
2. Great roads to connect their huge empire. The Appian Way, south of Rome, is a Roman road that is still in use today.
3. Aqueducts to bring water to the people in large cities.
4. Great sculpture. Roman statues can still be seen in Europe.
5. Great architecture. The Colosseum, which still stands in Rome today, is an example of great Roman architecture.
6. Great writers, such as the poet Vergil, who wrote the Aeneid.

49 B.C. A civil war breaks out that destroys Rome's republican form of government.

45 B.C. Julius Caesar becomes the sole ruler of Rome but is murdered one year later by rivals in the Roman army. ▶

27 B.C. Octavian becomes the first emperor of Rome. He takes the name Augustus. A peaceful period of almost 200 years begins.

THE CHRISTIAN FAITH Christians believe that Jesus Christ is the Son of God. The history and beliefs of Christianity are found in the New Testament of the Bible. Christianity spread slowly throughout the Roman Empire. The Romans tried to stop the new religion and persecuted the Christians. They were forced to hold their services in hiding, and some were crucified. Eventually, more and more Romans became Christian.

337 The Roman Emperor Constantine becomes a Christian. He is the first Roman emperor to be a Christian.

410 The Visigoths and other barbarian tribes from northern Europe invade the Roman Empire and begin to take over its lands.

476 The last Roman emperor is overthrown.

THE BYZANTINE EMPIRE, centered in modern-day Turkey, was made up of the eastern half of the old Roman Empire. Byzantine rulers extended their power into western Europe. The great Byzantine Emperor Justinian ruled parts of Spain, North Africa, and Italy. The city of Constantinople (now Istanbul, Turkey) became the capital of the Byzantine Empire in 330.

768 Charlemagne becomes king of the Franks in northern Europe. He rules a kingdom that includes parts of France, Germany, and northern Italy.

800 Feudalism becomes important in Europe. Feudalism means that poor farmers are allowed to farm a lord's land in return for certain services to the lord.

▼ *The Colosseum, Rome*

The Temple of Saturn, Rome

EUROPE 800s–1500s

896 Magyar peoples from lands east of Russia found Hungary.

Viking helmet ▼

800s–900s Viking warriors and traders from Scandinavia begin to move into the British Isles, France, and parts of the Mediterranean.

989 The Russian state of Kiev becomes Christian.

1066 William of Normandy, a Frenchman, successfully invades England and makes himself king. He is known as William the Conqueror.

1096–1291 THE CRUSADES In 1096, Christian European kings and nobles sent a series of armies to the Middle East to try to capture the city of Jerusalem from the Muslims. Between 1096 and 1291 there were about ten Crusades. During the Crusades the Europeans briefly captured Jerusalem. But in the end, the Crusades did not succeed in their aim.

One of the most important results of the Crusades had nothing to do with religion: trade increased greatly between the Middle East and Europe.

1215 THE MAGNA CARTA The Magna Carta was a document agreed to by King John of England and the English nobility. The English king agreed that he did not have absolute power and had to obey the laws of the land. The Magna Carta was an important step toward democracy.

1290 The Ottoman Empire begins. It is controlled by Turkish Muslims who conquer lands in the eastern Mediterranean and the Middle East.

1337–1453 WAR AND PLAGUE IN EUROPE

❶ The Hundred Years' War (1337) begins in Europe between France and England. The war lasts until 1453 when France wins.

❷ The bubonic plague begins in Europe (1348). The plague, also called the Black Death, is a deadly disease caused by the bite of infected fleas. Perhaps as much as one third of the whole population of Europe dies from the plague.

1453 The Ottoman Turks capture the city of Constantinople and rename it Istanbul.

1517 THE REFORMATION The Reformation led to the breakup of the Christian church into Protestant and Roman Catholic branches in Europe. It started when the German priest Martin Luther opposed some teachings of the Church. He broke away from the pope (the leader of the Catholic church) and had many followers.

1534 King Henry VIII of England breaks away from the Roman Catholic church. He names himself head of the English (Anglican) church.

▲ *Queen Elizabeth I*

1558 The reign of King Henry's daughter Elizabeth I begins in England. During her long rule, England's power grows.

1588 The Spanish Armada (fleet of warships) is defeated by the English navy as Spain tries to invade England.

◄ *Ottoman Palace of Ciragan, Istanbul*

1600s The Ottoman Turks expand their empire through most of eastern and central Europe.

1618 The Thirty Years' War begins in Europe. The war is fought over religious issues. Much of Europe is destroyed in the conflict, which ends in 1648.

1642 The English civil war begins. King Charles I fights against the forces of the Parliament (legislature). The king's forces are defeated, and he is executed in 1649. But his son, Charles II, eventually returns as king in 1660.

Vladimir Lenin

1762 Catherine the Great becomes the Empress of Russia. She allows some religious freedom and extends the Russian Empire.

1789 THE FRENCH REVOLUTION The French Revolution ended the rule of kings in France and led to democracy there. At first, however, there were wars, much bloodshed, and times when dictators took control. Many people were executed. King Louis XVI and Queen Marie Antoinette were overthrown in the Revolution, and both were executed in 1793.

1799 Napoleon Bonaparte, an army officer, becomes dictator of France. Under his rule, France conquers most of Europe by 1812.

1815 Napoleon's forces are defeated by the British and German armies at Waterloo (in Belgium). Napoleon is exiled to a remote island and dies there in 1821.

1848 Revolutions break out in countries of Europe. People force their rulers to make more democratic changes.

1914–1918 WORLD WAR I IN EUROPE At the start of World War I in Europe, Germany, Austria-Hungary and the Ottoman Empire opposed England, France, Russia, and, later, the U.S. (the Allies). The Allies won in 1918.

1917 The czar is overthrown in the Russian Revolution. The Bolsheviks (Communists) under Vladimir Lenin take control. Millions are starved, sent to labor camps, or executed under Joseph Stalin (1929-1953).

THE RISE OF HITLER Adolf Hitler became dictator of Germany in 1933. He joined forces with rulers in Italy and Japan to form the Axis powers. In World War II (1939-1945), the Axis powers were defeated by the Allies—Great Britain, the Soviet Union, and the U.S. During his rule, Hitler's Nazis killed millions of Jews and other people in what we now call the Holocaust.

1945 The Cold War begins. It is a long period of tension between the United States and the Soviet Union. Both countries build up their armies and make nuclear weapons but do not go to war against each other.

THE 1990s Communist governments in Eastern Europe are replaced by democratic ones. Divided Germany becomes one nation. The Soviet Union breaks up, leaving a weakened Russia. The European Union (EU) takes steps toward European unity. The North Atlantic Treaty Organization (NATO) bombs Yugoslavia in an effort to protect Albanians driven out of the Kosovo region.

2002 The euro becomes the single currency in 12 European Union nations.

◀ *Napoleon Bonaparte*

THE AMERICAS 10,000 B.C.–A.D. 1600s

10,000–8000 B.C. People in North and South America gather plants for food and hunt animals using stone-pointed spears.

▲ *The landing of Columbus*

AROUND 3000 B.C. People in Central America begin farming, growing corn and beans for food.

1500 B.C. Mayan people in Central America begin to live in small villages.

500 B.C. People in North America begin to hunt buffalo to use for meat and for clothing.

100 B.C. The city of Teotihuacán is founded in Mexico. It becomes the center of a huge empire extending from central Mexico to Guatemala. Teotihuacán contains many large pyramids and temples.

A.D. 150 Mayan people in Guatemala build many centers for religious ceremonies. They create a calendar and learn mathematics and astronomy.

900 Toltec warriors in Mexico begin to invade lands of Mayan people. Mayans leave their old cities and move to the Yucatan Peninsula of Mexico.

1000 Native Americans in the southwestern United States begin to live in settlements called pueblos. They learn to farm.

1325 Mexican Indians known as Aztecs create huge city of Tenochtitlán and rule a large empire in Mexico. They are warriors who practice human sacrifice.

Mayan pyramid, Yucatan Peninsula, Mexico ▶

1492 Christopher Columbus sails from Europe across the Atlantic Ocean and lands in the Bahamas, in the Caribbean Sea. This marked the first step toward the founding of European settlements in the Americas.

1500 Portuguese explorers reach Brazil and claim it for Portugal.

1519 Spanish conqueror Hernán Cortés travels into the Aztec Empire in search of gold. The Aztecs are defeated in 1521 by Cortés. The Spanish take control of Mexico.

WHY DID THE SPANISH WIN? How did the Spanish defeat the powerful Aztec Empire in such a short time? One reason is that the Spanish had better weapons. Another is that the Aztecs became sick and died from diseases brought to the New World by the Spanish. The Aztecs had never had these illnesses before and, as a result, did not have immunity to them. Also, many neighboring Indians hated the Aztecs as conquerors. Those Indians helped the Spanish to defeat them.

1534 Jacques Cartier of France explores Canada.

1583 The first English colony in Canada is set up in Newfoundland.

1607 English colonists led by Captain John Smith settle in Jamestown, Virginia. Virginia was the oldest of the Thirteen Colonies that turned into the United States.

1619 First African slaves arrive in English-controlled America.

1682 The French explorer Robert Cavelier, sieur de la Salle, sails down the Mississippi River. The area is named Louisiana after the French King Louis XIV.

THE AMERICAS 1700s–2000s

EUROPEAN COLONIES By 1700, most of the Americas are under the control of Europeans:

Spain: Florida, southwestern United States, Mexico, Central America, western South America.

Portugal: eastern South America.

France: central United States, parts of Canada.

England: eastern U.S., parts of Canada.

Holland: eastern U.S., West Indies, eastern South America.

1700 European colonies in North and South America begin to grow in population and wealth.

1775–1783
AMERICAN REVOLUTION The American Revolution begins in 1775 when the first shot is fired in Lexington, Massachusetts. The thirteen original British colonies in North America become independent under the Treaty of Paris, signed in 1783.

SIMÓN BOLÍVAR: LIBERATOR OF SOUTH AMERICA In 1810, Simón Bolívar began a revolt against Spain. He fought for more than 10 years against the Spanish and became president of the independent country of Greater Colombia in 1824. As a result of his leadership, ten South American countries had become independent from Spain by 1830. However, Bolívar himself was criticized as being a dictator. ▶

1810–1910 **MEXICO'S REVOLUTION** In 1846, Mexico and the United States go to war. Mexico loses parts of the Southwest and California to the U.S. A revolution in 1910 overthrows Porfirio Díaz.

Becoming Independent

Most countries of Latin America became independent of Spain in the early 1800s. Some took longer.

COUNTRY	YEAR OF INDEPENDENCE
Argentina	1816
Bolivia	1825
Brazil	1822[1]
Chile	1818
Colombia	1819
Ecuador	1822
Guyana	1966[2]
Mexico	1821
Paraguay	1811
Peru	1824
Suriname	1975[3]
Uruguay	1825
Venezuela	1821

[1]From Portugal.
[2]From Britain.
[3]From the Netherlands.

1867 The Canadian provinces are united as the Dominion of Canada.

1898 **THE SPANISH-AMERICAN WAR** Spain and the U.S. fight a brief war in 1898. Spain loses its colonies Cuba, Puerto Rico, and the Philippines.

U.S. POWER IN THE 1900s During the 1900s the U.S. strongly influenced affairs in the Americas. The U.S. sent troops to various countries, including Mexico (1914; 1916–1917), Nicaragua (1912–1933), Haiti (1915–1934; 1994–1995), and Panama (1989). In 1962, the U.S. went on alert when the Soviet Union put missiles on Cuba.

1994 The North American Free Trade Agreement (NAFTA) is signed to increase trade between the U.S., Canada, and Mexico.

2001 Terrorists crash planes into U.S. targets, killing about 3,000 people; the U.S. launches a "war on terrorism."

2003 U.S.-led forces invade Iraq and overthrow the regime of Saddam Hussein.

Looking Back

From 2004

50 YEARS AGO—1954

► In a landmark decision, the U.S. Supreme Court ruled that segregating white and black students into different schools violated the U.S. Constitution. ►

► Sir Roger Bannister, a British doctor, broke the 4-minute barrier for the mile when he ran the mile in a world-record 3 minutes, 59.4 seconds.

► A vaccine against polio, developed by Dr. Jonas Salk, came into use and nearly wiped out this crippling disease.

► Disc jockey Dewey Phillips put on "That's All Right (Mama)," making radio station WHBQ in Memphis the first to play an Elvis Presley record.

► The TV show *Lassie* aired on CBS. It first starred Pal from the 1943 movie *Lassie, Come Home*, based on Eric Knight's book of the same name.

► The first Burger King restaurant was opened in Miami, Florida, by James McLamore and David Edgerton.

100 YEARS AGO—1904

► More than 1,500 buildings burned to the ground in the Great Baltimore Fire. Amazingly, only 5 people died.

The New York City subway system opened. It grew to become the biggest in the U.S., and one of the biggest in the world.

► The first Olympic Games in the U.S. were held in St. Louis, Missouri, along with the 1904 World's Fair, which celebrated the 100th anniversary of the Louisiana Purchase.

Frenchman Louis Emile Rigolly became the first driver to break the 100 mph barrier, setting a record of 103.55 mph in Belgium.

► Prizewinning children's book author Theodor Seuss Geisel, better known as Dr. Seuss, was born in Springfield, Massachusetts.

From 2005

50 YEARS AGO—1955

Rosa Parks, a black woman, refused to give up her seat to a white person on a bus in Montgomery, Alabama, and was arrested for violating segregation laws. Reverend Martin Luther King Jr. led a bus boycott there that became a major victory for the civil rights movement.

► *The Return of the King*, the last book of J.R.R. Tolkien's "Lord of the Rings" trilogy, was published. The popular 2003 movie based on the book won 11 oscars.

McDonald's founder Ray Kroc opened his first hamburger restaurant, in Des Plaines, Illinois.

► The Brooklyn Dodgers won their only World Series (defeating the Yankees). Two years later, the Dodgers moved to Los Angeles. Disneyland opened in Anaheim, California, and *The Mickey Mouse Club* started on TV.

► The *Sam and Friends* TV show, starring Jim Henson's first muppets, first aired in Washington, D.C.

100 YEARS AGO—1905

► President Theodore Roosevelt hosted a peace conference that settled a war between Russia and Japan. A year later he won the Nobel Peace Prize for his efforts.

► Albert Einstein, then 26 years old, published some of his key scientific discoveries, including the special theory of relativity.

► Alberta and Saskatchewan, which had been part of the Northwest Territories, officially became provinces of Canada. ►

► The rules of college football were changed to make the forward pass a legal play.

► After leaving a cup of powdered fruit-flavored soda and water on the porch overnight, 11-year-old Frank Epperson discovered that the sweet mix was solid ice. The "Ep-sicle" (later popsicle) was born.

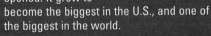

WOMEN IN HISTORY

The following women played important roles in shaping some of history's biggest events.

CATHERINE THE GREAT (1729-1796), empress of Russia (1762-1796). Catherine made Russia a European power and greatly expanded the territory of the Russian Empire. She raised the status of the nobles by granting them privileges such as freedom from military service and legal control over their serfs. She promoted culture as well as the education of women and religious tolerance.

Catherine the Great

SACAGAWEA (c. 1788-1812), Shoshone Indian who served as an interpreter, guide, and peacemaker on the Lewis and Clark Expedition across America from 1804 to 1806. Kidnapped by Indian warriors when she was 12 years old, Sacagawea was sold as a slave to Toussaint Charbonneau, a French-Canadian fur trader who made her his wife. With their infant son and 31 other people, they explored the wilderness, traveling from Fort Mandan, North Dakota, to the Pacific Ocean and back. She was a vital help because of her knowledge of the land and of Native American languages and customs.

SOJOURNER TRUTH (c. 1797-1883), abolitionist and women's rights activist (born Isabella Baumfree). She was raised as a slave on an estate in upstate New York. When she escaped in 1826, she went to New York City and worked as a cleaning woman. In 1843, she became a traveling preacher and took the name Sojourner Truth. She traveled widely speaking out against slavery and in favor of equal rights for women. She worked as a nurse and teacher during the Civil War and helped recruit African-American troops for the Union Army.

ELIZABETH CADY STANTON (1815-1902), social reformer and leader of the women's rights movement. Along with Lucretia Mott, she organized the first women's rights convention (1848), and won passage of a resolution demanding voting rights for women. She was president of the National Woman Suffrage Association, which she and Susan B. Anthony founded in 1869.

Elizabeth Cady Stanton & Susan B. Anthony

SUSAN B. ANTHONY (1820-1906), social reformer who, with Elizabeth Cady Stanton, led the struggle for women's rights. She was a lifelong campaigner for woman suffrage, but died 14 years before the adoption of the 19th Amendment, which allowed women to vote. She opposed the use of liquor and worked to free slaves. In 1979, the U.S. Mint issued the Susan B. Anthony dollar coin in her honor.

FLORENCE NIGHTINGALE (1820-1910), British nurse and founder of modern nursing. She was a Superintendent of Female Nurses in Turkey during the Crimean War, where she trained nurses and helped set up the first large-scale modern hospital, saving many lives. In 1860 she founded the the first professional nursing school, at Saint Thomas's Hospital in London. In 1907, she became the first woman to receive the British Order of Merit.

MARIE CURIE (1867-1934), Polish-French physical chemist known for discovering the element radium, which is used to treat some diseases. She also discovered the rare element Polonium (named after Poland, her country of birth). She won the Nobel Prize for chemistry in 1911. She and her husband, Pierre Curie, also won the Nobel Prize for physics in 1903 for their work in radiation.

◀ *Sojourner Truth*

HELEN KELLER

(1880-1968), author and lecturer who was stricken with an illness that left her both deaf and blind at 19 months old. With the help of

Hellen Keller and Anne Sullivan

her teacher, Anne Sullivan (known as "the Miracle Worker"), Keller learned to read Braille and write, and went on to graduate with honors from Radcliffe College. She wrote 14 books and gave speeches around the world, using her life story to inspire others. Her story was also told in a famous play, *The Miracle Worker* (1960), which was made into an award-winning movie (1962).

AMELIA EARHART

(1897-1937), American flier who in 1932 became the first woman—and the second person—to fly by herself across the Atlantic Ocean. She was also the first person to fly solo across the Pacific, and broke many altitude, speed, and distance records. In 1937, on a trip around the world, Earhart's plane disappeared near the coast of Howland Island in the Pacific and was never found, despite many air and sea searches.

GOLDA MEIR

(1898-1978), Israeli prime minister (1969-1974). She was born in Kiev, Russia, but she and her family emigrated to the U.S. when she was a child. In 1921, she and her husband moved to Palestine (now Israel). She came out of retirement at the age of 71 to become prime minister of Israel. Her government was known for its open-door policy, which encouraged thousands of Soviet Jews to come to Israel. Her biggest crisis came in 1973 when Israel was invaded in the Yom Kippur War.

BABE DIDRIKSON ZAHARIAS

(1914-1956), athlete who was widely considered to be the greatest woman sports figure of the early 20th century. In the 1932 Olympics she set two world records and won gold medals in the javelin throw and the 80-meter hurdles, as well as a silver medal in the high jump. Between 1936 and 1954, she captured each of the major women's golf championships, and helped stir wide interest in women's golf. She was named to the National Women's Hall of Fame in 1976.

KATHARINE GRAHAM

(1917-2001), publisher of *The Washington Post* and one of the most powerful women in American media. Her father bought *The Post* at an auction, and her husband published it from 1946 until his death in 1963. At the age of 46, she took over the paper and guided it to become one of the most influential and

Katharine Graham

respected newspapers in the country. In 1998, she received a Pulitzer Prize for her best-selling autobiography, *Personal History*.

MARGARET THATCHER

(born 1925), the first woman to become prime minister of Great Britain (1979-1990) and the first British prime minister in the 20th century to win three terms in a row. She started out as a research chemist and tax lawyer, then joined Britain's Conservative Party and became minister of education and science (1970-1974). As prime minister, she was known as "The Iron Lady" because of the tough stands she took over economic policy and relations with the Soviet Union.

Margaret Thatcher

TONI MORRISON

(born 1931), American writer whose powerful novels detail the lives of African American families. She received the National Book Critics Circle Award in 1977 for *Song of Solomon* and a Pulitzer Prize for fiction for the novel *Beloved* in 1988. In 1993 she became the first African American to win a Nobel Prize in literature.

AUNG SAN SUU KYI

(born 1945), Burmese political leader who received the Nobel Peace Prize in 1991 for her nonviolent activism. She was the daughter of nationalist leader U Aung San, who was assassinated in 1947. Educated in England, she

Aung San Suu Kyi

returned to Burma (now Myanmar) to care for her dying mother and became involved in pro-democracy movements. After a military junta took control of the country in 1988 she was frequently put under house arrest.

Dragon Maze

Throughout Chinese history, the dragon has been considered a symbol of good fortune, wisdom, and generosity. Chinese mythology associates the dragon with weather, particularly wind and water. It was believed that helpful dragons were responsible for the rainfalls that replenished the crops and that floods were caused by angry dragons.

START

FINISH

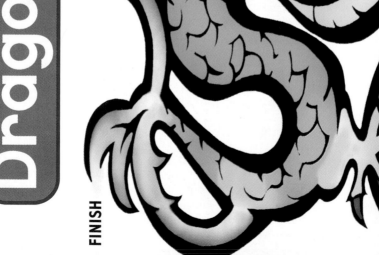

Answers

CAMPS Page 53: QUIZ

1: C) 1861: The Gunnery Camp, Washington, Connecticut, is considered the first organized camp in the U.S.

2: E) all of the above: You can do all of these activities and more at camp.

3: E) all of the above: Your camp director can help you decide what you should bring to camp.

COMPUTERS Page 58: COMPUTER MAZE

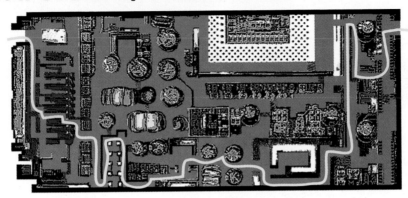

DINOSAURS Page 62: WORD SEARCH

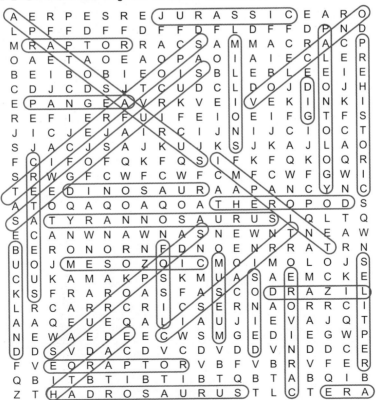

GEOGRAPHY Page 89: QUICK QUIZ

1: A. legend; 2: A. near the poles ; 3: C. the equator; 4: C. 1/360;
5: B the prime meridian; 6: A. 45° N

HEALTH Page 95: OPTICAL ILLUSIONS

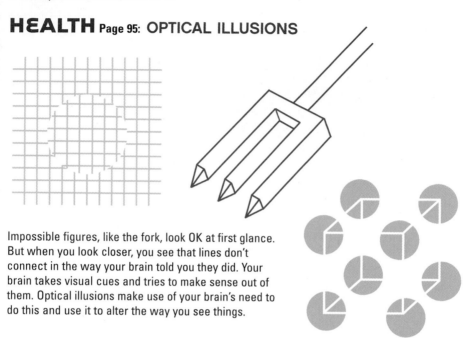

Impossible figures, like the fork, look OK at first glance.
But when you look closer, you see that lines don't
connect in the way your brain told you they did. Your
brain takes visual cues and tries to make sense out of
them. Optical illusions make use of your brain's need to
do this and use it to alter the way you see things.

INVENTIONS Page 106: CROSSWORD

¹T	E	²L	E	G	R	A	³P	H	
		O					R		
⁴E	S	C	A	⁵L	A	T	O	R	⁶S
		K		A			P		A
	⁷C		⁸S	M	O	K	E		L
⁹P	O	P		P			L		K
	M				¹⁰B	E	L	L	
¹¹O	P	T	I	C			E		
	U			¹²G		¹³R	¹⁴C	A	
	¹⁵T	H	O	M	A	S		A	
	E			M			S		
¹⁶T	R	U	M	P	E	T		H	

FOR MORE PUZZLES GO TO
WWW.WORLDALMANACFORKIDS.COM

LANGUAGE PUZZLES

Page 112: SECRET CODES: 1. Shrek Two; 2. Lemony Scent

Page 113: JOKES & RIDDLES

Why did the T-rex cross the road? *The chicken hadn't evolved yet.*

What's a boxer's favorite drink? *Punch.*

Which nail does a carpenter hate to hit? *A thumbnail.*

Why did the tomato blush? *It saw the salad dressing.*

What do you call a 100-year-old ant? *Ant-ique.*

Which day of the week starts with the letter "Y"? *Yesterday.*

What did the sick freight elevator say? *I think I'm coming down with something.*

What's a tree's favorite drink? *Root beer.*

What's black and white and eats like a horse? *A zebra.*

What's broken when you say it? *Silence.*

What can travel around the world without leaving the corner? *A stamp on an envelope.*

What kind of street does a ghost live on? *A dead end.*

Why did the cow cross the road? *To get to the udder side.*

Why did the turkey cross the road? *The chicken was on vacation.*

How do you stop a bull from charging? *Take away its credit card.*

Why was the computer cold at night? *It forgot to close its windows.*

Two legs I have, and this will confound: only at rest do they touch the ground! What am I? *A wheelbarrow.*

How far can a deer run into the woods? *Halfway. Any farther and it'll be running out.*

I run but cannot walk. I have hands but no arms, and a face but no head. What am I? *A clock.*

If you spell out the numbers, how far do you have to go before you need the letter "a"? *One thousand.*

Can you name a word in the English language that has 8 consonants and one vowel? *Strengths*

Which side of a chicken has the most feathers? *The outside.*

MOVIES & TV Page 125: MOVIE & TV MATCH-UPS

Woody & Buzz: *Toy Story*

Manfred & Sid: *Ice Age*

Jade & Uncle: *Jackie Chan Adventures*

Patrick & Squidward: *SpongeBob SquarePants*

Donkey & Fiona: *Shrek*

Mike & Sully: *Monsters, Inc.*

Pumbaa & Timon: *The Lion King*

Carl & Sheen: *Jimmy Neutron: Boy Genius*

Cosmo & Wanda: *The Fairly OddParents*

Eustace & Muriel: *Courage The Cowardly Dog*

Bart & Lisa: *The Simpsons*

Marlin & Dory: *Finding Nemo*

FOR MORE PUZZLES GO TO WWW.WORLDALMANACFORKIDS.COM

NUMBER PUZZLES

Page 179: ROMAN NUMERALS: CDLXXVI

Page 184: COIN PREDICTION TRICK

The success of this trick depends on two things: your powers of observation and a closed odd-even system. The "trick" works for you as long as pairs of coins are flipped.

When you first look at the coins, count up the number of heads (to yourself). The number of heads showing will increase by two, decrease by two, or stay the same. So if the number of heads you counted was odd, it will stay odd no matter how many pairs are turned over.

Before you make you prediction, count the number of heads again. If the number of heads showing is odd and was odd before (or even and was even before), then the hidden coin is a TAIL.

If the number of heads showing is odd now but was even before (or even now but was odd at the beginning) the hidden coin is a HEAD.

Page 184: SIX NINES: 99 + 99/99 = 100

Page 184: APPLE PICKERS

Ten. The same pickers picking 10 apples in 10 seconds are picking an apple a second and so can pick 60 apples in 60 seconds, a minute.

SCIENCE Page 204: QUICK QUIZ

1: B. carbon; 2: C. 10,000; 3: C. climate; 4: A. earthquakes; 5: C. atmosphere; 6: B: geometry ; 7: B. stomata; 8: D. Latin; 9: B. chimpanzee; 10: C. cells

SPACE Page 216: THE RIDDLE OF MARS

This cannot be done.

UNITED STATES Page 270: QUICK QUIZ

1: C. Wyoming; 2: A. South Carolina; 3: B. 2; 4: C. Franklin Roosevelt; 5: C. 10: 6: B. John Adams; 7: D. University of Pennsylvania; 8: C. New York City; 9: C. Yellowstone; 10: B. Hilo, HI; 11: C. Apache; 12: A. John Glenn; 13: C. Alaska; 14: C. Lou Hoover

WORLD HISTORY Page 318: DRAGON MAZE

FOR MORE PUZZLES GO TO
WWW.WORLDALMANACFORKIDS.COM

INDEX